STATE, CAPITALISM, AND FINANCE IN EMERGING MARKETS

Business, Finance, and International Development

Series Editors: **Catherine Dolan**, SOAS, University of London, **Paul Gilbert**, University of Sussex, **Lena Lavinas**, The Federal University of Rio de Janeiro, **Emma Mawdsley**, University of Cambridge, **Dinah Rajak**, University of Sussex, **Farwa Sial**, Eurodad and University of Manchester, **Jessica Sklair**, University of Cambridge

---

This series is dedicated to interdisciplinary work on business, finance, and international development, drawing on crosscutting conversations in the disciplines of anthropology, critical management studies, development studies, economics, geography, and socio-legal studies.

Also available in the series:

- *Feminism in Public Debt* edited by Juan Bohoslavsky and Mariana Rulli

Find out more at:

bristoluniversitypress.co.uk/
business-finance-and-international-development

STATE, CAPITALISM, AND FINANCE IN EMERGING MARKETS

Between Subordination and Statecraft

Edited by
Johannes Petry and Andreas Nölke

BRISTOL
UNIVERSITY
PRESS

First published in Great Britain in 2025 by

Bristol University Press
University of Bristol
1–9 Old Park Hill
Bristol
BS2 8BB
UK
t: +44 (0)117 374 6645
e: bup-info@bristol.ac.uk

Details of international sales and distribution partners are available at bristoluniversitypress.co.uk

British Library Cataloguing in Publication Data
A catalogue record for this book is available from the British Library

ISBN 978-1-5292-4334-5 hardcover
ISBN 978-1-5292-4336-9 ePub
ISBN 978-1-5292-4337-6 ePdf

Cover design: Nicky Borowiec
Front cover image: Getty/Craig Hastings
Bristol University Press uses environmentally responsible print partners.
Printed and bound in Great Britain by CPI Group (UK) Ltd, Croydon, CR0 4YY

Bristol University Press' authorised representative in the European Union is:
Easy Access System Europe, Mustamäe tee 50, 10621 Tallinn, Estonia,
Email: gpsr.requests@easproject.com

FSC
www.fsc.org
MIX
Paper | Supporting responsible forestry
FSC® C013604

Contents

PART III

Series Editors' Preface

Time and again, development organizations and policy makers tout plans to mobilize, catalyze, or leverage new flows of private finance as solutions to seemingly intractable development problems. The UN Climate Change Conference ('COP 29') in Baku in 2024 resulted in yet more commitments for catalyzing private finance. High-profile scandals hitting lauded 'impact investment' firms have done little to dull policy makers' enthusiasm in this regard. Aid is increasingly dispersed through development finance institutions that look and behave like private investment firms, while philanthropies become tangled up with donors and private contractors alike. Structural adjustment and policy conditionality for heavily indebted countries has returned (if it ever left), although efforts to restructure sovereign debt are often frustrated by the megalithic asset management firms that hold growing shares of Southern debt. Businesses loudly and proudly declare their intention to fight poverty and shape policy norms through 'multistakeholder' forums. Public private partnerships are once again being promoted as vehicles for the delivery of assorted development goals. Meanwhile for-profit consultancies (rather than civil society organizations or public policy experts) have the ear of policy makers and development ministries. As private sector actors become increasingly central to the design and delivery of international development, critical, interdisciplinary research on business, finance, and development has never been more pressing.

This series is intended as a home for works which examine the multiple forms that new public–private 'state-capital hybrids' take in contemporary international development. This includes: the role that private sector entities play in producing and legitimating knowledge in/of development; the impact of emerging financial architectures and innovations on the Global South; labour and human rights issues in global supply chains; the place of business and finance in resource extraction and conservation; as well as methodological and ethical issues in the study of private sector actors and international development. It is interdisciplinary by design and by necessity. Efforts to engage with some dimension of business, finance, and international development have been ongoing for some time in the editors' respective disciplines (anthropology, business and management, development studies, economics, geography, science and technology studies). Drawing together the approaches, methods, and normative concerns that have animated this work across disciplines allows contributions to the series to examine issues such as the technicalities of sovereign debt and impact investing, as well as their distributional consequences and entanglements with racialized and gendered power relations and post-colonial geographies.

Our goal is to spark dialogue across disciplines, and between scholars situated in the academy and those who work in civil society or advocacy organizations or in policy settings. The first volume in this series, Bohoslavsky and Rulli's *Feminism in Public Debt* (2024) emerged from civil society mobilization around the gendered impacts of debt and austerity in Latin America. *Varieties of Impact Investing*, edited by Philip Balsiger, Daniel Burnier, and Noé Kabouche, continued with the series' commitment to interdisciplinary explorations of international development, exploring a fuzzily defined but ubiquitous development 'model solution' as it takes shape across geographies, sectors, and through different disciplinary lenses. With this volume, *State, Capitalism, and Finance in Emerging Markets: Between Subordination and Statecraft*, Johannes Petry and Andreas Nölke continue the series' commitment to interdisciplinary exchange, and to examining the impact of established and emerging financial architectures and innovations on the Global South.

This volume brings into dialogue two strands in the scholarship of finance, the state and development, which are organized under the rubrics of 'international financial subordination' and 'international financial statecraft' respectively. Petry and Nölke bring these two perspectives together in an effort to unpick what occurs when developing and 'emerging' markets play an increasing role driving global economic production but remain beholden to financial institutions and markets located in the Global North. Alongside theoretical contributions from key proponents of both approaches, the chapters in the volume explore the relationship between financial subordination and statecraft in each of the 'BRICS', as well as the specific role of stock exchanges and central bank digital currencies in configuring the relationship between subordination and statecraft.

As might be expected when different schools of thought, rooted in varying disciplinary epistemologies and political commitments, collide, there are tensions within the volume. Some contributors ask when financial institutions are a 'source of subordination' and when they 'contribute to statecraft', posit potential indices of subordination, and explore states' capacity to undertake 'offensive' or 'defensive' forms of international statecraft. Others, who root their understanding of subordination in a longer lineage of dependency thinking, resist such an either/or framing, eschewing questions like 'can the state do statecraft' in favour of an approach that examines statecraft within the context of forces that generate uneven development across the globe.

From this perspective, subordination is not an end state, but a 'set of power relations which are internalized by state actors'.

But the tensions are productive, and the concepts of subordination and of statecraft are stretched as they encounter each other. Kapadia and Musthaq's chapter on India, for instance, is more directly engaged with the statecraft literature than the subordination literature. Yet, by exploring fiscal and monetary interventions undertaken by organs of the Indian state in light of the delicate domestic 'political settlement' with big business, farmers, and globalizing professionals, they almost converge on Alami's and Kvangraven's approach, which emphasizes how states mediate international financial subordination in relation to domestic and global class struggles.

Debt crises and attendant currency crises are unfolding across the Global South, and the dominant approach to climate finance is set to increase developing countries' indebtedness. Numerous (incomplete) proposals for reforming the international financial architecture have been articulated. Against this backdrop it is abundantly clear how desperately we need to deepen our understanding of how and to what end states in the Global South exercise control over finance and money, within an uneven and inequitable global economic order. We are pleased to be able to include a volume that seeks to do just that within the Business, Finance & International Development series.

List of Figures and Tables

Figures

Tables

List of Abbreviations

AIIB	Asian Infrastructure Investment Bank
ANC	African National Congress
ASEAN	Association of Southeast Asian Nations
ATM	automated teller machine
B3	Brazil Stock Exchange
BCB	Central Bank of Brazil
BIS	Bank for International Settlements
BNDES	Banco Nacional de Desenvolvimento Econômico e Social
BRI	Belt and Road Initiative
BRICs	Brazil, Russia, India, China
BRICS	Brazil, Russia, India, China, South Africa
BSE	Bombay Stock Exchange
CBDC	central bank digital currency
CBR	Central Bank of Russia
CCP	Chinese Communist Party
CFMMC	China Futures Market Monitoring Center
CIPS	Cross-Border Interbank Payment System
CMIM	Chiang Mai Initiative Multilateralization
CRA	Contingent Reserve Arrangement
DCEP	digital currency/electronic payments
DEE	developing and emerging market economies
DLT	distributed ledger technology
DSSI	Debt Service Suspension Initiative
EACOP	East African Crude Oil Pipeline
ECE	emerging capitalist economies
ECLAC	Economic Commission for Latin America and the Caribbean
EM	emerging market
EUR	Euro
FDI	foreign direct investment
FII	Foreign Institutional Investors (India)
FIMS	Foreign Investment Management System (South Korea)

FIX	Financial Information eXchange
FPI	Foreign Portfolio Investors (India)
FS	financial statecraft
FX	foreign exchange
G20	Group of 20
G7	Group of Seven
GBP	Pound Sterling
GCC	Gulf Cooperation Council
GDP	gross domestic product
GFC	global financial crisis
GFO	global financial order
GMFPS	Global Monetary and Financial Powers of States
HCA	historic cost accounting
HKMA	Hong Kong Monetary Authority
IASB	International Accounting Standards Board
IFRS	International Financial Reporting Standards
IFS	international financial subordination
IMF	International Monetary Fund
IMS	International Monetary System
IPE	International Political Economy
IPO	initial public offering
IRC	Investment Registration Certificate
ISDS	investors-state-dispute-settlement
JSE	Johannesburg Stock Exchange
JV	joint venture
KDB	Korea Development Bank
KRX	Korea Exchange
M&A	mergers and acquisitions
MCI	material capabilities index
MMT	Modern Monetary Theory
MOEX	Moscow Exchange
NATO	North Atlantic Treaty Organization
NCM	New Consensus on Macroeconomics
NDB	New Development Bank
NFCs	non-financial corporations
NIEO	New International Economic Order
NIIP	net international investment position
NPS	National Pension Fund (South Korea)
NSE	National Stock Exchange of India
NSPC	National System of Payment Cards (Russia)
ODA	official development assistance
OECD	Organisation for Economic Co-operation and Development

OPEC	Organization of the Petroleum Exporting Countries
PBoC	People's Bank of China
PGII	Partnership for Global Infrastructure Investment
PPP	public–private partnership
PT	Partido dos Trabalhadores (Brazil)
QE	quantitative easing
QFII	Qualified Foreign Institutional Investors (China)
RBI	Reserve Bank of India
RQFII	RMB Qualified Foreign Institutional Investors (China)
SAFE	State Administration of Foreign Exchange (China)
SARB	South African Reserve Bank
SBI	State Bank of India
SDRM	sovereign debt restructuring mechanism
SDRs	Special Drawing Rights
SML	Local Currency Payments System (Brazil/Argentina)
SPFS	System for the Transfer of Financial Messages (Russia)
SWF	sovereign wealth fund
SWIFT	Society for Worldwide Interbank Financial Telecommunication
TJLP	*Taxa de Juros de Longo Prazo*/long-term interest rate
TLP	*Taxa de Longo Prazo*/long-term rate
TPPPs	third-party payment providers
UAE	United Arab Emirates
UN	United Nations
UNCTAD	United Nations Conference on Trade and Development
USD	US Dollar
WC	Washington Consensus
ZAR	Zuid Afrikaanse Rand

Notes on the Contributors

Ilias Alami is Assistant Professor in the Political Economy of Development at the University of Cambridge. His research and teaching interests are in the areas of global political economy, political ecology, money and finance, state capitalism, economic geography, international capital flows, green transitions, theories of the state, and the articulations between race/class/coloniality. He is the author of *Money Power and Financial Capital in Emerging Markets: Facing the Liquidity Tsunami* (Routledge, 2019) and (with Adam Dixon) *The Spectre of State Capitalism* (Oxford University Press, 2024).

Leslie Elliott Armijo holds research affiliations with Simon Fraser University, School of International Studies, and Boston University, Global Development Policy Center. She did her PhD at the University of California, Berkeley (1989). Specializing in the international relations of the Global South and the politics of finance, her recent publications include *South American Policy Regionalism: Drivers and Barriers to International Problem Solving* (editor, with M. Fraundorfer and S.D. Rhodes, Routledge, 2025) and *The BRICS and Collective Financial Statecraft* (with C. Roberts and S. Katada, Oxford University Press, 2017).

Patrick Bond is Professor at the Department of Sociology, University of Johannesburg, South Africa. His research interests include political economy, environment, social policy, and geopolitics, primarily the political economy of Africa, international and local finance, eco-social development and political ecology, and development issues in contemporary South Africa and Zimbabwe.

Roxana Ehlke is a research assistant at the Institute of Sociology at Justus Liebig University Giessen, Germany, and a PhD candidate at the 'Dynamics of Security' Collaborative Research Centre in the 'Financial infrastructures and geoeconomic security' subproject. Her work addresses the geopolitical implications of securing financial transactions and the interrelations of economic and political security in Russia and Central Asia in the context of the sanctions regime imposed on Russia after the full-scale invasion of Ukraine in 2022.

Luiz Fernando de Paula is Associate Professor at the Institute of Economics of the Federal University of Rio de Janeiro (IE-UFRJ) and Professor of Economics at the Institute of Social and Political Studies of the State University of Rio de Janeiro (IESP-UERJ), Brazil. His main areas of research include economic development, monetary and financial economics, macroeconomics, and post-Keynesian theory. He is currently working on currency hierarchy, financial globalization, and policy space in emerging economies.

Annina Kaltenbrunner is Associate Professor for Economics of Globalization and International Economy at Leeds University Business School, UK. She is a pluralist macro-development economist with an interest in cross-border capital flows and international financial integration and the implications these processes have for macroeconomic and monetary policy. She is working on currency internationalization and financialization in emerging economies.

Elif Karaçimen is Associate Professor of Economics at Recep Tayyip Erdoğan University, Turkey. She obtained her PhD in economics from SOAS. Her research interests include the financialization of households and non-financial corporations in emerging capitalist economies, and feminist political economy. She is currently working on the intersections of agricultural production and financialization in Turkey.

Anush Kapadia is Associate Professor in the Department of Humanities and Social Sciences at IIT Bombay. He holds a PhD in anthropology from Columbia University and has previously held positions at Harvard University and City, University of London. He is the author most recently of *A Political Theory of Money* (Cambridge University Press, 2024). He is also the principal investigator of the New Political Economy Initiative based at IIT Bombay.

Ingrid Harvold Kvangraven is Senior Lecturer in International Development at King's College, London. Her research covers questions of uneven development, international financial subordination, and decolonizing economics. In addition to many academic articles, she has recently published the co-authored book *Decolonizing Economics: An Introduction* (Polity Press, 2025).

Pedro Lange Machado is a postdoctoral fellow at the Brazilian Center for Analysis and Planning (Cebrap) and holds a PhD in political science from the Rio de Janeiro State University (UERJ). His research interests lie in the field of international political economy, with a focus on the politics of finance and the political economy of green finance.

Eduardo Mantoan is a PhD candidate at the Institute of Economics of the Federal University of Rio de Janeiro (IE-UFRJ) and was an assistant lecturer of macroeconomics and public finance at the Fluminense Federal University (UFF) in Brazil. His main research areas include monetary and financial economics, macroeconomics, Post-Keynesian theory, financialization, and stock-flow consistent models. He currently works on monetary policy, financial globalization, and policy space in emerging economies.

Christopher A. McNally is Professor of Political Economy at Chaminade University and an adjunct senior fellow at the East-West Center in Honolulu, US. His research focuses on comparative capitalisms, especially the nature and logic of China's capitalist transition, and Sino-capitalism. He is also working on a research project that studies the implications of China's international re-emergence on the global order.

Fathimath Musthaq is Assistant Professor of Political Science at Reed College. Areas of ongoing research include sovereign debt and climate justice in small island developing states, legacies of developmentalist states, financial statecraft, and the integration of Asian economies into the global financial order. Her work has appeared in *New Political Economy*, *Review of International Political Economy*, *Review of African Political Economy*, and the *Journal of Democracy*.

Andreas Nölke is Professor of Political Science at Goethe University (Frankfurt) and a research fellow at the Leibniz Institute for Financial Research SAFE. Before joining Goethe University, he has taught at the universities of Konstanz, Leipzig, Amsterdam, and Utrecht. He also served as a consultant in the field of development cooperation, mainly for the German Agency for International Cooperation (GIZ), but also for the European Commission and the World Bank. His research areas are at the intersection of comparative and international political economy. He is the author of *Post-Corona Capitalism* (Bristol University Press, 2022).

Joel Rabinovich is Lecturer in International Political Economy at King's College London. His research focuses on the changing mechanisms that define the generation (both in terms of income and expenses) and use of funds in the non-financial corporate sector in advanced and peripheral economies, with special attention to finance, global value chains, and the increasing intangibilization of business models.

Johannes Petry is the principal investigator of the German Research Foundation (DFG) funded StateCapFinance project at Goethe University (Frankfurt) and a Centre for the Study of Globalisation and Regionalisation research fellow at the University of Warwick. His work explores the politics of global finance and post-crisis transformation of the global financial system, especially the internationalization of China's capital markets, financial market infrastructures, the development of non-Western financial systems, and the geopolitics of global finance. He is the co-author of *BRICS and the Global Financial Order: Liberalism Contested?* (with Andreas Nölke; Cambridge University Press, 2024).

Tim Salzer is a research assistant at Justus Liebig University Giessen (JLU) and a PhD candidate in sociology and history, jointly affiliated with JLU and the School for Advanced Studies in the Social Sciences in Paris. As a member of the 'Dynamics of Security' Collaborative Research Centre he studies the social and political impacts of payment system reforms and the political use of economic knowledge, focusing on Chinese-speaking East Asia in the 20th and 21st centuries.

Carola Westermeier leads the Lise Meitner Research Group on Technology and Sovereignty at the Max Planck Institute for the Study of Societies, Cologne. Her research connects economic sociology, international political economy, and (critical) security studies. Together with Malcolm Campbell-Verduyn and Barbara Brandl she is co-editor of *The Cambridge Global Handbook of Financial Infrastructure* (Cambridge University Press, 2025).

Preface and Acknowledgements

This book project is an outcome of the StateCapFinance project that explores the relationship between state, capitalism, and finance in emerging markets. The idea for this volume emerged in July 2022 during a workshop with our international cooperation partners in Frankfurt – each an expert in their respective areas and country cases. What transpired during this event was that while we came from different theoretical traditions and engaged in different debates and might not agree on all these issues, we all had a common aim of inquiry that bound us together – which was to understand the agency of emerging markets within the context of the global financial system. This book is an extension of this dialogue. Rather than following one paradigm, it ought to be understood as a space for conversation in trying to come to a better understanding of our common goal.

We also would like to thank those who participated in our ongoing conversations but were unable to join the book project for various reasons, especially Alexander Abramov, Muyang Chen, Indradeep Ghosh, Thomas Kalinowski, Nancy Kim, Kai Koddenbrock, Ilja Viktorov, and Jing Wang. Our thanks goes also to Isobel, Ellen, and Inga from Bristol University Press for their enthusiasm, patience, and guidance as well as to Niklas Kullick for his research and editorial assistance. We also acknowledge the generous funding by the German Research Foundation/Deutsche Forschungsgemeinschaft (NO 855/7-1) who financed this project. Finally, we would like to thank our families – Becky, Robin, and Sarah, and Andrea, Anouk, and Antonia – for their patience and support throughout this process.

PART I

1

Introduction: Subordination, Statecraft, and Comparative Capitalism

Johannes Petry and Andreas Nölke

Introduction

One of the most profound transformations of the global economy in the 21st century has been the rise of emerging markets. Whereas developing and emerging economies (DEEs) accounted for only 37 per cent of global gross domestic product (GDP) in 1990, their share rose to 59 per cent by 2024 (IMF, 2024a). As a recent International Monetary Fund (IMF) report put it, emerging markets – especially from Asia as well as the BRICS – are increasingly 'trading places' with Western high-income economies since they have become drivers of global growth and are evermore integrated with global trade and production (IMF, 2024b: Chapter 4). Global patterns of trade, consumption, production, and innovation are no longer solely defined by the West as emerging markets occupy ever more important roles within the global economy. However, in this context emerging markets have increasingly financialized (Bonizzi, 2013).[1] On the one hand, financial markets, actors, and industries have become much more prominent and central for the functioning of emerging market economies at the domestic level (Hardie, 2012; Karwowski, 2020). On the other hand, emerging markets are increasingly integrated into global financial circuits and thus subject and more vulnerable to global market conditions and sentiment (Bortz and Kaltenbrunner, 2018; Naqvi, 2019a). Despite their growing economic importance, emerging markets are situated within a global *financial* system that was created by – and is continuously dominated by – Western, global financial institutions.

Given this setup, what is the role and position of emerging markets in the global financial system? Are they subordinated within global financial hierarchies and restricted in their policy choices? Or do they (also) have autonomy, even power, to use finance to pursue state objectives? And is this power limited to the domestic realm or can it be exercised internationally as a form of economic statecraft? By addressing these questions, this book brings into conversation the academic literatures on financial statecraft – a discussion mostly between US scholars that focuses on countries' ability to achieve foreign policy objectives through financial means – and on international financial subordination, a discourse largely held among scholars in Europe and the Global South that investigates the restrictions placed on emerging markets within a hierarchically structured global financial system. Up until today there has been only limited interaction between these two literatures which paint very different pictures of the role and capacity of DEEs within the global financial system.

Further, few attempts have been made to explain differences between these different outcomes, that is (degrees of) subordination and/or statecraft between emerging markets. This book aims to address this lacuna, by bringing together these two strands of literature and enriching the debate by bringing it into conversation with insights from the comparative capitalism literature (Jackson and Deeg, 2008; Clift, 2021), specifically the emerging literature on state(-permeated) capitalism (Musacchio and Lazzarini, 2013; Alami and Dixon, 2020; Nölke et al, 2020). By drawing on the state capitalism literature which analyzes the role and power of the state within the institutional configurations of national capitalisms, we explain variation in the degree and reach of state capacity and how it conditions different patterns in the relationship between states and domestic as well as international finance.

Exploring the relationship between states and financial markets is ever more important within the current period of increasing financialization which engulfs both developed and developing countries (Epstein, 2005; Braun and Koddenbrock, 2021; Alves et al, 2022; Dafe et al, 2022) as well as within a situation where the established global economic order is cast into doubt, in particular in the context of global political tensions and a potential decoupling between a Western bloc and its Asian challengers (Stuenkel, 2013; Öniş and Kutlay, 2020; Economy, 2022; Petry and Nölke, 2024). We primarily focus on the BRICS as those emerging markets with the largest financial footprint and which are also most prominent and internationally institutionalized as a group, even if this does not allow us to generalize our findings to emerging economies in general.[2]

In doing so, our edited volume makes several contributions to political economy literature. First, it demonstrates that emerging market economies are not helpless victims of financialization. Even under conditions of a subordinated position within the global financial system, they can potentially exercise control over the domestic financial sector and even engage in powerful financial statecraft. However, large emerging economies differ substantially in the degree to which they mobilize this potential state capacity effectively.

Second, our combination of country-related case studies and cross-country comparisons allows us not only to identify different degrees and reach of state capacity in emerging markets, but also to explain how these different features come about. By placing emphasis on the conditions that characterize different state–finance relationships which explain varying patterns of subordination and statecraft, our edited volume thus contributes to current debates on the rise of emerging markets within an increasingly financializing global economy (Huotari and Hanemann, 2014; Roberts et al, 2018; Pape and Petry, 2024).

Third, by taking the perspective of emerging markets, our analysis also provides additional insights for international political economy (IPE) discussions about the power of global finance which in recent analyses of the global financial system has placed more analytical emphasis on global financial actors rather than on the role of states (Braun and Koddenbrock, 2021; Petry et al, 2021; Dafe et al, 2022; Nölke, 2024).

Finally, our combination of insights from the comparative/state capitalism literature with debates on financial statecraft and international financial subordination also contributes to the ongoing endeavour of integrating conceptual tools and research agendas between international and comparative political economy (Phillips, 2005; Kalinowski, 2019; Weinhardt and ten Brink, 2020; Chen and Petry, 2023; Nölke, 2023).

This introduction first sketches the state of the debate on the two established concepts of subordination and statecraft, before articulating the core argument of the volume – namely the importance of the categories developed in comparative capitalism/state capitalism research for understanding differences in state capacity and reach that inform countries' scope of action within these two positions. We then highlight how each chapter of the book contributes to this research agenda.

Between subordination and statecraft: two sides of a coin?

Within the academic debate there are two literatures that investigate questions about the nature and effects of state–finance relationships in DEEs. On the one hand, there is the emerging debate on 'international financial subordination' (IFS) (Kvangraven et al, 2021; Alami et al, 2023; Green, 2023; Bonizzi and Kaltenbrunner, 2024; Moyo, 2024) which is largely held in British and European academic circles and which draws on a wider set of anti-colonial and South-centred scholarship such as dependency theory (Santos, 1970; Amin, 1974; Bhambra, 2021).[3] As Alami et al (2023, p 4) note, international financial subordination suggests a 'relation of domination, inferiority and subjugation between different spaces across the world market, expressed in and through money and finance, which penalizes actors in DEEs disproportionally'. This literature focuses on the hierarchical nature of a global financial and monetary system characterized by core–periphery relationships (Kvangraven, 2021; Cerpa Vielma and Dymski, 2022; Kvangraven and Styve, 2023) where despite their economic rise, DEEs maintain a subordinate position at the bottom of global financial hierarchies (Kaltenbrunner and Painceira, 2018; Bernards, 2022; Kaltenbrunner, 2022). This is not only characterized by recurring periods of financial volatility (Naqvi, 2019a; Alami, 2020), but also embodied within permanent structural features of their integration into the global financial system such as USD hegemony (Norrlöf, 2014; Bonizzi et al, 2022), exchange rate regimes (Andrade and Prates, 2013), development (finance) paradigms (Naqvi et al, 2018; Gabor, 2021), volatile capital flows (Bonizzi and Kaltenbrunner, 2018), or the colonial financial relations that pre-structure contemporary global economic activity (Koddenbrock and Sylla, 2019; Akolgo, 2022; Bernards, 2022; Sylla, 2023). While subordination has tended to breed innovative policy responses so that countries are (somewhat) protected from the vagaries of global capital, from an IFS perspective the agency of states in DEEs is significantly constrained through their embeddedness within global finance.

On the other hand, there is the somewhat more established literature on 'financial statecraft' (FS) which mostly US scholars engage in. Whereas IFS emphasizes the subordination of DEEs resulting from often privately organized, hierarchically organized financial structures, the FS literature places greater emphasis on the state as the primary unit of analysis and its ability to facilitate economic policies through financial means, both defensively and offensively. Armijo and Katada (2015, p 43) define financial statecraft as 'the intentional use, by national governments, of domestic or international monetary or financial capabilities for the purpose of achieving ongoing foreign policy goals, whether political, economic, or financial'. Thereby, financial statecraft can be 'bilateral' or 'systemic' in scope, utilize 'monetary' or 'financial' means, and can be 'offensive' or 'defensive' in character – that is, directed outwards to exercise power vis-à-vis other actors ('sword') or used as a 'shield' to preserve policy autonomy (Andrews, 2006, p 19; Armijo and Katada, 2015, pp 46–7). Financial statecraft therefore is a subset of economic statecraft that facilitates the achievement of foreign policy through economic means (Baldwin, 2020). Thereby, scholars have for instance pointed towards the importance of financial innovation (Lagna, 2016; Munoz Martinez, 2016), infrastructure investment (Pacheco Pardo, 2018; Lim et al, 2021), currencies (Cohen, 2019), swap lines (McDowell, 2019), or financial infrastructures (Petry, 2023) in facilitating financial statecraft (Armijo and Katada, 2015; Roberts et al, 2018; Armijo et al, 2020). The focus is here often put on the policy space that is available to countries (Gallagher, 2015; Grabel, 2015). Rather than subordinated, the FS perspective highlights the policy space and (potential) capacity of states in DEEs for utilizing finance to achieve foreign and domestic economic policy (Grabel, 2017; Naqvi, 2019b).

However, up until today there has been only limited interaction between these two literatures which paint two very different pictures of the role and capacity of DEEs within the global financial system. Further, few attempts have been made to explain these different outcomes, that is, (degrees of) subordination and/or statecraft between emerging markets. We address this lacuna by bringing together these two strands of literature and further enriching the debate by bringing it into conversation with insights from the comparative capitalism literature. As the following section illustrates, the core argument of this book is that variety in national capitalist institutional settings is crucial for understanding state capacity and state reach of emerging markets in the realm of finance. It provides us with a conceptual lens to understand how emerging markets can navigate tensions and their positionality between subordination and statecraft, leading to very different outcomes.

Bridging the gap: taking national capitalist institutions seriously

The approaches that can be grouped under the umbrella of 'comparative capitalism' relate precisely to the structural or institutional level covered by the distinction between subordination and statecraft. They do not compare differences in economic policy between countries, but rather the more abstract institutional mechanisms by which national capitalisms function differently in the first place.

It is the 'Varieties of Capitalism' approach that has been defining comparative capitalism research since the early 2000s. In their introductory chapter to the anthology of the same title, Peter Hall and David Soskice (2001) outline the main features of this research programme. They decided to take a 'business management' approach to the question of capitalist diversity: on the one hand, by making companies – as central actors in capitalism – the focus of the analysis, and on the other hand, by applying a decidedly rationalist theory of institutions. Hall and Soskice analyze capitalism from a supply-side perspective; implicitly, they are always concerned with the competitiveness of companies and the national economies formed by these companies.

During the last decades, several shortcomings of the original 'Varieties of Capitalism' approach have been identified in the literature (May et al, 2024, pp 27–30), two of which are particularly pertinent for the discussion of subordination and statecraft. For one, the 'Varieties' literature treats national economic systems as quasi-containers, neglecting the power of transnational economic relations that is a crucial precondition within the financial subordination literature (Alami et al, 2023). Moreover, the original 'Varieties' literature focused exclusively on high-income economies within the OECD, neglecting the rise of emerging markets outside of the core of the global economy, with their completely different instruments for financial statecraft (Roberts et al, 2018).

Recent theoretical developments in the study of comparative capitalism have helped to overcome these weaknesses. On the one hand, scholars have developed models of capitalism that are better suited to the analysis of emerging economies (Wood and Schnyder, 2020). Among the most prominent of these models are those of 'dependent market economies' found in small emerging economies in the semi-periphery such as in East Central Europe (Nölke and Vliegenthart, 2009), 'hierarchical market economies' found in Latin America (Schneider, 2009), and 'state-permeated capitalism' (Nölke et al, 2020) in large emerging economies such as China and India. On the other hand, comparative capitalism has branched out to cover the demand side of the economy. The new research programme on 'growth models' incorporates global financial dependencies much more prominently (Baccaro et al, 2022; Mertens et al, 2022). Compared to the traditional (microeconomic) varieties of capitalism perspective with its focus on (long-term) institutional complementarities, the (macroeconomic) growth model perspective with its emphasis on (short-term) economic policies lends itself more towards an identification of economic agency, also with regard to finance.

Especially with respect to emerging markets, this literature has illustrated how different institutional configurations of state–finance relationships can tilt the power relations between public and private actors, between the state and financial markets. These include state ownership of financial institutions (Musacchio and Lazzarini, 2013; Wang, 2015), increased regulatory capacity (Collins and Gottwald, 2014; Jain and Gabor, 2020), the state as market creator (Rethel and Sinclair, 2014; Lee, 2024), as well as the (subsequent) political control of market outcomes (Petry, 2020; Viktorov and Abramov, 2022). The defining difference between neoliberal and state-capitalist institutional logic is not the existence or growing importance of financial markets per se but rather the principles that underlie market organization (profit creation vs state objectives) and the actors that dominate/shape these markets (private finance capital vs state institutions) (Petry, 2021).

The comparative/state capitalism literature thus provides us with the conceptual tools to better understand the *degree* and *reach* of state capacity within DEEs. On the one hand, we can distinguish between low and high degrees of state capacity: whether the state has the capacity to resist pressures to conform with or even exercise power vis-à-vis financial actors/markets or whether the state has relatively little power and instead financial actors

Figure 1.1: Varieties of state–finance relationships in emerging markets

Degree of state capacity / ***Reach of state capacity***	*Domestic*	*International*
Low	full subordination (A)	international subordination (B)
High	domestic autonomy (C)	international influence (D)

themselves are able to dominate state policies. On the other hand, we can distinguish between the domestic and international reach of state capacity. Whether the potential ability of the state to exercise control over finance is restricted to the domestic sphere or whether it is able to utilize finance for its foreign economic policy.

Overall, this framework produces a taxonomy with four ideal-typical outcomes (Figure 1.1). While real countries in a specific historical situation never completely match ideal types, the combination of types and countries nevertheless helps us to illustrate the specific challenges involved.

First, if degree and reach of state capacity are low, we end up with a situation of what we would call 'full subordination' (A). As Patrick Bond shows in his analysis of South Africa, in this constellation the state is largely subordinated to international *as well as* domestic finance and has little capacity to productively steer domestic (let alone international) financial actors due to a combination of extensive malevolent innovation, weak regulation, and intellectual capture exemplified by orthodox monetary policy.

Second, while the state might have some control over finance domestically, states can still be subject to 'international subordination' (B). In their study of Brazil, Pedro Lange Machado, Luiz Fernando de Paula, and Eduardo Mantoan demonstrate how domestic political cycles and institutional configurations severely constrain the room to manoeuvre for the state. While the boundary between these two categories is blurry, we do see different dynamics unfolding between full and international subordination. However, we can observe situations where states have higher degrees of control over finance.

While in some cases the state's capacity to utilize finance might have little international reach, the state does have a high degree of control over the domestic financial system which it can use for defensive purposes, so-called 'domestic autonomy' (C).[4] As Anush Kapadia and Fathimath Musthaq demonstrate in their chapter, the Indian state has considerable power and capacity to control its domestic financial system, but with little international reach. While India is able to relax its survival constraint, within the context of its national institutional setup this creates a fiscal and current account deficit which limits its ability to successfully execute offensive financial statecraft.

Fourth, we can also observe cases where the state has both a high degree of capacity domestically as well as internationally, which provides it with the ability to also utilize finance to exercise international influence (D). Christopher McNally demonstrates this with respect to the case of China and its development of the digital yuan through which the Chinese authorities are attempting to chart a new course beyond liberal convergence.

Overall, these contributions highlight how differences in the institutional settings of national capitalisms facilitate a diversity of outcomes with respect to states' ability to (successfully) exercise financial statecraft within a context of international financial subordination and thus reduce the negative effects resulting from their subordinate position. The subsequent chapters in the book not only further develop this taxonomy, but also explore the reasons behind these very different country developments and their relationship towards subordination and statecraft.

Plan of the book

The edited volume comprises three parts. The first section focuses on conceptual issues around the relationship between state capitalism, financial subordination, and statecraft. After this introduction, Ilias Alami explores the concept of international financial subordination, its historic roots and contemporary relevance for understanding the reproduction of core–periphery relations within the global financial system and its relationship to financial innovation and statecraft. First, it provides a genealogy of international financial subordination as a concept and a research agenda dedicated to explaining why the structural power of finance takes a particularly violent form in developing countries and emerging markets. Second, drawing on recent scholarship, the chapter provides an overview of some of the key features of international financial subordination and their implications. Third, it reviews what we know about the historical, geographic, and political–economic factors that contribute to international financial subordination. The chapter then turns to the relationship between financial subordination and statecraft. It highlights some of the problematic ways in which the relationship between the two has been conceived, such as when they are seen as two poles of a continuum. While financial subordination imposes real and identifiable constraints on policy making, this does not mean that state agency and capacity are denied. On the contrary, financial subordination can be (and has been) a powerful catalyst for institutional innovation, regulatory experimentation, and resource mobilization in developing countries and emerging markets, whether to accommodate, mitigate, or resist the effects of financial subordination or to enhance a state's position in global financial and monetary relations. Thus, the chapter argues for understanding financial subordination not as an end state (in which state autonomy and agency are denied), but as a set of power relations that are internalized by state actors, shape policy making, and are thus crystallized in variegated configurations of financial statecraft. The chapter concludes with some open questions and avenues for future research.

In the following chapter, Leslie Armijo explores the concept of financial statecraft which she defines as the attempt, by incumbent national political leaders of a sovereign state, to employ financial or monetary resources controlled or influenced by the central government in order to achieve larger foreign policy ends, and it can be used defensively or offensively. A state's ability to exercise financial statecraft, Armijo argues, depends both on sufficient central government competence ('state capacity') to articulate and execute such statecraft as well as on its relative international power capabilities based on net external public debt, creditor capability, network capability, and financial governance capability. However, after discussing differences in financial statecraft and power capabilities within the Global North and Global South, the chapter argues that most developing and emerging economies cannot successfully pursue financial statecraft – especially not bilateral offensive measures. Looking specifically at countries in the Global South, Armijo argues that defensive FS may be a necessary evil given their subordinate position within global markets, thus states try to achieve a degree thereof given their power capabilities. However, these measures always impose costs on these states. Overall, the largest returns for DEEs likely derive from collectively using financial statecraft in order to reform global financial governance arrangements, which is also these countries' best hope for combatting international financial subordination.

After Part I explores the core concepts and sides of the theoretical debate, Part II of the book comprises in-depth country case studies which explore the state–finance relationship in four emerging markets – South Africa, Brazil, India, and China. As the case studies illustrate, the diverse national institutional settings of these economies' financial systems facilitate different outcomes (see Figure 1.1). As Patrick Bond states, no other major economy has experienced such an extreme combination of financial 'deepening' (that is, measured by the ratio of financial assets to the real economy), predatory banking, and uneven financial development than South Africa. The reach and capacity of the South African state to reign in domestic as well as international finance is severely limited, reflecting South Africa's fully subordinated position within the global financial system. The reasons for this position within the global financial system are extensive malevolent innovation, weak state regulation, and orthodox monetary policy – jointly resulting in a situation of extreme financial subordination where state capacity is minimal at best. A persistent dialectical relationship between innovation and degradation exists in South African finance, in part resulting from long-standing contradictions found deep within the local capital accumulation cycle, added to which are processes that reflect the politicization of the economy. At particular moments, the double-movement combination of a deregulatory, pro-corporate ideology and penetration of the commodity form, met by popular discontent – as theorized by Karl Polanyi – caused major upheavals. These require careful dissection, because only rarely did civil society capitalize on the extreme degradation associated with financial innovation to demand and win vitally needed reforms to overcome the loss of state reach and capacity resulting from South Africa's financialization.

The chapter by Pedro Lange Machado, Luiz Fernando de Paula, and Eduardo Mantoan seeks to understand Brazil's position in the international financial order. Studies on financial subordination show that Brazil's policy space is constrained by the subordinate nature of its integration into international financial markets. Meanwhile, compared to its BRICS peers, Brazil presents an intermediate level of financial statecraft, which triggers an ambiguous contestation of the liberal financial order. Machado et al link these two strands of literature by arguing that Brazil's faltering financial statecraft is related to its internal political dynamics, where there has been a power shift between governments more or less aligned with the underlying ideology of the liberal financial order. This political divide helps to maintain its subordinate position in the global financial order, to the detriment of its policy space. Machado et al analyze some of the economic policies adopted by each of Brazil's governments (from Lula da Silva's first term to Bolsonaro's), as well as the institutional changes promoted by them, framing them as liberal or state-capitalist. This allows them to draw conclusions about Brazil's ambiguous position with regard to the contestation of the international financial order made possible by the other BRICS. It also sheds light on some of the roots of its resilient financial subordination, which continues to limit its policy space and make it vulnerable to international financial conditions.

Drawing on Hyman Minsky's ideas, the chapter on India by Anush Kapadia and Fathimath Musthaq conceptualizes financial statecraft as a state lever for easing its 'survival constraint'. First, they argue that India's survival constraint, both domestically and internationally, is generated by its specific political regime and India's position in the global division of labour. Domestically, the state's inability to effectively tax (large) corporations as well as the salaried and property-owning classes results in weak fiscal capacity, which is compounded by a large informal economy, a low tax/GDP ratio, and a net import position, especially in energy, thanks to a failed industrial policy. A robust electoral polity mobilized by machine/patronage politics combines with low fiscal capacity to produce structural fiscal deficits. India's political economy thus requires the external account to be balanced by foreign borrowing; this is now achieved by selling domestic private rather than public debt to foreign investors. The twin deficits and the political constraint on inflation leave India little room to manoeuvre. India addresses its survival constraints (captured by its fiscal and current account deficits) through financial repression, borrowed reserves, a managed rupee, a high degree of capital controls, and limited external/dollar-denominated public debt – thus an exercise in defensive financial statecraft that facilitates greater domestic autonomy. Most government debt is held domestically by the nationalized banking system. Thus, a welcoming environment for foreign investment (subject to capital controls) combines with its apparent opposite, a nationalized banking system, to ease India's survival constraint. India manages its survival constraint in a way that gives it little international clout, but is functional for supporting its main product: electoral democracy in a poor, populous nation.

The chapter by Christopher McNally examines the emergence of a unique form of financial statecraft in China. He argues that Chinese financial statecraft is shaped by two factors: China's subordinate position within the international financial system; and domestic political–economic arrangements, namely the nature and logic of Sino-capitalism. As a case study, the chapter examines the People's Bank of China's recent efforts to develop a central bank digital currency (CBDC), the digital yuan or e-CNY. This fintech innovation could potentially revolutionize monetary relations in China and beyond. A digital currency can provide traceability of all transactions, providing unprecedented insight into the economy. The launch of the e-CNY shows that China is not a helpless victim of financialization, but rather seeking to proactively combine aspects of market-based (neoliberal) finance with efforts to strengthen state capacity. Chinese authorities are attempting to chart a new course beyond liberal convergence to establish novel instruments of financial statecraft whose influence might even expand abroad through China-led projects like mBridge, a non-Western multilateral CBDC project with the potential to upend global currency hierarchies, thus attaining a degree of international influence. The rationalities of market efficiency are merging with the logics of state-directed capitalism, creating a new paradigm of monetary affairs with significant, but as yet uncertain, global spillover effects.

In Part III of the book, comparative studies of three important issue areas provide additional insights about the similarities and differences in state–finance relationships in major emerging economies. Focusing on the nexus between finance, the state, and non-financial corporations, Annina

Kaltenbrunner, Elif Karaçimen, and Joel Rabinovich place the spotlight on the crucial role of the state within subordinated financialized capitalisms, generating insights from comparing Brazil and Turkey. Their chapter analyzes the role of the state in mediating the international financial subordination of emerging capitalist economies through an analysis of the financialization of non-financial corporations in Brazil and Turkey. According to a growing number of scholars, under financialized capitalism the state has been restructured on the basis of the interests of finance capital and due to the impositions of the world. Their chapter shows how this restructuring is fundamentally shaped by the spatial configurations of emerging capitalist economies (ECEs), both in terms of their shared experience of uneven and subordinate integration into the global capitalist system and their historical and institutional specificities. Combining insights from published corporate reports, balance sheet data, and semi-structured interviews with corporate representatives and financial experts, the chapter makes two main arguments. First, it shows how state intervention is a characteristic and even necessary feature of international financial subordination. Rather than being inconsistent with international financial subordination, state interventions – such as the reorganization of the regulatory and supervisory framework for financial activities, the management of cross-border finance, and the creation of sovereign debt markets and public–private partnerships – have been crucial in supporting the participation of non-financial corporations from ECEs in the global circuits of capital and the hierarchical and unstable global financial system. Second, it shows that the variety and differentiation of state interventions have been fundamentally shaped by the two countries' accumulation regimes and differential integration into global financial markets.

Johannes Petry then examines the role of stock markets as important intermediaries in the relationship between financial subordination and statecraft in six emerging markets – Brazil, Russia, India, China, South Africa, and South Korea. The spread of stock markets is central to financialization processes that have engulfed not only the core but also the periphery of the global economy. On the one hand, they can increase the power of global institutional investors and thus exacerbate the negative effects of financial subordination. On the other hand, stock markets can facilitate financial statecraft by organizing markets in ways that they are directing market outcomes towards state objectives and policies. Stock markets are thus important intermediaries for the position and power of emerging markets with global finance, and their institutional embeddedness significantly influences these outcomes. Investigating the ownership of stock exchanges and listed companies as well as restrictions on capital flows, the chapter analyses patterns of subordination and statecraft in six countries. While exchanges in China enable the state to utilize stock markets for financial statecraft both domestically and abroad, in India, South Korea, and Russia exchanges are rather organized in a way that secures autonomy from global markets. In contrast, stock markets in Brazil and especially South Africa contribute to a more subordinate position within the global financial system.

Carola Westermeier, Roxana Ehlke, and Tim Salzer finally focus on CBDCs and their potential to be a major instrument of financial statecraft by reducing the dependency on access to the US-dominated global cross-border payments infrastructure, comparing CBDCs in China and Russia. Central banks around the world develop CBDCs amidst growing geopolitical tensions. While the motivation of central banks to create and implement new digital currencies differs from case to case, the chapter focuses on two projects that are of particular geo-economic relevance: the digital yuan and the digital rouble. Based on an analysis of official publications by the relevant central banks, statements of board members, as well as reports and commentaries by other financial and political actors, they provide a comparative analysis of both CBDC projects with a focus on the anticipated domestic and international reach of state capacity. The CBDC projects are potential instruments for financial statecraft. However, this potential is addressed very differently in the discussions surrounding the two projects. While the defensive character of the digital rouble is spelled out prominently, the potential international effects of the digital yuan are rarely discussed. Regarding the domestic sphere, both projects are meant to increase state capacity while the specific mechanism of this strengthening is shaped by the role of the state vis-à-vis the financial economy and specifically the payment sector. Instead of a straightforward dominance of one field, they find new forms of synergy and mutual dependency between central banks and private finance and technology firms that are currently being hardwired into the new monetary architecture. Thus, state capacity is not restricted but rather enabled by financial actors and increasingly the technology industry.

The final chapter is written by Ingrid Kvangraven who critically reviews the contributions of this volume in light of recent debates on financial hierarchies, subordination, and dependencies. She argues that our search for more differentiated empirical and theoretical positions should not lead to the neglect of capitalism as such, including the embedding of states within this socio-economic formation. Instead of arguing in favour of a dialogue between theoretical traditions – such as financial statecraft, comparative capitalism, and international financial subordination – she highlights potential tensions between the (in part, very) different theoretical assumptions underlying some contributions to these traditions. She thus pleads for sticking to more orthodox approaches with a common grounding in historical materialism, emphasizing in particular decolonial perspectives.

Overall, the contributions to this volume highlight the diverse positionalities of emerging markets within the global financial system – and the diversity of theoretical positions for exploring these. They illustrate the different ways of how national capitalisms, subordination, and statecraft can interact within the context of domestic and international financialization. In contrast to previous debates on finance in the Global South which remained within their established paradigmatic shells, these contributions open up space for cross-paradigmatic debates, though this can only be a first point of departure for more thorough, critical engagements.

Notes

1 Following Epstein (2005: 3), we define financialization as 'the increasing role of financial motives, financial markets, financial actors and financial institutions in the operation of the domestic and international economies'.

2 However, the comparative chapter by Annina Kaltenbrunner, Elif Karaçimen, and Joel Rabinovich (on Brazil and Turkey), and the chapter by Johannes Petry (on Brazil, Russia, India, China, South Africa, and South Korea) offer valuable additions as they provide additional insights into non-BRICS emerging markets.

3 While this book focuses mostly on the more narrow issue of *financial* subordination, the broader issues of subordination and core-periphery relations have long been central to intellectual debates emerging from the Global South; for a recent overview, see Kvangraven (2021).

4 While similar, there is an important difference between international subordination (B) and domestic autonomy (C). In the former, the degree of state capacity within the financial system does not extend into the international realm making the country vulnerable to international financial activity, in the latter state capacity on the domestic level is strong enough to counter these effects.

References

Akolgo, I.A. (2022) 'Collapsing banks and the cost of finance capitalism in Ghana', *Review of African Political Economy*, 49(174): 624–33.

Alami, I. (2020) *Money Power and Financial Capital in Emerging Markets: Facing the Liquidity Tsunami*, London: Routledge.

Alami, I. and Dixon, A. (2020) 'State capitalism(s) redux? Theories, tensions, controversies', *Competition & Change*, 24(1): 70–94.

Alami, I., Alves, C., Bonizzi, B., Kaltenbrunner, A., Koddenbrock, K., Kvangraven, I., et al (2023) 'International financial subordination: a critical research agenda', *Review of International Political Economy*, 30(4): 1360–86.

Alves, C., Bonizzi, B., Kaltenbrunner, A., and Palma, J.G. (2022) 'Conceptualising financialisation in developing and emerging economies: Systemic and global perspectives', *Cambridge Journal of Economics*, 46(4): 619–28.

Amin, S. (1974) *Accumulation on a World Scale: A Critique of the Theory of Underdevelopment*, New York: Monthly Review Press.

Andrade, R.P. and Prates, D.M. (2013) 'Exchange rate dynamics in a peripheral monetary economy', *Journal of Post Keynesian Economics*, 35(3): 399–416.

Andrews, D. (2006) 'Monetary power and monetary statecraft', in D. Andrews (ed) *International Monetary Power*, Ithaca: Cornell University Press, p 7–28.

Armijo, L.E. and Katada, S.N. (2015) 'Theorizing the financial statecraft of emerging powers', *New Political Economy*, 20(1): 42–62.

Armijo, L.E., Tirone, D.C., and Chey, H. (2020) 'The monetary and financial powers of states: Theory, dataset, and observations on the trajectory of American dominance', *New Political Economy*, 25(2): 174–94.

Baccaro, L., Blyth, M., and Pontusson, J. (2022) *Diminishing Returns: The New Politics of Growth and Stagnation*, Oxford: Oxford University Press.

Baldwin, D.A. (2020) *Economic Statecraft: New Edition*, Princeton, NJ: Princeton University Press.

Bernards, N. (2022) 'States, money and the persistence of colonial financial hierarchies in British West Africa', *Development and Change*, 54(1): 64–86.

Bhambra, G.K. (2021) 'Colonial global economy: Towards a theoretical reorientation of political economy', *Review of International Political Economy*, 28(2): 307–22.

Bonizzi, B. (2013) 'Financialization in developing and emerging countries', *International Journal of Political Economy*, 42(4): 83–107.

Bonizzi, B. and Kaltenbrunner, A. (2018) 'Liability-driven investment and pension fund exposure to emerging markets: A Minskyan analysis' *Environment and Planning A: Economy and Space*, 51(2): 420–39.

Bonizzi, B. and Kaltenbrunner, A. (2024) 'International financial subordination in the age of asset manager capitalism', *Environment and Planning A: Economy and Space*, 56(2): 603–26.

Bonizzi, B., Kaltenbrunner, A., and Powell, J. (2022) 'Financialised capitalism and the subordination of emerging capitalist economies', *Cambridge Journal of Economics*, 46(4): 651–78.

Bortz, P.G. and Kaltenbrunner, A. (2018) 'The international dimension of financialization in developing and emerging economies', *Development & Change*, 49(2): 375–93.

Braun, B. and Koddenbrock, K. (2021) *Capital Claims: Power and Global Finance*, London: Routledge.

Cerpa Vielma, N. and Dymski, G. (2022) 'A core–periphery framework for understanding the place of Latin America in the global architecture of finance', *Cambridge Journal of Economics*, 46(4): 629–50.

Chen, M. and Petry, J. (2023) 'What about the dragon in the room? Incorporating China into international political economy (IPE) teaching', *Review of International Political Economy*, 30(3): 801–22.

Clift, B. (2021) *Comparative Political Economy: States, Markets and Global Capitalism*, London: Palgrave Macmillan.

Cohen, B.J. (2019) *Currency Statecraft: Monetary Rivalry and Geopolitical Ambition*, Chicago: University of Chicago Press.

Collins, N. and Gottwald, J.-C. (2014) 'Market creation by Leninist means: The regulation of financial services in the People's Republic of China', *Asian Studies Review*, 38(4): 620–38.

Dafe, F., Hager, S.B., Naqvi, N., and Wansleben, L. (2022) 'Introduction: The structural power of finance meets financialization', *Politics & Society*, 50(4): 523–42.

Economy, E. (2022) 'Xi Jinping's new world order: Can China remake the international system?', *Foreign Affairs*, 101(1): 52–67.

Epstein, G.A. (2005) 'Introduction: financialization and the world economy', in G.A. Epstein (ed) *Financialization and the World Economy*, Cheltenham: Edward Elgar, pp 3–16.

Gabor, D. (2021) 'The Wall Street consensus', *Development and Change*, 52(3): 429–59.

Gallagher, K.P. (2015) 'Countervailing monetary power: Re-regulating capital flows in Brazil and South Korea', *Review of International Political Economy*, 22(1): 77–102.

Grabel, I. (2015) 'The rebranding of capital controls in an era of productive incoherence', *Review of International Political Economy*, 22(1): 7–43.

Grabel, I. (2017) *When Things Don't Fall Apart: Global Financial Governance and Developmental Finance in an Age of Productive Incoherence*, Cambridge, MA: MIT Press.

Green, W.N. (2023) 'Financial inclusion or subordination? The monetary politics of debt in Cambodia', *Antipode*, 55(4): 1172–92.

Hall, P.A. and Soskice, D. (2001) 'An introduction to varieties of capitalism', in P.A. Hall and D. Soskice (eds) *Varieties of Capitalism: The Institutional Foundations of Comparative Advantage*, Oxford: Oxford University Press, pp 1–68.

Hardie, I. (2012) *Financialization and Government Borrowing Capacity in Emerging Markets*, Basingstoke: Palgrave Macmillan.

Huotari, M. and Hanemann, T. (2014) 'Emerging powers and change in the global financial order', *Global Policy*, 5(3): 298–310.

IMF (2024a) IMF Datamapper: GDP based on PPP, share of world, Available from:https://www.imf.org/external/datamapper/PPPSH@WEO/OEMDC/ADVEC/WEOWORLD

IMF (2024b) *World Economic Outlook: Steady but Slow, Resilience amid Divergence*, Washington DC: International Monetary Fund.

Jackson, G. and Deeg, R. (2008) 'From comparing capitalisms to the politics of institutional change', *Review of International Political Economy*, 15(4): 680–709.

Jain, S. and Gabor, D. (2020) 'The rise of digital financialisation: The case of India', *New Political Economy*, 25(5): 813–28.

Kalinowski, T. (2019) *Why International Cooperation is Failing: How the Clash of Capitalisms Undermines the Regulation of Finance*, Oxford: Oxford University Press.

Kaltenbrunner, A. (2022) 'International monetary and financial hierarchies: Macroeconomic implications for emerging market economies', *Ensayos Económicos, Central Bank of Argentina*, 1(79): 159–67.
Kaltenbrunner, A. and Painceira, J.P. (2018) 'Subordinated financial integration and financialisation in emerging capitalist economies: The Brazilian experience', *New Political Economy*, 23(3): 290–313.
Karwowski, E. (2020) 'Economic development and variegated financialization in emerging economies', in P. Mader, D. Mertens, and N. Van der Zwan, (eds) *The Routledge International Handbook of Financialization*, London: Routledge, pp 162–76.
Koddenbrock, K. and Sylla, N.S. (2019) 'Towards a political economy of monetary dependency: The case of the CFA franc in West Africa', *MaxPo Discussion Paper*, 19(2).
Kvangraven, I.H. (2021) 'Beyond the stereotype: Restating the relevance of the dependency research programme', *Development and Change*, 52(1): 76–112.
Kvangraven, I.H., and Dyveke Styve, M. (2023) 'The hierarchies of global finance: An anti-disciplinary research agenda', *Review of Political Economy*, 36(2): 504–27.
Kvangraven, I.H., Koddenbrock, K., and Sylla, N.S. (2021) 'Financial subordination and uneven financialization in 21st century Africa', *Community Development Journal*, 56(1): 119–40.
Lagna, A. (2016) 'Derivatives and the financialisation of the Italian state', *New Political Economy*, 21(2): 167–86.
Lee, Y. (2024) 'Financial liberalization or state capitalism? The developmental state and the special purpose bond market in South Korea', *Contemporary Politics*: 1–20.
Lim, G., Li, C., and Ji, X. (2021) 'Chinese financial statecraft in Southeast Asia: An analysis of China's infrastructure provision in Malaysia', *The Pacific Review*, 35(4): 647–75.
May, C., Mertens, D., Nölke, A., and Schedelik, M. (2024) 'Theoretical foundations of comparative political economy', in C. May, D. Mertens, A. Nölke, and M. Schedelik (eds) *Political Economy: Comparative, International and Historical Perspectives*, Cham: Springer Nature Switzerland, pp 13–36.
McDowell, D. (2019) 'The (ineffective) financial statecraft of China's bilateral swap agreements', *Development and Change*, 50(1): 122–43.
Mertens, D., Nölke, A., May, C., Schedelik, M., ten Brink, T., and Gomes, A. (2022) 'Moving the center: Adapting the toolbox of growth model research to emerging capitalist economies' (Working Paper No 188), Berlin: Institute for International Political Economy.
Moyo, G. (2024) 'Global financial subordination and the pathologies of sovereign debt', in G. Moyo (ed) *Africa in the Global Economy: Capital Flight, Enablers, and Decolonial Responses*, Cham: Springer Nature Switzerland, pp 81–101.

Munoz Martinez, H. (2016) 'Hedging neoliberalism: Derivatives as state policy in Mexico', *New Political Economy*, 21(3): 291–304.

Musacchio, A. and Lazzarini, S.G. (2013) *Reinventing State Capitalism: Leviathan in Business, Brazil and Beyond*, Cambridge, MA: Harvard University Press.

Naqvi, N. (2019a) 'Manias, panics and crashes in emerging markets: An empirical investigation of the post-2008 crisis period', *New Political Economy*, 24(6): 759–79.

Naqvi, N. (2019b) 'Renationalizing finance for development: Policy space and public economic control in Bolivia', *Review of International Political Economy*, 28(3): 1–32.

Naqvi, N., Henow, A., and Chang, H-J. (2018) 'Kicking away the financial ladder? German development banking under economic globalisation', *Review of International Political Economy*, 25(5): 672–98.

Nölke, A. (2023) *Second Image IPE: Bridging the Gap between Comparative and International Political Economy*, London: Palgrave.

Nölke, A. (2024) 'Private institutions in infrastructural geoeconomics: limits to the rise of emerging economies in global finance', *Finance and Space*, 1(1): 282–98.

Nölke, A. and Vliegenthart, A. (2009) 'Enlarging the varieties of capitalism: The emergence of dependent market economies in East Central Europe', *World Politics*, 61(4): 670–702.

Nölke, A., ten Brink, T., May, C., and Claar, S. (2020) *State-Permeated Capitalism in Large Emerging Economies*, London: Routledge.

Norrlöf, C. (2014) 'Dollar hegemony: A power analysis', *Review of International Political Economy*, 21(5): 1042–70.

Öniş, Z. and Kutlay, M. (2020) 'The new age of hybridity and clash of norms: China, BRICS, and challenges of global governance in a postliberal international order', *Alternatives*, 45(3): 123–42.

Pacheco Pardo, R. (2018) 'Europe's financial security and Chinese economic statecraft: The case of the Belt and Road initiative', *Asia Europe Journal* 16(3): 237–50.

Pape, F. and Petry, J. (2024) 'East Asia and the politics of global finance: A developmental challenge to the neoliberal consensus?', *Review of International Political Economy*, 31(1): 224–52.

Petry, J. (2020) 'Financialization with Chinese characteristics? Exchanges, control and capital markets in authoritarian capitalism', *Economy & Society*, 49(2): 213–38.

Petry, J. (2021) 'Same same, but different: Varieties of capital markets, Chinese state capitalism and the global financial order', *Competition & Change*, 25(5): 605–30.

Petry, J. (2023) 'Beyond ports, roads and railways: Chinese economic statecraft, the Belt and Road initiative and the politics of financial infrastructures', *European Journal of International Relations*, 29(2): 319–51.

Petry, J. and Nölke, A. (2024) *BRICS and the Global Financial Order: Neoliberalism Contested?*, Cambridge: Cambridge University Press.

Petry, J., Fichtner, J., and Heemskerk, E.M. (2021) 'Steering capital: The growing private authority of index providers in the age of passive asset management', *Review of International Political Economy*, 28(1): 152–76.

Phillips, N. (2005) 'Globalizing the study of international political economy', in N. Phillips (ed) (2005) *Globalizing International Political Economy*, Basingstoke: Palgrave Macmillan, pp 1–19.

Rethel, L. and Sinclair, T.J. (2014) 'Innovation and the entrepreneurial state in Asia: Mechanisms of bond market development', *Asian Studies Review*, 38(4): 564–81.

Roberts, C.A., Armijo, L.E., and Katada, S.N. (2018) *The BRICS and Collective Financial Statecraft*, Oxford: Oxford University Press.

Santos, T.D. (1970) 'The structure of dependence', *The American Economic Review* 60(2): 231–36.

Schneider, B.R. 'Hierarchical market economies and varieties of capitalism in Latin America', *Journal of Latin American Studies*, 41(3): 553–75.

Stuenkel, O. (2013) 'The financial crisis, contested legitimacy, and the genesis of Intra-BRICS cooperation', *Global Governance*, 19(4): 611–30.

Sylla, N.S. (2023) *Imperialism and the Political Economy of Global South's Debt*, Leeds: Emerald.

Viktorov, I. and Abramov, A. (2022) 'The rise of collateral-based finance under state capitalism in Russia', *Post-Communist Economies*, 34(1): 15–51.

Wang, Y. (2015) 'The rise of the "shareholding state": financialization of economic management in China', *Socio-Economic Review*, 13(3): 603–25.

Weinhardt, C. and ten Brink, T. (2020) 'Varieties of contestation: China's rise and the liberal trade order', *Review of International Political Economy*, 27(2): 258–80.

Wood, G. and Schnyder, G. (2020) 'Intro: comparative capitalism research in emerging markets – A new generation', *New Political Economy*, 26(4): 509–13.

2

Political Economy of International Financial Subordination: From Genesis to Varieties of Financial Statecraft

Ilias Alami

Introduction

An enduring fact of international political economy (IPE) is the profound inequalities between less developed and richer, more powerful economies. There only exist few historical cases where economies have 'graduated' from the periphery to the core of the world economy, that is, achieved rates of capital accumulation, labour productivity growth, technological development, and structural change that enabled a significant degree of economic 'catch-up' with advanced capitalist economies. This suggests that there are powerful centrifugal forces at play, which significantly constrain the developmental prospects of developing and emerging economies and contribute to reproducing enduring lines of inequalities between a small group of advanced capitalist economies and the rest of the world. There is of course a long and rich tradition of writings dedicated to explaining this structural phenomenon (with the aim of ultimately abolishing it), from Latin American structuralism and dependency theory to various strands of developmentalism and Third World Marxism(s). International financial subordination (IFS), as a concept and research agenda, sits within these research efforts. It focuses on questions of *money* and *finance*, and their substantive role in perpetuating abiding lines of division between a handful of wealthy capitalist economies and the spaces of the world economy successively referred to as the colonies, the peripheries, the Third World, and the Global South. How do the operations of capitalist money and finance keep reproducing deeply unequal power relations across the world market, and continue to penalize economic and political actors in developing and emerging economies? How to explain this phenomenon and its reproduction over time? What are its manifestations and associated policy dilemmas?

This chapter introduces the reader to IFS, one of the core conceptual tools deployed in this book, and expounds its connection to financial statecraft. IFS, as both an umbrella concept and a research agenda, was developed to address a series of determinate developmental and economic challenges. The chapter therefore starts by offering a definition of its object of investigation, it spells out the research questions that it sets out to answer, and it briefly reviews some of its main theoretical inspirations. Next, the chapter offers an overview of some of the main sources, features, and implications of IFS, particularly those that exert constraints and pressures on state policy making and development trajectories in the Global South. The chapter then turns to the relationship between financial subordination and statecraft. It highlights some of the problematic ways in which the relationship between the two has been conceived, such as when they are seen as two poles of a continuum. While IFS exerts real and identifiable constraints on policy making, this, however, does not mean that state agency and capacity are denied. On the contrary, IFS can be a powerful catalyst of institutional innovation, regulatory experimentation, and resource mobilization in developing and emerging economies, whether it is to accommodate, mitigate, or resist the impacts of IFS, or to ameliorate a state's position in global financial and monetary relations. Thus, the chapter makes the case for understanding financial subordination not as an end state or static, inescapable condition (where state autonomy and agency are denied), but as a set of power relations which are internalized by state actors, shape policy making, and therefore become crystallized in financial statecraft. State capabilities and capacities, then, are not denied by IFS, but structured by it, resulting in variegated configurations of financial statecraft. The chapter concludes with some open questions and avenues for future research.

Genesis of international financial subordination

IFS was born out of a collective research project (funded by a grant from the Independent Social Research Foundation), conducted by Annina Kaltenbrunner, Bruno Bonizzi, Ingrid Kvangraven, Jeff Powell, Carolina Alves, Kai Koddenbrock, and myself, between 2018 and 2021. All of us had previously researched a range of subject matters related to money, finance, financialization, and capital flows in development contexts, including in Brazil, Mexico, South Africa, Senegal, Ghana, Thailand, Colombia, and Peru (cf Powell, 2013; Bonizzi, 2013; Kaltenbrunner and Painceira, 2015; 2018; Alves, 2017; Alami, 2018a; 2018b; 2018c; 2019a; 2019b; Bonizzi et al,

2019; 2021a; Koddenbrock, 2020; Kvangraven et al, 2021; Alves et al, 2022; Koddenbrock et al, 2022). The project rationale was to bring together a team of researchers from various academic disciplines (heterodox economics, international political economy, development studies, and economic geography, with many of us having a foot in more than one discipline) to systematize our respective research findings, identify overlapping research interests, think collectively about theory and method, foster cross-fertilization between our approaches, and identify potential avenues for future research.

Several key cross-cutting themes emerged from our discussions. First, concerning our research objects: we were all, in different ways, concerned with the specific form that monetary and financial phenomena take in developing and emerging economies. In short, the management of monetary and financial affairs appears to be more difficult in these economies than it is in richer, more powerful countries. This manifests, inter alia, as repeated financial and debt crises, monetary instability, vulnerability to external financial conditions, capital flight, and financial fragility (cf de Paula et al, 2020). What makes financial crises so recurrent in developing and emerging economies? How and why is financial fragility and vulnerability exported to those spaces of the global capitalist economy? Our research showed that this phenomenon does not manifest only during periods of crisis, monetary instability, and financial distress. It also shapes everyday economic and financial relations, in ways that are consequential for developmental prospects, from policy making at various levels of government, to dynamics of industrial capital accumulation and productive structures, patterns of urban growth and regional development, class relations and distributional conflicts, as well as geographical value transfers within and across territorial borders. Several of us had started to think of this built-in asymmetry in world financial and monetary relations in terms of *subordination* (see, for instance, Powell, 2013 on 'subordinate financialization'; Kaltenbrunner and Painceira, 2018 on 'subordinated financial integration'; Alami, 2018b; 2019a on the 'subordinate positionality of developing countries within the global financial system'). It was clear that this notion of international financial subordination (IFS, which is the term we collectively agreed upon, for reasons that are further explicated later) required fuller conceptual development and empirical substantiation.

Second, we thought that the notion of financial subordination was all the more suggestive as it raised a number of theoretical and methodological challenges: how to theorize IFS as a phenomenon that is simultaneously highly *general* (in the sense that it structurally affects most, if not all, developing and emerging economies) and *variegated* (in the sense that it can take highly differentiated forms depending on local specificities and institutional configurations of state–finance relations, and in the sense that there could potentially be different degrees and shades of subordination)? Put differently, the theoretical and methodological challenge here is to develop a conception of IFS as a global–structural yet geographically variegated phenomenon across world regions, national states, and local economies. Such a conception would allow comparing and analyzing the similarities and differences in how IFS is expressed in, say, a rapidly growing East Asian economy, a post-Soviet central Asian commodity exporter, a lower-income West African country, or a large South American emerging market. (I return to the question of differences in IFS and how it relates to variegated financial statecraft later.) A related challenge is to account for both the specificity of IFS at the *present historical juncture* (that is, in our highly economically integrated and financialized capitalism, cf Bonizzi et al, 2022), while also uncovering *historical patterns and legacies* (including how entangled histories of finance, empire, and imperialism continue to shape IFS) (Alami, 2019c; Koddenbrock, 2020; Bernards, 2021; 2022; 2023a; 2023b; Koddenbrock et al, 2022). This is important to understand the factors that contribute to IFS and its reproduction over time, but also the historical transformations in its modalities of expression.

The third cross-cutting theme that emerged from our discussions is that the causes, manifestations, and consequences of IFS are *multifaceted*. They involve a complex mix of monetary, financial, macroeconomic, (geo)political, historical, geographic, institutional, technological, and environmental factors (I'll discuss some of these factors later). Moreover, there are multiple feedback loops and reciprocal mechanisms between these factors. For instance, a country with weak productive structures is likely to develop a form of external financial integration that renders it highly vulnerable to international financial liquidity cycles, which, in turn, acts as an impediment to economic upgrading and structural change in this economy. The point is that the multifaceted nature of IFS demands that we develop *systemic* explanations of IFS, that is, explanations capable of accounting for multiple factors, how they interact and combine, and contribute to the constitution of IFS as a general phenomenon. Avowedly, this is easier said than done. But we thought that, at the very least, this requires multidisciplinary perspectives. Due to their diverse theoretical proclivities and empirical orientations, disciplines such as IPE, historical institutionalism, heterodox economics, financial geography, economic anthropology, and so on, could all have a role to play in reconstructing systemic conceptualization(s) of IFS. More pointedly, this also demands that we develop collective and cumulative efforts at theory building. Indeed, research efforts into the causes and consequences of IFS had so far remained relatively fragmented, with little attempt at systematizing findings, comparing cases, confronting causal explanations, and developing broader theorizations. This, in our view, was a significant epistemological hurdle to understanding IFS in its multifaceted and systemic dimensions.

Our proposition of IFS as an *umbrella concept* and *research agenda*, outlined in Alami et al (2023), followed from these reflections. It is worth briefly explaining our choice to conceive of IFS in those terms, rather than the (perhaps more obvious) choice of developing a particular analytical framework. Simply put, we were less interested in making the case for a single analytical or conceptual apparatus, than in providing a platform for bringing into conversation a wide range of investigations into various aspects, properties, and features of IFS. At the core of our proposition is an attempt at generating an interdisciplinary and pluralist encounter involving various social scientific traditions around a focused research agenda on IFS. Given these objectives, it seemed to us that a single analytical framework would be too rigid to accommodate for experimentation and creative combinations of approaches and methods to address the various theoretical and epistemological challenges raised earlier. By contrast, the notion of an umbrella concept (think of prominent umbrella concepts such as neoliberalism or financialization) could help anchor and channel research efforts towards a cumulative theory-building endeavour, while offering the necessary scope and flexibility for creative experimentation and pluralist dialogue. At least this is our hope.

IFS: what's in a term?

The argument so far is that IFS as an umbrella concept and research agenda was motivated by a series of determinate developmental challenges, and associated research puzzles and policy dilemmas. IFS is about focusing scholarly efforts on the set of processes, mechanisms, and relations that maintain developing and emerging market economies (DEEs) in a subordinate position in the global monetary and financial system, and the implications thereof. Let me now zoom in on each term: 'international', 'financial', and 'subordination'.

By *international*, we mean that financial subordination is a global phenomenon, in the sense that it refers to structured hierarchies within the world market, and it manifests as an unequal relation between national states. The term also refers to the tightly integrated character of global finance, and the now unprecedented degree of interconnection between national financial systems. This does not mean, however, that the international and the national are the only relevant scales in analyzing IFS. Recent studies have emphasized that other factors contributing to IFS can be constituted or manifest at other scales (such as the body, local, urban, regional, continental, and so on) (see Büdenbender and Aalbers, 2019; Fernandez and Aalbers, 2020; Socoloff, 2020; Guermond, 2022; Haag, 2023; Reis and Lukas 2022; Reyes and Basile, 2022; Bernards, 2023a; Green, 2023). Elsewhere, we made the case for conceiving of IFS as a process that is reproduced through a nested hierarchy of socially produced and interrelated scales, from the investment practices of individual economic actors to the structures of the global financial system, interstate relations, and international financial governance, and a multitude of scalar levels in between (Alami, 2018a; Alami et al, 2023).

The term *financial* reflects our interest in the operations of capitalist money and finance, and in the causes and consequences of developing and emerging economies' enhanced vulnerability to the movement of financial capital across the world market. We approach money, finance, and finance capital not only from the angle of their technicalities, but also (and foremost) as expressions of power. This way, we draw attention to the eminently political nature of IFS, and we directly connect IFS to cognate debates on the structural power of finance in developing and emerging economies (see Gallagher, 2015; Grabel, 2018; Naqvi, 2019; Gabor, 2021; Petry et al, 2021; Akolgo, 2022; Dafe and Rethel, 2022; Schedelik et al, 2022; Bernards, 2023b; Gort and Brooks, 2023; Pataccini, 2024). Thus, we suggest that the questions that IFS as a research agenda must aim to elucidate are why the structural power of finance takes a particularly violent form of expression in DEEs, what sort of power is expressed (state power, capitalist class power, the power and interest of specific class fractions or economic actors), how, and to what effect.

Finally, we chose the term *subordination* to convey the idea that IFS is made of relations that are both spatial and saturated with power, and that it is part and parcel of the structured hierarchies of the world economy. We see IFS as composed of relations of domination, inferiority, and subjugation between different spaces across the world market, expressed in and through money and finance. These relations shape the possibilities of governments, firms, and other actors (institutional investors, international financial institutions, and so on) in both developed and developing economies, but they penalize actors in developing and emerging economies disproportionally. Consider, for instance, the case of flight-to-safety during financial crises, when international investors (often located in world financial centres) dump their emerging market assets, and purchase 'safe-haven' assets denominated in the currencies of advanced capitalist economies. Insofar as the asymmetric flows of financial capital triggered by flight-to-safety simultaneously worsen the crisis in developing and emerging economies (currency depreciation, dislocation of financial systems, increase in perceived investment risk, and so on), and facilitate the management of the crisis in advanced capitalist economies (financial institutions can repatriate assets and consolidate activities, financial systems benefit from the inflow of financial capital, which helps stabilizing exchange rates, and so on), it is an example of the subordinated character of crisis resolution in developing and emerging economies.

Causes, manifestations, and consequences of IFS

What do we know about the causes, manifestations, and consequences of IFS? Let us state at the outset that mainstream economics approaches offer an inadequate answer to these questions. Typically, the difficulties faced by developing and emerging economies in the management of monetary and financial affairs are attributed to a combination of factors internal to these political economies: the alleged underdevelopment of domestic financial systems, bad governance, fiscal and monetary mismanagement, the weakness of macroeconomic fundamentals, and an insufficiently attractive business environment. These factors may well be important, but by themselves cannot explain IFS as a general and enduring global phenomenon, nor can they explain why the developing and emerging economies that have made considerable efforts on all these fronts remain prone to financial crises and highly vulnerable to volatile capital flows. More generally, mainstream economics has little to say about the relationship between IFS and the structure of the world economy, contemporary processes of accumulation (notably the specificities of capital accumulation in the periphery), and the turbulent histories of the relation between finance and (post)colonial development.

Three heterodox traditions offer a much richer intellectual source to start theorizing and empirically documenting IFS, given their long-standing interest in the specific nature of financial and monetary phenomena in developing economies: dependency theory, post-Keynesian economics, and Marxist scholarship (see Figure 2.1). This is not the place to explore in detail each of these approaches and their arguments on the causes and manifestations of IFS (see Alami et al, 2023 for a systematic review). Rather, in this section, I briefly discuss some of the most relevant factors to understand the nature and diversity of financial statecraft under IFS, which is the core topic of this book.

Let us start with the structure of the global financial system. The latter is organized in a highly hierarchical way: some of the most powerful financial institutions (banks, insurance companies, pension funds, asset managers, and so on) and financial markets (money markets, foreign exchange markets, commodity markets, and derivatives markets) dominate this hierarchy, and are concentrated in a small number of world financial centres (Haberly and Wójcik, 2022). Many of these world financial centres (New York, London, Paris, Frankfurt, Amsterdam, and so on) remain located in advanced capitalist economies, and concentrate command-and-control functions, which profoundly shape global financial operations, including investment into (and out of) developing and emerging economies. Financial investors organize their scale of operations and diversification into other geographical markets from these world financial centres, and tend to treat investment into 'emerging' and 'frontier' markets as risky (with the assistance of credit rating agencies, see de Conti et al, 2022). The implication is that assets from these economies must not only deliver high returns (insofar as a

Figure 2.1: Arguments on IFS from three heterodox traditions

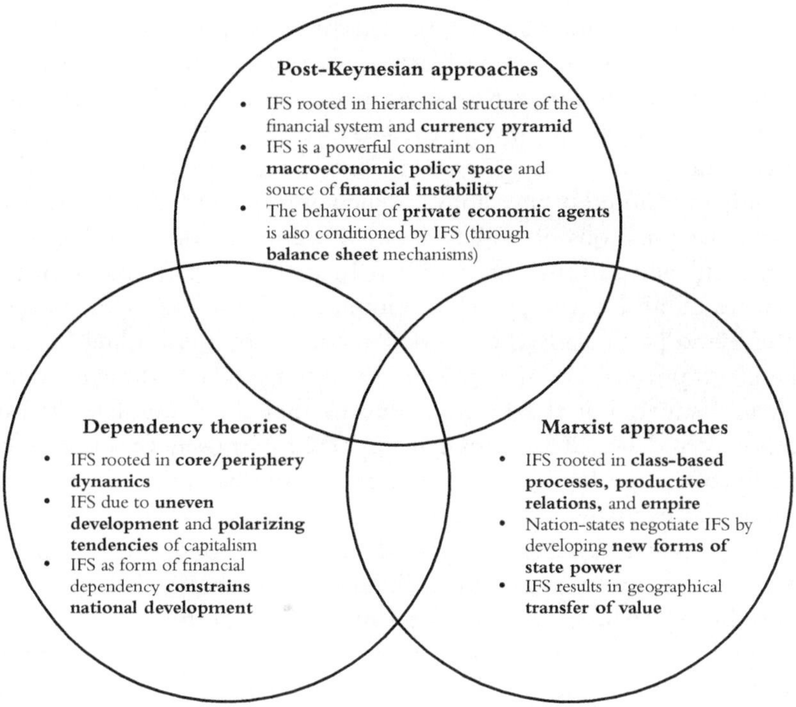

Note: The Venn diagram suggests that there are multiple overlaps between the three traditions, in the form of cross-fertilization as well as authors combining all three traditions. It is possible to identify distinct lines of argumentation on the causes, manifestations, and consequences of IFS in these three traditions, as shown on this figure.

high-risk perception leads investors to demand a high premium), they are also the first to be liquidated during periods of financial distress. The parastatal institutions in charge of the governance of the global financial system (think about the IMF, the Bank of International Settlements, or the US Federal Reserve) are also located in these world financial centres, as well as other actors producing financial information and governance standards (credit rating agencies, professional financial and legal services firms). Thus, most of the private and public financial institutions that developing states borrow from are located in these world financial centres (although some large emerging economies borrow mostly domestically). These institutional–geographical features of the global financial system significantly matter for IFS. They shape the terms according to which developing and emerging economies access international capital markets, the type of finance they have access to, and how debt crises are resolved when they happen, such as who of the borrowers or lenders bears the brunt of the costs of deflationary adjustment. This hierarchical structure of the global financial system is therefore a key factor of IFS.

Let us now look at the monetary basis of the global financial system, which compounds some of the financial factors contributing to IFS. Of particular interest here is what post-Keynesian economists call the international currency hierarchy (or pyramid) (de Paula et al, 2017; Bonizzi et al, 2021b). The current global monetary system is made of a hierarchy of currencies with different 'liquidity premiums', depending on their relative ability to perform the functions of money (unit of account, store of value, means of payment, and settling international financial obligations). While the currencies of advanced capitalist economies sit at the top of the currency pyramid (and particularly the US dollar, backed by the leading hegemon and military power), the currencies of developing and emerging economies are firmly situated at the bottom, due to their low liquidity premium (Prates and Andrade, 2013; Murau et al, 2022). As a result of this monetary subordination, developing and emerging economies tend to experience financial and exchange rate instability, high exposure to large and sudden changes in global liquidity conditions, and strong constraints on national policy making. These constraints include a high cost of borrowing (due to the need to offer higher interest rates to compensate for their currencies' low liquidity premium), the need to accumulate vast amounts of foreign exchange reserves (which can be costly, given the limited amount of locally available resources), and, in the case of the poorer economies, an inability to issue debt in domestic currency. Monetary subordination also shapes the corporate behaviour and decisions of economic agents (borrowing, lending, investment, and so on), such as how firms in developing economies borrow internationally (often in US dollars) or hedge interest and foreign exchange risks, or how large institutional investors (often located in advanced capitalist economies) invest in developing economies (such as the carry trade operations of hedge funds, or how pension funds invest in infrastructure) (Bonizzi and Kaltenbrunner, 2019; Pryke and Allen, 2022; Andreoni et al, 2023). This in turn leads to the build-up of financial fragilities on balance sheets, which not only constrain firms, but also pose additional policy making challenges, notably in terms of managing exchange rates and maintaining domestic financial stability.

These financial and monetary factors interact and combine with so-called 'real economy' factors, such as weak and dependent productive economic structures, compounding the effects of IFS (Bonizzi et al, 2022; de Almeida Oliveira and de Conti, 2022). Developing and emerging economies are indeed often characterized by low labour productivity levels, a low degree of sectoral diversification, a focus on low-value added activities, and a strong orientation towards the export of primary commodities and natural resources. Their firms and regions are often integrated as subordinate actors within regional and global value chains and production networks, which are governed by lead transnational corporations (Newman, 2022). These are largely headquartered in advanced capitalist economies, and often exercise monopoly control over advanced intellectual property, core technologies, and strategic intangibles (Durand and Milberg, 2020; Baglioni et al, 2021; Hauge, 2023). This maintains economic actors in developing economies (in addition to their dependence on dollar funding to trade with partners in global value chains) in a situation of external dependence on technologies and capital goods, which they must import. In addition, these economies often suffer from a structural dependence on energy and food imports (the international prices of which can be highly volatile), which translates at the aggregate national level into severe balance-of-payments constraints and additional external debt burden. Furthermore, the weakness and dependent character of productive capital accumulation combines with often extremely hierarchical and oppressive configurations of postcolonial class relations and regressive tax systems (where comprador elites are deeply committed to illicit capital flight and other forms of transferring locally produced wealth to tax havens and the world financial centres mentioned earlier), resulting in a narrow fiscal base, and difficulties mobilizing local resources for investment in development and structural change (Ashman et al, 2011; Ndikumana and Boyce, 2022).

Crucially, these mutually reinforcing hierarchical financial, monetary, and productive relations contribute to the intensification of highly destructive environmental regimes of capital accumulation and unsustainable socioecological relations across the Global South (Bernards, 2021; Althouse and Svartzman, 2022). Repeated financial crises, debt servicing, the pursuit of foreign exchange at any costs, and other manifestations of IFS push developing economies to deepen specialization in low value-added activities, as well as extractive and polluting sectors. IFS-induced pressures to intensify resource extraction of mining, energy, and other raw materials for exports further expose developing and emerging economies to ecological degradation, which often directly affects the most vulnerable communities (Franz and McNelly, 2023). Moreover, climate change risks tend to translate into higher external financial fragility, deteriorating currencies' liquidity premia and sovereign credit ratings, thereby worsening financial and monetary subordination (Löscher and Kaltenbrunner, 2022). Of the countries most vulnerable to climate impacts, 93 per cent are currently in or near debt distress (ActionAid, 2023). In short, IFS is rooted in (and contributes to reproduce) deeply unequal and violent global political ecologies that penalize workers, peasants, the poor, and their livelihoods across the Global South (Althouse and Svartzman, 2022). In an age of accelerating climate change, it is only likely that this nexus of IFS and environmental destruction will deepen.

To sum up this section, the combination of monetary, financial, productive, and environmental factors renders IFS a particularly persistent phenomenon which strongly constrains patterns of policy making. Developing and emerging economies are forced to conduct monetary, fiscal, and exchange rate policies in reaction to rapid changes in global liquidity preference (which are determined by global risk sentiment and monetary policy choices in advanced capitalist countries), rather than following domestic developmental priorities. IFS generates a profound asymmetry between how states in advanced capitalist economies and those in the Global South face the competitive pressures of the world market, and how they can handle the crises and contradictions of capital accumulation. Furthermore, low liquidity premia and low credit ratings force peripheral states to implement investor-friendly policies and offer high returns to attract external finance and sustain continuous inflows. This acts as a drag on the local social surplus product and significantly reduces fiscal space. This constrains the capacity of states to invest in developmental projects (infrastructure, climate transition, and so on), engage in social redistribution, or simply manage aggregate demand.

Despite efforts (including painful structural reforms) to make themselves attractive to international investors, the poorer states often face rationed credit and can temporarily lose access to international bond markets. As a result of global interest rate hikes, capital flight and currency depreciation can rapidly increase the cost of borrowing and servicing external debt. Money is expensive for the poor. Many poor countries spend far more on interest payments than on health, education, and green transition and decarbonization goals. At the time of writing (June 2023), as many as sixty-one countries are in (or in high risk of) debt distress (Global Development Policy Center, 2023).

Varieties of financial statecraft under financial subordination

Let me now turn to the core subject matter of this book, the relationship between IFS and financial statecraft, that is, the deployment of financial or monetary instruments by governments to achieve policy ends (as defined in the introduction and next chapter of this collection). How to understand the relation between the two? What does statecraft look like under IFS? In the remainder of this chapter, I make three arguments in response to these questions. As we have just seen, IFS exerts strong pressures on peripheral states, on what they can do, and on how they do it. The constraints on policy making, patterns of capital accumulation, and development trajectories are real, consequential, and identifiable. This, however, does not mean that state agency and capacity are denied. Thus, my first argument on the relationship between financial statecraft and IFS is that it would be a mistake to conceive of the state in developing and emerging economies as a passive actor, or a helpless victim of IFS.[1] A few examples of state financial activism across the developing world will suffice to illustrate this point.

The 1997–98 Asian financial crisis, the early 2000s 'emerging markets' crises (in Brazil, Argentina, Russia, South Africa, Turkey, and many others), and the 2008 global financial crisis have been watersheds in spurring remarkable processes of institutional innovation and policy experimentation, notably in policy areas such as cross-border finance management and financial stabilization. Many peripheral states deliberately accumulated massive amounts of foreign exchange reserves throughout the 2000s as a war chest to 'self-insure' against sudden capital account reversals and capital flight. State-financial apparatuses (central banks, national treasuries, and financial regulatory authorities) were empowered and adopted strict macroprudential regulations (Marois, 2012). They also strictly regulated, monitored, and supervised domestic banking systems. Some of these regulations were often tighter than international norms and best practices.

These policy and institutional developments however failed to provide sufficient financial and macroeconomic stability in the aftermath of the 2008 global financial crisis. Indeed, between 2009 and 2014, developing and emerging economies faced extraordinarily volatile patterns of cross-border finance, the procyclicality of which was enhanced by the expansionary monetary policies conducted by central banks and governments in advanced capitalist economies (particularly the United States, the United Kingdom, the Eurozone, and Japan). As a result of these policies, peripheral states faced a 'liquidity tsunami', most of which was in the form of speculative financial capital flows, which proved particularly thorny to manage (Alami, 2019a). Consequently, developing and emerging economies engaged in another round of policy experimentation in the immediate 2008 global financial crisis period. Countries as diverse as Brazil, South Korea, Indonesia, China, Costa Rica, Uruguay, the Philippines, Peru, Taiwan, Colombia, Argentina, Thailand, Turkey, and India deployed a wide range of measures to manage cross-border financial flows in a context of acute financial instability, from diverse capital controls (on both portfolio flows and bank loans), to stricter macroprudential regulations, foreign exchange derivatives regulations, unconventional monetary policy tools, and 'aggressive' foreign exchange market interventions (Gallagher, 2015; Prates and Fritz, 2016; Grabel, 2018; da Silva, 2022).

Many governments also experimented with various forms of state financial ownership. Some created new sovereign wealth funds (or vastly expanded the mandates and prerogatives of already existing ones) to buffer the economy from external macro-financial shocks or economic downturns. Some of these funds invested in domestic equities to help mitigate externally induced financial markets volatility. Other sovereign funds used revenues from natural resources exports and invested them in highly liquid low-risk assets offshore (Dixon et al, 2022). Sovereign funds also played a role in fiscal policy, by smoothing resource revenue spending over time, and in monetary policy, by limiting the appreciation of the exchange rate. During crises, they helped sustain government spending or bail out certain industries. Governments could thus avoid the need for international assistance from the Bretton Woods institutions and the accompanying conditionalities, which often mean severe cuts to public spending and other politically contentious economic reforms. Examples of sovereign funds created over the past two decades to play a stabilizing role (simultaneously managing financial stability and revenues from energy and mining exports) include the *Fondo Mexicano del Petroleo*, the *Fundo Soberano de Angola*, the Petroleum Fund of Timor-Leste, the Ghana Stabilization Fund, Chile's Economic and Social Stabilization Fund, Botswana's Pula Fund, and the Stabilization Fund of the Russian Federation.

Other countries turned to state-owned banking as a tool for counter-cyclical management (Griffith-Jones and Ocampo, 2018; Marois, 2021). They vastly expanded the loan portfolios and financial capacities of their national policy and development banks to channel finance and credit. For example, in Bolivia, the *Movimiento al Socialismo*, empowered by popular pressure from below, re-established state-owned banks and implemented a financial reform in a bid to reduce external vulnerabilities and ensure political stability (Naqvi, 2021). In Indonesia under the Jokowi administration the state responded to the instabilities generated by shrinking external development finance and underdeveloped domestic capital markets by enhancing its role as patient capitalist and development financier since the early 2000s, via state banks such as *Bank Rakyat Indonesia*, *Bank Mandiri*, and *Bank Negara Indonesia* (Kim, 2019; 2021). In Brazil, under the *Partido dos Trabalhadores,* the *Banco Nacional de Desenvolvimento Econômico e Social* and other federal banks played a vital counter-cyclical role which helped the country withstand the global financial crisis (von Mettenheim, 2015). Central banks in developing and emerging economies have also developed new instruments to maintain the 'plumbing' of financial markets and guarantee market liquidity, to accompany the institutional development and deepening of market-based financial systems. In the process they have concentrated extraordinary discretionary authority to govern in and through financial markets (Musthaq, 2023).

These examples of state financial activism show that peripheral states assert their agency in the realms of money and finance in all sorts of ways, including by developing new institutional forms, or expanding their financial statecraft toolkit. IFS therefore does not deny state agency; on the contrary, these examples suggest that, because of the very pressures and constraints that it generates, IFS can be a powerful catalyst of institutional innovation, regulatory experimentation, and resource mobilization in developing and emerging economies. Consequently, the relationship between IFS and state power is not a zero-sum game. Put differently, financial statecraft and financial subordination are not the two opposite poles of a continuum of state autonomy. Accordingly, the relevant question to ask is not if this or that particular emerging capitalist state is capable of exercising financial statecraft or not. Rather, we should ask: How does IFS shape the interaction of states and financial markets in developing and emerging economies? How do various modalities of state financial activism respond to, and *negotiate*, the pressures and constraints emanating from IFS? How does financial statecraft *internalize* the power relations and structured hierarchies that characterize IFS? How do different institutional configurations of state–finance relations influence developing countries' abilities to engage in varieties of financial statecraft within the context of IFS?

Hence, my second argument: state financial activism, even in cases that demonstrate a remarkably high degree and reach of state capacity, must not necessarily be understood as an attempt to escape IFS, or decrease its intensity. Let me flesh out this point by offering a brief (and sympathetic) critique of two bodies of literature, both of which have offered valuable studies of state financial activism in developing and emerging economies over the past few years, the literature on 'policy space' and that on 'financial statecraft'. The literature on 'policy space' tends to interpret policies such as capital controls, the introduction of strong regulations on financial systems, or the expansion of state-owned banking and financial entities, as measures working towards decreasing IFS, with the explicit objective of regaining policy space (that is, the scope for domestic policies that is available for each country at a particular point in time to implement an autonomous national development strategy) (cf Gallagher, 2015; Grabel, 2018; Ban and Bohle, 2021; Naqvi, 2021). The literature on financial statecraft also tends to interpret the multiplication of financial initiatives on the part of developing and emerging economies as expressions of 'defensive' tactics – whereby states resist against 'pernicious influences from global financial markets', or 'offensive' strategies – designed to 'fend off disruptive influences from the global financial system' (Armijo and Katada, 2015, p 53; see Leslie Armijo's chapter in the present collection). My objection here is not that notions of policy space and offensive/defensive financial statecraft cannot be helpful analytical lenses. Rather, it is the tendency to automatically associate state financial activism with these particular logics that I find potentially problematic (as well as the tendency across both literatures to reproduce a binary opposition between state power/agency and financial market constraint) (see an early critique in Alami, 2018a).

To substantiate my critique, let me briefly return to the deployment of various types of capital controls discussed earlier. To be clear, these policies did affect the cross-border operations of finance, notably the most short-term and speculative ones, and in some cases they clashed with the interests of financiers and other business actors who (unsurprisingly) strongly opposed them. This was the case, for instance, in countries like Brazil. Yet, for the most part, these policies neither challenged long-term commitments to capital account liberalization, nor did they signal a break with neoliberal norms of free capital mobility and other pillars of orthodox macroeconomic policy making (such as central bank independence, inflation targeting, and relatively tight fiscal discipline). Moreover, they often had the explicit objective of securing the continuous inflow of financial capital, to sustain ongoing development models relying on external finance. Overall, they were designed and implemented *not to alter the status quo but to maintain it.* In my reading, rather than attempts to preserve and expand policy autonomy, or experimentations in defensive financial statecraft, these capital controls are best seen as the emergence of novel forms of state power in emerging economies to allow for the continuation of finance-led strategies of accumulation, while limiting the build-up of financial vulnerability and fragility, and mitigating some of its worst short-term consequences. One can see here that although these capital controls aimed to tame speculative finance (and, in some cases, successfully did so), they did not aim at challenging the structures of IFS, nor did they aim at improving developing countries' positions within such structures. Put simply, this was about coping with IFS, rather than extricating oneself from it, or exerting a countervailing power against it.

Turning to another major form of financial activism over the past decade, which is the proliferation of state-owned financial entities, it is equally difficult to argue that those unequivocally signalled a retreat of IFS, or an attempt to resist it. As argued earlier, many sovereign wealth funds have been recently created or repurposed to help manage some of the contradictions, instabilities, and policy dilemmas associated with IFS. Yet, partly because they strive to normalize their status as legitimate financial market actors, sovereign funds generally do so by following a market-oriented logic, and by mimicking the practices and organizational goals of comparable private-sector financial entities (such as supplementary occupational pension funds). For instance, they often purposefully embrace the tools of modern financial management such as shareholder-value logics in the administration of state assets. Overall, sovereign funds have adopted the institutional, cultural, and social norms of neoliberalized global finance, and have become deeply embedded into the global financial system (Dixon et al, 2022). Consequently, they have also become tightly enmeshed with the structured hierarchies of IFS. Hence the paradoxical role they play with respect to IFS: the (geo)political and developmental functions that sovereign funds can play (for instance, by investing strategically across a range of sectors and assets both domestically and internationally) may well help their state sponsors ameliorate their respective positions in global financial relations (see for instance Liu, 2024), but their deep integration into the global financial system, their adoption of conventional investment practices, and their embrace of financialized norms arguably also contribute to the overall consolidation of IFS as a global phenomenon.

This succinct discussion suggests that IFS does not only act as a force which externally constrains state power and agency, it is also *reproduced in and through practices of state financial activism* in developing and emerging economies. These, of course, include policies that deregulate and open financial systems and liberalize cross-border flows of finance. But they can also include policies that otherwise demonstrate strong state capacities and statecraft, whether it is by taming speculative finance, keeping financial interests under control, exercising authority over domestic financial systems, or directing flows of credit and investment. Thus, to understand the motivations and outcomes of policies and practices of state financial activism in developing and emerging economies, it is insufficient to try and assess the extent to which they appear to accommodate, mitigate, or resist pressures emanating from IFS. Understanding the relationship between statecraft and IFS solely in these terms necessarily leads to an incomplete picture.

My third and final argument follows from this: developing a richer understanding of state agency and statecraft under IFS requires introducing a *class* lens. State policies, regulations, and institutions, including various practices of state financial activism, have class-based determinants and distributive consequences. Indeed, under capitalism, states face the double imperative of fostering capital accumulation and managing class relations. To do that, they attempt to engineer accumulation strategies (or development models) as well as social contracts between classes. The crisis-ridden character of capital accumulation and the antagonistic nature of class relations render these attempts at engineering growth strategies and social contracts necessarily unstable, precarious, fragile, and riven with tensions.

All of this to say that being attentive to domestic class-based interests, strategies, and conflicts is essential to explaining the variegated ways in which states navigate and negotiate the constraints and pressures of IFS. Various business interests and social groups may be differently exposed to financial risks and vulnerability, or indeed they may be differently positioned to profit from financial opportunities, as a result of both IFS and state policies. Thus, state financial activism in developing and emerging economies must be understood as *politically mediating* the impacts of IFS, with uneven consequences across classes and social groups. This allows studying the development of policies, regulations, and institutions in the realms of money and finance in light of states' attempt to negotiate IFS in ways that are more or less consistent with their accumulation strategies, growth models, and attempts to engineer particular social contracts between classes.

Again, let me illustrate this claim by returning to one of the modalities of state financial activism in emerging economies mentioned earlier: the renationalization of banking systems and the expansion of state-owned banking. A wide range of political regimes in developing and emerging economies have recently relied upon state-owned banking to engineer particular social contracts with various segments of the population, notably by facilitating the expansion of consumer debt and the asset valuation in real estate markets. In Hungary, for example, the nationalization of a large share of foreign-owned commercial banks, and the re-politicization of the central bank in 2014–15 enhanced the ability of the state to contain the destabilizing effects of foreign capital inflows but also facilitated a centralization of political control over credit provision. The Hungarian state used this power to engineer a boom in construction and housing markets, to further financialize social policy, and to earmark lending to small-and-medium enterprises, in order to strike 'rentier' bargains between state and society (Scheiring, 2020; Karas, 2022; Piroska, 2022). Relatively similar processes took place in Turkey (Öniş and Kutlay, 2021; Altınörs and Akçay, 2022), as well as in Russia, where resurgent state activism has been a direct response to the IFS-induced fragilities of the 2000s, namely speculative patterns of cross-border finance and volatile hydrocarbon prices. A wave of renationalization and banking sector concentration facilitated the emergence of several state-controlled national champions, which allowed the state to exert considerable political control over the financial system, consolidate authoritarian tendencies, and catalyze forms of financialization that served its interests and benefitted political factions and economic interests closely associated with state power (Viktorov and Abramov, 2020; Mishura and Ageeva, 2022).

In sum, to use an expression famously coined by state theorist Nicos Poulantzas (1978), I submit that financial statecraft and state–finance institutional arrangements in developing and emerging economies must be conceived as the *material condensation of two types of social relations, IFS and domestic class configurations*. Importantly, these two types of social relations do not simply overlap or intersect, they are mutually constitutive: the ways in which states politically mediate IFS shape domestic processes of class formation and struggle. Reciprocally, class forces and sociopolitical conflicts affect how states navigate the pressures and constraints of IFS at national and subnational levels. This, in turn, contributes to shaping the overall trajectory of IFS, that is, how it is reproduced as an aggregate, global phenomenon. The argument is summed up visually in Figure 2.2.

Conclusion: Future research on IFS and financial statecraft

This chapter aimed to demonstrate the analytical value and political salience of IFS. As an umbrella concept and research agenda, it focuses on the mechanisms that maintain developing countries in a subordinate position in

Figure 2.2: IFS and variegated financial statecraft: a conceptual framework

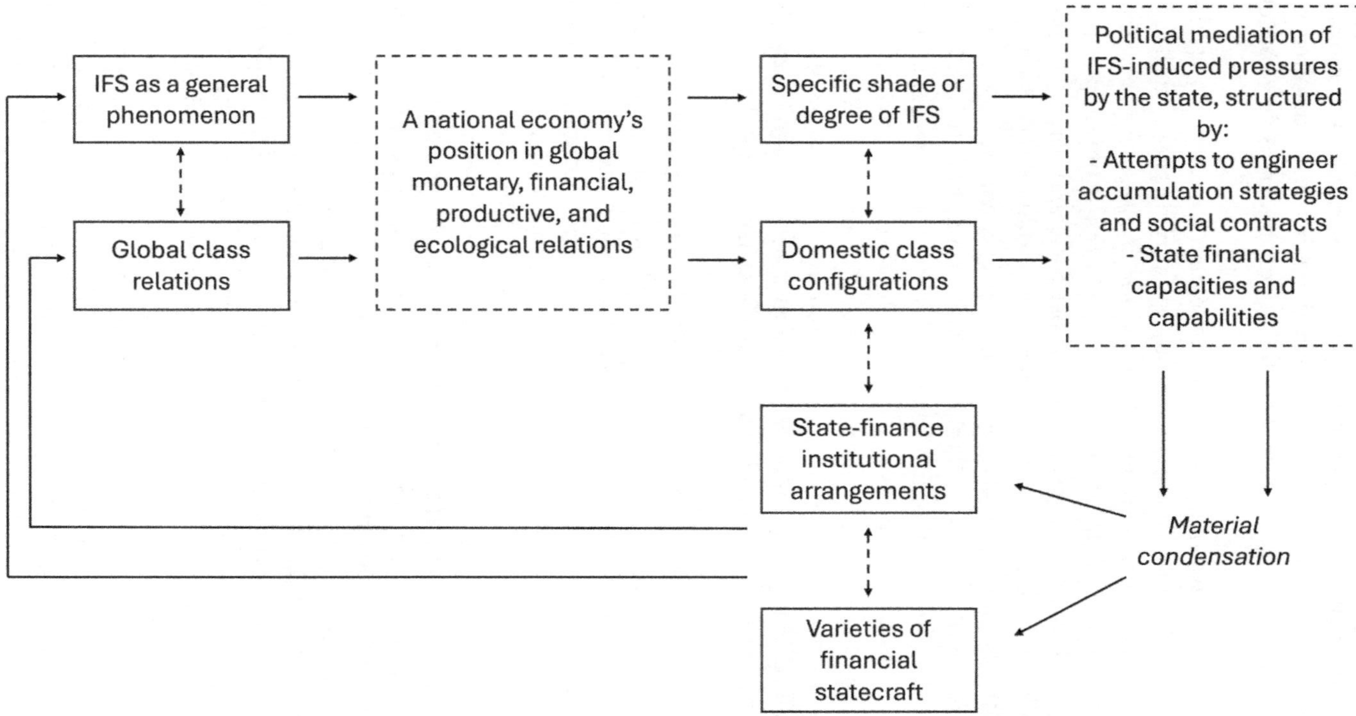

Note: One-direction arrows do not represent successive causal steps, but rather different layers of national and political mediation. Dashed arrows suggest mutual constitution.

the global monetary and financial system, as well as how such mechanisms shape variegated patterns of state–finance relations. By means of conclusion, let me briefly mention some avenues for future research on IFS and financial statecraft. While much work remains to be done on the multifaceted aspects, properties, and features of IFS, in what follows my remarks solely concentrate on two dimensions.

First, future research may investigate the extent to which IFS is mutating in an age of geoeconomic fragmentation, intensifying geopolitical tensions, turbulent reconfiguration of global production and financial networks, and resurgent state capitalism. If, as argued earlier, IFS is indeed a remarkably enduring and resilient phenomenon, whose form and nature has changed historically according to prevailing monetary, productive, geopolitical, and ecological relations, then we may wonder how it will develop in reaction to these trends. Relatedly, researchers may scrutinize how IFS is influencing how states in the Global South adjust and participate in ongoing processes of (post-)globalization. If history is of any lesson, we can hypothesize that this will involve dynamics of crises and policy innovation. Whether these twin dynamics will simply lead to a reconfigured financial policy toolkit and renewed state–financial activism, or to a deeper restructuring of the relationship between states and financial markets in developing and emerging economies, is an open question. Ultimately, these questions matter for social forces concerned with identifying opportunities for progressive social change.

Second, in an era of catastrophic climate change there is a crucial need for further research into the nexus of IFS and environmental degradation discussed earlier. By now we know that adequately addressing the climate crisis will require a thorough overhaul of the international financial and monetary architecture, or what Dafermos (2023) calls 'a climate just financial system'. My wager here is that, in order to be *just*, such a system must explicitly address IFS. At the very least, this would mean making sure developing and emerging economies are less exposed to IFS-induced pressures, constraints, financial risks, and vulnerabilities. This would also mean setting up robust global and regional governance mechanisms to mitigate the impacts of IFS, and redesigning financial and monetary arrangements so that risks and fragilities are not exported to the peripheries and disproportionately borne out by developing and emerging economies. Furthermore, a climate just financial and monetary architecture must not only help finance rapid climate action and decarbonization in both the Global North and South, it must also help address the other (non-monetary and financial) sources and roots of IFS, notably those that relate to technology, energy, food, and other dependencies. Research efforts to improve our collective knowledge of the nexus of IFS and environmental degradation could therefore help inform struggles to bring into being a climate just financial system.

Note

[1] Curiously, this is a view that Gabriel Palma attributes to us, despite our insistence (in our collectively written paper and individual works cited earlier) that domestic class configurations, sociopolitical conflicts, and state policies are fundamental to understanding patterns of IFS and state-finance relations (I further flesh out this important point later). Palma writes: 'some heterodox narratives that like to understand emerging countries as somehow helpless victims trapped in a hierarchical world economy that coerced them to do what is against their own interest (for example, the "International Financial Subordination Hypothesis") should also think again' (2023, p 34).

References

ActionAid (2023) 'The Vicious Cycle. Connections between the debt crisis and climate crisis', *ActionAid*, [online], Available from: https://actionaid.org/publications/2023/vicious-cycle [Accessed 6 May 2024].

Akolgo, I.A. (2022) 'Collapsing banks and the cost of finance capitalism in Ghana', *Review of African Political Economy*, 49(174): 624–33.

Alami, I. (2018a) 'Money power of capital and production of "New State Spaces": A view from the global south', *New Political Economy*, 23(4): 512–29.

Alami, I. (2018b) 'Capital accumulation and capital controls in South Africa: A class perspective', *Review of African Political Economy*, 45(156): 223–49.

Alami, I. (2018c) 'On the terrorism of money and national policy-making in emerging capitalist economies', *Geoforum*, 96: 21–31.

Alami, I. (2019a) *Money Power and Financial Capital in Emerging Markets: Facing the Liquidity Tsunami*, London: Routledge.

Alami, I. (2019b) 'Post-crisis capital controls in developing and emerging countries: Regaining policy space? A historical materialist engagement', *Review of Radical Political Economics*, 51(4): 629–49.

Alami, I. (2019c) 'Global finance capital and Third World debt', in Z. Cope and I. Ness (eds) (2019) *The Palgrave Encyclopedia of Imperialism and Anti-imperialism* (2nd edn), London: Palgrave Macmillan, pp 1050–68.

Alami, I., Alves, C., Bonizzi, B., Kaltenbrunner, A., Koddenbrock, K., Kvangraven, I., et al (2023) 'International financial subordination: a critical research agenda', *Review of International Political Economy*, 30(4): 1360–86.

Althouse, J. and Svartzman, R. (2022) 'Bringing subordinated financialisation down to earth: The political ecology of finance-dominated capitalism', *Cambridge Journal of Economics*, 46(4): 679–702.

Altınörs, G., and Akçay, Ü. (2022) 'Authoritarian neoliberalism, crisis, and consolidation: The political economy of regime change in Turkey', *Globalizations*, 19(7): 1029–53.

Alves, C.C. (2017) 'Stabilisation or financialisation: Examining the dynamics of the Brazilian public debt', Doctoral dissertation, SOAS University of London.

Alves, C., Bonizzi, B., Kaltenbrunner, A., and Palma, G.J. (2022) 'Conceptualising financialisation in developing and emerging economies: Systemic and global perspectives', *Cambridge Journal of Economics*, 46(4): 619–28.

Andreoni, A., van Huellen, S., and Robb, N. (2023) 'Financialisation of Non-Financial Corporations in South Africa: An integrated framework to study variations across sectors, value chains and firms' (Working Paper No 255), SOAS Department of Economics.

Armijo, L.E. and Katada, S.N. (2015) 'Theorizing the financial statecraft of emerging powers', *New Political Economy*, 20(1): 42–62.

Ashman, S., Fine, B., and Newman, S. (2011) 'Amnesty International? The nature, scale and impact of capital flight from South Africa', *Journal of Southern African Studies*, 37(1): 7–25.

Baglioni, E., Campling, L., and Hanlon, G. (2021) 'Beyond rentiership: Standardisation, intangibles and value capture in global production', *Environment and Planning A: Economy and Space*, 55(6): 1528–47.

Ban, C., and Bohle, D. (2021) 'Definancialization, financial repression and policy continuity in East-Central Europe', *Review of International Political Economy*, 28(4): 874–97.

Bernards, N. (2021) 'Poverty finance and the durable contradictions of colonial capitalism: Placing "financial inclusion" in the long run in Ghana', *Geoforum,* 123: 89–98.

Bernards, N. (2022) *A Critical History of Poverty Finance: Colonial Roots and Neoliberal Failures*, London: Pluto Press.

Bernards, N. (2023a) 'States, money and the persistence of colonial financial hierarchies in British West Africa', *Development and Change*, 54(1): 64–86.

Bernards, N. (2023b) 'Where is finance in the financialization of development?', *Globalizations*, 21(1): 88–102.

Bonizzi, B. (2013) 'Financialization in developing and emerging countries: a survey', *International Journal of Political Economy*, 42(4): 83–107.

Bonizzi, B. and Kaltenbrunner, A. (2019) 'Liability-driven investment and pension fund exposure to emerging markets: A Minskyan analysis', *Environment and Planning A: Economy and Space*, 51(2): 420–39.

Bonizzi, B., Laskaridis, C., and Toporowski, J. (2019) 'Global liquidity, the private sector and debt sustainability in Sub-Saharan Africa', *Development and Change*, 50(5): 1430–54.

Bonizzi, B., Churchill, J., and Guevara, D. (2021a) 'Variegated financialization and pension fund asset demand: the case of Colombia and Perú', *Socio-Economic Review*, 19(2): 789–815.

Bonizzi, B., Kaltenbrunner, A., and Ramos, R.A. (eds) (2021b) *Emerging Economies and the Global Financial System: Post-Keynesian Analysis*, London: Routledge.

Bonizzi, B., Kaltenbrunner, A., and Powell, J. (2022) 'Financialised capitalism and the subordination of emerging capitalist economies', *Cambridge Journal of Economics*, 46(4): 651–78.

Büdenbender, M. and Aalbers, M.B. (2019) 'How subordinate financialization shapes urban development: The rise and fall of Warsaw's Służewiec business district', *International Journal of Urban and Regional Research*, 43(4): 666–84.

da Silva, P.P. (2022) 'The reregulation of capital flows in Latin America: Assessing the impact of post-neoliberal governments', *Review of International Political Economy*, 29(5): 1497–524.

Dafe, F. and Rethel, L. (2022) 'Domestic bank reform and the contingent nature of the structural power of finance in emerging markets', *Politics & Society*, 50(4): 571–98.

Dafermos, Y. (2023) 'Towards a climate just financial system' (Working Paper No 259), SOAS Department of Economics.

de Almeida Oliveira, É. and de Conti, B. (2022) 'The international division of finance: reassessing the peripheral condition in a financialised capitalism', *26th Annual Conference of the Forum for Macroeconomics and Macroeconomic Policies (FMM)*, Berlin, 20–22 October 2022.

de Conti, B., Borsari, P., and Martínez, M. (2022) 'Credit rating agencies as policymakers: the different stances in regard to core and peripheral countries during the pandemic', *Instituto de Economia*, UNICAMP.

de Paula, L.F., Fritz, B., and Prates, D.M. (2017) 'Keynes at the periphery: Currency hierarchy and challenges for economic policy in emerging economies', *Journal of Post Keynesian Economics*, 40(2): 183–202.

de Paula, L.F., Fritz, B., and Prates, D.M. (2020) 'The metamorphosis of external vulnerability from original sin to original sin redux: Currency hierarchy and financial globalisation in emerging economies', IE-UFRJ, Discussion Paper 033.

Dixon, A.D., Schena, P.J., and Capapé, J. (2022) *Sovereign Wealth Funds, between the State and Markets*, New York: Agenda Publishing.

Durand, C. and Milberg, W. (2020) 'Intellectual monopoly in global value chains', *Review of International Political Economy*, 27(2): 404–29.

Fernandez, R. and Aalbers, M.B. (2020) 'Housing financialization in the Global South: In search of a comparative framework', *Housing Policy Debate*, 30(4): 680–701.

Franz, T. and McNelly, A. (2023) 'The "Finance-Extraction-Transitions Nexus": Towards A Critical Research Agenda Exploring the Scramble for Transition Minerals' (Working Paper No 257), SOAS Department of Economics.

Gabor, D. (2021) 'The Wall Street consensus', *Development & Change*, 52(3): 429–59.

Gallagher, K.P. (2015) *Ruling Capital: Emerging Markets and the Reregulation of Cross-Border Finance*, Ithaca: Cornell University Press.

Global Development Policy Center (2023) 'Debt relief for a green and inclusive recovery: Guaranteeing sustainable development', *Global Development Policy Center*, [online], Available from: https://www.bu.edu/gdp/2023/03/31/debt-relief-for-a-green-and-inclusive-recovery-guaranteeing-sustainable-development/ [Accessed 6 May 2024].

Gort, J. and Brooks, A. (2023) 'Africa's next debt crisis: A relational comparison of Chinese and Western lending to Zambia', *Antipode*, 55(3): 830–52.

Grabel, I. (2018) *When Things Don't Fall Apart – Global Financial Governance and Developmental Finance in an Age of Productive Incoherence*, Cambridge, MA: MIT Press.

Green, W.N. (2023) 'Financial inclusion or subordination? The monetary politics of debt in Cambodia', *Antipode*, 55(4): 1172–92.

Griffith-Jones, S. and Ocampo, J.A. (2018) *The Future of National Development Banks*, Oxford: Oxford University Press.

Guermond, V. (2022) 'Remittance-scapes: The contested geographies of remittance management', *Progress in Human Geography*, 46(2): 372–97.

Haag, S. (2023) 'Old colonial power in new green financing instruments. Approaching financial subordination from the perspective of racial capitalism in renewable energy finance in Senegal', *Geoforum*, 145: 103641.

Haberly, D. and Wójcik, D. (2022) *Sticky Power: Global Financial Networks in the World Economy*, Oxford: Oxford University Press.

Hauge, J. (2023). *The Future of the Factory. How Megatrends are Changing Industrialization.* Oxford: Oxford University Press.

Kaltenbrunner, A. and Painceira, J.P. (2015) 'Developing countries' changing nature of financial integration and new forms of external vulnerability: The Brazilian experience', *Cambridge Journal of Economics*, 39(5): 1281–306.

Kaltenbrunner, A. and Painceira, J.P. (2018) 'Subordinated financial integration and financialisation in emerging capitalist economies: The Brazilian experience', *New Political Economy*, 23(3): 290–313.

Karas, D. (2022) 'Financialization and state capitalism in Hungary after the Global Financial Crisis', *Competition & Change,* 26(1): 29–52.

Kim, K. (2019) 'Using partially state-owned enterprises for development in Indonesia', *Asia Pacific Business Review*, 25(3): 317–37.

Kim, K. (2021) 'Indonesia's restrained state capitalism: Development and policy challenges', *Journal of Contemporary Asia*, 51(3): 419–46.

Koddenbrock, K. (2020) 'Hierarchical multiplicity in the international monetary system: From the slave trade to the Franc CFA in West Africa', *Globalizations*, 17(3): 516–31.

Koddenbrock, K., Kvangraven, I.H., and Sylla, N.S. (2022) 'Beyond financialisation: The longue durée of finance and production in the Global South', *Cambridge Journal of Economics*, 46(4): 703–33.

Kvangraven, I.H., Koddenbrock, K., and Sylla, N.S. (2021) 'Financial subordination and uneven financialization in 21st century Africa', *Community Development Journal*, 56(1): 119–40.

Liu, I.T. (2024) 'Beyond the spatial fix: Towards a finance-sensitive reading of the Belt and Road in Serbia', *Area Development and Policy*, 9(3): 343–64.

Löscher, A. and Kaltenbrunner, A. (2022) 'Climate change and macroeconomic policy space in developing and emerging economies', *Journal of Post Keynesian Economics*, 46(1): 113–41.

Marois, T. (2012) *States, Banks and Crisis: Emerging Finance Capitalism in Mexico and Turkey*, Cheltenham, UK: Edward Elgar.

Marois, T. (2021) *Public Banks: Decarbonisation, Definancialisation and Democratisation* (1st edn), New York: Cambridge University Press.

Mishura, A. and Ageeva, S. (2022) 'Financialisation and the authoritarian state: the case of Russia', *Cambridge Journal of Economics*, 46(5): 1109–40.

Murau, S., Pape, F., and Pforr, T. (2022) 'International monetary hierarchy through emergency US-dollar liquidity: A key currency approach', *Competition & Change*, 27(3–4): 495–515. DOI: 10245294221118661.

Musthaq, F. (2023) 'Unconventional central banking and the politics of liquidity', *Review of International Political Economy*, 30(1): 281–306.

Naqvi, N. (2019) 'Manias, panics and crashes in emerging markets: An Empirical investigation of the post-2008 crisis period', *New Political Economy*, 24(6): 759–79.

Naqvi, N. (2021) 'Renationalizing finance for development: Policy space and public economic control in Bolivia', *Review of International Political Economy*, 28(3): 447–78.

Ndikumana, L. and Boyce, J.K. (eds) (2022) *On the Trail of Capital Flight from Africa: The Takers and the Enablers*, Oxford: Oxford University Press.

Newman, S. (2022) 'Global value chains and global value transfer', in Z. Cope and I. Ness (eds) *The Oxford Handbook of Economic Imperialism*, Oxford: Oxford University Press, pp 213–29.

Öniş, Z. and Kutlay, M. (2021) 'The anatomy of Turkey's new heterodox crisis: the interplay of domestic politics and global dynamics', *Turkish Studies*, 22(4): 499–529.

Palma, J.G. (2023) 'Ricardo was surely right: the abundance of "easy" rents leads to greedy and lazy elites. Rentier-capitalism as an exercise in "non-creative" destruction. A tribute to Geoff Harcourt', Cambridge Working Paper in Economics.

Pataccini, L. (2024) 'The (un)usual suspects? Exploring the links between illicit financial flows, Russian money laundering and dependent financialization in the Baltic states', *Competition & Change*, 28(1): 3–22.

Petry, J., Fichtner, J., and Heemskerk, E. (2021) 'Steering capital: The growing private authority of index providers in the age of passive asset management', *Review of International Political Economy*, 28(1): 152–76.

Piroska, D. (2022) 'Financial nationalism and democracy', in A. Pickel (ed) *Handbook of Economic Nationalism*, Cheltenham: Edward Elgar, pp 256–74.

Poulantzas, N. (1978) *State, Power, Socialism*, London: Verso.

Powell, J. (2013) 'Subordinate financialisation: A study of Mexico and its non-financial corporations', Doctoral dissertation, SOAS University of London.

Prates, D.M. and Andrade, R. (2013) 'Exchange rate dynamics in a peripheral monetary economy', *Journal of Post Keynesian Economics*, 35(3): 399–416.

Prates, D.M. and B. Fritz. (2016) 'Más allá de los controles de capital: Regulación de los mercados de derivados en moneda extranjera en la República de Corea y el Brasil después de la crisis financiera mundial', *Revista de la CEPAL*, 2016(118): 193–213.

Pryke, M. and Allen, J. (2022) 'The everyday construction of value: A Canadian investment fund, Chilean water infrastructure and financial subordination', *Finance and Society*, 8(2): 189–208.

Reis, N. and Lukas, M. (eds) (2022) *Beyond the Megacity: New Dimensions of Peripheral Urbanization in Latin America*, Toronto: University of Toronto Press.

Reyes, A. and Basile, P. (2022) 'The distinctive evolution of housing financialization in Brazil and Mexico', *International Journal of Urban and Regional Research*, 46(6): 933–53.

Schedelik, M., Nölke, A., May, C., and Gomes, A. (2022) 'Dependency revisited: Commodities, commodity-related capital flows and growth models in emerging economies', *European Journal of Economics and Economic Policies*, 20(3): 515–38.

Scheiring, G. (2020) *The Retreat of Liberal Democracy: Authoritarian Capitalism and the Accumulative State in Hungary*, Cham: Palgrave Macmillan.

Socoloff, I. (2020) 'Subordinate financialization and housing finance: The case of indexed mortgage loans' coalition in Argentina', *Housing Policy Debate*, 30(4): 585–605.

Viktorov, I. and Abramov, A. (2020) 'The 2014–15 financial crisis in Russia and the foundations of weak monetary power autonomy in the international political economy', *New Political Economy*, 25(4): 487–510.

von Mettenheim, K. (2015) *Monetary Statecraft in Brazil: 1808–2014*, London: Routledge.

3

International Financial Statecraft: How, Who, and with What Expectations of Success?

Leslie Elliott Armijo

Introduction and theoretical priors

This volume sets up a dialogue among social scientists from different traditions, each of which employs different frameworks to analyze the connections among states, private financial actors, and global money and credit markets. This introduction clarifies how this chapter fits within this dialogue. Most of the included authors implicitly or explicitly adhere to the theoretical priors of one of three traditions: international financial *subordination,* as most clearly articulated in Chapter 2 by Ilias Alami and the concluding chapter by Ingrid Harvold Kvangraven; international financial *statecraft*, as in this chapter; or political and economic *survival constraints* for the state, as in Anush Kapadia and Fathimath Musthaq's discussion of India. One way to frame the dialogue is to highlight differences in their underlying assumptions. To begin, note that 'the state' has two distinct meanings for included authors. The first definition is incumbent national political leaders (senior policy makers) plus the permanent central government administrative bureaucracy. Thus, one might investigate the degree of independence of 'the state' from private financial capital. The second meaning is independent country, as in 'the structure of the interstate system is determined by the distribution of capabilities among its units, who are sovereign states'.

International financial *subordination* (IFS) researchers begin from the thesis that both international markets and legally sovereign countries are penetrated by, and often subordinated to, the wishes of private financial actors, as the latter are driven to expand their control and their profits. National political incumbents (representatives of 'the state') in each industrial core country mainly interact with private capital based within their own borders, with senior politicians acting on behalf of private financiers, whether consciously or not. However, policy makers in these core states (today termed the 'Global North') may be able to deflect many of the most dangerous consequences of financial actors' single-minded drive for profits away from their home countries and toward peripheral countries and peoples. Historically, such deflection was achieved via overt imperialism, but today redirection toward developing and emerging economies (DEEs) occurs through more subtle neo-imperialist predations, for example, being imposed by global economic governance institutions and 'neutral' rules favouring Northern firms and countries. National political incumbents and their bureaucracies in the Global South, meanwhile, are doubly vulnerable, once to their own private financial sector and again to international financial capital, which is closely entwined with the foreign policies of core states. Given these assumptions, the essential research question is: 'How can we identify and expose the pathways by which international financial actors control and constrain DEE states and peoples?'

In contrast, the international financial *statecraft* (FS) literature begins from the assumption that state incumbents, in both the Global North and South, are mostly self-aware decision makers, rationally manipulating national policy levers to achieve desired outcomes. Private financial actors constitute one interest group among many, albeit a perennially influential one. Statecraft occurs when incumbent leaders use national economic levers under their control – including bank regulations, investment laws, capital controls, taxes, subsidies, sanctions, and bilateral investment treaties – to achieve goals that primarily (in the judgement of an outside observer) serve larger foreign policy ends, such as instigating or avoiding interstate war, or intimidating foreign leaders, rather than goals that are primarily economic, such as stimulating national economic growth or maintaining price stability. The core research question for statecraft researchers is: 'What types of economic statecraft instruments have been, or might be, used by sovereign states to achieve their foreign policy goals – and with what results?' In other words, while the subordination researchers implicitly assume that private financial actors act as puppeteers moving state institutions and incumbents, the statecraft researchers begin from the reverse assumption: it is the state, with its monopoly of the legitimate use of force, that ultimately calls the shots.

Volume editors Andreas Nölke and Johannes Petry suggest bridging the two approaches by conceptualizing them as problem and potential solution. They lament the international financial subordination of DEEs, yet hope that thoughtful international financial statecraft might reduce such dependence. They define *state capacity* as high if the central government in a DEE state can avoid being controlled by private financial capital, whether local or originating abroad, and low if the state is captured by private finance capital. By framing the debate thus, Nölke and Petry suggest that the degree of subordination or autonomy in a particular DEE during a specific time period is a question subject to empirical investigation. The chapter by Petry comparing stock markets in six major DEE countries responds to this overarching question most explicitly, suggesting that the openness to foreign ownership of domestic financial assets is an important variable in explaining subsequent financialization and subordination.

A third broad approach, the *political survival* framing, also lends itself to empirical research and provides another path for potential dialogue between competing traditions. Kapadia and Musthaq begin from the standard rational choice assumption that political incumbents (the 'state') want to 'survive', a formulation that can mean either that a dictator wants a lifetime appointment or simply that a particular set of political institutions, such as parliamentary democracy, endures over time, while specific political incumbents rotate. In assuming that the state can be modelled as a unitary rational actor with a set of concrete goals, the political survival approach approximates the economic statecraft tradition. At the same time, the political survival approach is less concerned with how state incumbents might use financial resources as foreign policy instruments (the major preoccupation of statecraft researchers), instead focusing on the struggle of state incumbents to pay for all their survival needs and policy choices, whether through taxes, fees for state services, or public debt, voluntarily lent by national or international private financial actors, or sometimes by other sovereign states. The core research question in a political survival investigation is, 'How have national political incumbents, in this country and time period, attempted to secure the funding necessary to pay for the expenses of the state itself and for execution of their preferred policies?' This formulation gives private, possibly foreign, bankers and investors a great deal of potential influence over state policy, which for some DEEs in some periods may amount to full international financial subordination. At the same time, private financial capital per se is not necessarily the dominant thread in a country's national political economy, for example, if the financial sector itself is mostly nationalized, or if ample funding for the state's maintenance and activities can be raised in some other fashion, from taxing salt to the sale of public appointments or aristocratic titles to possession of a suddenly valuable and scarce natural resource such as petroleum.

The remainder of this chapter unpacks and illustrates the international financial statecraft approach. The chapter's next major section further examines assumptions, terms, and categories undergirding the FS approach. The third section examines classic instruments of financial statecraft, distinguishing between those that are primarily assertive ('offensive') and those usually understood as defensive. Section four proposes that relative interstate power capabilities strongly condition which instruments of financial statecraft incumbent leaders might be tempted to employ, setting the stage for the chapter's fifth and sixth sections, which consider the contemporary financial statecraft options for important states in the Global North and Global South, respectively. The chapter's conclusions are pragmatic and cautionary, suggesting that in most cases FS, especially the use of offensive instruments, will not yield the results policy makers intend.

International financial statecraft: definitions and categories

The FS approach uses 'state' in both senses: to mean a country's senior central government political incumbents and the bureaucracy they command, and also the country itself, as in the 'interstate system'. The FS approach does not assume a unique and overwhelmingly important role for private financial capital: instead, the domestic political support base of incumbent state leaders is a question for empirical question. The FS approach understands state capacity as the ability of incumbent political leaders to conceptualize and implement public policies plausibly related to some desired goal. While state capacity and the preferences of incumbents' key political support groups are assumed important, the primary research focus lies with the country's interactions with the international system.

Financial statecraft is a subset of international *economic statecraft*, encompassing instruments (the means of economic statecraft) such as tariffs, foreign aid, trade embargoes, preemptive purchases of a scarce commodity, investment guarantees, direct purchases from the target, and many others (Baldwin, 1985, pp 58–69 and passim). Significantly, economic statecraft lies on a continuum of instruments of statecraft ranging from peaceful suasion via diplomacy to psychological warfare to military attack, as each is a 'branch of political activity', as famously observed by Prussian General Carl von Clausewitz (translation of 1976) in the early 19th century (Baldwin, 1985, p 64). That is, economic statecraft is about the use, by incumbent political leaders, of their state's economic power capabilities to achieve a wide range of foreign policy goals. Economic statecraft, including FS, thus may be discussed in terms of an *actor* or initiating state, its economic *means* or instruments, its *target* or targets (often but not always another state), and a foreign policy *goal* or desired outcomes. While the instruments themselves need not be exclusively international, they are being used by national leaders to influence international outcomes, including foreign behaviours, international processes, and perceptions. The foreign policy goals of FS are political, although they also may include an economic or financial dimension. For example, an import tariff applied equally to all trading partners for the purpose of raising revenues or protecting domestic industry is not FS. However, an import tariff applied only to states considered to be political rivals or as a punishment for the target state's undesirable behaviour is FS, even if the tariff also raises revenue.

The FS actors are always sovereign states, but the targets can be states, international institutions, foreign investors, foreign populations, or even decentralized global market sentiment (Armijo and Katada, 2014; Katada et al, 2017). For example, a creditor state (the actor) may offer (or decline to provide) a loan to a recipient country or international organization (the target) whose policy choices please (displease) the creditor state. Financial statecraft may be offensive, although 'assertive' is often a better label, as 'offense' in international relations often is understood to imply the use or threat of military force, which is not meant here, or it may be 'defensive'.

In offensive or *assertive* FS, state A (the actor) attempts to induce, persuade, or coerce state B (the target) into taking some action that state B's leaders otherwise would not choose. For example, in 2022 the United States, the United Kingdom, the European Union, and other countries (the actors) intensified preexisting financial sanctions on Russia (the target) in response to Russia's February invasion of Ukraine, in the stated hopes that these financial penalties would cause President Vladimir Putin to order his troops to withdraw. Note that Ukraine itself is neither actor nor target in this example. Financial statecraft may also be reactive or *defensive*. In the case of defensive FS, state A (the actor) is attempting to defend itself from pressure coming from state(s) B. For example, the defensive FS reactions of Russia (in this example the actor) to the financial sanctions of the US and others (now the targets) have included loud assertions that Western (Northern) financial sanctions were illegal, while also transferring its official foreign exchange reserves out of US dollar-denominated assets and into gold or the liquid assets of third countries, such as China.

International financial statecraft is often *bilateral*, involving only an actor and a target, but may also be *collective*, as when the countries in the BRICS club (originally Brazil, Russia, India, and China, plus South Africa from late 2010) joined together in 2009 and after to press for certain reforms of global financial rules and institutions, such as larger voting shares within the International Monetary Fund for countries of the Global South (Roberts et al, 2018). Bilateral, and especially collective, FS may be aimed at reforming international governance arrangements or influencing global market conditions (as by talking down or up a particular currency or investment option).

Instruments of financial statecraft

The means, or instruments, through which national policy makers engage in FS vary. Table 3.1 lists eight major categories of FS instruments or potential instruments, including four conceptualized as primarily assertive, and four which are largely defensive. This list is illustrative, not comprehensive.

Instruments that incumbent state leaders can employ to exercise assertive FS include foreign aid, debt forgiveness, access of others to their home

Table 3.1: Principal instruments of contemporary financial statecraft

Assertive financial statecraft	**Examples**
Foreign aid and public investment	• Provide official development assistance (ODA) (loans, grants), outward foreign direct investment (FDI), and portfolio investment via sovereign wealth funds (SWFs)
Debt forgiveness	• Support bilateral and multilateral debt restructuring
Financial market access	• Permit foreign accounts and investments in home banks and capital markets • Permit access to financial services, for example, lawyers and courts for initial public offerings (IPOs), mergers and acquisitions (M&A), SWIFT • Encourage foreign governments to hold official reserves in one's currency • Extend currency swaps
Financial sanctions	• Withdraw components of financial market access, promised loans, and so on
Defensive financial statecraft	**Examples**
Capital controls	• Outward capital controls (taxes, quantity limits) • Inward capital controls (taxes, penalties for early repatriation)
Diversify foreign financial links	• Accept loans, investment from both China and the Global North
Collective voice	• 'Inside options' or pressure for greater influence within existing global governance institutions
Collective alternative institution building	• 'Outside options' or creation of new institutions

financial market, and financial sanctions. First, governments usually present their *foreign aid and public investment* as purely altruistic, but it often supports informal influence by the aid-giving or investing state.[1] Aid may arrive in the form of loans, grants, or subsidized goods or services directed from one state (the actor) to another (the target). Such financial assistance may be extended bilaterally, or via a multilateral financial institution, such as the World Bank or IMF, in which the state exercising FS is able to exert significant influence. Official development assistance (ODA) builds up diffuse reservoirs of good will, but occasionally, the FS link is more direct. For example, state A may vote in favour of a loan to state B, the target country, in a multilateral financial institution such as the World Bank in disguised or explicit exchange for state B's vote on a United Nations General Assembly vote of importance to state A or some other concrete policy shift by state B.[2] The early 21st century witnessed the rise of a new financial vehicle known as sovereign wealth funds (SWFs), or state-run investment institutions funded by excess foreign exchange held by the country's central bank, most often due to large earnings from fossil fuel exports, but also as a consequence of persistent current account surpluses resulting from other causes. They often invest in countries with which the owner of the SWF would like to have closer political or economic links.[3] Foreign aid and public investment benefit the initiating state by cementing alliances and strategically winning friends (and/or imposing the donor state's economic preferences) abroad (Bearce and Tirone, 2010; Andersen et al, 2024).

Second, an important means by which creditor countries have exercised direct or indirect FS is via *foreign debt forgiveness* and rescheduling. This can occur through bilateral write-downs or debt cancellations or via state A employing its votes or influence in multilateral financial institutions or clubs to support or oppose a loan or a policy exemption sought by state B. Even when the formal rules are clear, powerful governments can use their de facto influence over granting exemptions for special circumstances to reward friends (Armijo and Sood, 2023). This said, multilateral financial institutions in general will be less biased than national creditors.

A third category of historically important and assertive FS is the grant of *access to a state's home financial markets.* This can take many forms, and a financially central country may thus gain influence over foreign governments, banks, non-financial firms, or citizens. Foreign governments in soft currency countries want to hold their official reserves in safe assets, such as US Treasury securities. Foreign banks may borrow funds in core country markets and relend them at home at attractive margins, engaging in the so-called 'carry trade'. Foreign firms may arrange initial public offerings on the stock exchanges of Frankfurt or London, or may wish to incorporate in jurisdictions such as the US state of Delaware, whose courts they trust to be impartial (or pro-business, see Pistor, 2020). Countries with large and liquid capital markets also offer foreign citizens and businesses attractive earnings opportunities via portfolio investments in corporate shares, or corporate and government bonds. Foreign citizens may wish to open bank accounts with their hard currency earnings, rather than surrendering them to their own government's central bank in exchange for a local currency that tends to lose value vis-à-vis the US dollar or the Euro. Access to each of these financial services increases the safety and profitability with which foreigners, including foreign governments, can manage their money. Opening one's home financial markets, institutions, and services, including the presence of trusted regulatory oversight, to foreigners is a clear choice by the initiating state, although seldom one associated with a specific short-term foreign policy goal. Granting access to domestic financial transactions can cement alliances and less-formalized friendly relations with foreign governments and their citizens. An interesting twist is that, in contrast to the transfer of real resources implicit in concessional foreign aid, when an already financially powerful country opens its home financial markets, it serves to increase the acting state's centrality in global financial markets. If China, for example, invests a significant share of its official foreign exchange reserves in US Treasury assets, then China's future prosperity is tied to the future health of the US currency and economy.

Fourth, the imposition of *financial sanctions* imposes direct, immediate costs on a target state or states by reversing the grant of access to a country's home financial markets. An escalating list of financial sanctions begins with state A, the actor, freezing the bank accounts of top officials and supporters of state B, the target. The sanctioning country subsequently may decide to freeze all financial assets owned by state B's government held in state A, or even to invoke third party sanctions, by which the initiating state threatens exclusion from state A's home financial markets and services to any institutions from states C or D who transact financial business with state B. The US has claimed the right to repossess all US dollar-denominated deposits owned by 'rogue' states everywhere in the world, although this is difficult to enforce. Such financial sanctions impose costs on targets. Meanwhile political leaders in the initiating state receive the political benefit of looking tough to domestic constituents, while avoiding more costly foreign policy actions such as initiating a military response to the target's foreign policy choices.

Table 3.1's lower portion lists major instruments of defensive financial statecraft, including capital controls, diversifying international financial links, collective action to increase voice, and collective action to establish new, alternative financial institutions, services, and markets. *Capital controls* slow or prevent the movement of financial flows (except for limited purposes such as trade clearing or essential travel) across national borders. Typically, their economic goal is to prevent the rapid, large-scale inflows or exit of capital (in the form of hard currency) from the country, which can destabilize the domestic currency and banking system. Capital controls also may be employed politically as defensive FS, for example, when only home country citizens and those from favoured foreign countries may own specific domestic financial assets. A sixth type of FS, also defensive, is a decision by central government incumbents to *diversify the foreign sources of official capital*, including development assistance or other inflows of foreign aid, concessional loans, or SWF investments. Recognizing that creditor governments often attempt to gain political influence over debtor governments, borrowing countries may actively seek to play off one foreign patron against another. This is the same calculation that leads thoughtful national leaders to attempt to diversify their trade relations in terms of both partners and products. In the case of defending against financial sanctions, a country may try to diversify its official foreign exchange holdings in favour of another hard currency or even gold.

A seventh major instrument of defensive FS is the exercise of *collective voice*, especially by less-influential state actors, within existing global financial governance forums, from the IMF and World Bank, to the Financial Stability Forum, to influential yet public–private or fully private venues ranging from voluntary international financial market standard-setting and regulatory bodies to informal yet influential gatherings like the World Economic Forum in Davos. This constitutes an 'inside option', in that it does not directly challenge, nor seek to supplant, existing institutions, but instead aims at expanding participation within them.

An eighth category of FS instruments is the 'outside option' of the *collective creation of alternative multilateral institutions* that implicitly or explicitly challenge the major institutions of the postwar Western-dominated order created in the decade following the Second World War. In the financial and monetary sphere among the most important of these new international financial institutions may be the New Development Bank (NDB) of the BRICS club countries and the Asian Infrastructure Investment Bank (AIIB), which now has over 100 member countries but in which China retains a controlling interest. In addition to formal institutions, informal clubs of countries with common goals for reforms of global or regional financial or monetary governance may become an important option.

Assessing national power capabilities

Different categories of states have options to exercise different types of international financial statecraft. Basic administrative competence ('state capacity') is essential to any type of FS. Assuming basic capacity, a state's (country's) position in the global distribution of power capabilities among all countries is the most important dimension shaping its leaders' FS options. International 'soft power', or the ability of a country to exercise influence through the attractiveness of its culture, language, values, or reputation abroad, is relevant and important, but difficult to measure comparatively. However, it is possible to assess different countries' hard power and financial power capabilities to understand which types of FS their leaders might be tempted to wield.

Hard power capabilities are relative and thus necessarily zero-sum in their conceptualization. They are best assessed vis-à-vis other states within the relevant interstate system. While many discussions of relative power simply rank countries by the size of their overall economies, this chapter employs an index that combines five different empirical measures of national power capabilities. The material capabilities index (MCI) from the Global Monetary and Financial Powers of States (GMFPS) dataset includes almost all countries, and is calculated as the mean of each country's annual shares of total world quantities in five critical dimensions: economic size (as measured by nominal

GDP), population, industrial innovativeness (assessed as patents plus industrial value-added), trade, and military spending (for details see Armijo et al, 2020).

In addition to basic state competence and overall hard power capabilities, finance-specific vulnerabilities or capabilities also matter. Five dimensions are especially important: external debt buildup, ability to act as a creditor to other states, currency power, network centrality, and influence in global financial governance. Countries may vary in terms of their *net external public debt*, measured relative to the size of a country's own economy. In general, high foreign sovereign debt should impede a state's ability to carry out any type of consistent, goal-oriented international financial statecraft. High foreign debt makes a country vulnerable and more likely to lead to the country becoming a target of domineering FS by others. The only exception is a dominant reserve currency country, whose money (which constitutes claims against the reserve currency government) foreign central banks wish to hold as a hedge against exchange rate movements against their own currencies. So long as countries B, C, and D wish to invest indefinitely in country A's government securities or currency, A can accumulate foreign debt without pain.

In contrast, higher scores on another four financial dimensions increase FS options. These dimensions can, like the MCI, be assessed as shares of the global total (Armijo et al, 2020). *Creditor capability* represents a country's ability to send financing abroad in the form of loans, portfolio investment, and foreign direct investment or donated as foreign aid. A creditor state, for example, can target its allies to receive more generous bilateral ODA on a per capita basis than similar target states with whom the creditor has frosty relations. The potential for creditor capability can be measured as a country's share of the total surplus of all countries running a balance of payments (current account) surplus in a year. Actual creditor capability can be assessed as a stock, for example, by calculating a country's share in all official foreign exchange holdings each year, or the country's accumulated share in the total ownership of net financial assets among all countries with a surplus. The index reported here is a mean of the latter two components. As with the measure of external public debt, the key reserve currency country(ies) will have an anomalous share. At present, because the US dollar remains the dominant reserve currency, the US central bank need not accumulate large quantities of government bonds of other hard currency countries as insurance against capital flight or international financial volatility.

Currency capability means the dominance of a country's home currency in global markets, for example, as the currency in which countries hold their official foreign exchange reserves or in which trade is invoiced or international corporate bonds are priced. The historical record as well as political economic theory suggests that currency power tends to be centralized, giving enormous power capabilities to the country at the centre of a regional or global trading and financial system (Cohen, 2018). Moreover, as noted, a state at the peak of the global currency hierarchy is largely exempt from needing to worry about its net foreign indebtedness, as foreigners choose to hold its currency, nor does the key currency country need to self-insure via large foreign exchange reserves. For this reason, both the IFS and the FS approaches pay great attention to global currency hierarchy.

Network capability is a country's centrality to global financial markets, or the degree to which its major financial city or cities function as nodes for cross-border transactions within international financial networks. Network nodes can be discovered by observing a country's share of global bilateral trades of financial assets. Like currency dominance, network centrality is self-reinforcing; the more central a node already is, the more necessary it is for other global players to be represented there and do business there. Network centrality requires large, sophisticated, diverse, and well-regulated home financial markets, the size of which can be mapped as a share of world totals. The higher a country's network capability, the easier it is to attract an array of transnational public–private financial service providers, controlling such essential infrastructure as custodial services for financial assets such as government bonds, nearly instantaneous price information flows, secure messaging for financial asset transfers, highly specialized legal advice, trusted business courts, and access to voice within specialized regulatory bodies. The network measure reported here is the mean of a country's share of home financial market size and presence as one party to all bilateral financial transactions.

Finally, *financial governance capability* refers to the influence a country has in shaping consensual standards for financial regulation, such as the lending priorities of international financial institutions, the conditions of debt restructuring following financial crises, or the capital adequacy standards for guiding the operations of multinational banks. Governance capability can be measured as a country's share of votes, leadership positions, and any other globally summable dimension mirroring influence in major global financial governance institutions. Global financial governance influence is also relevant to a country's ability to employ most other types of FS instruments. For example, consider capital controls, quintessentially a defensive weapon of relatively weak states. IMF strictures on permissible versus disqualifying capital controls for member states wishing access to IMF benefits, such as emergency liquidity support, have been the subject of recurrent fights within the Fund's Executive Board, especially in the runup to and aftermath of the Asian financial crisis of the late 1990s (Blustein, 2003).

The chapter's next two sections link countries' relative power capabilities to their possible options for employing different instruments of international financial statecraft.

Power capabilities and financial statecraft options of the Global North

The advanced capitalist democracies of the Global North designed and continue to dominate the complex of multilateral global governance institutions formed in the aftermath of the Second World War. Among the most significant international organizations in terms of their enduring influence on global politics are the United Nations (UN), the North Atlantic Treaty Organization (NATO), and the two peak international financial institutions, the International Monetary Fund (IMF) and World Bank. Arguably the most important core countries have been the members of the Group of Seven (G7): the United States, Japan, Germany, United Kingdom, France, Italy, and Canada. These are the status quo powers, leaders of the post-Second World War global order.

This set of countries scores high on basic state capacity: their central governments articulate and implement reasonably coherent policies across a wide range of issue arenas, from infrastructure planning, to national monetary policy, to consumer safety regulations. They also score very high on a composite measure of hard power, the MCI, and a wide variety of financial and monetary power capabilities, which do not all move together: some lead, and others lag. As shown in Table 3.2, in the most recent year available for this dataset, the G7 accounted for only around 10 per cent of the world's population, but 37 per cent of global hard power capabilities, and 28 per cent of creditor power. They overwhelmingly dominated the other financial capabilities measured, including currency power (93 per cent), network power (62 per cent), and influence in global financial governance institutions (52 per cent). The table also includes figures for less powerful advanced capitalist countries with outsize financial capabilities: South Korea, once a DEE but in the 21st century a high-income democracy, Switzerland, and Norway. Although Table 3.2 also reveals significant redistribution of power capabilities away from the G7 since the beginning of the 21st century, the US and its major allies still dominate global power resources. This means that this is the set of countries most able to exercise assertive FS. The remainder of this section connects each type of financial power capability to related instruments of FS.

A state needs creditor capability to employ the assertive FS instruments of offering a target state foreign aid and public investment or forgiving or rescheduling its troubled sovereign debt. Table 3.2 tracks the G7's total creditor capability as falling from about 40 per cent of the global total to 28 per cent in the final year measured. Consequently, it is increasingly difficult for national leaders in the political West (Global North) to offer large quantities of ODA or public loans and investment. And one cannot forgive bilateral sovereign debts if the loans were never made. True, the

Table 3.2: The power capabilities of the Global North (as per cent of global total)

Country	Population		Material capabilities		Creditor power		Currency power		Network power		Governance power	
	2000	2019	2000	2019	2000	2013	2000	2013	2000	2011	2000	2013
US	4.3	4.0	24.0	19.3	1.5	0.6	63.4	59.7	29.0	24.7	16.2	14.5
Japan	2.1	1.6	11.2	5.0	28.9	16.8	9.3	3.8	15.3	10.8	9.5	8.4
Germany	1.3	1.1	4.5	3.6	1.5	9.6	17.5	22.4	7.0	5.9	8.3	6.9
UK	0.9	0.9	3.7	3.3	1.0	0.4	1.7	2.5	9.4	9.8	7.9	6.2
France	1.0	0.9	3.3	2.4	5.5	0.2	2.2	2.8	5.3	5.7	7.9	6.2
Italy	0.9	0.8	2.5	1.7	0.7	0.2	0.0	0.0	3.4	3.0	6.8	5.2
Canada	0.5	0.5	1.8	1.4	0.9	0.3	0.1	1.1	2.2	2.2	6.7	4.3
G6 Total	**6.7**	**5.8**	**27.0**	**17.4**	**38.5**	**27.5**	**30.8**	**32.6**	**42.6**	**37.4**	**47.8**	**37.2**
G7 Total	**11.0**	**9.8**	**51.0**	**36.7**	**40.0**	**28.1**	**94.2**	**92.5**	**71.6**	**62.1**	**63.3**	**51.7**
Others with notable hard power or international financial capabilities												
Korea, Rep.	0.8	0.7	2.3	2.8	2.6	1.5	0.0	0.0	0.8	1.2	0.6	1.8
Switzerland	0.1	0.1	0.7	0.7	6.5	4.0	0.1	0.2	2.5	2.0	1.1	1.0
Norway	0.1	0.1	0.4	0.4	1.2	4.0	0.0	0.0	0.4	0.7	0.5	0.5

Notes: All figures are for dates noted, or latest available. For Canada's material capabilities index (MCI), the latest available date is 2017. The MCI in 2019 for other states often caucusing with the Global North was: Spain 1.1, Australia 1.1, Turkey 0.9, and Sweden 0.5.

Source: Armijo et al, 2020

major reserve currency countries could expand their domestic money supplies for this purpose, but they will not. They have been willing to work collectively to expand credit by modifying some rules within the multilateral financial institutions (as by easing the constraints on the use of IMF's Special Drawing Rights quasi-currency, SDRs) or to approve modest collective projects for debt relief from multilateral banks. Nonetheless, the point holds. Examining a different measure of creditor capability, the IMF's net international investment position (NIIP), which calculates absolute figures for country stocks of net foreign financial assets, leads to similar conclusions about eroded creditor capabilities in the Global North.[4] For example, among the G7, only three had significant surpluses in late 2022: Japan (US$3.2 trillion), Germany (US$2.9) trillion, and Canada (US$0.8 trillion).[5] Other advanced industrial countries with surpluses included South Korea, Norway, and Switzerland. In contrast, the NIIP positions of the remaining major Northern powers in Table 3.2 reflect their accumulated international indebtedness. The US' negative NIIP (that is, its net foreign liabilities) figure is US$16.2 trillion. For now, global investors continue to view the US as a 'safe haven' for footloose global private capital, and foreign governments acquire its currency for official foreign exchange reserves. At some unknown future date these accumulated foreign liabilities may become problematic for the US dollar and US economy. Meanwhile, these large inward capital flows of foreign investment in US Treasury securities ease US domestic budget constraints.

In place of offering DEEs direct government-to-government funds as grants or low-cost loans, as in the past, declining creditor capabilities mean that policy makers in the Global North (or political West) thus increasingly focus on improving their technical assistance and encouraging private foreign investment by their transnational firms. For example, in 2023, the G7 club of major advanced industrial democracies reaffirmed their commitment to infrastructure financing going to DEEs via their Partnership for Global Infrastructure Investment (PGII), which promises to 'mobilize' billions of dollars of investment in high-quality infrastructure, by 'catalyzing' private investment in 'transformative ecosystems of infrastructure investment' in sectors such as green energy, digital upgrading, and health care.[6] Decoded, this means that the PGII-initiating governments wish to play a critical technical assistance and organizational role in helping low and middle-income countries use their existing infrastructure more wisely, but the bulk of investible funds is to come from profit-seeking private investors, whose participation is voluntary. This shift can be told as one reflecting 'financialization' and the increasing power of private financial interests within the US and other major advanced capitalist democracies (Gabor, 2021; Gabor and Sylla, 2023), but it clearly also has been driven by underlying structural shifts in international creditor capabilities.

The Global North's options to use bilateral sovereign debt forgiveness as an instrument of direct foreign policy also have shrunk, as the management of financial crises and troubled sovereign debt of DEEs is now largely handled by multilateral institutions, with the IMF playing a leading role. This said, the US and other G7 countries continue to hold greater influence in the status quo international financial institutions such as the IMF and World Bank than would be predicted by their populations or economic size. Observers such as Kharas and Linn (2008) argue that the IMF has been more generous with the peripheral countries of the Global North than the Global South.

The continuing high concentration of currency, network, and financial governance capabilities in the US and its G7 partners revealed in Table 3.2 enables these countries to employ access to their home financial markets, home currency, and even to a host of 'global' financial institutions necessary to transacting business, such as the SWIFT network for transnational financial messaging, as a reward or a sanction for other countries. Currency capability interacts with and bolsters financial network capability (Perez, 2022). An important FS use for currency capability is that financial sanctions against foreign countries are readily enabled if those deposits are held in the issuing countries financial institutions. The US even imposes sanctions on third country financial institutions domiciled outside the US that hold US dollar-denominated deposits for sanctioned individuals and countries. Russia, Iran, Venezuela, and Cuba have been major targets of Northern/Western financial sanctions, and China also has felt their bite

Dominant currency capabilities also allow the US to remain the most important issuer of emergency currency swap arrangements, differentially extended to countries whose stability is important to the global economy – but also to US friends and allies (Cassetta, 2022).

So long as the US' network capabilities remain high, foreign firms need access to US financial markets and services to launch initial public offerings (IPOs) or incorporate in predictable, business-friendly jurisdictions. Recently, the US has begun employing inward capital controls targeted at Chinese high-tech firms, denying them the opportunity to engage in foreign direct investment partnerships in the US (Li et al, 2023). Finally, the overweighting of global financial governance power vis-à-vis underlying hard power for most of the political West (all except the US and South Korea, among the countries listed in Table 3.2) reflects these countries' dominant role in constructing the complex of postwar global governance institutions. Overall, the countries of the Global North (or political West) control most of the underlying international financial power capabilities that enable the use of assertive FS. However, the secular trend is for a power shift toward rising powers of the Global South.

Table 3.3: Power capabilities of major and selected middle powers caucusing with Global South (as per cent of global total)

Country	**Population**		**Material capabilities**		**Creditor power**		**Currency power**		**Network power**		**Governance power**	
	2000	**2019**	**2000**	**2019**	**2000**	**2013**	**2000**	**2013**	**2000**	**2011**	**2000**	**2013**
Major powers												
China*	20.7	18.2	6.8	18.4	4.5	16.3	0.0	0.0	2.0	5.8	2.0	4.1
Hong Kong	*0.1*	*0.1*	*NA*	*NA*	*5.7*	*4.2*	*0.0*	*0.0*	*2.0*	*1.6*	*NA*	*NA*
India	17.3	17.8	4.4	5.7	1.0	1.2	0.0	0.0	0.3	1.0	1.6	2.7
Russia	2.4	1.9	1.7	2.3	1.1	2.0	0.0	0.0	0.6	0.9	1.9	2.5
Brazil	2.9	2.8	1.6	1.6	0.9	1.5	0.0	0.0	0.9	2.0	1.2	2.1
Indonesia	3.5	3.5	1.0	1.4	0.8	0.4	0.0	0.0	0.2	0.3	0.6	1.5
Middle powers with notable financial capabilities												
Saudi Arabia	0.3	0.4	1.0	1.3	1.8	5.3	0.0	0.0	0.1	0.2	2.0	2.7
UAE	0.1	0.1	0.4	0.8	5.0	3.4	0.0	0.0	0.2	0.2	0.1	0.1
Singapore	0.1	0.1	0.6	0.8	3.5	3.5	0.0	0.0	0.7	1.1	0.1	0.2
South Africa	0.7	0.8	0.4	0.5	0.2	0.2	0.0	0.0	0.3	0.4	0.6	1.4

Notes: All figures are for dates noted, or earliest or latest available. * Figures for China exclude Hong Kong.

Source: Armijo et al, 2020

Power and financial statecraft options in the Global South

What of the Global South? Table 3.3 displays overall hard power and financial power capabilities for developing and emerging economies countries falling into two sub-categories. The first sub-category is 'Southern' countries that are clearly major powers. The most significant is China, an aspiring superpower, followed by India, the world's most populous democracy and its third largest economy in purchasing power parity terms, and Russia, a longtime major power possessed of nuclear weapons and ample fossil fuel resources. Brazil and Indonesia, although often understood as mere regional powers, are potential global major powers. Both have been top ten economies since the 1950s,[7] and Brazil displays rising financial capabilities in the 21st century, although beginning from low levels. Table 3.3's second sub-category includes four smaller jurisdictions that are not major global powers: Saudi Arabia, United Arab Emirates (UAE), Singapore, and South Africa. Despite small populations, each reveals large creditor and/or financial network power as of the end of the period. Confirming their importance to this discussion, South Africa, Indonesia, and Saudi Arabia are members of the G20 group of large economies that collectively proved essential to managing the global financial crisis of 2008–09, and Indonesia, Saudi Arabia, and the UAE have been invited to join South Africa in the expanded BRICS+ group.

The previous section's discussion of the Global North's FS linked specific international financial capabilities to types of assertive FS. That framing worked because the G7 countries are relatively similar in their international political and financial profiles. However, the Global South is a more disparate group, even if we limit ourselves to the nine countries profiled in Table 3.3. Consequently, this section's discussion primarily is organized by country.

China is of course in a category by itself. China's increasing prominence in the global political economy reflects both its hard power capabilities (MCI) and its financial capabilities, but especially its enormous creditor power, which is second only to that of Japan, by either of the measures referenced here. In terms of the GMFPS dataset referenced in Tables 3.2 and 3.3, China's creditor capability expanded almost fourfold in a little over a decade. According to the NIIP, calculated slightly differently and reporting absolute figures, in September 2022 mainland China had a net surplus of US$2.5 trillion, with another US$1.7 trillion in Hong Kong. China, whose overseas grants and loans are not included in the ODA statistics, is now the world's most important bilateral lender to DEE governments (Gelpern et al, 2021). A Chinese-affiliated think tank recently estimated that financial flows associated with China's Belt and Road Initiative (BRI), first announced in 2013 and focusing on funding traditional heavy infrastructure in energy, transportation, mining, and communications throughout the Global South, had now passed the symbolic US$1trillion level, including US$634 billion in 'construction contracts' (or loans tied to the purchase of Chinese equipment and services) and US$419 billion in 'non-financial investments' (that is, equity participation by Chinese banks and firms, often ostensibly private, but with obligatory close ties to the state), with the latter category slated to increase (Nedopil, 2024, p 7 and passim). The BRI sums for 2022 (US$75 billion) and 2023 (US$92 billion) are only about three quarters of recent bilateral ODA flows from the political North, but the types of goods provided by Chinese aid and investment are closer to the dams, roads, and power plants on which the West (now Global North) concentrated its foreign assistance from the 1950s through the early 1980s.

As noted earlier in this chapter, a country with a large international creditor presence can exercise the FS instrument of debt forgiveness, sometimes extracting reciprocal favours. Because the majority of BRI funding has been via loans, China now is having to deal with the problem of how to treat defaulting sovereign debtors. Public–private transnational committees from the Global North, such as the Sovereign Debt Working Group of the Bretton Woods Committee (2021), worry because China will not join with them as official and private creditors to DEE governments, but instead prefers to wield the important FS instrument of sovereign debt restructuring unilaterally. China also has moved into financial crisis management, becoming increasingly consequential as a potential global lender of last resort by offering emergency swap lines and other facilities, including to countries, such as Argentina, that the US foreign policy establishment continues to view as its own 'backyard' (Bradsher, 2023; Tett, 2023). As of end 2020, China had bilateral swap arrangements with 31 countries, including several advanced industrial democracies such as Australia, Canada, Japan, South Korea, and the United Kingdom (Perks et al, 2021, p 36). Thus far, Chinese swaps seldom have been used, in contrast to those extended by the US (Perez-Saíz and Zhang, 2023).

In Table 3.3's measure, for which unfortunately 2013 is the latest year available for all countries, neither China nor any other Global South country profiled has any currency capabilities, yet this is changing. In late 2016, in a decision that was as much a political calculation as an economic necessity, the IMF incorporated the yuan (renminbi) into the basket of hard currencies used to compose its SDRs with an initial weight of just under 11 per cent.[8] Subsequently, China's currency capabilities have gradually expanded, particularly in terms of the yuan's use as a trade currency in Southeast Asia and to denominate its swap arrangements with DEEs of political interest to China's government. These emergency swap arrangements indirectly bolster Chinese currency and network capabilities. Nonetheless, China also continues to employ extensive capital controls as a form of defensive FS, thus demonstrating considerable reluctance to expand its international financial network role. Despite recent increases in China's financial governance roles within the global institutions and clubs dominated by the Global North, its leaders also have experimented with constructing alternative global financial institutions and clubs, such as the BRICS' New Development Bank (NDB), its companion stabilization fund, the Contingent Reserve Association (CRA), and the Asian Infrastructure Investment Bank (AIIB), all created in 2011–12. More recently, China's focus has been on promoting its central bank digital currency (CBDC) (McNally, Chapter 7 this volume), similar to Russia's digital ruble (Ehlke, Salzer, and Westermeier, Chapter 10 this volume), and on the de-dollarization of international transactions more generally (Peruffo et al, 2024).

Table 3.3 also shows the following interesting patterns among the remaining countries profiled. As a group, these major emerging economies have increased their creditor capability, although mainly in East Asia and among natural resource exporters. In addition to China (and Hong Kong), the IMF's NIIP measure shows late 2022 surpluses for Singapore (US$0.8 trillion); Saudi Arabia (US$0.7 trillion); and Russia (US$0.8), the latter despite Russia being the subject of financial sanctions from the political West.[9] Countries with large net external financial liabilities included Brazil (US$0.8 trillion), India (US$0.4 trillion), and Indonesia (US$0.3 trillion). Over the period measured, none had any currency power, but all increased their financial network and governance capabilities.

The overall hard power capabilities of *Russia*, a natural resource exporter and nuclear weapons power, are undervalued by the MCI index employed in Table 3.3, as neither of these dimensions is included. The original promoter of the BRICs as a multilateral political club in the first decade of the 21st century, Russia also has had sufficient creditor and financial governance capabilities to shield itself from financial sanctions imposed by the West, beginning in response to the 2014 annexation of Crimea, but vastly expanded following Russia's February 2022 attack on Ukraine. However, there have been costs. The knock-on effects of financial sanctions led by the Global North have impeded Russia's technological modernization, reinforcing its identity as a natural resource exporter, and now to destinations prominently including its BRICS partners China, India, and Brazil, each of whom increased deliveries from Russia (Prokopenko, 2023). Nonetheless, Russia's considerable creditor power, along with its indefatigable efforts to paint the Global North as an aggressor and its sanctions as criminal, have enabled the country to avoid too much direct pain from the sanctions. Russia has keenly promoted concrete alternatives to the US dollar, including a CBDC, the digital ruble, which policy makers openly describe as a tool of geopolitical competition with the West, and the possible option of a BRICS currency, initially for settling bilateral international balances (Ehlke, Salzer, and Westermeier, Chapter 10 this volume; Economist, 2024b).

India is a major power by overall hard power capabilities, but its national financial profile remains that of a lower-middle income DEE, albeit one with considerable global financial governance capabilities. Its choices in FS have been to continue to defend its autonomy via capital controls, extend very modest foreign assistance in areas of its historic special interest, such as Anglophone East Africa, and participate in collective FS via the BRICS (Roberts et al, 2018). This said, the most problematic, even hostile, bilateral relationship within the five BRICS is the India–China one, so India is quite reluctant to act in any fashion that would increase its vulnerability to China.[10] As detailed by Kapadia and Musthaq (Chapter 6, this volume), India has adopted a policy of encouraging foreign borrowing by its private sector, on the theory that any future external debt crises might provoke private bankruptcies but will not destabilize public finances. However, the experiences of Latin America in the early 1980s and East Asia in the late 1990s suggest that large private bank creditors and institutional investors based in the G7 in the past have been able to call on their home governments to force DEE governments to assume the foreign private, non-guaranteed debts of their banks (Armijo and Sood, 2023). Where the foreign creditors are dispersed, as in the thousands of Spanish and Italian pensioners and small funds who purchased Argentine bonds in the 1990s and were subject to default in late 2001, this did not occur. Power matters.

Brazil's leaders have used tools of bilateral international financial statecraft primarily for defensive purposes, having decades of experience with creative and flexible use of capital controls to cope with the exchange complexities of a very high-inflation economy, ending only in the mid-1990s. In the late 1990s, Brazil inaugurated modest foreign aid and technical cooperation programmes, particularly with Lusophone Africa. In the early 21st century, Brazil participated enthusiastically in the collective FS projects of the BRICS and somewhat less enthusiastically with its regional neighbours in South America (Henderson and Clarkson, 2016; Armijo and Sepehr, 2025). Brazil, which experienced external debt crises in 1982, 1999, and 2002, subsequently followed a defensive FS strategy for minimizing external vulnerability of substituting domestic debt for international borrowing, bringing the foreign-to-domestic public debt ratio down from 11 per cent in 2002 to under 4 per cent in 2020. Domestic financial regulations encouraged private borrowers to do likewise, halving the foreign-to-domestic private debt ratio from 63 to 31 per cent from 2003 to 2020. This said, the ratio of Brazil's total external debt to GDP, which fell from 19 per cent in 2003 to only 7 per cent in 2008, by 2020 was back at 18 per cent.[11] In any case, only DEE countries such as Brazil with large and liquid domestic financial markets, approximated by the financial network capabilities shown in Tables 3.2 and 3.3, can successfully reorient government and business borrowing from foreign to domestic sources of credit.[12]

Indonesia, although the world's fourth largest country by population, lacks independent financial capabilities, and thus focuses mainly on defensive actions, such as diversifying the sources of its inward foreign investment. Indonesia's neighbour, *Singapore*, however, has outsize financial capabilities in both the creditor and network dimensions. Together with other members of the original ASEAN-5 (Indonesia, Thailand, Malaysia, and the Philippines) Singapore and its neighbours have large joint creditor capabilities, totaling 5.5 per cent of the world's financial surplus in 2013 (Armijo et al, 2020). Their location next to China largely neutralizes their hard power capabilities, yet the ASEAN-5 have engaged in considerable collective financial institution-building on behalf of themselves and the five poorer, newer ASEAN countries, including by pushing forward the Chiang Mai Initiative Multilateralization (CMIM) regional emergency swap arrangement of all ten countries plus China, Japan, and South Korea (Katada, 2020), as well as a new initiative to provide a joint trading platform for members' sovereign debt (Rethel, 2021).

Saudi Arabia is not a major power in overall material capabilities, yet its leaders, along with neighbouring fossil fuel exporters *UAE* and Kuwait, wield very considerable creditor capabilities. These governments' preferred vehicle for assertive FS is the sovereign wealth fund (SWF), an often-opaque type of investment fund operated by national governments, and which frequently seeks some balance of political influence and profits in its portfolio and foreign direct investment (FDI) holdings. Of the eleven largest SWFs as of end 2022, each with at least US$300 billion in assets under management, four were from China or Hong Kong, with a total portfolio of US$3.3 trillion, five from Persian Gulf petroleum exporters, totalling US$3.1 trillion, and the governments of Norway and Singapore owned the remaining two.[13] *South Africa,* the final country in the Global South mentioned here separately, possesses fewer overall hard power capabilities than a larger country such as Nigeria, yet is notable for being a member of the BRICS and the G20, and for possessing creditor, financial network, and financial governance capabilities that are significant for its region. Nonetheless, South Africa's abilities to initiate bilateral financial statecraft, except possibly vis-à-vis its immediate subregion, are quite limited.[14]

A final (implicit) group consists of all the remaining countries in the Global South. Most countries in this thoroughly heterogenous group lack both the hard power and financial power capabilities for assertive FS. They are not able to extend public sector aid, credit, or investment to their neighbours, forgive others' foreign debts, offer access to their attractive home financial markets, or exercise financial sanctions. Even with respect to defensive FS, most DEEs cannot contemplate individual action, except to erect defensive capital controls when they fear being destabilized by capital flight, or to take up opportunities to diversify their sources of external capital. They can, in principle, join in collective FS, for example by pursuing 'inside options' such as joint campaigns to reallocate votes and quotas within the international financial institutions or to free up more emergency lending by the IMF through loosening restrictions on the uses of SDRs. Some participate actively in collective efforts to reform the treatment of troubled sovereign debt, both by participating in debt reduction efforts led by the Global North, such as the G20's Debt Service Suspension Initiative (DSSI) to postpone, but not cancel, sovereign debt to official creditors during the height of the global COVID-19 pandemic, or by the Global South, as in the Bridgetown Initiative led by Barbados.[15] A more radical alternative is the pursuit of 'outside options' such as attempting to diversify away from the US dollar or to promote collective financial institutions not controlled by the Global North, such as regional development banks that try to operate independently of the major global powers, including the ultimately unsuccessful Bank of the South (Armijo and Sepehr, 2025).

Conclusions: Can international financial statecraft in the name of the Global South mitigate international financial subordination?

These conclusions circle back to the larger inquiries motivating this collective volume, particularly the question of whether thoughtful *international financial statecraft* (FS) from leaders of countries identifying with the Global South can act to mitigate *international financial subordination* (IFS) (Alami et al, 2023, and see Chapter 2 and the Afterword in this volume). IFS is both a political and an economic concept, coined by a group of scholars attempting to unify a large body of work under a common label. IFS is also a social science theory, by which is meant a related, mutually consistent set of propositions, or hypotheses, about cause-and-effect relationships. Theories may be credible or implausible, but they are not easily falsifiable. Unlike the *law* of gravity, which always holds on earth except under highly specialized conditions such as within a vacuum tube, a causal relationship posited by a social science *theory* is almost always only probabilistically true, making efforts to prove or disprove it even more difficult.

The theory of IFS makes at least two related claims. First, the norms and customary procedures within global financial and currency markets, as well as the rules and regulations adopted by international organizations tasked with global financial governance (collectively, the 'global financial architecture') operate as a system that is structurally biased against fair treatment for DEEs. Moreover, and second, this bias is both deeply embedded and usually unperceived, either by its victims or its beneficiaries, who suffer from false consciousness. Examples of such systemic bias are not difficult to locate. Consider, for example, the difficulties experienced by countries that cannot borrow internationally or pay for imports in their home currencies, but instead must exchange their national monies for so-called hard currencies, preeminently the US dollar. This is the so-called problem of currency 'original sin' (Eichengreen et al, 2022; Armijo, 2023).

Can the exercise of FS by countries self-identified with the Global South help? Even assuming that degrees of IFS could be measured or assessed, even qualitatively, which is not how the existing academic literature reads, is FS a useful response? This chapter's investigation suggests four somewhat sobering conclusions.

First, it is by no means clear that the assertive FS increasingly used by powerful states of the Global North, especially the financial sanctions imposed on 'rogue states' by the US and G7, is a useful strategy, at least in terms of its stated goals. Financial sanctions seldom achieve their announced goals of deterring or reversing actions by rogue states, although calibrated economic sanctions against close allies with lesser hard power capabilities than the sanctioning state (as in the Suez Crisis of 1956) likely have the best chance for success. Moreover, financial sanctions directly undercut the very capabilities on which this FS instrument relies (Farrell and Newman, 2020; McDowell, 2021). Not only have countries directly subject to US financial sanctions – including Iran, Venezuela, and Russia – suffered from them, but so have many other states, who find their own financial institutions and transactions blocked when they wish to remain neutral. For example, India, historically reliant on Russian petroleum, has also been inconvenienced by the costs imposed by US-led sanctions (Economist, 2024a). Even core states of the political West, such as Germany, have experienced large transaction costs due to US-led financial sanctions. Arguably the main actual benefit to US and EU politicians of financial sanctions on Russia in 2022–24 over its attacks on Ukraine has been that of being seen to have acted, without risking direct military involvement and major power war. Russia has not been deterred.

Second, much FS is bilateral and zero-sum, and developing and emerging economies at best can anticipate the same ambiguous results as experienced by the Global North. Individual FS, even relatively generous actions such as the incumbent leaders of a powerful state resolving to extend foreign aid or sovereign debt relief, inevitably is characterized by mixed motives, some of which are positive sum ('it is in our national interest that our neighbours and allies are prosperous and peaceful') while others are zero-sum ('however, we don't wish our allies to become less dependent on us or less willing to follow our lead on UN votes'). In other words, it is inherent in the definition of FS that its primary goals are not to improve the efficiency of financial intermediation or promote regional or global economic growth. Moreover, overt manipulation by one state invites retaliation and a shrinking and more politicized global financial and monetary system overall, an unpredictable and undesirable outcome. Sometimes sanctions can be defended as an option short of war, but they are seldom a first best foreign policy choice, and hardly ever a sound economic policy.

Third, as argued throughout this chapter, a country's options for exercising FS cannot be divorced from the country's underlying relative power capabilities: smaller or weaker powers are necessarily disadvantaged when international relations devolve into sheer power politics. Ceteris paribus, DEEs have every incentive to prefer multilateral cooperation to the spread of a combative FS perspective.

In the end, and fourth, the best opportunities for DEEs to employ intentional FS to mitigate or ameliorate financial subordination will derive from their exercise of collective international financial statecraft, directed at reforms of global financial governance. Such reform coalitions are challenging to organize. Developing and emerging economies, roughly, the countries of the Global South, first need to pursue international cooperation among themselves to achieve greater international voice (Armijo, 2023). Coordination might occur within a regional neighbourhood, as evidenced by financial cooperation within ASEAN or the Gulf Cooperation Council, or via a cross-regional coalition of countries, as within the five BRICS from 2000 to 2019, or, as by the Alliance of Small Island States through which members advocate for international financing of climate adaptation and resilience activities.[16]

In other words, in the end, FS is … simply statecraft. Lesser powers operating in the global space generally have two options: they may bandwagon with a great or major power, accepting subordinate status in exchange for concrete benefits, or they may laboriously form a coalition with other middle or small powers to aggregate their voices around common goals. Country leaders need not select the same foreign policy partners across all international issue arenas, incidentally an important thesis of the 'active non-alignment' option being promoted by norm entrepreneurs from Latin American middle powers (Fortín et al, 2023). Thus, Brazil or Argentina might caucus with the self-proclaimed representatives of the Global South on some issues, but with the political North on others. In the international issue arena of global financial governance there are many attractive reform ideas already under discussion including, for example, allowing for Global North countries to 'share' their SDR allocations, establishing a multilateral sovereign debt restructuring mechanism (SDRM) or institution, expanding options for wealthy countries to subsidize environmental and climate protection via revived 'debt-for-nature' swaps, or for Global South groups such as the BRICS to innovate new instruments including currencies (Batista Jr, 2024). Ultimately, the core solutions to IFS are as much or more about old-fashioned international political cooperation as about the use of national financial capabilities or FS instruments, per se.

Notes

1 The US national security establishment, for example, considers Chinese and Russian loans and investment in Latin America threatening (Kroenig et al, 2024).

2 For example, in early 2021, just days before leaving office, the US Trump administration arranged a US$3.5 billion loan to Ecuador, conditioned behind-the-scenes on privatization and refusing Chinese 5G telecommunications technology (Gallagher and Heine, 2021).

3 Concerns in the Global North around SWFs derive from the fact that most of the largest are owned by authoritarian countries, including China and Middle Eastern petroleum exporters. Although blatant examples of political pressure are relatively few, the possibility clearly exists and has sparked Northern-led efforts at collective self-regulation, as through the 2008 Santiago Principles (Fry et al, 2011; Carney, 2018). Consider also European SWFs that pride themselves on investing profitably, prudently, and largely within Europe: these resources certainly will be tapped during a financial crisis.

4 Country-level NIIP data are available from the IMF's Balance of Payments data portal (https://data.imf.org/?sk=7a51304b-6426-40c0-83dd-ca473ca1fd52, accessed April 2024). The NIIP differs from the GMFPS' creditor capability index in that the latter is calculated as global percentage shares, not absolute US dollar values. Moreover, the GMFPS dataset assesses official foreign exchange positions as part of its currency pillar, not the creditor pillar (Armijo et al, 2020).

5 Canada, with its long, shared border and deeply entwined economy with the US retains large USD reserves to manage that bilateral relationship. It constitutes a special case, and seldom employs FS vis-à-vis third parties except in concert with the US.

6 See Moses and Zhu, 2022; US Government, 2023.

7 Using data from Maddison, 2006, 'GDP in 1990 international dollars' and from 1999 forward as per the World Bank's 'World Development Indicators', 'GDP at purchasing power parity'.

8 See https://www.imf.org/en/News/Articles/2016/09/29/AM16-NA093016IMF-Adds-Chinese-Renminbi-to-Special-Drawing-Rights-Basket [Accessed 10 February 2025].

9 The IMF doesn't calculate NIIP for the UAE, but presumably this number also would be strongly in surplus.

10 The incorporation of five Middle Eastern fossil fuel exporters and/or Red Sea powers into a new BRICS+ club in January 2024 was a Chinese preference, initially opposed by both India and Brazil.

11 See https://fred.stlouisfed.org [Accessed 10 February 2025].

12 Machado, de Paula, and Mantoan (Chapter 5, this volume) identify partisan rotation between developmentalist and neoliberal presidential administrations as a principal source for macroeconomic and FS outcomes, while Kaltenbrunner, Karaçimen, and Rabinovich (Chapter 8, this volume) emphasize financial differences between Brazil and Turkey, yet stress each country's IFS. Armijo (2017) identifies a comparatively competent Brazilian state with multiple goals for public banks.

13 See https://www.statista.com/statistics/276617/sovereign-wealth-funds-worldwide-based-on-assets-under-management/ [Accessed 10 February 2025].

14 Patrick Bond (Chapter 4, this volume) and Johannes Petry (Chapter 9, this volume) agree that South Africa enjoys scant autonomy in FS, crediting the state's financial subordination as the main cause.

15 See https://www.un.org/sustainabledevelopment/blog/2023/04/press-release-with-clock-ticking-for-the-sdgs-un-chief-and-barbados-prime-minister-call-for-urgent-action-to-transform-broken-global-financial-system/ [Accessed 10 February 2025].

16 See https://www.dlapiper.com/en-us/insights/topics/cop-conference-of-the-parties/mitigation-adaptation-and-resilience [Accessed 10 February 2025].

References

Alami, I., Alves, C., Bonizzi, B., Kaltenbrunner, A., Koddenbrock, K., Kvangraven, I., et al (2023) 'International financial subordination: A critical research agenda', *Review of International Political Economy*, 30(4): 1360–86.

Andersen, M.S., Cooley, A. and Nexon, D.H. (eds) (2024) *Undermining American Hegemony: Goods Substitution in World Politics*, Cambridge: Cambridge University Press.

Armijo, L.E. (2017) 'The public bank trilemma: The BNDES and Brazil's new developmentalism', in P. Kingstone and T. Timothy Power (eds) *Democratic Brazil Divided*, Pittsburgh: University of Pittsburgh Press, pp 230–47.

Armijo, L.E. (2023) 'Regionalism, multilateralism, and sovereign debt: Observations from a Latin Americanist', *Global Perspectives*, 4(1): 57547.

Armijo, L.E. and Katada, S.N. (eds) (2014) *The Financial Statecraft of Emerging Powers: Shield and Sword in Asia and Latin America*, New York: Palgrave Macmillan.

Armijo, L.E. and Sood, P. (2023) 'Voice at the point of sovereign default', *Ethics and International Affairs*, [online] 13 March, Available from: https://www.ethicsandinternationalaffairs.org/online-exclusives/voice-at-the-point-of-sovereign-default [Accessed 10 February 2025].

Armijo, L.E. and Sepehr, V.R. (2025) 'Long-term finance: The challenging international politics of regional development banks', in L.E. Armijo, M. Fraundorfer, and S.D. Rhodes (eds) *South American Policy Regionalism: Drivers and Barriers to International Problem Solving*, London: Routledge.

Armijo, L.E., Tirone, D.C., and Chey, K. (2020) 'The monetary and financial powers of states: Theory, dataset, and observations on the trajectory of American dominance', *New Political Economy*, 25(2): 174–94.

Baldwin, D.A. (1985) *Economic Statecraft*, Princeton, NJ: Princeton University Press.

Batista Jr., P.N. (2024) 'BRICS: How to arrive at a new international reserve currency?', *Red.org*, [online] 18 October, Available from: https://red.org.br/noticia/brics-como-chegar-a-uma-nova-moeda-de-reserva-internacional/ [Accessed 28 November 2024].

Bearce, D.H. and Tirone, D.C. (2010) 'Foreign aid effectiveness and the strategic goals of donor governments', *The Journal of Politics*, 72(3): 837–71.

Blustein, P. (2003) *The Chastening: Inside the Crisis that Rocked the Global Financial System and Humbled the IMF,* New York: Public Affairs.

Bradsher, K. (2023) 'After doling out huge loans, China is now bailing out countries', *New York Times,* [online] 27 March, Available at https://www.nytimes.com/2023/03/27/business/china-loans-bailouts-debt.html [Accessed 7 May 2024].

Carney, R.W. (2018) *Authoritarian Capitalism: Sovereign Wealth Funds and State-Owned Enterprises in East Asia and Beyond*, Cambridge: Cambridge University Press.

Cassetta, J.M. (2022) 'The geopolitics of swap lines' (M-RCBG Working Paper Series 181), Cambridge, MA: Harvard University Press.

Cohen, B.J. (2018) *Currency Power: Understanding Monetary Rivalry*, Princeton, NJ: Princeton University Press.

Economist (2024a) 'How India's imports of Russian oil have lubricated global markets', *Economist*, [online] 11 April, Available from: https://www.economist.com/asia/2024/04/11/how-indias-imports-of-russian-oil-have-lubricated-global-markets [Accessed 28 November 2024].

Economist (2024b) 'Putin's plan to dethrone the dollar,' *Economist*, [online] 20 October, Available from: https://www.economist.com/international/2024/10/20/putins-plan-to-dethrone-the-dollar [Accessed 28 November 2024].

Eichengreen, B., Hausmann, R., and Panizzi, U. (2022) 'Yet still it endures: The persistence of original sin' (CEPR Discussion Paper DP17691), London: Centre for Economic Policy Research.

Farrell, H. and Newman, A. (2020) 'The twilight of America's financial empire: Washington's economic bullying will erode its power', *Foreign Affairs*, [online] 24 January, Available from: https://www.foreignaffairs.com/united-states/twilight-americas-financial-empire [Accessed 7 May 2024].

Fortín, C., Ominami, C., and Heine, J. (eds) (2023) *Latin American Foreign Policies in the New World Order: The Active Non-Alignment Option*, London: Anthem Press.

Fry, R.A., McKibbin, W.J., and O'Brien, J. (eds) (2011) *Sovereign Wealth: The Role of State Capital in the New Financial Order*, London: Imperial College Press.

Gabor, D. (2021) 'The Wall Street consensus', *Development and Change*, 52(3): 429–59.

Gabor, D. and Sylla, N.S. (2023) *Development and Change*, 54(5): 1169–96.

Gallagher, K.P. and Heine, J. (2021) 'Biden needs to reverse Trump's economic policy in Ecuador', *The Hill,* [online] 26 January, Available from: https://thehill.com/opinion/international/535838-biden-needs-to-reverse-trumps-crony-capitalism-in-ecuador/ [Accessed 7 May 2024].

Gelpern, A., Horn, S., Morris, S., Parks, B., and Trebesch, C. (2021) *How China Lends: A Rare Look into 100 Debt Contracts with Foreign Governments*, AIDDATA Policy Report, Available from: https://www.aiddata.org/publications/how-china-lends [Accessed 10 February 2025].

Henderson, J. and Clarkson, S. (2016) 'International public finance and the rise of Brazil: Comparing Brazil's use of regionalism with its unilateralism and bilateralism', *Latin American Research Review*, 51(4): 43–61.

Katada, S.N. (2020) *Japan's New Regional Reality: Geoeconomic Strategy in the Asia-Pacific*, New York: Columbia University Press.

Katada, S.N., Roberts, C., and Armijo, L.E. (2017) 'The varieties of collective financial statecraft: The BRICS and China', *Political Science Quarterly*, 132(3): 403–33.

Kharas, H. and Linn, J.F. (2008) 'Hypocrisy in financial crisis response: East Asia 1998 versus the USA 2008', *Brookings Institution*, [online], Available from: https://www.brookings.edu/articles/hypocrisy-in-financial-crisis-response-east-asia-1998-versus-the-usa-2008/ [Accessed 7 May 2024].

Kroenig, M., Marczak, J., and Cimmino, J. (2024) 'A strategy to counter malign Chinese and Russian influence in Latin America and the Caribbean', *Atlantic Council*, [online] 12 February, Available from: https://www.atlanticcouncil.org/content-series/atlantic-council-strategy-paper-series/a-strategy-to-counter-malign-chinese-and-russian-influence-in-latin-america-and-the-caribbean/ [Accessed 7 May 2024].

Li, J., Shapiro, D., and Ufimtseva. A. (2023) 'Regulating inbound foreign direct investment in a world of hegemonic rivalry: The evolution and diffusion of US policy', *Journal of International Business Policy*, 7: 147–65.

Maddison, A. (2006) *The World Economy*, Paris: Development Centre, Organisation for Economic Co-operation and Development (OECD).

McDowell, D. (2021) 'Financial sanctions and currency risk in the international financial system', *Review of International Political Economy*, (28)3: 635–61.

Moses, O. and Zhu, K. (2022) 'The Belt and Road Initiative and the Partnership for Global Infrastructure and Investment' (GCI Working Paper 026), Boston: Boston University.

Nedopil, C. (2024) *China Belt and Road Initiative (BRI) Investment Report 2023*, Brisbane: Griffith Asia Institute.

Perez, C. (2022) 'What does Russia's removal from SWIFT mean for the future of global commerce?' *Foreign Policy*, [online] 8 March, Available from: https://foreignpolicy.com/2022/03/08/swift-sanctions-ukraine-russia-nato-putin-war-global-finance/ [Accessed 7 May 2024].

Perez-Saíz, H. and Zhang, L. (2023) 'Renminbi usage in cross-border payments: Regional patterns and the role of swaps lines and offshore clearing banks' (IMF Working Papers 2023/77), Washington, DC: IMF.

Perks, M., Rao, Y., Shin, J., and Tokuoka, K. (2021) 'Evolution of bilateral swap lines' (IMF Working Paper 21/210), Washington, DC: IMF.

Peruffo, L., Cunha, A.M., and Haines, A.F.H. (2024) 'Moving away from a dollar dominated international monetary and financial system? The BRICS grouping as an arena to promote the e-CNY', in Y. Li, F.J.B.S. Leandro, J.T. Silva, and C. Rodrigues (eds) *The Palgrave Handbook on China-Europe-Africa Relations*, Singapore: Palgrave Macmillan, pp 1149–65.

Pistor, K. (2020) *The Code of Capital: How the Law Creates Wealth and Inequality*, Princeton, NJ: Princeton University Press.

Prokopenko, A. (2023) *How Sanctions Have Changed Russian Economic Policy*, Washington, DC: Carnegie Endowment for International Peace.

Rethel, L. (2021) 'State–state and state–market alliances in the forging of the ASEAN economic community: The case of capital markets', unpublished manuscript, Warwick: University of Warwick.

Roberts, C., Katada, S.N., and Armijo, L.E. (2018) *The BRICS and Collective Financial Statecraft*, New York: Oxford University Press.

Tett, G. (2023) 'Argentina's IMF deal should be a wake-up call on emerging market debt', *Financial Times,* [online] February 3, Available from: https://www.ft.com/content/c4aee76a-0415-47ed-b1ab-285bdc2baa4e [Accessed 7 May 2024].

US Government (2023) *Fact Sheet: Partnership for Global Infrastructure and Investment at the G7 Summit*, Press Briefing, 20 May 2024.

PART II

4

South African Financial System Innovation and Degradation under Conditions of Extreme Uneven Development

Patrick Bond

Introduction

South Africa's financial system is both a source of innovation and social degradation within a context of extreme uneven development. This chapter analyzes the interplay of these two factors, and illustrates the insufficient role of the state in regulating finance and the havoc it is wreaking on its economic and social life. Given the extraordinary extent of unfettered financialization within South African finance and the state's capture by neoliberal economic ideology, the resulting institutional structure of the economy provides the state with neither the capability (or willingness) to tame finance domestically, nor to exercise any meaningful degree of financial statecraft abroad. Instead, we can observe the development of a socio-economic system that is fully subordinated (see Petry and Nölke, Introduction, this volume) to the imperatives of financial accumulation and thus subject to the whims of financial investors, causing tremendous societal degradation in the process.

South African 'settler-colonial' capitalism was traditionally adjusted when successive modes of extra-economic oppression had the effect of raising the rate of capital accumulation, as Ben Magubane's (2001) historic periodization of the race–class relationship illustrated. In its most recent manifestation, financial institutions have recorded the fastest growth and wield the most power, in an era following the discovery of diamonds and gold in the 1870s–80s when a 'minerals energy complex' emerged. This entailed multinational corporate mining houses, smelters, petrochemical plants, refineries, and the coal-reliant parastatal electricity company Eskom, which were financed in the postwar era through an innovative oligopolistic form of corporate structure (Innes, 1984). The extreme form of uneven development of South Africa's productive forces that resulted, characterized by the world's worst inequality, social unrest, and corporate corruption, in turn profoundly affected modes of financial innovation. Today, a 'minerals-energy-finance complex' is the resulting description of the most recent force driving an exceptionally distorted political economy, as framed by Samantha Ashman (2018).

In recent decades, two of the most extreme forms of innovation within African financial markets have been witnessed in Zimbabwe and South Africa. In the former, after a century of uneven development between financial repression and speculative bubbles (Bond, 1998), from the late 1990s the Reserve Bank of Zimbabwe adopted desperate forms of (corruption-riddled) quantitative easing, that is, excessive printing of money on many occasions to facilitate the elites' primitive accumulation. This led to the world's second-worst-ever hyperinflation (more than a trillion per cent by 2008) and compelled the repeated reintroductions of local currencies (in 2024, one that is supposedly gold-backed, although the US dollar remained dominant for 80 per cent of transactions). This degenerate monetary status represents what may be the core problem behind financial management in Zimbabwe, alongside an underlying inability to circulate surpluses from the mining industry (Bond, 1998).

In South Africa, in contrast, controversies mainly surround the extreme *orthodoxy* associated with the financial system, especially the introduction of monetarism in 1989 – resulting in a devastating interest rate increase (of 13 per cent) just at the time the transition to democracy began, resulting in the modern economy's longest-ever depression – followed by a deregulatory (broadly considered 'neoliberal') approach to finance during the 1990s. The problems were only somewhat corrected by sporadic, shallow forms of reregulation, and periodic bouts of social resistance. The resulting degradation of the economy ranged from the local household balance sheet up to global interactions with global monetary and financial power, manifesting South Africa's full subordination vis-à-vis both domestic and global finance (see Petry and Nölke, Introduction, this volume).

In this context, the innovative zeal associated with Wild West-type 'economic crime and fraud' (as PwC terms the phenomenon) is manifest in South African finance. To illustrate, local-level predatory finance affects even the poorest social grant recipients as well as rural municipalities which during the 2010s deposited their funds in a bankrupted institution (VBS Mutual Bank). But the problems range upwards in scale to prolific international 'illicit financial flows' which reached a point of such degeneracy that in 2023 two major events dominated market news: a 'grey listing' of the South African banking system by the Paris-based Financial Action Task Force, and the long-overdue prosecution of blatant currency manipulation against the Rand. Excessive household-scale indebtedness was reflected in a scandal in which during the 2010s, state grants of as little as $20/child/month served as the collateralization basis for debit orders facilitated by Mastercard's then chief executive Ajay Banga, to pay for unwanted microfinance and burial-insurance products. This form of predatory behaviour led to the 2018 prosecution of – and 2020 fine and ultimately bankruptcy for – Net1's Cash Paymaster Services, a World Bank 'financial inclusion' subsidiary (Bateman et al, 2023; Bond, 2024b).

The following pages track, first, the ways South African financial markets were celebrated for innovations dating to the 19th century when discoveries were made of the world's richest diamond field (Kimberley in 1867) and then the richest gold seam (Johannesburg in 1884) (Bond, 2003). Not only were new banks amenable to financing resource extraction – for example, the original Standard Chartered (founded in 1857 in one of South Africa's major cities, Port Elizabeth) – but so too were foreign loans and equity available, especially from the City of London in the late 19th century, from New York banker J.P. Morgan in 1917 (to create the Anglo American Corporation), and from the World Bank from 1951 to 1967 (even though in the latter case, loans that financed coal-fired power plants generated electricity that was not provided to the vast majority of Black South Africans due to apartheid policies).

Moreover, one of the world's major stock markets (especially during the 20th century), in Johannesburg, proved capable of providing innovative financing for ever-deeper mining (down to 4 km), smelting, electrification, petrochemicals, and associated minerals-energy complex activities. These firms were responsible for the economy's enormous contribution to the climate crisis, ranking as the world's third-highest contributor by the 2020s, measured as annual greenhouse gas emissions per unit of per capita GDP (among countries with 10 million or more inhabitants): a typical 500 million tonnes emissions for 62 million people producing $400 billion in GDP, lagging behind only Kazakhstan and the Czech Republic (Bond, 2021b). Also, both during apartheid and in current times, shortages of affordable electricity adversely affect the Black majority, given that an enormous share (more than 40 per cent) is consumed by just two dozen 'Energy Intensive Users Group' member corporations which exert enormous influence (for example, regular authorship of the government's Integrated Resource Plan, highly discounted electricity prices, and unmatched defensive capacities against disconnections during supply shortages).

There was, as well, sociopolitical innovation in retail banking that allowed financiers to serve not only traditional White customers but also middle-class Black borrowers from the 1980s, and even low-income recipients of social welfare by the 2010s. However, there arose an obvious dialectic fusing

South Africa's excessive financial deepening – for example, 2021 bank assets worth 130 per cent of GDP and other investment funds worth 250 per cent of GDP (IMF, 2022, p 10) – with rapid degradation of balance sheets and living conditions. As a result, a few top-down reactions have resulted, such as belated financial reregulation for domestic customers. Relatively weak laws were passed in 2005, 2008, 2017, and 2022 (the latter to fend off imminent grey listing), alongside various court judgements against unjust salary debit orders (Bond, 2015; Sibanyoni et al, 2024).

In addition, rare prosecutions of financial fraud recently tackled the VBS Mutual Bank in 2018 – revealing a high degree of corruption that benefited politicians from the ruling party and third-largest party (ironically, one with self-avowed socialist aspirations) – and also one of the main predatory lenders, Net1, in 2020. Civil cases were also important, for example against illegitimate debit orders on salaries imposed by microfinancier Capitec, in 2024 (Sibanyoni et al, 2024). However, although Competition Tribunal prosecutors attempted in 2023 to punish local and international commercial banks for Rand currency manipulation (a decade earlier), the case was considered to reflect overreach and in an appeals court judgment was diminished to reflect some of the banks' complaints. An attempted prosecution of the country's largest-ever financial fraud case, involving the Steinhoff South African–German retail empire, was making progress until March 2024 when the leading principal, Markus Jooste, committed suicide.

The limitations of South Africa's legislative reforms, regulatory strengthening, criminal prosecution, and moral suasion were unveiled in mid-2024 when the parliament, Treasury, Reserve Bank, and National Prosecuting Authority failed to impress the Financial Action Task Force with their finance-sector oversight improvements, in seeking to be removed from its grey list. Moreover, bottom-up resistances in civil society also emerged, providing at least a hint of how to cease both innovation and degradation, *by making finance a public utility* not a source of illegitimate profit. All these cases are discussed later, following a review of the destructive forms of financial innovation that have helped make South Africa such an extreme case of uneven development.

Recognition of financialized innovation

Within the global financial system, South Africa was typically celebrated as among the most innovative, Western-gazing economies, one of the most mature and deepest (in terms of financial assets/GDP), and also most expansive in regional scope. Turan Subasat and Stavros Mavroudeas (2023, p 220) note that that during the 1990s–2010s, South Africa was the world's 'fastest financializing' economy (of the world's 41 largest). Standard Bank and Amalgamated Banks of South Africa (ABSA) have the main bank branch networks across sub-Saharan Africa, making them, the International Monetary Fund (IMF) (2022, p 10) noted, 'systemically important in many host countries, for example, Botswana, Lesotho, Malawi, Mauritius, Mozambique, Namibia, Swaziland, Uganda, and Zambia.'

Other financiers have explored down-market and by the 2010s, microfinance lenders reached tens of millions of low-income South Africans (Bateman et al, 2023). This suited orthodox analysts, for the quality and durability of banking, accounting, and state financial regulation were rated among the best in World Economic Forum (2018) *Global Competitiveness Reports* during the 2010s, even if the harsh reality of financial innovation was better characterized as customer *degradation*. As a share of GDP, the same document rated South Africa's insurance premiums as third highest in the world, and the share of domestic credit to the private sector as 11th highest, implying there is a deep, broad store of consumer wealth to draw upon.

To illustrate with another data point, the fast-rising 'Buffett Indicator' concept applied to the Johannesburg Stock Exchange (JSE) – that is, market capitalization as a share of GDP – put South Africa consistently at the top of the world charts. As the world's 17th largest stock market in 2024 (as against 36th highest GDP), the JSE has been a dynamic source of corporate funding dating to its 1887 founding, when it was mutually owned by listed companies, a status that lasted until 2005. Today it trades in equities, bonds, and three types of derivatives (financial assets, commodities, and interest rates). It has an exchange dedicated to small and mid-sized listings, a futures exchange, and a bond market.

In this context, the South African state's managers of finance, monetary policy, and currency flows were held in unusually high regard, until the grey listing. Several finance ministers and central bank governors who repeatedly opposed leftwing populism within the ruling African National Congress (ANC) – especially Trevor Manuel, Tito Mboweni, and Lesetja Kganyago – were given extremely influential positions at the Bretton Woods Institutions as well as *Euromoney* 'Central Banker of the Year' and 'African Finance Minister of the Year' recognition. Thanks in part to their facilitation, financial innovations came easily in a city that once sat atop half the world's gold reserves, whose tycoons ranged from the Oppenheimers (responsible for attracting Morgan to Anglo American) to (teenager) Elon Musk, and whose post-apartheid political elite was remarkably finance-friendly.

South African financial institutions periodically led the world in innovations. In August 2023, Johannesburg hosted a cutting-edge debate on de-dollarization at the heads-of-state summit of the BRICS bloc, at which the chief executive of the Western-oriented (albeit 20 per cent Chinese-owned) Standard Bank (Sim Tshabalala) decisively rejected a change in global currency arrangements (Bond, 2023b). In 2013, South Africa's foreign ministry had speculated that Johannesburg would host the BRICS

New Development Bank headquarters, and although Shanghai won that honour, the BRICS Bank branch established in Sandton was the institution's first regional outpost (Bond, 2021a). As noted, South African financiers had discovered a way of using algorithmic information on spending facilitated by Mastercard that allowed the leveraging of social welfare grants with credit during the 2010s. During the early 2000s, carbon offsets promoted by the World Bank were marked for the first time from an African country, initially from a Durban landfill where methane was converted to energy (Bond, 2019). As discussed later, the innovations turned to degradation as uneven development was amplified by finance, consistent with the general Marxist theory (Bond, 1998).

Going back further in time, other innovations reflected the dialectic of financial power and vulnerability. In 1944, for example, South African delegates to the Bretton Woods Conference projected the country's strength in gold production, thus bucking the country's expected support for the British position against the US, resulting in the $35/ounce set price of gold which put the dollar at the heart of the world economy, after which the wild gyrations in the gold price played havoc with South Africa's currency and sovereignty. In 1932, South Africa's financial delinking began once the London-centric gold standard was abandoned, after which the economy recorded its fastest-ever GDP growth (8 per cent annually) with far greater credit availability and financial deepening than ever before. A 1921 independent central bank proved both an ally of London but also a source of strength for the quasi-colony's eventual status as a full-fledged independent country in 1960. At its origins, a commercial banking network had solidified in the main (mainly agrarian-grounded) cities by the 1850s (Bond, 2003).

Yet over time, South Africa's once-proud gold, monetary, and fiscal sovereignty eroded and was often subordinated to chaotic global financial power. This was especially obvious when in 1971 US President Richard Nixon defaulted on the $35-per-ounce-of-gold Bretton Woods deal cut a quarter century earlier (that is, ignoring liabilities to pay gold worth an estimated $80 billion). Then after US consumer price inflation soared during the late 1970s, the Federal Reserve raised interest rates to unprecedented levels in 1979 so as to reduce effective demand. The gold price then quickly collapsed from $850/ounce in 1980 to $250/ounce two years later, causing a financial crisis in a South African economy which had welcomed gold's role as a safe haven from inflation, and had taken on an unprecedented level of foreign debt during the 1970s as a result (Bond, 2003).

The 1970s–80s anti-apartheid financial sanctions campaigns also contributed to the South African debt crisis of 1985, which caused not only a state default on $13 billion of unpayable short-term debt, but also the imposition of strict exchange controls, in turn catalyzing a fatal break between White business interests and the racist Pretoria government. Activists followed this success by enforcing a disinvestment policy on London-based Barclays and Standard Chartered banks (Bond, 2003). The anti-apartheid movement's innovation in political punishment, in the form of financial sanctions, degraded the unified White state-business power of the apartheid system, as much as any other single factor (Fields, 2010).

Post-apartheid financial deregulation and degradation

Nine years after the 1985 debt crisis, what major financial institutions had initially feared would be fatal to their interests was ultimately achieved: a one-person, one-vote democracy. However, because they were increasingly confident that Nelson Mandela's government, elected by a landslide in 1994, would not nationalize or reregulate finance, the largest banks stayed the course and turned their attention to influencing public policy (Bond, 2014). Early reform proposals such as a Community Reinvestment Act were shelved. And more generally, economic policy making associated with sustained ANC rule was akin to the 'low-intensity democracy' that, at the time across the world, reflected an unprecedented degree of 'Washington Consensus' influence (Gill et al, 1993).

Partly as a result of ANC neoliberal economic policy and also due to fast-rising imports (devastating the labour-intensive footwear, clothing, textiles, appliances, and electronics sectors) and higher capital intensity as machinery replaced workers, unemployment doubled and inequality soared during Mandela's five years in office from 1994 to 1999 (Bond, 2014). And even though international financial volatility intensified in the mid-1990s, so too did the Treasury and South African Reserve Bank (SARB) become ever more committed to exchange control deregulation (Bond, 2003). The withdrawal of the Finrand occurred in early 1995, just weeks after the Mexican 'Tequila Effect' crash should have cautioned the opposite course, that is, the tightening of capital controls and delinking from the most parasitical, speculative circuits of world finance (as did Malaysia in mid-1988, to good effect, even winning the endorsement of Paul Krugman, after its currency was subject to extreme trading volatility) (Bond, 2003).

To mitigate against capital flight in 1995, following the first exchange control relaxation, required the SARB to permanently ratchet up the real interest rate by 5 per cent in subsequent weeks. Monetary tightening was repeated in mid-1998 amidst a global panic, with Russia, South Korea, and many other major middle-income economies having defaulted or buckled. In a failed bid to retain money within the country and to defend the fast-sliding Rand currency, the SARB imposed a 7 per cent interest rate increase within two weeks in July 1998. One result of the consequent financial vulnerability was the April–September 1998 near-halving of local stock market values, especially of the new Black empowerment companies where ownership was based on debt-based share acquisition, with interest rates to be serviced by a gradual sale of shares. This innovation led to sudden degradation of Black owners' assets, as the financial models crashed due to the much higher rates and much lower stock market capitalization witnessed in 1998 (Bond, 2003; 2014).

The underlying conditions amplifying financial vulnerability were then exacerbated again in 1999 by the Mandela government's decision to allow most of the largest South African firms to delist their corporate headquarters from Johannesburg and relist in London. Dozens more exchange-control liberalizations occurred during the 2000s, with the Treasury conceding in 2019 that up to 7 per cent worth of GDP was fleeing the country annually as illicit financial flows (Planting, 2019). Further international capital flight took the form of cyber currency purchases, which by 2019 had reached among the world's highest rates, with 10.7 per cent of South African internet users owning Bitcoin and other cryptocurrencies (just ahead of Thailand and Indonesia), nearly double the global average (Bond, 2020b). Several major financial institutions also suffered from cyber crime and major database leaks, confirming the IMF's (2022, p 27) concern of the 'medium-likelihood' that 'attacks on critical infrastructure and financial systems [could] trigger systemic financial instability or widespread disruptions in socio-economic activities.'

The Treasury's (2024, p 7) 'terrorism financing risk assessment' in mid-2024 acknowledged major problems due to banking innovations; for example, the 'burgeoning fintech ecosystem with an active crypto asset community consisting of vendors, suppliers of crypto mining equipment, crypto ATMs, exchanges, meet-up groups, service providers, network infrastructures, protocols, users and wallets.' Specifically, since both 'startups and established financial institutions are exploring blockchain technology and crypto assets,' a long-standing concern remains: 'Weaknesses in South Africa's beneficial ownership transparency regime and customer due diligence practices of financial and non-financial businesses may be exploited.' Reforms could readily have been addressed within multiple financial-legislative opportunities but, tellingly, have not been.

The failure to address such malevolent international financial relationships can be traced to the desire of elites to escape a prior period of tight exchange controls, from 1985 to 1995. Within a democracy led initially by Mandela, transitional regulatory arrangements were adversely affected by apartheid beneficiaries' desire to externalize their wealth, but also by the new government's desire for international financial respectability. This entailed taking on an unnecessary $850 million IMF loan in late 1993, gaining an investment-grade credit rating in mid-1994, and steadily repaying the $25 billion worth of apartheid-era foreign debt, a move controversially agreed to in 1993 in spite of the ANC's history of lobbying against banks which made such loans (Bond, 2006; 2014). Harmful symptoms of entering the globally financializing economy were soon evident, as the Rand currency became one of the world's most volatile, collapsing by more than 10 per cent over a fewer than two-month period in 1998, 2001, 2006, 2008, 2015, and 2020. Measured in broad terms, the finance-insurance-real estate sector's share of GDP nearly doubled to 21 per cent by the early 2000s. The stock market periodically crashed by more than 40 per cent – in 1996, 1998, 2008, 2011, 2016, and 2020 – yet usually ranked as one of the world's most overvalued. In terms of market capitalization/GDP, the JSE's 'Buffett Indicator' was bested only by Hong Kong and in the early 2020s by Saudi Arabia and Iran, due to the three economies' particular market conditions.

There were racial overtones to South Africa's financialization, because such rentier-style capital accumulation occurred primarily on behalf of White beneficiaries of apartheid. As neighbouring Zimbabwe (also settler-colonial in character) unravelled during the 2000s and hyperinflation destroyed historic financial wealth (wiping out pension holdings), South Africans feared a similar process. This is one reason that illicit financial outflows rose to what the Treasury admitted was 3–7 per cent of GDP annually (Planting, 2019). The results of declining investor confidence in the real economy – aside from mining during occasional upticks in commodity prices (2002–08, 2009–14, and 2020–22) – were just as extreme. Fixed investment plummeted from apartheid-era levels, and unemployment soared from its post-apartheid low of 16 per cent to 34 per cent before COVID-19 hit. The Gini coefficient on income overtook Brazil to become the world's most unequal, and was higher even than Russia's on wealth. Poverty rates rose to two thirds of the society (measured by a \$3.50/day corrected 'Upper Bound Poverty Line'). And the working class was often measured by the World Economic Forum (2018) *Global Competitiveness Report* as the world's most militant.

In this context, consumer credit expansion and financial-inclusion innovations occasionally caused extreme stresses. Household non-performing loans (including both three-month arrears and default rates) reported by formal-sector lenders rose to more than 50 per cent of households by 2008 in the wake of a rapid interest rate increase (Bond, 2015), and again to 37 per cent by 2023 in the wake of renewed rate hikes. The household debt/income ratio had been as low as 55 per cent in 2004 but soared to 90 per cent in 2008, and again rose rapidly during COVID-19's lockdown (see Figure 4.1). Consumer overindebtedness implicated 'loan pushing' institutions ranging from local *mashonisas* (informal money lenders) to global institutions like Mastercard and the World Bank, whose financial-inclusion innovations not only lowered the 'unbanked' from near 30 per cent of adults to below 10 per cent during the 2010s, but led to

Figure 4.1: South African households' debt/income ratio, 1969–2021

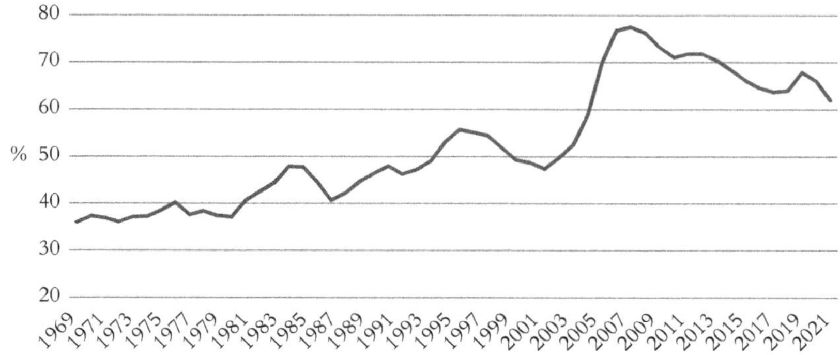

Source: IMF (2022)

Figure 4.2: Adults using financial services, percentage, 2010–19

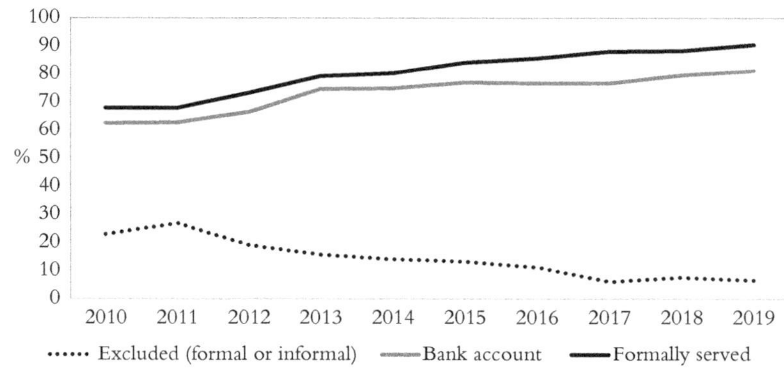

Source: IMF (2022)

much greater exposure of low-income households to predatory 'emolument attachment orders' debited from monthly wages, salaries, and state grants (see Figure 4.2). The extent of debit-order salary reductions was a major contributing factor to platinum industry strikes and then the Marikana massacre (Bond, 2013; 2015; 2018).

Weak regulation was also a major factor in increasing both the zeal to innovate and vulnerabilities in household and corporate financial balance sheets. In 2023, the grey listing of South Africa by the Financial Action Task Force revealed the extent of damage caused by the state's sloppy, deregulatory philosophy, as discussed later. To illustrate, Finance Minister Enoch Godongwana (cited in Magubane, 2024) was asked in February 2024 about his relaxation of exchange controls two years earlier – in the form of a much-decreased requirement on institutional investors' local asset holdings (from 70 to 55 per cent) – and confessed, 'We are agreed that it was a grave mistake. If you ask me, it was a grave mistake. But the question is, is it easy to undo? The answer is no … Look, we accept in my view it was a grave mistake.' The relaxation allowed 'a marked increase in domestic investors' foreign asset allocation, with a sharp increase in exposure to foreign equities at the expense of domestic equities and exposure to domestic property portfolios,' according to a SARB (2024a, pp 12–13) Financial Stability Review. South Africans' offshore asset allocation as a share of GDP rose from 84 to 106 per cent in 2022 alone, up from 46 per cent in 2012.

These are the licit financial outflows but there was a grey line between offshore investments as well as repatriation of profits, dividends, and interest, and formally illicit financial flows (see Figure 4.3). In three well-publicized cases, President Cyril Ramaphosa – considered a *reformer* in the wake of Jacob Zuma's 2009–18 rule, partly on the basis of his lead role in authoring a 1996 constitution that gave corporations juristic personhood and made private property a foundational right – personified South Africa's foreign-exchange controversies.

First, his Black investment firm Shanduka encouraged the shifting of Lonmin's Marikana platinum mine profits to Bermuda during the early 2010s at the same time underpaying workers, as the Farlam Commission determined (Alternative Information and Development Centre, 2014). A wildcat strike resulted in the infamous 2012 massacre of 34 mineworkers because Ramaphosa sent emails (for which he later apologized) to senior Lonmin colleagues and the government's police and mining ministers, terming the underpaid labourers 'dastardly criminal' and calling for a 'pointed response' (Saul and Bond, 2014).

Figure 4.3: South Africans' offshore asset allocation as a share of GDP, 2013–24

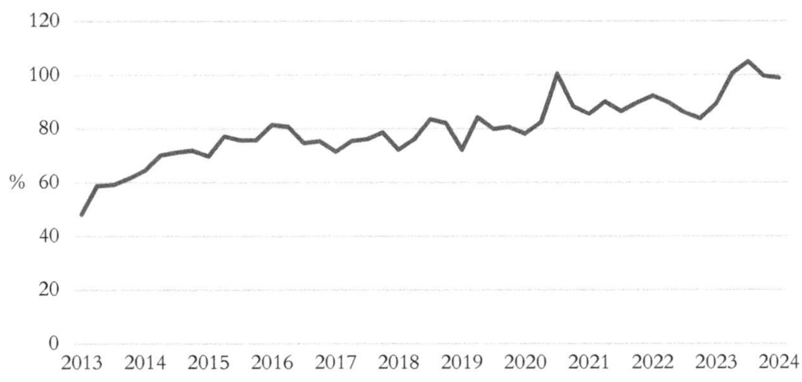

Source: SARB (2024b, p 13)

Second, in 2020, Ramaphosa hid at least $580,000 worth of undeclared and hence illegal US dollars under cushions in a couch at his cattle ranch, *while president of the country* (though the money was soon stolen, resulting in a controversy that nearly ended his presidency in 2022). Third, Ramaphosa's close partnership with Glencore's Ivan Glasenberg is also of interest, given that the world's largest commodity trader was fined $1.5 billion in 2022 for corrupting African states (15 per cent of the company's pretax profit the year before), which as *Business Maverick* editor Tim Cohen (2022) pointed out, 'is, in all honesty, a parking ticket.' Reflecting prosecutorial laxity, there was no local investigation of Johannesburg-born Glasenberg's prolific role in South Africa, including illicit financial flows, even though these featured prominently in former President Thabo Mbeki's (2015) critique of Glencore's transfer-pricing role in underdeveloping the Zambian economy. Ramaphosa was also accused by a former CEO of the state electricity company of supporting Glencore's sale of much higher-priced coal when he took over the paratatal's 'war room' in late 2014, even though seven months earlier he had chaired the same Glencore mine (Optimum) that was the main beneficiary of the purchase price increase (South African Federation of Trade Unions, 2021).

The capital flight that Ramaphosa, the Treasury, and the Reserve Bank hastened for so long had raised pressure on South African debt repayment, because to attract capital inflows, local interest rates typically remained higher in real terms by 5 per cent than prior to the first post-apartheid exchange control liberalization in 1995 (Bond, 2003; 2014). This proved an important debilitating factor in not only borrowing, but – alongside the regular bursts of currency depreciation – also in servicing a sustained foreign debt of $160 billion in 2024 (that is, $2,580/person including private sector borrowers). Of that, $13.5 billion is owed to the IMF and World Bank (not including prolific International Finance Corporation equity investments), and since mid-2020 has carried strict fiscal-austerity conditions. The trade surplus that began with import compression during COVID-19 continued into 2024, but was by early 2022 outweighed by the much more serious problem of net income outflows – through profit and dividend repatriation plus interest payments – leaving the current account in substantial deficit (in 2023, often in excess of 3 per cent) (SARB, 2024b).

The country's foreign debt had risen from $25 billion at the end of apartheid in 1994 in part because of many new, dubious borrowings – such as the controversial 2010 credit of $3.75 billion from the World Bank (its biggest-ever project loan) for a corrupt coal-fired power plant – and in part because of currency devaluation. The Rand's decline was especially severe as the commodity supercycle faded in the mid-2010s (from R3.5/$ in 1994 to R6.3/$ in 2011 to R18.6/$ in 2024). The foreign debt had peaked at more than $185 billion in 2019 prior to a COVID-19 panic sale of South African securities by overseas creditors, when it represented nearly a quarter of the entire African continent's debt (that is, 60 million South Africans owed five times per person more than the average of 1.4 billion other Africans) (SARB, 2024b).

That debt was extremely expensive. The interest rate paid on South Africa's foreign borrowings is typically higher (at 10.5 per cent in mid-2024) than any other country issuing ten-year bonds aside from Turkey, Pakistan, Brazil, and Colombia (The Economist, 2024). From 2017, when a finance minister presumed to be a populist was appointed, and again in 2020 as COVID-19 hit hard, the New York credit rating agencies declared South Africa's securities to be 'junk' in quality (Figure 4.4). Given the exchange control liberalization that would always present a risk of capital flight, there was no prospect that the neoliberal SARB would lower rates; its main excuse was a self-mandate to keep inflation within a 3–6 per cent band.

All this international financial-market opprobrium was then reflected in domestic loan repayment pressure and in the extremely uneven valuation of financial assets. Domestic public debt had been repaid down to a level of less than 30 per cent of GDP by the time of the 2008 crash, but soared during the 2010s as tax revenues declined when commodity prices fell, and especially during COVID-19, reaching 72 per cent of GDP by 2024. In the private sector, a spectacular rise in property values from 1998 to 2007 offered an example of a 'Kuznets Cycle', with the world's highest real estate price increase at the time (double even the rates of second- and third-place Ireland and Spain). After official concerns about housing inflation at the peak in 2007 led Reserve Bank Governor Tito Mboweni to raise interest rates dramatically in 2008, there was a steady decline in residential, commercial,

Figure 4.4: South Africa sovereign debt ratings, 2008–20

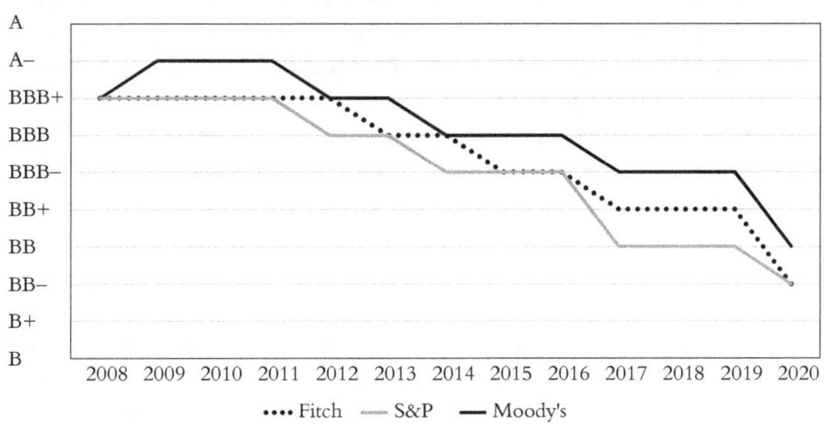

Source: IMF (2022)

and industrial property markets (aside from Cape Town's ultra-hedonistic Atlantic coastline).

With a 42 per cent rate of unemployment, which has been triple the worst such figures in peer economies, and with interest rates rising dramatically in 2022–23 (as the US Federal Reserve initiated a worldwide tightening), South Africa again began experiencing high levels of household debt distress, with close to 35 per cent of formal-sector borrowers falling at least three months behind on their loan repayments. In poorer households, the most advanced financial innovation – the 2013–18 effort at collateralizing low-income people's state grants – was a dramatic failure, resulting in Banga's financial-inclusion strategy being declared guilty of the predatory imposition of debit orders, and as a result, his Net1 ally was forced into bankruptcy in 2020 (although incongruously, in mid-2023 Banga was appointed World Bank president by Joe Biden, *with no BRICS opposition or alternative candidates*). The broader problem of debit orders continued to bedevil South African consumers even after a major Constitutional Court confirmation of the responsibility of magistrates to assure they were not burdensome to the debtor (Sibanyoni et al, 2024).

Other corporate crashes occurred during the 2010s, illustrating extremely weak accounting standards, practices, and oversight, including the international Steinhoff retail chain and several major state-owned enterprises which were effectively bankrupt. The latter occurred, in part, because corrupt elements within the leading international consulting and accountancy firms had illegitimately given their books a clean bill of health (Thompson, 2020). Moreover, major financial liabilities, such as the world's two largest coal-fired power plants under construction, were obviously classifiable as 'odious debt' because of blatant corruption by Hitachi in league with the South African ruling party (Bond, 2024a). Although they should not have been repaid, the loans were never written off by the World Bank, Western bilateral credit agencies, commercial banks, and even the BRICS New Development Bank and Chinese state banks.

This degree of graft should not have been surprising because more broadly, during the 2010s, the South African business community was rated the PwC (2016) title of world's worst for 'economic crime and fraud' (although by 2020 India had taken over with South Africa tied for second with China) (PwC, 2020). At the same time, during the 2010s, Transparency International's Corruption Perception Index rated South African politicians and bureaucrats between 135th to 108th most corrupt out of 180 states, though under Ramaphosa, the index fell to 100th most corrupt in 2024 (Bond, 2024a).

Corruption also suffused nearly all the BRICS New Development Bank's 2010s loans to Pretoria and its parastatal agencies (Bond, 2020a; 2021a). In spite of extensive rhetoric against Western finance, the BRICS never challenged the Bretton Woods Institutions: instead, Bank and IMF staff had since 1994 included many coopted South Africans. Nor did the BRICS finance ministers and central bank governors dare to challenge the dollar-based trade finance system. South Africa's hosting of the bloc's 2023 summit revealed the extent to which domestic banking interests opposed global innovation such as de-dollarization, or even South–South trade finance options and use of the BRICS' so-called Contingent Reserve Arrangement (a supposed alternative to the IMF which in reality strengthens the IMF's conditionality leverage) (Bond, 2023b).

The SARB (2024b, p 5) offered a 'Risks and Vulnerabilities Matrix' in mid-2024 (see Figure 4.5) that ignored many of these factors, but did include 'perpetual risks' – low, inequitable economic growth, climate change, and cyber attacks – whereas there was more immediate concern with the state's 'weak fiscal position' and its implications for a 'sovereign-financial sector nexus' pushing the junk credit rating into the banking sector, as well as the risk of South Africa 'remaining on the grey list beyond June 2025'.

The climate crisis is a clear example of the tension between financial innovation and degradation. The IMF (2022, p 55) itself began to recognize the 'higher frequency and severity of natural disasters related to climate change and transition risks due to [South Africa's] highly CO2 intensive economy', making the economy 'vulnerable to both physical and long-term transition risks' since 'increased damage from storms, floods and droughts can weigh on the economy and adversely impact the financial sector through credit risk, a decline in profitability, and valuation losses.' Ending South African corporations' coal addiction is also a problem, because 'transition risks can reduce corporate profits, with potential credit risk implications for the banking system.'

But solutions are lacking. For example, the pricing of carbon which in South Africa is only \$0.30/tonne of CO_2 emissions for the largest polluters (Eskom and Sasol), at least through 2025. One example of a financial innovation aiming to address South African leaders' reluctance to end the coal addiction is the Just Energy Transition Partnership offered since the 2021 UN climate summit in Glasgow, by governments of the US, Britain, Germany, France, and the European Union. The intention was to provide an incentive to close coal-fired power plants early. But in part because of the coal addiction (especially what with major 'black diamond' coal-sector entrepreneurs contributing to the ANC, including Ramaphosa himself until 2014), and in part because the \$8.5 billion package is comprised 97 per cent of new foreign debt – a small fraction of which is concessional, at below-market rates, due to the hard-currency character of the financing (in spite of major locally paid expenses such as labour and materials) – the South African government has taken the position since 2023 that the coal-fired power plants will stay open *longer* than originally scheduled (Bond, 2024c).

Figure 4.5: South African Reserve Bank Risks and Vulnerabilities Matrix, 2024

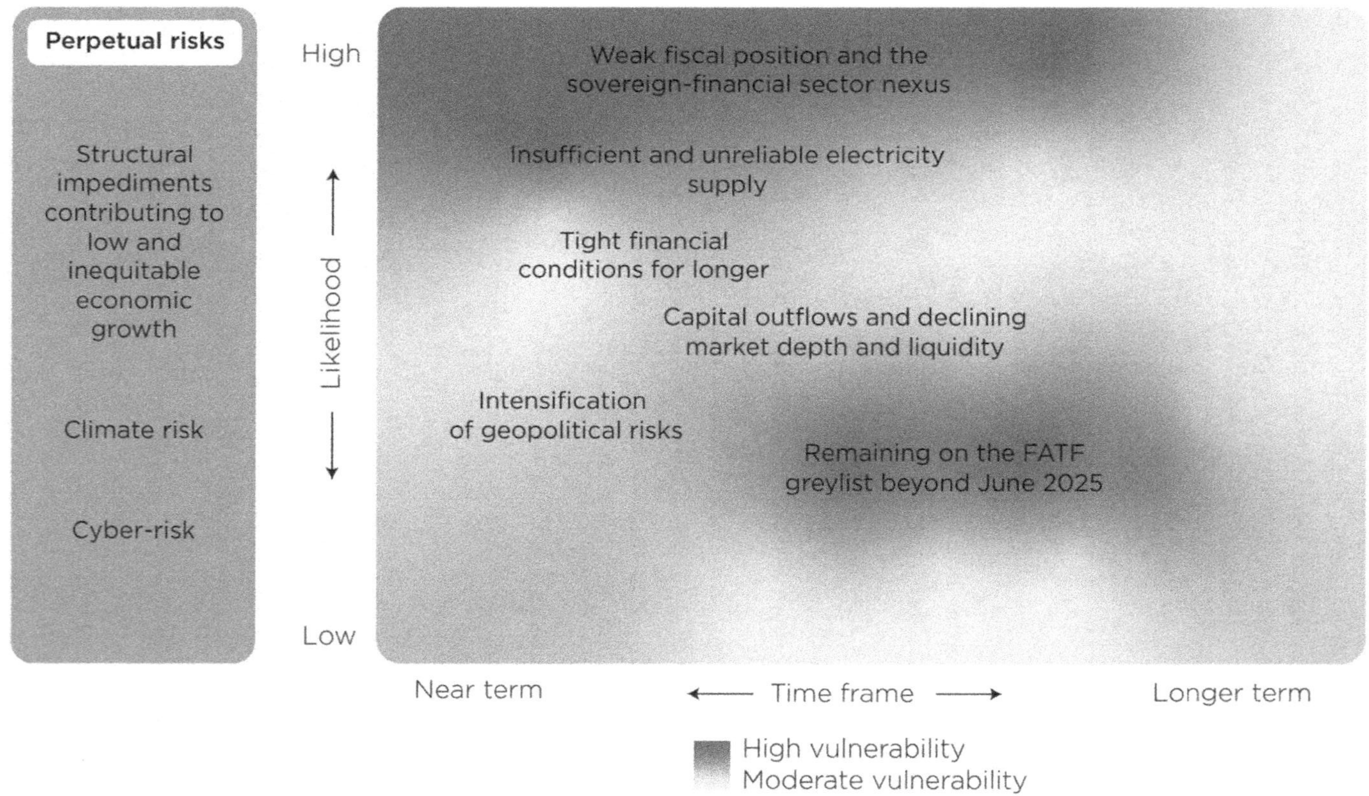

Source: SARB (2024b, p 5)

Real economic degradation in the context of financialization fraud

These examples of financial-system depravity – instead of economically, environmentally, and socially useful innovation – reflected *underlying* conditions of deindustrialization and intensified extractivism (that is, uncompensated non-renewable resource depletion). Moreover, South Africa's overall economic context was characterized by bursts of productive capital overaccumulation within a context of declining manufacturing/GDP from 24 per cent in 1990 to below 12 per cent in the early 2020s, once trade liberalization became decisive (Bond and Malikane, 2019). There has also been a sustained net negative 'adjusted net savings' as calculated by even the World Bank, namely a decline in national wealth, once the adverse externalities from mining, smelting, and petrochemicals – especially pollution, greenhouse gas emissions, and mineral depletion – are considered (Bond and Basu, 2021).

Meanwhile, a much greater degree of productive-capital accumulation occurred within the minerals-energy complex especially after the 2002–14 commodity supercycle had helped raise South African corporate profitability to a level that the IMF (2016) measured as the third highest in the world among major economies. At the same time, the power to defend the interests of the financial lobby also grew yet more formidable. In 1990 as liberalization began, extremely high industry concentration characterized especially the main financial asset holders, for example the two main insurers Old Mutual and Sanlam (which were once both mutually owned but in the late 1990s converted to listed, thus turning an historic equity base into a dramatic wealth boost for mainly White policy holders) (Bond, 2014).

After the 'building society' (home mortgage lending) component of banking faded away by the early 1990s and such loans were incorporated in commercial banks, five institutions dominated the market: Standard (the rump of Standard Chartered following its disinvestment), First National (formerly Barclays), ABSA (pulled together from several failing institutions including Afrikaner financiers Bankorp and Volksas), Nedbank, and Ninety One (formerly Investec, founded in 1991 in Cape Town but a decade later relisted in London). Together these five manage 90 per cent of the country's banking assets.

But while the major institutions generally prospered in the post-apartheid period, smaller retail banks were, on at least a dozen occasions, felled by curatorship, receivership, or outright liquidation due to 'bad management', excessive operating expenses, and liquidity crises: Sechold Bank, 1994; Prima Bank, 1994; African Bank, 1995 and 2014; Community Mutual Bank, 1996; Islamic Bank, 1997; FBC Fidelity Bank, 1999; Regal Treasury Bank, 2002; New Republic Bank, 2002; Saambou Bank, 2002;

VBS Mutual Bank, 2018; Ubank, 2022; and Habib Overseas Bank, 2024 (Havemann, 2019; SARB, 2024b). Only in 2024 did the SARB finally begin implementation of a deposits-insurance facility to minimize losses by such banks' innocent depositors.

In this context of high banking-sector concentration and small-bank volatility, a distortion arose, as explained by Harvard economist Dani Rodrik (2008, p 792): 'A post-1994 investor – domestic or foreign – considering an investment in South Africa would have been far less likely (than s/he would have been in the 1980s) to commit resources to manufacturing, compared to banking, insurance, or other services oriented towards the home market.' The reason was simple, according to Ewa Karwowski, Ben Fine, and Samantha Ashman:

> Since the end of apartheid, access to international capital markets for large South African conglomerates, and their subsequent internationalisation, was advocated as ways to achieve higher investment, boosting growth and employment. Instead, the rise of finance in South Africa has coincided with a strong decline of the manufacturing sector whose contribution to GDP has halved. (Ashman, 2018, p 383)

The relative rates of return favoured the former – thanks to high real interest rates and financial asset speculation – not the latter. Indeed, overall corporate profitability in South Africa is also correlated to commodity price increases, so in the late 2010s the much higher rates of profit achieved in South Africa over the prior 15 years suddenly receded to the emerging market norm (IMF, 2022, p 32).

Regardless of the vicissitudes of corporate profits, by the early 2010s, according to Gilad Isaacs (2014), pension funds, insurance companies, hedge funds, and private equity had 'assumed a new prominence in South African markets, with their assets quadrupling since the early 1990s and their share of ownership on the JSE doubling.' As a result of the 'short-termism' thereby introduced, continued Isaacs, 'Dividends paid out by South African non-financial corporations rose from 25% of their gross operating surplus in 1995 to a height of 45% in 2007. The same firms have also increasingly engaged directly in financial market trading and speculation.' Even the COVID-19 crisis of the early 2020s, including the final junk rating by Moody's as lockdowns began, was brushed off, as 'the financial industry remained profitable and was throughout the crisis, in contrast to many other financial systems', according to the IMF (2022, p 27).

Another result of the relatively high rates of return gained from the speculative markets and high real interest rates (and the banks' high spread between lending and deposit rates), added to much lower fixed investment rates after apartheid than even in its 1970s–80s decline, was that idle cash tended to pile up in corporate treasuries, instead of being reinvested. Redge

Nkosi blamed the Treasury and the Reserve Bank for the incentive structure that produced such results:

> Channelling finance away from real capital development, economic transformation and structural transformation towards financialisation is the hallmark of SA's macroeconomic policy framework and its institutional design. And as all public policy is distributional, without redound to the vast majority of citizens, the South African macroeconomic policy regime and its institutional design can only be described as abject failure. They have created a high distributional bias towards financial income at the expense of earned income. And as expected, the outcomes are unambiguous: failed structural transformation, including premature deindustrialisation; unreformed ownership patterns; inequality of the order unmatched by any other nation on earth; an unemployment level only typical of nations ravaged by war; untold poverty; and the financialisation of all forms of commerce and industry. (Nkosi, 2019, p 2)

To explain this policy framing and the predictable results, South African Communist Party deputy leader Jeremy Cronin admitted in the house journal *Umsebenzi*,

> Part of the implicit elite economic pact that shadowed the more open democratic constitutional settlement involved the sweeping liberalisation of the financial markets … [which] grabbed the opportunity in a massive flurry of capital flight out of the country. Some of it was now legal, much of it illicit. Dual listings, tax havens, transfer pricing and the headlong financialisation of what had once been mining and manufacturing giants all contributed to this massive loss of investible South African wealth. According to the most comprehensive study of this, capital flight as a percentage of GDP rose from an average of 5.4% per year between 1980 and 1993, to 9.2% between 1994 and 2000, and averaged 12% between 2001 and 2007, finally peaking at a staggering 23% in 2007. (Cronin, 2020)

The dysfunctionality in the broader economy was also conceded by Rob Davies (2010) during his tenure as Minister of Trade and Industry, even if nothing he did in his term of service (2009–19) changed this reality:

- The existing growth path is led by the consumption-driven sectors, which are growing twice as fast as the productive sectors.
- The economy is import intensive especially with respect to value-added products.

- Stronger domestic growth in the manufacturing sector is imperative.
- High structural unemployment is a constant, oscillating between 22.5% and 25% if the narrow definition is used.
- The economy is characterised by extensive financialisation, but only a small percentage of investment is channelled to the productive sectors.

Revealing how fruitless internal reform had become, Davies himself was regularly implicated in promoting irrational megaprojects in the extractive sector (Sole, 2020). What he could have done, Seeraj Mohamed (2018, p 34) argued, was to have adopted 'policies that promote economic restructuring in a way that shifts the core of the economy away from financial services and mining and minerals related activities toward more labor intensive, downstream, value-added activities in manufacturing and associated productive services sectors.'

But the terrain of neoliberal public policy, deregulatory sloth, and corporate corruption – all inherited from apartheid – adds needed context. To illustrate with the most current cases of financial innovation occurring *against* the interests of the South African majority, consider two case studies: weak prosecution of currency manipulation (mostly in the US from 2013–19, but in Pretoria in 2023–24), and the Financial Action Task Force's 2023 grey listing of South Africa. Those sobering events are followed – in the Conclusion – by consideration of vitally needed, bottom-up civil society pressure. While broadly reflective of a critical perspective on South Africa's banks, social advocacy was regrettably absent in a sustained manner in both the two 2023 sites of conflict, especially compared to climate-financing protest at the largest bank, Standard, where disruption of the annual general meetings and subsequent Extinction Rebellion demonstrations led to arrests and rising controversy.

Controversies over currency manipulation and South Africa's grey listing

The long rise and sudden fall of the South African Competition Commission's charges of currency manipulation against major banks revealed deep fault lines in the society and huge holes in the financial regulatory apparatus. Foreign exchange traders from at least five banks faced trial in 2023–24 for their collusion during Rand trades within a Bloomberg chat room carrying the name 'ZAR Domination' (in Afrikaans, the Zuid Afrikaanse Rand is abbreviated as 'ZAR'). According to recorded notes that the banks were loathe to disclose but finally did as part of plea deals, from 2007–13 that international chat room featured macho language, such as by Standard Chartered traders: 'I think we need an Old Gits meeting [that is, ZAR Domination] to discuss good ole [rand] manipulation. We should be able to bully people now far more than any other [currency]' (Tshwane, 2019). New York State financial regulators won guilty pleas in 2019 (and plea bargains followed in 2023 in South Africa). However, in Pretoria sloppiness characterized the state's attempt at prosecution – leading to other banks being dropped from the charges in 2024 (although a Constitutional Court appeal remained to be heard).

For a few weeks, from late November 2023 until early January 2024, social outrage rose against the banking industry because, according to the Competition Commission, leading institutions conspired 'to manipulate prices … [and] to assist each other by allowing a trader with a significant open risk position to complete trades before others and by manipulating liquidity' (Wasserman, 2023). The specific techniques entailed:

- Colluding on USD/ZAR currency pair by fixing bids; offers; bid-offer spreads; the spot exchange rate; and the exchange rate at the FIX.
- Dividing markets by allocating customers in terms of which one trader withholds or pulls his existing bid or offer from the market to allow the other trader to execute and complete his trade.
- Cartel behaviour: Buying and selling money on behalf of their clients as well as on their own behalf – either buying or selling USD with ZAR or ZAR with USD – and fixing of buying and/or selling price of these currencies and fixing the spread (profit margin);
- Traders taking turns to buy or sell currencies or giving each other opportunity to buy or sell currencies without interference from each other (Nkosi, 2017).

However, the widespread anger in society did not result in substantial mobilizations and protests. To be sure, Competition Appeal Court Judge Dennis Davis (2024) ruled that most of the 28 banks did not deserve to be charged with a 'single overarching conspiracy'; for many institutions, their traders' malevolent roles in the dubious chat rooms were not confirmed. The Competition Commission appealed soon afterwards that Davis was too generous to the banks when he ruled the prosecutors had overreached, and the Constitutional Court heard the case in 2024.

But New York State regulators had already prosecuted JPMorgan Chase, BNP Paribas, HSBC, and Credit Suisse for manipulating the Rand in prior years. Several others acknowledged guilt, including Standard Chartered (in November 2023 having settled in New York State courts in 2019), Citibank (in 2017), Barclays, Barclays Capital, and Johannesburg-based ABSA. The first two paid fines of $2.3 million and $3.7 million respectively. (One other South African bank, Investec, did not file objections alongside other local banks, whose traders were not found to have participated in the manipulation, although doubts remain.) In March 2023 following a long series of disputes, including over jurisdiction, the Competition Tribunal (2023) finally ruled against these and other banks, for their 'conduct considered the most egregious in competition law. Furthermore, the alleged conduct relates to fixing and manipulating the rand:dollar exchange rate, which has a central and crucial role in the South African economy.'

In contrast, four years earlier, then Finance Minister (and former Reserve Bank Governor) Mboweni had claimed in Parliament that since 'the currency market is a deep and liquid market, and it is difficult to determine any material or long-lasting impact of any one transaction on the level or value of the currency', the manipulation charges against the banks should not be taken too seriously. As he put it, 'The investigation before the Competition Commission appears to be related more to the conduct of bank traders towards clients, rather than providing evidence of their affecting the actual value of the rand' (Phakathi, 2019).

Davis' 2024 decision was unsatisfactory, since some of the criticism levelled against the Commission case was procedural in nature, based on relatively minor incorrect specifications or failure to identify bank employees' names engaged in the chat rooms. (For example, according to Davis, 'A holding company which is not registered as a bank, not authorized to trade in foreign currency and whose role is simply shown to be that one of the subsidiaries traded in foreign currency cannot on this alone be included in the referral affidavit' – which appears to dodge an obvious line of ownership accountability.) Meanwhile, even as the Competition Tribunal had labelled the act an 'egregious' legal violation, the other logical authorities – Reserve Bank, Treasury (and its Financial Intelligence Centre), the South African Police Service (and its investigative Hawks unit for priority crimes), and the National Prosecuting Authority – continued to prove notoriously soft on corporate fraud.

Hence, as the New York State prosecution against the currency manipulators indicated, when South African financial regulation was terribly weak, an embarrassing international intervention may well be needed. To illustrate with another case, it took a February 2023 grey listing of South Africa by the Financial Action Task Force (2023) to alert society about the systemic character of banking-sector crime, following that agency's 2019 warnings about illicit financial flows, money laundering, drug financing, and terrorist money transfers. Regulators in both the Treasury and the Reserve Bank – owned by the very banks engaged in Rand rigging and other illegal acts – ignored these until late in 2022, when three new laws were passed and regulatory procedures tightened.

Comprising international regulatory bodies, the Financial Action Task Force's (2023) judgment is not difficult to reverse (many governments have done so, including Namibia in 2023). But nor is it impossible for South Africa to slip further onto a 'black list' that in 2024 contained the

Democratic People's Republic of Korea, Iran, and Myanmar. On the grey list alongside South Africa in 2023–24 were Albania, Barbados, Burkina Faso, Cameroon, Cayman Islands, Croatia, Democratic Republic of Congo, Gibraltar, Haiti, Jamaica, Jordan, Mali, Mozambique, Nigeria, Panama, Philippines, Senegal, South Sudan, Syria, Tanzania, Turkey, Uganda, United Arab Emirates, Vietnam, and Yemen. This kind of peer group is a profound embarrassment, reflecting a regulatory apparatus in Pretoria that appears to have been utterly coopted by financial fraudsters, or neoliberal deregulatory ideologues, or both.

The Reserve Bank (2024a) occasionally took these problems semi-seriously, for example, issuing 'administrative sanctions' (often in excess of $500,000 per violation) to the following banks from 2014 to 2024: ABSA (twice), FirstRand, Nedbank, Standard (twice), Capitec, Deutsche Bank (twice), GBS Mutual, Habib Overseas (twice), Investec, Standard Chartered, South African Bank of Athens (twice), Société Générale, VBS Mutual, China Construction, HSBC, Bidvest, Sasfin, Baroda, Bank of China (twice), and Ubank. In 2019, for example, Bank of China and four others were fined due to weaknesses in each of the banks' money laundering control measures and in 2024 Bank of China again was fined (this time much more, $1.65 million) because its staff 'failed to conduct customer due diligence and enhanced due diligence on sampled customer relationships … to timeously report suspicious transactions and/or activities … to timeously attend to its automated transaction monitoring system alerts … [and] to properly identify, assess, monitor, mitigate and/or manage its risks' (SARB, 2024c).

The repeated violations of international financial regulations, in spite of such administrative sanctions, appear to reflect a low incentive for complying, for in 2023 a high-profile Al Jazeera (2023) report on a Zimbabwean 'gold mafia' ring proved the complicity of Standard, ABSA, and Sasfin. Ultimately, Sasfin finally faced Reserve Bank fines of $280 million for money laundering, bribery, and a variety of other infringements in 2024 and was forced to delist from the JSE and (from 2026) to close its banking subsidiary entirely, announcing that 'Since discovering this syndicate, Sasfin took significant steps, which included laying criminal charges against the implicated employees, responsibly exiting the forex business at a considerable cost, and taking steps to further strengthen its compliance and control environments' (Pillay, 2024).

Shortages of international financial integrity are not only local in nature, but also reflect lack of will in global corporate headquarters and especially competing hot money centres (Tax Justice Network, 2024). International accountancy firms were responsible for giving a clean bill of health to some of the most notorious South African corporations and parastatals: Steinhoff retail (Deloitte), VBS bank (KPMG), South African Airways (PwC), Tongaat Hulett sugar (Deloitte), Eskom (Deloitte and McKinsey), Transnet

(McKinsey), and the South African Revenue Service (KPMG and Bain) (Thompson, 2020). And these problems of international contagion can become so obvious – such as the 'ZAR Domination' currency manipulators – that occasionally, as in the case of Minister in the Presidency Khumbudzo Ntshavheni, forceful statements emanate from the top of the South African state (in this case fighting business conservatives who ridiculed her in November 2023):

> What are the challenges confronting this government that delegitimises it from even speaking for the poor against corporate criminals that have already conceded and paid fines in other jurisdictions? What of Standard Bank SA, which has already lost several court challenges against the Competition Commission on the rand manipulation scandal, but has yet to file its affidavit responding to the commission's affidavit? The question is why it is not filing its affidavit if it did not manipulate the rand, or is Standard Bank's position the same as that of Bank of America and Barclays in the US? Does SA's top bank not want to compensate the poor for its conduct? It is also entitled to use the courts to drag this matter out, hoping we will have collective memory loss because there is nobody to accuse it of Stalingrad antics. (Ntshavheni, 2023)

Conclusion: Resistance from below

Contradictions associated with skewed forms of financial innovation on the one hand, and widespread balance-sheet degradation on the other, adversely affect the South African economy, society, and environment within global markets, at national level and at firm and household scales. The dialectics involved, boiling down to the interplay of financial power and vulnerability, are relatively straightforward. In this constellation, South Africa is fully subordinated to international and domestic finance with very limited capacity to influence the, in part, malicious activities of financial actors due to a combination of extensive innovation, weak regulation, and intellectual capture exemplified by orthodox monetary policy.

The most obvious proof of this *sub-imperial* financial stance occurred in August 2023 with the South African elites' failure to advance a vital innovation – de-dollarization – when Ramaphosa hosted the BRICS leaders' summit (Bond, 2023b). Leslie Armijo (Chapter 3, this volume) is correct to conclude, 'South Africa's abilities to initiate bilateral financial statecraft, except possibly vis-à-vis its immediate subregion, are quite limited.'

As Petry and Nölke (Introduction, this volume) note, there are enormous variances in 'the role and power of the state within the institutional configurations of national capitalisms', and the regulatory system in Pretoria typically appears feeble compared, certainly, to the Beijing and New Delhi central banks and finance ministries. Indeed the subordination to international financial power is most explicit when it comes to Pretoria's state regulatory and prosecutorial laziness, and especially the lack of apparent willingness by the Treasury and the Reserve Bank to clamp down (for example, by properly enforcing and also tightening exchange controls). Consequently, solutions are not likely to come from ruling-party politicians or even the Financial Action Task Force and Competition Commission. In 2023–24, while both rose to address innovation-degradation processes very late in the day, they appeared unable to garner sufficient political will and institutional power so as to achieve the needed reforms.

Instead, we have much more to learn about disciplining finance from South Africa's many civil society campaigns, dating at least to the 1980s. First, anti-apartheid sanctions were wide-ranging, but in mid-1985 they hit particularly hard in the financial sphere, where social acceptance grew that banks were criminal for providing loans to the apartheid state, its agents, and even companies operating in South Africa, leading to an international financial 'run' on the South African economy (Bond, 2003). A second instance was the 'bond boycott' arranged by community groups in Black townships starting in the late 1980s, against payment of mortgage bonds (Bond, 2024b). A third case was the 'Red October' financial transformation campaign mounted by the South African Communist Party starting in 1999 and civil society allies in a Financial Sector Campaigns Coalition, especially to win the removal of aspirant members of the petite bourgeoisie from financial blacklisting when they had defaulted. Fourth, from 2014 to 2020, the Black Sash social welfare rights movement successfully attacked and ultimately halted Net1's Cash Paymaster Services subsidiary's abuse of social grant recipients (Torkelson, 2020). One part of the conviction related to Net1's corruption of the Minister of Social Welfare; yet the World Bank (which since 2016 had owned 22 per cent of the firm) issued a 2022–26 South Africa Country Partnership Framework whose assessment of Net1 objectives were, the Bank (2021) claimed, 'mostly achieved', with a blank space in the section about Net1 labelled 'Lessons'.

Fifth, in the early 2020s, Standard Bank was the main target of pressure by civil society activists attempting to achieve (relatively narrow) financing reform consistent with the world's 'divest-invest' movement to replace fossil-fuel lending with renewable energy investments. In 2023, Africa's largest private financial institution advanced $5.4 billion in new loans and investments for fossil-related projects, amplified in 2024 by a controversial decision to lead the international financing syndicate for the East African Crude Oil Pipeline (EACOP). Two major oil firms – TotalEnergies and China National Overseas Oil Corporation – intend to extract and transport 848 million barrels of oil over 25 years, that in turn will be responsible for

379 million tonnes of $CO2$ emissions (Bond, 2022a; 2022b). By using a $1,056 social cost of carbon, the 'polluter pays' price for the (indirect Scope 3) emissions would be $400 billion, but Standard did not factor in such damage or liabilities, nor did their shareholders object aside from the NGO Just Share (2024) and a few others. Standard's fossil investment also included the 'Blood Methane' of Cabo Delgado, Mozambique (Bond, 2022a; 2022b), and the 'Blood Coal' of Somkhele in KwaZulu-Natal Province where leading activist Fikile Ntshangase was assassinated in 2020 (Bond, 2023a). In addressing the various Johannesburg critics of EACOP protesting at Standard regularly (including Extinction Rebellion, Earthlife Africa, Stop EACOP, 350.org, Mining Communities United in Action, Sisonke Revolutionary Movement, and Greenpeace), Standard argued that it was still in line with Paris Climate Agreement commitments to limit warning to 1.5 degrees (Evans, 2024). That claim, untrue though it was, reflected the arrogance of South Africa's main bank, and its confidence in a kind of multilateral climate politics that regularly favoured status quo polluters (Bond, 2024c).

In all these respects, the particular targets – funders of apartheid and predatory schemes, as well as fossil-fuel financiers – were either formally guilty of anti-social behaviour and outright corruption, or widely perceived to be. What is critical in the period ahead, is the ability to unite the large disaffected movements in South African civil society – labour, community, anti-racism, feminist, student and youth, public health advocacy, gender identity, and many others – whose former affiliation to the ANC in the 1994–2004 period of up to 67 per cent voter support (and 57 per cent in 2019) had plunged in 2024 to a 40 per cent electoral tally. But as the prior decades had illustrated, the unity was best derived from concrete forms of struggle, transcending narrow silo-based interest politics. At that stage, the processes behind anti-social corporate and bank behaviour at an individual level can be explored, in order to then address not only the financial innovation that leads to such extreme socio-economic-ecological degradation, but beyond that, as Ingrid Harvold Kvangraven (Chapter 11, this volume) suggests, we dare to name and explain the South African capitalist system's laws of extreme uneven development.

References

Al Jazeera (2023) 'How a 'Gold Mafia' is looting Southern Africa, washing dirty cash', *Al Jazeera*, [online] 23 March, Available from: https://www.aljazeera.com/news/2023/3/23/gold-mafia-looting-southern-africa [Accessed 28 November 2024].

Alternative Information and Development Centre (2014) 'Lonmin, the Marikana massacre and the Bermuda connection', *Alternative Information and Development Centre*, [online] 2 June, Available from: https://aidc.org.za/lonmin-the-marikana-massacre-and-the-bermuda-connection-seminar-and-press-conference/ [Accessed 28 November 2024].

Ashman, S. (2018) 'The minerals-energy-finance complex redubbed?', in G. Khadiagala, P. Naidoo, D. Pillay, and R. Southall (eds) *New South African Review 5*, Johannesburg: Wits University Press, pp 67–84.

Bateman, M., Bond, P., Lavinas, L., and Torkelson, E. (2023) 'Incoming World Bank President Ajay Banga's predatory-finance background threatens even more prolific Bank poverty-creation', *CADTM,* [online] 12 April, Available from: https://www.cadtm.org/Incoming-World-Bank-President-Ajay-Banga-s-predatory-finance-background [Accessed 28 November 2024].

Bond, P. (1998) *Uneven Zimbabwe,* Trenton: Africa World Press.

Bond, P. (2003) *Against Global Apartheid,* London: Zed Books.

Bond, P. (2006) *Looting Africa,* London: Zed Books.

Bond, P. (2013) 'Debt, uneven development and capitalist crisis in South Africa', *Third World Quarterly,* (34)4: 569–92.

Bond, P. (2014) *Elite Transition,* London: Pluto Press.

Bond, P. (2015) 'Contradictions in consumer credit: Innovations in South African super-exploitation', *Critical Arts,* 29(2): 218–39.

Bond, P. (2018) 'German fingerprints at the scene of Lonmin's Marikana Massacre: From BASF to Volkswagen and the World Bank', in M. Grimm, J. Krameritsch, and B. Bekker (eds) *Business as Usual after Marikana: Corporate Power and Human Rights,* Johannesburg: Jacana, pp 312–33.

Bond, P. (2019) 'Contradictory time horizons of Durban energy piping in an era of looming climate chaos', *City,* 23(4): 631–45.

Bond, P. (2020a) 'BRICS banking and the demise of alternatives to the IMF and World Bank', in J. Puppim de Oliveira and Y. Jing (eds) *International Development Assistance and the BRICS*, London: Palgrave Macmillan, pp 189–218.

Bond, P. (2020b) 'Who really 'state-captured' South Africa? Revealing silences in poverty, inequality and structurally-corrupt capitalism', in E. Durojaye and M. Mirugi-Mukundi (eds) *Exploring the Link between Poverty and Human Rights in Africa,* Pretoria: Pretoria University Law Press, pp 59–94.

Bond, P. (2021a) 'The BRICS New Development Bank's false dawn', in A. Shaw and R. Bhattacharya (eds) *Urban Housing, Livelihoods and Environmental Challenges in Emerging Market Economies*, Delhi: Orient Blackswan, pp 100–20.

Bond, P. (2021b) 'Luxemburg's contemporary resonances in South Africa: Capital's renewed super-exploitation of people and nature', in D. Cornell and J. Gordon (eds) *Creolizing Rosa Luxemburg*, New York: Rowman and Littlefield, pp 287–316.

Bond, P. (2022a) 'South Africa's pro-military lobby risks worsening multiple injustices in northern Mozambique', *The Thinker*, 90: 69–80.

Bond, P. (2022b) 'L'impérialisme fossile Français, le sous-impérialisme Sud-Africain et la résistance anti-impériale', *Actuel Marx*, 72(2): 78–97.

Bond, P. (2023a) 'Climate, violence, resource extraction and ecological debt: Global implications of an assassination on South Africa's coal mining belt', *Globalizations,* 20(8): 1411–25.

Bond, P. (2023b) 'After Johannesburg, BRICS humbled as sub- not anti- or inter-imperialist', *Counterpunch*, August 31.

Bond, P. (2024a) 'Corporate corruption of South African politics and economics', *New Agenda,* 93: 33–46.

Bond, P. (2024b) 'South Africa's housing financialisation crises and social resistance', *Critical Housing Analysis,* 11(1): 81–93.

Bond, P. (2024c) 'Elite summits amplify Africa's climate catastrophes', *The Journal of Peasant Studies,* 51(3): 738–56.

Bond, P. and Malikane, C. (2019) 'Inequality caused by macro-economic policies during overaccumulation crisis', *Development Southern Africa,* 36(6): 803–20.

Bond, P. and Basu, R. (2021) 'Intergenerational equity and the geographical ebb and flow of resources: The time and space of natural capital accounting', in M. Himley and E. Havice (eds) *Handbook of Critical Resource Geography,* New York: Palgrave Macmillan, pp 260–73.

Cohen, T. (2022) 'Coming to an understanding about Glencore', *Daily Maverick,* [online] 26 May, Available from: https://www.dailymaverick.co.za/article/2022-05-26-coming-to-an-understanding-about-glencore/ [Accessed 28 November 2024].

Competition Tribunal (2023) 'Tribunal rules that it has jurisdiction to hear the 'Forex Cartel case' against foreign and local banks', *Competition Tribunal,* [online] 30 March, Available from: www.comptrib.co.za/info-library/case-press-releases/tribunal-rules-that-it-has-jurisdiction-to-hear-the-forex-cartel-case-against-foreign-and-local-banks [Accessed 28 November 2024].

Cronin, J. (2020) 'Red alert: Johnson's track-record as a futurologist is pretty dismal', *Umsebenzi Online,* [online], Available from: https://groups.google.com/forum/#!topic/umsebenzi-online/0jzHdQfNC9c [Accessed 28 November 2024].

Davies, R. (2010) *National Assembly Statement on IPAP2*, 18 February, Pretoria: Department of Trade and Industry.

Davis, D. (2024) 'In the Competition Appeal Court of South Africa. Case No: 215/CAC/APR23', *SAFLII*, [online] 8 January, Available from: https://www.saflii.org/za/cases/ZACAC/2024/1.rtf [Accessed 28 November 2024].

Evans, J. (2024) 'Climate activists stand in solidarity after arrests outside Standard Bank', *Daily Maverick,* [online] 13 March, Available from: https://www.dailymaverick.co.za/article/2024-03-13-climate-activists-stand-in-solidarity-after-arrests-outside-standard-bank/ [Accessed 28 November 2024].

Fields, C. (2010) *Have you heard from Johannesburg: The Bottom Line,* [Video], Available from: https://vimeo.com/ondemand/haveyouheard/66941278 [Accessed 28 November 2024].

Financial Action Task Force (2023) '"Black and grey" lists', *Financial Action Task Force,* [online], Available from: www.fatf-gafi.org/en/countries/black-and-grey-lists.html [Accessed 28 November 2024].

Gills, B., Rocamora, J., and Wilson, R. (1993) *Low Intensity Democracy: Power in the New World Order,* London: Pluto Press.

Havemann, R. (2019) 'Lessons from South African bank failures. 2002 to 2014', PhD Thesis, Stellenbosch University Department of Economics.

Innes, D. (1984) *Anglo American and the Making of Modern South Africa,* New York: Monthly Review Press.

International Monetary Fund (2016) *South Africa: Article IV Consultation 2016,* Washington, DC: IMF.

International Monetary Fund (2022) *South Africa: Financial System Stability Assessment,* Washington, DC: IMF.

Isaacs, G. (2014) 'The financialisation of the SA economy and the havoc it wreaks', *Sacsis,* [online], Available from: https://sacsis.org.za/site/article/1959 [Accessed 14 February 2025].

Just Share (2024) 'Redirecting capital flows', *Just Share,* [online], Available from: https://justshare.org.za/redirecting-capital-flows/ [Accessed 28 November 2024].

Karwowski, E., Fine, B., and Ashman, S. (2018) 'Introduction to the special section "Financialization in South Africa"', *Competition and Change,* 22(4): 383–7.

Magubane, B. (2001) 'The social construction of race and citizenship in South Africa' (Working paper), Geneva: UN Research Institute for Social Development.

Magubane, K. (2024) 'Godongwana's big offshore boo-boo', *Business Day,* [online], Available from: https://www.businesslive.co.za/bt/business-and-economy/2024-02-25-godongwanas-big-offshore-boo-boo/ [Accessed 28 November 2024].

Mbeki, T. (2015) *Report of the High Level Panel on Illicit Financial Flows from Africa, Commissioned by the AU/ECA Conference of Ministers of Finance, Planning and Economic Development,* Addis Ababa.

Mohamed, S. (2018) 'The state of the South African economy', in J. Daniel, R. Southall, P. Naidoo, and D. Pillay (eds) *New South African Review,* Johannesburg: Wits University Press.

Nkosi, R. (2017) 'Currency manipulation, collusion, and other corrupt practices', *IndraStra Global,* 3: 1–3.

Nkosi, R. (2019) *South Africa's Moribund Economy,* London: Prime Policy Research in Macroeconomics.

Ntshavheni, K. (2023) 'I won't back down', *Business Day,* [online] 28 November, Available from: https://www.businesslive.co.za/bd/opinion/2023-11-28-khumbudzo-ntshavheni-i-wont-back-down/ [Accessed 28 November 2024].

Phakathi, B. (2019) 'No evidence of currency manipulation, says Tito Mboweni', *Business Day,* [online] 11 August, Available from: https://www.businesslive.co.za/bd/national/2019-08-11-no-evidence-of-currency-manipulation-says-tito-mboweni/ [Accessed 28 November 2024].

Pillay, V. (2024) 'Sasfin kills its banking operation: A tale of how fraud can destroy a business', *IOL*, [online] 23 October, Available from: https://www.iol.co.za/business/jobs/sasfin-kills-its-banking-operation-a-tale-of-how-fraud-can-destroy-a-business-38a3a810-cc10-4fda-b832-044bd86acfaf [Accessed 28 November 2024].

Planting, S. (2019) 'SA's anti-money laundering measures under global spotlight', *Daily Maverick,* [online] 27 October, Available from: https://www.dailymaverick.co.za/article/2019-10-27-sas-anti-money-laundering-measures-under-global-spotlight/ [Accessed 28 November 2024].

PwC (2016) Global Economic Crime Survey, Available from: https://www.pwc.com/gx/en/assets/gecs/gecs-fs-industry-cut-2016.pdf [Accessed 14 February 2025].

PwC (2020) Global Economic Crime and Fraud Survey 2020, Available from: https://www.global-screeningsolutions.com/industries/global-economic-crime-and-fraud-survey-2020-1.pdf [Accessed 14 February 2025].

Rodrik, D. (2018) *Understanding South Africa*, Cambridge: Harvard University.

Saul, J. and Bond, P. (2014) *South Africa – The Present as History,* Johannesburg: Jacana Media.

Sibanyoni, B., van Rensburg, D., and Mndebele, M. (2024) 'Past sins come back to haunt microlenders, with Capitec on the frontline', *Amabhungane*, [online] 24 July, Available from: https://amabhungane.org/past-sins-come-back-to-haunt-microlenders-with-capitec-on-the-frontline/ [Accessed 28 November 2024].

Sole, S. (2020) 'Limpopo's dirty great white elephant', *Amabhungane*, [online] 7 April, Available from: https://amabhungane.org/stories/earthcrimes-limpopos-dirty-great-white-elephant/ [Accessed 28 November 2024].

South African Federation of Trade Unions (2021) *SAFTU Calls on Deputy Justice Zondo to Demand Testimony from President Ramaphosa*, Johannesburg: South African Federation of Trade Unions.

South African Reserve Bank (SARB) (2024a) *South African Reserve Bank Imposes Administrative Sanctions on Five Banks*, Pretoria: South African Reserve Bank.

SARB (2024b) *Risks and Vulnerabilities Matrix*, Pretoria: South African Reserve Bank.

SARB (2024c) *South African Reserve Bank Imposes Administrative Sanctions on Bank of Chine Limited Johannesburg Branch*, Pretoria: South African Reserve Bank.

South African Treasury (2024) *National Terrorism Financing Risk Assessment*, Pretoria: South African Treasury.

Subasat, T. and Mavroudeas, S. (2023) 'Financialization hypothesis: A theoretical and empirical critique', *World Review of Political Economy*, 14(2): 204–33.

Tax Justice Network (2024) 'Corporate tax haven index methodology', *Tax Justice Network*, [online], Available from: https://res.cloudinary.com/dybieo1nh/image/upload/workspace_QQiCKdxM4JCLtU/CTHIMethodology2024_g2lwgq [Accessed 28 November 2024].

Tshwane, T. (2019) 'US fine bolsters SA's rand-fixing case', *Mail & Guardian,* [online] 8 February, Available from: https://mg.co.za/article/2019-02-08-00-us-fine-bolsters-sas-rand-fixing-case/ [Accessed 28 November 2024].

The Economist (2024) 'Economic and financial indicators', *The Economist*, [online], Available from: https://www.economist.com/economic-and-financial-indicators [Accessed 28 November 2024].

Thompson, W. (2020) 'When good auditors go bad', *Financial Mail*, [online] 2 July, Available from: www.businesslive.co.za/fm/features/cover-story/2020-07-02-when-good-auditors-go-bad/ [Accessed 28 November 2024].

Torkelson, E. (2020) 'Collateral damages: Cash transfer and debt transfer in South Africa', *World Development,* 126: 104711.

Wasserman, H. (2023) 'Fact check: Here's what we know about rand rigging and the banks', *News24*, [online] 4 December, Available from: https://www.news24.com/fin24/markets/fact-check-heres-what-we-know-about-rand-rigging-and-the-banks-20231204-2 [Accessed 28 November 2024].

World Bank (2021) *World Bank-South Africa Country Partnership Framework. Report No. 154318-ZA*, Washington, DC: World Bank.

World Economic Forum (2018) *Global Competitiveness Report 2018*, Davos: WEF.

5

Brazil in the Global Financial Order: How Domestic Politics Trigger Ambiguous Contestation

Pedro Lange Machado, Luiz Fernando de Paula, and Eduardo Mantoan

Introduction

Scholarship on stages of capitalism posits that the liberal order is in crisis, which may lead to the configuration of a new order in the medium term (for example, Nölke, 2017; 2022; Lake et al, 2021; Saad-Filho and Feil, 2023). This is partially being triggered by the adoption of financial statecraft policies[1] by developing and emerging market economies (DEEs), which suffer the negative effects of the subordinated condition of their integration into the global financial order (GFO). International financial subordination (IFS) is an umbrella concept related to 'an important set of process and relations that maintain DEEs in a subordinate position in the global monetary and financial system. In short, IFS is about unearthing why the structural power of finance takes a particularly violent form of expression in DEEs, and the implications thereof' (Alami et al, 2023, p 1360).

As Alami states (Chapter 2, this volume), while IFS imposes real and identifiable constraints on policy making in DEEs, this does not necessarily mean that state agency and capacity are denied. In fact, IFS can serve as a powerful catalyst for institutional innovation and regulatory experimentation in these economies, potentially improving a country's position in global financial and monetary relations. DEEs are subordinated financially to different degrees, depending on, among other factors, the manner of their international financial integration in the global monetary and financial system, and a set of domestic institutions and policies implemented in each country.

An illustrative example of the contestation of the liberal order is the adoption of state capitalist policies by the countries that make up the

BRICS (Brazil, Russia, India, China, and South Africa), as opposed to the hegemonic liberal capitalist policies in the global financial order configured in the last quarter of the 20th century (Petry and Nölke, 2024). By doing so, the BRICS, as other DEEs, seek to curb the restrictions imposed on their policy space to pursue alternative development strategies to the liberal script.

This contestation of liberal capitalism, however, varies in intensity depending on the country in question. While China emerges as the main challenger of the hegemonic order, in a pole opposite to that of the United States and the United Kingdom, other emerging economies move between a position more or less complicit with the status quo. Among the BRICS, the case of Brazil draws attention due to its ambiguity in contesting the liberal financial order. On the one hand, Brazil has been notable for adopting economic policy instruments that confront the liberal agenda, while integrating a series of initiatives that challenge the hegemonic order at the international level. On the other hand, this process has always occurred in conciliation with liberal orthodox instruments, which have never been abandoned or explicitly confronted by Brazilian governments. What may explain this puzzling behaviour?

This chapter contributes to this debate by highlighting how financial statecraft can be dependent on domestic politics, in line with reflections made by Petry and Nölke (Chapter 1, this volume). It aims to understand Brazil's ambiguous contestation of the current global financial order by claiming that such ambiguity reflects Brazil's internal political dynamics, where there has been an alternation of power between governments to a greater or lesser extent more or less aligned with the underlying ideology of the liberal financial order. This argument develops from the analysis of the economic policy implemented by different Brazilian governments throughout the 21st century (2003–22), as well as of specific foreign policy initiatives, in light of the theoretical framework developed by Petry and Nölke (2024) to examine the contestation of the liberal financial order. In this way, this study also contributes to a better understanding of the contestation of the global financial order by emerging economies in general, and the case of Brazil in particular.

The chapter is divided into four sections, besides this introduction. Section 2 presents the theoretical framework that underlies our analysis, allowing us to identify government policies as 'liberal' or 'state capitalist'. The third section offers Brazil's economic overview, from the national-developmentalist model to the Washington Consensus (WC) model, and the conduct of economic policies during the Partido dos Trabalhadores (PT) governments, from the first election of Lula da Silva as president in 2002 until Rousseff's impeachment in 2016, followed by the implementation of a neoliberal agenda with the Temer and Bolsonaro governments. In the fourth section, we analyze the case of Brazil in light of the theoretical framework presented, which allows us to draw conclusions aligned with the hypothesis. Section 5 concludes this chapter.

Challenging the global financial order: the theoretical framework

A first step in developing our argument is to clarify what is meant by *global financial order* (GFO) and to present the theoretical framework that underpins our analysis. The literature on stages of capitalism has been debating the crisis of the current international order, which may be experiencing a disruptive moment inaugurated by the 2008 global financial crisis and its consequences (Sato, 2012; Nölke, 2017; Nölke and May, 2019), to which the COVID-19 pandemic (Nölke, 2022) and the climate and environmental crises (Saad-Filho and Feil, 2023) were added. However, as Petry and Nölke (2024) note, the financial dimension of the international order is constantly neglected in this debate, even though it constitutes one of its bedrocks. More than that, this is where financial statecraft policies have been employed by DEEs to mitigate the negative effects of their subordinated integration into the current GFO (Armijo, Chapter 3, this volume). As posited by the literature on IFS, this is a pattern of integration that originated from the financial asymmetries and monetary hierarchy of the current stage of global capitalism.[2] As a result, DEEs face serious restrictions on their policy space, resulting, among other factors, from the peripheral condition of their currencies and the shallowness of their financial markets (Paula et al, 2017).

For the sake of clarification, a GFO will be henceforth understood as the interweaving of the eleven issue areas shown in the first column of Table 5.1, which represent important elements of the global financial and monetary structures. This framework was developed by Petry and Nölke (2024), who posit that, given that an international order is built on the intertwining of international institutions, domestic features, and the stream of interactions across borders, each of these issue areas should be approached from a national, transnational, and international perspective. This concept gives nuances and develops other concepts present in the literature on stages of capitalism, such as the one of international economic order proposed by Sato (2012).[3] Moreover, this makes it possible to operationalize a taxonomic analysis of the different GFOs that run through the history of capitalism.

There is a certain consensus in the diagnosis that a first international order emerged at the end of the 19th century, under the aegis of the gold standard. After the Great Depression and the Second World War, the international order architected in Bretton Woods was in force until the crisis of the 1970s, which put its parameters and institutions in check. From the 1980s onwards, a neoliberal international order marked by financial globalization and the financialization of capitalism became hegemonic. However, as already pointed out, it might be experiencing a potentially disruptive moment (for example, Sato, 2012; Nölke and May, 2019).

One of the symptoms of this crisis would be initiatives to challenge the international order through financial statecraft, triggered by DEEs' attempts to mitigate the negative effects of their subordinated financial integration into the GFO, including the implementation of capital controls, greater participation of state-owned banks, and creation of new international institutions. In the current stage of capitalism, the use of financial statecraft to challenge the liberal order is being framed by the literature as state-capitalism (Musacchio and Lazzarini, 2013; Petry, 2023). To understand it, this is necessary to consider how the liberal nature of the international order (supposedly) in crisis translates into the GFO. According to Petry and Nölke (2024), the ideal type of *liberal capitalism* prevailing in the GFO is based on pro-market regulations in the economy, free international capital flows, promotion of shareholder value, and a global power structure centred on the hegemonic role of the dollar and backed by a private financial infrastructure that promotes it. On the other hand, the challenging ideal type, known as *state-capitalism,* seeks to preserve national sovereignty and policy space for industrial catch-up, which requires restrictions on shareholder value and a prominent role for the state in its relationship with the market and with global capital flows (see Chapter 1). The main features of liberal and state capitalism are depicted in Table 5.1.

An important contribution in the literature on contestation to the neoliberal international order is made by Grabel (2018), who, when analyzing several multilateral initiatives made by developing countries, such as the Chiang Mai Initiative Multilateralization (CMIM) and the New Development Bank (NDB) of the BRICS group, from a Hirschmanian view, highlights the relevance of 'small-scale, disconnected, experimental, and incremental adjustments in institutions that take root in the concrete demands facing policymakers' (Grabel, 2018, p 2). Such initiatives may result in 'institutional experimentation, expansion, and hybridization as a moment of pragmatic innovation that might yield institutions that do better than their predecessor in promoting financial stability and resilience, and as a consequence, provide the possibility for development that is more stable, inclusive, sustainable, and protective of autonomy' (Grabel, 2018, p 5). In other words, this perspective supports the diagnosis of the use of financial statecraft by DEEs seeking to avoid the harmful effects of their IFS.

These are, therefore, the theoretical parameters that guide the analysis of Brazil's insertion in the contemporary GFO. As shown in Table 5.1, Brazil has demonstrated an ambiguous position in contesting the liberal GFO, simultaneously engaging to initiatives that both support and confront it, although in general the country is structurally closer to liberal capitalism (see also Kaltenbrunner et al, Chapter 8, this volume): floating exchange

Table 5.1: Brazil in the global financial order

Issue areas	Liberal capitalism	State capitalism	Brazil in the GFO
Foreign exchange rate system	(i) Free floating exchange rate; (ii) large and liquid offshore currency markets; (iii) market decides on the lead currencies.	(i) Managed exchange rate; (ii) restrictions on offshore currency markets; (iii) promotion of a multipolar currency system.	(i) Floating regime with some interventions; (ii) no offshore currency markets; (iii) BRICS initiatives for a multipolar currency system.
Balance of payments	(i) One reserve currency (USD) based around a highly integrated and liquid market structure; (ii) swap lines based on the dollar; (iii) liquidity problems solved by the IMF.	(i) High reserve accumulation; (ii) swap lines based on other currencies; (iii) alternative arrangements for liquidity provision.	(i) Significant reserve accumulation; (ii) Brazil has both types of agreement; (iii) Brazil takes part in both initiatives.
Central banks and monetary policy	(i) Independent central banks with a focus on price stability and inflation targeting; (ii) not supportive of central banks' digital currencies; (iii) narrow mandate to fight inflation domestically.	(i) Central banks accountable to governments with multiple objectives; (ii) promotion of digital currencies; (iii) international management of monetary policies.	(i) Central bank is independent; (ii) involvement with digital currency projects; (iii) prevalence of inflation target regime.
International capital mobility	(i) Capital market openness; (ii) promotion of international capital mobility; (iii) international enforcement by OECD and IMF.	(i) Capital controls for maintaining state capacity; (ii) restrictions to international financial flows; (iii) contention of the enforcement for international capital mobility.	(i) Domestic restrictions on capital mobility; (ii, iii) resistance to conform with liberal norms.
Foreign direct investment	(i) Abolishment of national restrictions on foreign direct investment (FDI) flows; (ii, iii) prominence of the 'investors-state-dispute-settlement' (ISDS).	(i) Restrictions on inward FDI flows based on strategic considerations; (ii, iii) avoidance or withdrawal from institutions such as the ISDS.	(i) Liberalized FDI regime; (ii) Outward FDI promoted by the National Bank for Economic and Social Development (BNDES) and tax cuts.
Corporate ownership and governance	(i) Corporate ownership through institutional investors prompting shareholder value maximization; (ii) foreign ownership promoted through liberalized capital markets; (iii) Regulation of sovereign wealth funds.	(i) Significant degree of state ownership in listed companies; (ii) foreign ownership should be curtailed; (iii) free use of sovereign wealth funds.	(i) High degree of free float and institutional ownership and moderate levels of state ownership; (ii) low foreign ownership.
Commercial banks and banking regulations	(i) Private ownership and self-regulation; (ii) high level of foreign banks accounting for banking assets.	(i) Banks partially state-owned/controlled with state-centred regulations; (ii) low level of foreign banks accounting for banking assets and transnationalization of state-owned banks.	(i) Moderate state-ownership degree in the bank sector, and high volumes of state-directed lending; (ii) moderate-low level of foreign banks accounting for banking assets.

Table 5.1: Brazil in the global financial order (continued)

Issue areas	Liberal capitalism	State capitalism	Brazil in the GFO
Financial markets	(i) Exchanges are profit-oriented corporations mostly owned by international investors and driven by market forces; (ii) transnational standards and light regulation for derivatives market, which is organized on over-the-counter and high-frequency trading.	(i) Exchanges are (partially) state-oriented entities, less profit-oriented, and foreign ownership of exchanges is restricted; (ii) incompatibility between opaque markets for leveraged, speculative products and a state-capitalist logic of market organization.	(i) Exchange's state-ownership is non-existent, and foreign ownership is extensive; (ii) derivative trading conducted in the national exchange, with improvements in the infrastructure to promote high-frequency trading.
Financial infrastructures	(i) 'Fair value accounting/FVA'; (ii) application of the International Financial Reporting Standards (IFRS) as set by the International Accounting Standards Board (IASB); (iii) private governance and one central global standard.	(i) 'Historic cost accounting (HCA)'; (ii) resistance to the transnational spread of accounting standards that are wedded to liberal capitalism; (iii) prominent role for national governments and demands for reform of the IASB.	(i) Supportive of the IFRS.
International debt management	(ii, iii) Prominent role of international institutions designed to strengthen claim enforcement against national governments on behalf of private investors.	(ii, iii) Weaker role of global institutions, and more significant bilateral negotiations between national governments.	(i, iii) Integrated into the international institutions responsible for international debt management, while participating in BRICS initiatives for South–South cooperation.
Development finance	(i) Minor role domestically; (ii) coordinated through official development assistant (ODA) between countries; (iii) authority is concentrated in World Bank with which regional development banks coordinate.	(i) Domestically relevant; (ii) bilateral development finance utilizes different mechanisms and focuses more on political targets than commercial viability; (iii) creation of new international institutions to operate independently and differently from the World Bank.	(i, ii) Prominence of the BNDES domestically and regionally; (iii) New Development Bank (NDB) of the BRICS.

Notes: (i) Domestic dimension; (ii) transnational dimension; (iii) international dimension.

Source: Authors' elaboration based on Petry and Nölke (2024)

regime; independence of central bank; inflation target regime; liberalized foreign direct investment (FDI) regime; supportive to International Financial Reporting Standards (IFRS); integration to the international institutions responsible for international debt management. But at the same time, there have been some initiatives in the direction of contestation, which include, among others: BRICS initiatives for a multipolar currency system; domestic restrictions on capital mobility in some periods; moderate–low level of foreign banks accounting for banking assets; moderate (but somehow high) state-ownership share in the banking sector; participating in BRICS initiatives for South–South cooperation. As for development finance, the prominence of the National Bank for Economic and Social Development (BNDES) domestically and regionally and the establishment of the NDB by the BRICS countries in 2015. What can explain this ambiguous pattern of contestation? We now turn to Brazil's political and economic trajectory to address this question.

Brazilian economy in the liberal order

This section offers a descriptive examination of the trajectory of economic policy implemented by Brazilian governments to operationalize our argument that the use of financial statecraft in Brazil is dependent on its domestic politics. Some political developments and foreign policy initiatives are also addressed for this purpose. As our analysis will show, the implementation of policies that challenge the liberal script is always constrained by the subordinated condition of Brazil's integration into the GFO. The section is divided into two subsections. The first addresses the background of the time frame considered in our analysis, focusing on the transition from the period of military dictatorship in Brazil to the country's integration into the order of financial globalization. In the second subsection, the experience of Brazilian governments between 2003 and 2022 is explored.

From national-developmentalist model to the Washington Consensus

From the post-Second World War period until the beginning of the 1980s, Brazil had a steady economic growth with an average real GDP growth of 7.1 per cent in 1947–80, with the expansive economic dynamism driven mainly by the industrial sector (8.5 per cent p.a.), in particular by the manufacturing sector.[4] In this period, some significant structural changes happened in the Brazilian economy: there was a shift in its dynamic centre from the agro-exporter sector to the industrial sector, more oriented towards the domestic market; meanwhile, the economy also experienced a decrease in the import coefficient (13.7 per cent of GDP in 1947 to 7.6 per cent in 1980); and the country went through a quick process of urbanization, which was marked by increasing social inequalities and high margins of absolute poverty.[5]

Behind the post-Second World War changes in the Brazilian economy was the adoption of a national strategy of development known as 'national-developmentalist', strongly influenced by the Economic Commission for Latin America and the Caribbean's (ECLAC)[6] structuralism of the 1950s, that had as its main features: the inducement for the country's industrialization, from the lighter segments to the heavier ones, based on the process of import substitution industrialization;[7] and the active role of the state, performing as planner, financer, and producer (basic inputs, such as steel and oil, and infrastructure, such as roads and electric energy). In a model known as the 'tripod', the state was the protagonist together with the multinational enterprises that were present in the more dynamic segments of the manufacturing sector (such as vehicles), while the domestic enterprises were the small partner of the tripod. The autonomy of economic policy was assured by the restricted capital account convertibility (initially under the Bretton Woods order) that allowed the frequent use of expansionary policies, as was the case at the beginning of the so-called 'economic miracle' (1967–73),[8] and since 1967 the use of a crawling peg exchange rate regime.

The Brazilian economy entered a deep economic crisis at the beginning of the 1980s under the foreign debt crisis, resulting from the sudden increase of US interest rates after the 1970s external indebtedness cycle to finance current account deficits. The debt crisis contributed to the deterioration of public finance and the acceleration of inflation due to the shocks caused by maxi-devaluations of exchange rates (in 1979 and 1983) in an increasingly indexed economy. The economic crisis then weakened the Brazilian government's ability to intervene in the economy.

At the end of the 1980s and the beginning of the 1990s, a set of proposals aimed at promoting a new strategy for growth to Latin America after one decade of stagnation ('1980s lost decade') arose. They were first introduced by John Williamson (1990), and they were largely known as the 'Washington Consensus' (WC), as they served as inspiration for the liberalizing economic reforms imposed by Washington-based institutions, particularly in Latin America.

The recommendations aimed at stimulating economic growth towards a set of policies and liberalizing reforms, notably macroeconomic discipline, trade openness, privatization of state-owned firms, and market-friendly microeconomic policies. The proposal for capital account liberalization was not included in the original WC but was added to the proposal by multilateral institutions, such as the IMF and World Bank. Liberal reforms, in greater or lesser extension, were applied in many Latin American countries in the 1990s, including Argentina, Brazil, and Mexico. In other words, the WC's prescriptions aimed to integrate emerging economies into the GFO of financial globalization. However, the results of the implementation of WC strategy were somewhat disappointing, particularly regarding economic growth. Argentina, which was considered by the IMF during the 1990s as an example of the success of WC strategy, was in fact an enormous failure.

Brazil, like other Latin American countries, adopted liberal reforms and economic openness during the 1990s inspired partially by the WC. The economic openness, specifically in terms of reduced import tax, and the privatization of state-owned firms (in particular the steel sector) began during Collor de Melo's government (1990–92). Under Itamar Franco's government (1992–95), price stabilization was achieved in 1994 with the implementation of the 'Real Plan', with a stabilization programme that used an exchange rate anchor and economic deindexation. In the two terms of Fernando Cardoso's government (1995–98 and 1999–2003), besides the consolidation of price stabilization, the entry of FDI was stimulated, and new programmes of privatization were implemented in the telecommunication and electric energy sectors.

The 1990s in Brazil were also characterized by the process of capital account liberalization. In the first part of the decade, the Brazilian government permitted the acquisition of equities of domestic firms by foreign institutional investors, through special funds for this purpose, and made an important change in a special non-resident bank account (CC5), that operated by foreign financial institutions in practice permitted that both residents and non-residents could send freely abroad their domestic monetary resources. In the 2000s, financial liberalization continued through legislation that aimed at simplifying the norms related to foreign exchange operations (Paula, 2011).

Summing up, the 1990s in Brazil were marked by economic openness (trade and financial), the privatization of state-owned firms, and price stabilization. However, they were also characterized by the contagion of external crises – Mexican, Asian, and Russian ones – under a context of high external vulnerability. There were important structural changes in the Brazilian economy – economic openness, price stabilization, renegotiation of external debt, reinsertion of the economy in the international financial market – but the economic performance disappointed, due to the contagious crises and Brazilian crises in 1999 and 2002, so that the average GDP growth of the 1990s (2.5 per cent) was closer to the 1980s performance (2.3 per cent) than to the 1950–70 performance (7.1 per cent pa). Such crises expressed the problems related to the mode of international subordination of the Brazilian economy in the context of financial openness and the adoption of a stabilization plan based on an exchange rate anchor.

In 1999, after the crisis of the semi-fixed exchange rate regime, which was the fundamental basis of the Real Plan, the Brazilian government made some important changes in the structure of economic policy, by adopting a floating exchange rate regime and an inflation targeting system, that became the new anchor of prices. Under the conditions of the enhancement of financial liberalization, the new regime of macroeconomic policy can be characterized as inspired by what is currently called 'The New Consensus on Macroeconomics' (NCM). NCM supports that the main focus of economic policy is price stabilization and that the inflation targeting regime is the best arrangement for economic policy, as it provides some degree of freedom to accommodate output fluctuations due to non-anticipated shocks. In such an arrangement, fiscal policy is no longer viewed as a powerful macroeconomic instrument and should be aligned and subordinated to monetary policy (Mishkin, 2000). Monetary policy is a flexible instrument for achieving medium-term stabilization objectives, in that it can be adjusted quickly in response to macroeconomic developments.[9] In the Brazilian case, this macroeconomic arrangement was characterized by a sort of *tripod of economic policy*: a floating exchange regime, an inflation target regime, and the generation of primary fiscal surplus. A certain and moderate economic policy autonomy (for domestic purposes) is achieved under the context of capital account convertibility due to the working of a floating exchange rate regime.

At the beginning of the 2000s, the Brazilian economy initially suffered the impact of some international shocks (the slow-down in the US economy, and the Turkish and Argentine crises) and later a confidence crisis in 2002 due to the probable election of a more leftist government, that eventually caused a sudden stop in the inflow of foreign capital, and consequently a steady and abrupt exchange rate devaluation. Lula da Silva, the candidate of the centre-leftist Workers' Party (Partido dos Trabalhadores – PT), was then pressured to make explicit the moderation of his agenda, which culminated in the release of his 'Letter to the Brazilian people', where he pledged to fulfill the contracts signed and to maintain the economic policy guidelines previously established. This confidence crisis highlights the limitations of the policy space for left-wing governments with a redistributive agenda in the context of international financial integration, especially in critical events. At the end of 2002 he was elected president of Brazil.

From PT social-developmentalism to Temer–Bolsonaro neoliberalism

The 2002 elections significantly changed the correlation of political forces between representatives of capital – particularly financial capital, until then hegemonic – and labour, with the rise of previously marginalized sectors (Boito Júnior and Berringer, 2013). The difficulties of the Washington Consensus inspired policies in leveraging industrial growth favoured a partial degree of convergence between some domestic businesses and wage earners. This 'productivist' coalition was responsible for the gradual and partial flexibilization of the macroeconomic tripod via the mediation platform created by segments of Brazil's political, business, and civil society actors (Ianoni, 2018). The result of easing measures was a mix of policies now including actions focused on the productive sector and the fight against poverty. Prates et al (2020) have shown that the PT governments' developmentalist project combined elements of *social developmentalism*[10] with orthodox economic policies: these governments sought to stimulate growth based on mass consumption, which drew on increases in minimum wages, social transfers, and credit expansion – a predominantly wage-led growth strategy.[11]

Lula's government was pressured to adopt orthodox policies at the beginning of its first administration in 2003, and maintained the tripod of economic policy during his two terms: since international conditions (the commodities boom) were favourable, it implemented a more interventionist and distributive agenda while maintaining an orthodox macroeconomic policy. Furthermore, incentives for capital inflows in Brazil were maintained (see Chapter 9). Indeed, the economy was favoured by the benign international environment (a commodities boom and high liquidity in the international financial market) that allowed the Brazilian economy to grow at 4.8 per cent on average in 2004–08 (Table 5.2), an unprecedented performance compared to the 1980s and 1990s. During this period, the main engine of growth was household consumption (which responds to the biggest share of the Brazilian GDP, around 60 per cent), fostered by a real increase in the minimum wage[12] – that was the key policy of the government – and the continuous credit growth to households and enterprises.

While the Lula administration was undoubtedly favoured by the international economic context, discretionary domestic policies played an important role in increasing the autonomy of its economic policy. Two examples may be highlighted in this regard. On the one hand, the government launched a policy of international reserves accumulation, starting in 2004 from US$53 billion to US$194 billion in 2008 (reaching more than US$350 billion after 2011). On the other hand, it implemented a deliberate policy to reduce the external public debt (from US$132 billion in 2004 to US$84 billion in 2006), taking advantage of the abundance of international liquidity, which made the Brazilian government a creditor in dollars starting in 2007 (Figure 5.1). Indeed, at the end of 2008 the Brazilian economy was hit by the contagion of a global financial crisis (GFC), which caused an immediate and deep impact on the economy. However, the effect was relatively short, with the economy showing signals of recovery by the middle of 2009, due to the combination of countercycle policies and a benign external environment (mainly Chinese economic recovery).

In the context of the contagion effect of the GFC, Lula's second term responded to the financial crisis by adopting some countercyclical measures, including measures to strengthen the liquidity of the banking sector; a

Table 5.2: GDP growth in Brazil (per cent per annum)

Year	Real GDP	Agriculture	Industry	Services
2003	1.1	8.3	0.1	1.0
2004	5.8	2.0	8.2	5.0
2005	3.2	1.1	2.0	3.7
2006	4.0	4.6	2.0	4.3
2007	6.1	3.3	6.2	5.8
2008	5.1	5.8	4.1	4.8
2009	–0.1	–3.7	–4.7	2.1
2010	7.5	6.7	10.2	5.8
2011	4.0	5.6	4.1	3.5
2012	1.9	–3.1	–0.7	2.9
2013	3.0	8.4	2.2	2.8
2014	0.5	2.8	–1.5	1.0
2015	–3.6	3.3	–5.8	–2.7
2016	–3.3	–5.2	–4.6	–2.2
2017	1.3	14.2	–0.5	0.8
2018	1.8	1.3	0.7	2.1
2019	1.2	0.4	–0.7	1.5
2020	–3.3	4.2	–3.0	–3.7
2021	4.8	0.0	5.0	4.8
2022	3.0	–1.1	1.5	4.3

Source: Authors' calculation based on IPEADATA (2023)

temporary credit line for exports; interventions by the Central Bank of Brazil (BCB) in the foreign exchange market; stimulation of credit expansion by state-owned banks as they were encouraged to expand their credit operations to compensate for the sharp deceleration in the credit supply by private banks – see Figure 5.2; reduction of the tax on industrialized products for cars, household appliances, and construction products; extension of the period for granting unemployment insurance; and the creation of a programme to build low-income housing ('*Minha Casa, Minha Vida*') (Barbosa Filho, 2010). Clearly, there was a shift in the orientation of the economic policy in Lula da Silva's government after the GFC, with the implementation of more developmental and interventionist policies, making the economic tripod more flexible, but without breaking it (Prates et al, 2020).

It is also worth mentioning two other measures taken by the Lula government in the crisis context. First, it created the Sovereign Wealth Fund

Figure 5.1: Brazil's net external debt (US$ billion)

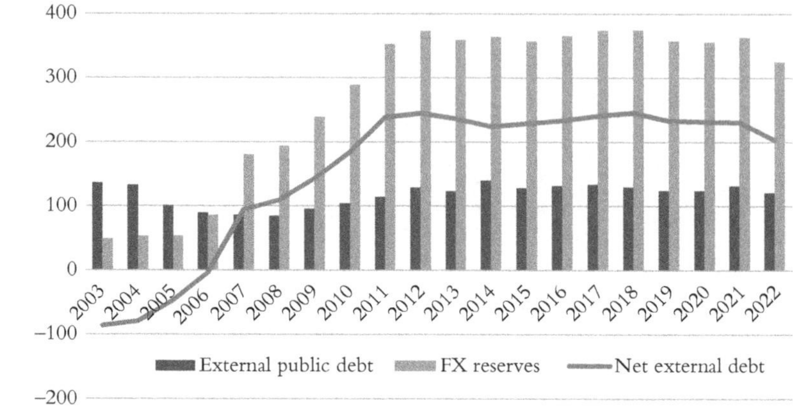

Note: Net external debt = International reserves minus external public debt.
Source: Authors' elaboration based on data from Banco Central do Brasil (2023)

Figure 5.2: Brazil's credit supply for ownership (percentage)

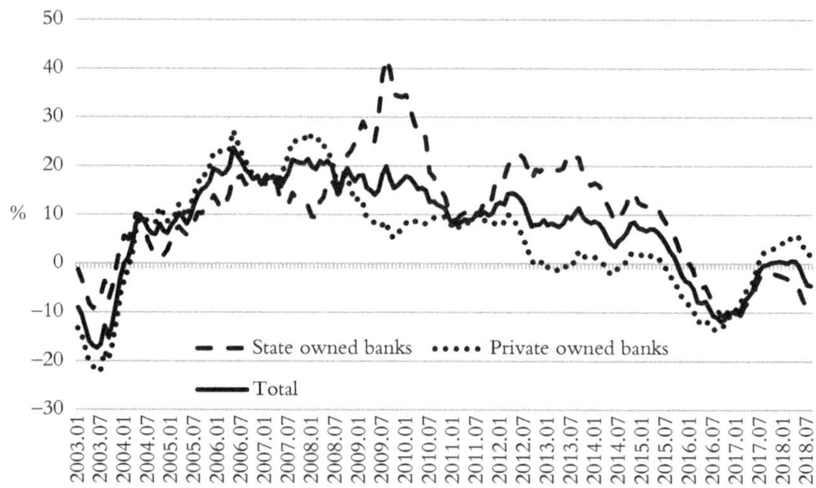

Note: Growth rate compared to 12 months before with data in real values (deflated by IPCA).
Source: Authors' calculation based on Banco Central do Brasil (2023)

of Brazil, still in 2008, receiving an initial contribution of US$7.9 billion, with the issuance of public domestic bonds by the National Treasury of Brazil. Second, it helped to create the Local Currency Payments System of Mercosur, which established a system for settling trade in local currencies without the intermediation of the dollar in Mercosur. Created in 2008 between Brazil and Argentina, the initiative would incorporate Uruguay in 2014 and Paraguay in 2016, aiming at consolidating itself as an official payment and settlement system of the Mercosur bloc. Both measures reflected emerging economies' needs, further evidenced by the 2008 crisis, to protect themselves from the instabilities arising from their integration into the global financial order.

After governing for two terms (2003–06 and 2007–10) and benefiting from Lula's high popularity rates, the Workers' Party easily elected as president his successor and former minister, Dilma Rousseff. In contrast with Lula, however, the domestic policy during Dilma Rousseff's first administration (2011–14) was faltering. Initially orthodox, it later combined orthodoxy with heterodox policies and finally returned to strongly contractionary policies in 2015 in her second term. Between 2010 and 2014, the government bet that the change in the economic policy mix (the reduction of the Selic policy rate and exchange rate devaluation) – the so-called 'New Economic Matrix' – added to the tax exemptions would be enough to jointly boost aggregate supply and demand for goods. In order to devalue the currency, the Ministry of Finance started imposing regulations on capital flows, which had already started with a tiny financial transaction tax on foreign portfolio investments in October 2009. One year later, these regulations were strengthened with the first measure targeting foreign exchange derivatives operations and administrative controls (Paula and Prates, 2017). The new matrix proved controversial and sparked debate about future tensions that would lead to the collapse of the government's supporting coalition.

By bringing about changes in interest and exchange rate policies, with a drastic reduction in the Selic rate[13] and bank spreads, Rousseff eventually strained the relationship with representatives of this financial-rentier segment (Singer, 2018). In addition to the strife with the Brazilian Federation of Banks, in June 2013 widespread demonstrations erupted in the country's capitals that produced a fundamental cleavage in the Rousseff government (Singer, 2018, p 99). The episode rattled the political climate of the country. The drop in the president's popularity put the federal government in a defensive stance, with setbacks such as the restoration of higher interest rates by the Central Bank in mid-2013 and 'the beginning of the mobilization of the middle class, which would eventually play a decisive role in the fall of Dilma' (Singer, 2018, p 103).

Due to the economic slowdown from 2011 onwards, the Rousseff government sought to implement ad hoc measures to stimulate growth, such as the extension of the payroll tax exemption to more sectors. This action, however, was not well coordinated and lacked consistency: the adoption of a countercyclical fiscal policy was justified in view of the poor performance of the economy, but it came late, favoured tax exemptions over public investments, and was poorly communicated to agents. The countercyclical policies adopted by the first Rousseff administration were poorly conceived on the fiscal issue – with ambitious targets being maintained through nonrecurring budget operations and exemption-oriented fiscal expansionism and excessive intervention in regulated markets (energy and oil), among other things (Paula et al, 2015). Meanwhile, it is worth mentioning that it was during Rousseff's first term that the NDB and the Contingent Reserve Arrangement (CRA) were established by the BRICS in the sixth summit at Fortaleza.

After Rousseff's reelection in a tight presidential race, in 2015–16 the economy suffered a series of shocks – deterioration of the terms of trade, fiscal adjustment, the acceleration of inflation, water crisis, currency devaluation, the increase in the Selic interest rate, and finally the impact of Operation Car Wash[14] on the economy, particularly the civil construction and oil and gas sectors – which contributed to further reducing economic growth, which decelerated sharply to −3.5 per cent on average over the period. The second Rousseff government (2015–16) faced a 'perfect storm'. In 2015, the government shifted its economic policy radically towards a more orthodox policy stance. This change led to the accusation of 'policy switch', with mass demonstrations intensifying in the streets concomitant with the deepening recession and dissatisfaction with the president, whose rejection rate jumped from 30 per cent to 70 per cent from September 2014 to September 2015 (Datafolha, 2015). The erosion of middle-class support for the PT was sharp, as was the very middle-class that backed the protests alongside right-wing political actors, movements, and business entities (Singer, 2018). The liberal rhetoric critical of interventionism ascribed to the PT – holding it responsible for the mistakes that had led the country to the crisis – gained momentum.

The main aim of the economic policy was to implement fiscal adjustment mainly on the side of public expenditures, understood as fundamental for retaking the agents' confidence as a precondition for economic recovery. Rousseff tried rather desperately to regain market confidence through an orthodox adjustment, but it turned out to be counterproductive in a recession that was already underway and in a quite adverse international and domestic context.

At the political level, the concatenation of a more conservative Congress and a new president of the Chamber of Deputies (Deputy Eduardo Cunha) colliding directly with the executive branch hindered any consensus on a common agenda between the two powers. It is in this context that Vice President Michel Temer gained strength as an alternative to Rousseff, whose impeachment had already been architected during the first year of her second term. Given the president's lack of popularity and communication problems, he became a relevant political coordinator, mediating with the Congress and specifically with his party, the Brazilian Democratic Movement – increasingly detached from Rousseff – for the approval of liberalizing and austerity measures. In October 2015, Temer's party – the Brazilian Democratic

Movement Party – released a government agenda explicitly informed by liberal orthodox principles and liberal reforms.

Months later, Rousseff's impeachment in 2016 was a victory for the coalition that opposed the PT governments and can be seen as the result of its progressive strengthening, especially since June 2013. In fact, the offensive of this neoliberal coalition – spearheading, in particular, societal groups aligned with financial interests – would have created the conditions for the removal of the president, which for many constituted a legal-parliamentary coup. Representing these interests, the Temer government advanced an agenda aligned with liberal orthodox precepts, guided by the implementation of liberalizing reforms in the economy and the imperative of fiscal austerity, which was associated with a conservative monetary policy.

As Oreiro and Paula (2021: Chapter 4) pointed out, the Temer government (2016–18) was a turning point in the developmentalist policies implemented by the PT governments, starting a series of orthodox and neoliberal policies that the authors termed as 'Brazilian Thatcherism', with a deliberate goal of reducing the role of the state in the economy, that was continued by the Bolsonaro government (2019–22).[15] Such policies comprised the conventional deployment of macroeconomic policies – monetary policy directed at inflation targets and austerity in fiscal policy and a floating exchange rate policy, combined (in the Bolsonaro government) with the privatization of state-owned enterprises.

The liberal reforms implemented by the Temer and Bolsonaro governments included among others: a labour reform approved in late 2016, introducing a series of measures to bring greater flexibility to the labour market; a spending cap, constitutional amendment also approved in 2016, which implemented a 20-year freeze on real government expenditures by stipulating that public spending would be adjusted by the prior year's inflation;[16] a social security reform approved on 12 November 2019; the extinction of the Sovereign Wealth Fund of Brazil in 2019; approval of a law (24 February 2021) granting independence to the Central Bank of Brazil and established four-year terms for its president and directors (with most of them, including the president, remaining in office beyond the presidential electoral cycle); the privatization of Eletrobras in 2022, a state-owned group oriented towards electricity generation and transmission systems through their own subsidiaries. In 2022, Bolsonaro announced the intention to privatize Petrobras, the giant state-owned oil firm, in the event of his reelection as president, which did not happen.

The effect of the liberal reforms on the performance of the Brazilian economy were very disappointing. After the semi-stagnant period of the Temer government (GDP average growth of only 1.6 per cent pa in 2017–18), economic performance also disappointed under the Bolsonaro administration, even considering the effect of the COVID-19 crisis: the average GDP growth in 2019–22 was 1.5 per cent pa (industry growth was only 0.733 per cent) compared to 3.2 per cent pa on average of the group of emerging and developing economies, according to data from IMF's World Economic Outlook Database. Indeed, economic growth during the Bolsonaro administration fluctuated widely, as a result of a rather erratic and inconsistent economic policy, sometimes contractionary, sometimes expansionist for purely electoral purposes (see Table 5.3).

In 2022, Bolsonaro was defeated by Lula in the presidential elections. After the failure of the orthodox agenda to promote socioeconomic development, the Worker's Party president promised the return of a more active role for the state in this regard during his third term. As one of his first symbolic measures in this direction, Lula indicated his support for former president Rousseff as the new governor of the BRICS' NDB with the aim of providing more activism to this multilateral bank. Furthermore, another important initiative of the Brazilian government, together with China's government, was the announcement of the BCB and the People's Bank of China that they would establish a bilateral local currency swap agreement (reais for yuan) at the amount of R$60 billion – CNY190 billion, valid for three years and with the possibility of renewal. The aim is to facilitate bilateral trade between the two countries.

Brazil's contestation in the international and domestic arena

The description presented in the previous section shows that, in Brazil's experience, the adoption of policies that challenge the liberal global financial order was conditioned by its domestic political dynamics. In the face of alternating power between ideologically divergent governments, it was up to the Workers' Party governments to adopt state capitalist policies, albeit always associating them to some degree with orthodox policies. The intensity with which such policies were adopted was also influenced by exogenous elements associated with the international context in which the different Workers' Party governments were situated. On the other hand, after the impeachment of President Rousseff, financial statecraft was abandoned in favour of the liberal agenda, in both the Temer and Bolsonaro governments, which has been partially reverted in Lula's third government since 2023. Table 5.3 depicts this scenario.

We have already pointed out that Lula's first electoral victory in 2002 was due to the ineffectiveness of the liberal economic agenda prevalent during the 1990s, inspired by the Washington Consensus, to promote socioeconomic development. The first Lula administration, however, faced internal and external constraints that restricted its policy space to adopt policies ideologically divergent from the liberal financial order.

Table 5.3: Brazilian governments between state and liberal capitalism

Lula I (2003–06)	**Lula II (2007–10)**	**Rousseff I (2011–14)**	**Rousseff II (2015–16)**	**Temer (2016–18)**	**Bolsonaro (2019–23)**	**Lula III (2023–…)**
Social-developmentalist policies	Social-developmentalist policies	Social-developmentalist policies	Social-developmentalist policies	Neoliberal policies (liberal reforms)	Neoliberal policies (liberal reforms)	Social-developmentalist policies
Orthodoxy macroeconomic framework	Orthodoxy macroeconomic framework	Orthodoxy and heterodoxy macroeconomic framework	Strict orthodoxy macroeconomic framework	Strict orthodoxy economic policy framework	Strict orthodoxy economic policy framework	Orthodox economic policy framework with some flexibility
Capital account liberalization (with foreign reserves accumulation)	Capital account liberalization (with foreign reserves accumulation)	Capital account liberalization (with some capital controls)	Capital account liberalization	Capital account liberalization	Capital account liberalization	Capital account liberalization
Independent foreign policy	Independent foreign policy	Independent foreign policy	Independent foreign policy	Foreign policy aligned with US interests	Foreign policy aligned with US interests	Independent foreign policy
	BRICS as priority in foreign policy	BRICS as priority in foreign policy	BRICS as priority in foreign policy	BRICS neglected in foreign policy	BRICS neglected in foreign policy (tensions with China)	BRICS as priority in foreign policy

Nevertheless, measures aimed at boosting the domestic market and the policy of accumulating international reserves gave a new dynamic to the national economy, albeit under the auspices of an orthodox macroeconomic policy. In its second term, the Lula government advanced in the contestation of the liberal order on a variety of fronts, but which were strongly associated with the prevailing international conjuncture. With the global financial crisis triggered in 2008, a series of countercyclical policies were adopted, deepening the social-developmentalist strategy of the government. Of particular importance, as already pointed out, was the countercyclical role of state-owned banks after the GFC, highlighting the role of the BNDES in long-term financing: the bank's total disbursements reached 4.3 per cent of GDP in 2010 (see also Chapter 8).

In addition, the Lula government promoted the creation of the Sovereign Wealth Fund of Brazil in 2008, as well as beginning to articulate a relationship with the BRICS.[17] Furthermore, Brazil and Argentina created the Local Currency Payments System (SML), which established a system for settling trade in local currencies without the intermediation of the dollar in Mercosur (the system incorporated Uruguay in 2014 and Paraguay in 2016).[18] This did not mean, however, a break with orthodox-liberal precepts: domestically, the macroeconomic policy framework, although made more flexible, remained under the auspices of the tripod established in 1999; externally, despite the independence of Brazilian foreign policy and the founding of the BRICS, there were no explicit challenges to the liberal order by Brazil.

The first Rousseff government continued to reconcile liberal and state capitalist policies, although it promoted economic policy changes, as seen in the previous section. These changes were not successful, which, added to the adverse domestic and international environment, led to the restriction of policy space for policies challenging the liberal order to continue to be adopted. In terms of the BRICS, an important initiative was the creation of the NDB in 2014, headquartered in Shanghai, China, in which the five partners – Brazil, China, India, Russia, and South Africa – have equal voting power. As a multilateral bank that began to operate in 2016, the NDB proposes to finance investments in infrastructure and sustainable development in the BRICS and has resources for other emerging economies as well.[19] In Rousseff's second term, to achieve confidence-building in the context of a political crisis already underway, the government adhered to the liberal agenda, which, as showed, failed and was not enough to contain the economic and political crises that culminated in her impeachment.

Temer's ascension to the presidency represented the end of a cycle in which elements of state capitalist policies were introduced by Workers' Party governments for around 13 years. Even before Rousseff's impeachment, the then vice-president was showing signs of his alignment with the liberal agenda. At the economic level, the strategy of liberal reforms and the institutionalization of fiscal austerity became hegemonic. At the Ministry of Foreign Affairs, Temer appointed a foreign minister who was not even sure about who and what the BRICS were.[20] In 2018, his government decided to totally zero out the Brazilian Sovereign Fund to pay off public debts. Furthermore, the Temer administration decided to decapitalize the BNDES and to introduce a new unsubsidized long-term interest rate; its total disbursements came to represent only 0.7 per cent of GDP in 2021. Therefore, any Brazilian initiative to challenge the liberal order was then decisively abandoned.

This process was accentuated by the Bolsonaro government, which deepened and radicalized the liberal economic policy that had begun to be implemented by Temer. The Brazilian Sovereign Fund was extinguished by Law No 13,874 on 20 September 2019. On the external front, the articulation with the BRICS reached a critical level, as the Bolsonaro government (as well as the president's sons who held parliamentary positions) uttered a series of hostilities against China, even though it had been Brazil's largest trading partner since 2009. It should be noted, however, that the strong anti-China rhetoric yielded to pragmatism over the course of his term, with bilateral trade relations not being affected and the president's participation in the BRICS summits. The failure of his government on a wide range of fronts, however, prevented his reelection and led to Lula being elected for a third term from 2023. With this, the expectation that state capitalist policies will be implemented again, resuming Brazil's contestation of the liberal financial order, appeared on the near horizon.

Once again, Lula's third term has been characterized by ambiguity: Finance Minister Fernando Haddad has maintained a reasonably orthodox fiscal policy – including a new fiscal framework approved in August 2023 that combines primary fiscal result targets with a rule for public spending, whose growth depends on the performance of revenues, and the guarantee of a minimum level for public investment – while adopting some measures aimed at greater progressivity in income distribution (taxing exclusive and offshore investment funds). In terms of international relations, Lula returned to the discourse of strengthening the South–South dialogue, and while holding the presidency of the G20 in 2024, the Brazilian government launched the motto 'Building a just world and a sustainable planet'.

Overall, therefore, Brazil's experience in contesting the international order reflects the comings and goings of its domestic political process. With the rise of the Workers' Party to power, state capitalist policies were adopted, especially in the wake of the 2008 global financial crisis, albeit always in conciliation with liberal capitalist policies. But the room for manoeuvre has narrowed as the international environment has become hostile to the adoption of measures that compromise the country's credibility in the financial market. Two observations follow from this.

On the one hand, the conditions of the international conjuncture appear as a non-negligible element for the policy space available for measures diverging from the liberal economic agenda to be implemented. On the other hand, this reflects the path-dependent character of the experience of an emerging economy already integrated into financial globalization: once such a process has already taken place, reversing it presents political, economic, and social costs that would probably not be tolerable within the frameworks of liberal democracy. As a result, the tendency is for Brazil's participation in the contestation of the liberal global financial order to remain marked by the ambiguities presented in this chapter.

Conclusion

This chapter examined Brazil's experience in contesting the contemporary global financial order. With its potential disruptive crisis triggered by the 2008 financial crisis and accentuated by the COVID-19 pandemic and the climate and environmental crises, the adoption of state capitalist policies by emerging economies appears as a sign that alternatives to liberal policies, hegemonic in this stage of capitalism, are being tried and implemented. In this process, the internal and external initiatives of the BRICS become particularly illustrative of the challenge to the liberal order, shedding light on how DEEs are resorting to financial statecraft to overcome the negative effects of their internationally subordinated condition in the liberal GFO. Containing and mitigating the adverse effects of asymmetric and subordinated financial insertion has become an indispensable objective.

When compared to its peers, however, Brazil presents an ambiguous stance in contesting the liberal financial order, in which state and liberal capitalist policies are often conflated. We argued that this is due to the country's domestic political dynamics, which have experienced an alternation of power between governments to a greater or lesser extent ideologically aligned with the current global financial order. Moreover, we showed that the adoption of state capitalist policies was accentuated in the wake of the 2008 global financial crisis, which represented a critical event for the order in question. This argument was based on the analysis of policies implemented by Brazilian governments between 2003 and 2022 in light of the theoretical framework proposed by Petry and Nölke (2024) to frame policies as state or liberal capitalist in the context of challenges to the liberal order.

This study therefore contributes to a better understanding of the process of contestation of the liberal order, in general, and the role played by Brazil in this process in particular. More specifically, it shows how domestic politics play a crucial role in this regard. This suggests that understanding how the internal reality of each country can limit or favour the experience of contestation is a condition for understanding the prospects for transforming the global financial order. Moreover, it underlines the importance of examining the experience of other emerging economies, for which the parameters of the liberal financial order are often dysfunctional to their development, reflected in the subordinated condition of their integration into the GFO, which constitutes a promising space for further research.

Notes

1 According to Armijo and Katada (2015, p 43), financial statecraft can be defined as 'the intentional use, by national governments, of domestic or international monetary or financial capabilities for the purpose of achieving ongoing foreign policy goals, whether political, economic, or financial'.

2 According to Paula et al (2024, p 95), financial subordination can be understood as the 'dependent manner in which PEEs [peripheral emerging economies] integrate internationally with the International Financial system. The unstable, pro-cyclical nature of capital flows, which are subject to boom-and-bust cycles strongly determined by exogenous factors, causes macroeconomic instability in the periphery and narrows its policy space.'

3 According to Sato (2012), an international economic order is composed of a financial regime, a monetary regime, and a trade regime. In addition to these international regimes, the author considers the pattern of international distribution of wealth and power and the development strategy implicit in the order.

4 Data extracted from Serra (1982).

5 According to Serra (1982), in 1975 one third of households in Brazil lived on less than the minimum wage.

6 ECLAC (the Spanish acronym is CEPAL) is headquartered in Santiago, Chile, and is one of the five regional commissions of the United Nations.

7 Import substitution industrialization is an industrial and economic policy based on the premise that a country should attempt to reduce its foreign dependency through the local production of industrialized products, that should be done by using domestic market protectionism and also by state-inducement industrialization.

8 During the economic miracle, average GDP growth was 11.2 per cent.

9 For a criticism on the New Consensus on Macroeconomics, see Arestis and Sawyer (2004), for whom the use of an inflation target regime can be a 'straitjacket' for output and employment growth, due to the negative effects of interest rate policy on productive accumulation rate.

10 Social-developmentalism refers to a strategy in which growth of the 'mass domestic market' should be stimulated by both expanding employment and improving income distribution due to redistributive government policies and stimulating consumer credit. For more on this, see Bielschowsky (2012) and Carneiro (2012). It differs from the new-developmentalism strategy, which assumes that countries that manage to implement a catch-up strategy of development should attack the foreign exchange overappreciation tendency, which stems from two structural factors: the 'Dutch disease' and an additional currency appreciation caused by net foreign capital flows that the policy of growth with foreign savings fosters (Bresser-Pereira et al, 2016).

11 According to Prates et al (2020), the proportion of wages in the GDP increased from 35.8 per cent in 2004 to 46.8 per cent in 2014.

12 The rule for adjusting the minimum wage adopted over this period was to add the inflation of the previous year and the GDP growth rate of the second year before the relevant one.

13 The Selic interest rate is the monetary policy interest rate, the key tool used by the Central Bank of Brazil in the implementation of monetary policy.

[14] Operation Car Wash was launched in 2014 by the Brazilian federal police to uncover corruption schemes. As the investigations progressed, a large part of the Brazilian political class became the target of accusations, which led to instabilities in the national political and economic process. Operation Car Wash would be harshly accused of political bias and of persecuting the Workers' Party, which was partially proven by the revelation of collusion between prosecutors and the judge in charge of the case, the result of a hacker attack on the mobile phone of one of the task force's members.

[15] It should be pointed out that in the first month of Bolsonaro's administration (January 2019), he allowed for Boeing to purchase Embraer, a Brazilian aerospace manufacturer, as due to the 'golden share' clause the Brazilian government has a veto power in strategic decisions, such as in the transfer of the shareholding control of a company. In April 2020, however, Boeing gave up the purchase because of the impact of the pandemic crisis on the aviation sector.

[16] These first two reforms were approved by the Temer government. Constitutional Amendment 95 imposing the spending cap prevented any fiscal policy management, which is a fundamental tool for smoothing out the economic cycle.

[17] Following the diplomatic ties established in 2006, the bloc had its first official summit in 2009, with Brazil, Russia, India, and China as members; later, in 2011, South Africa was incorporated to the bloc.

[18] In 2022, commercial transactions through the system totalled around BRL 5.5 billion (BCB, 2023). Although it has modest adherence, the system has attracted small and medium-sized importing and exporting companies, as it eliminates the need to access dollar exchange markets and thus enables a significant reduction in trade transaction costs (UNCTAD, 2015).

[19] For an analysis of the creation process of the NDB and an assessment of the first five years of its operation, see Batista Jr (2021). According to this author, the bank's evolution was slow and hesitant, for political reasons, falling short of the original ambitious design, which envisioned the establishment of a global, modern, innovative, and technically professional development bank.

[20] See Forum (2016).

References

Alami, I., Alves, C., Bonizzi, B., Kaltenbrunner, A., Koddenbrock, K., Kvangraven, I., and Powell, J. (2023) 'International financial subordination: A critical research agenda', *Review of International Political Economy*, 30(4): 1360–86.

Armijo L.E. and Katada, S.N. (2015) 'Theorizing the financial statecraft of emerging powers', *New Political Economy*, 20(1): 42–62.

Arestis, P. and Sawyer, M. (2004) *Re-examining Monetary and Fiscal Policy for the 21st Century*, Cheltenham: Edward Elgar.

Barbosa Filho, N. (2010) 'Latin America: Counter-cyclical policy in Brazil: 2008–09', *Journal of Globalization and Development*, 1(1): 1–12.

Batista Jr, P.N. (2021) *O Brasil Não Cabe no Quintal de Ninguém*, São Paulo: LeYa Brasil.

Banco Central do Brasil – BCB (2023), Available from: https://www3.bcb.gov.br/sgspub/localizarseries/localizarSeries.do?method=prepararTelaLocalizarSeries [Accessed 20 October 2023].

Bielschowsky, R. (2012) 'Estratégia de desenvolvimento e as três frentes de expansão no Brasil', *Economia e Sociedade*, 21, special issue: 729–48.

Boito Júnior, A. and Berringer T. (2013) 'Brasil: classes sociais, neodesenvolvimentismo e política externa nos governos Lula e Dilma', *Revista de Sociologia e Política*, 21(47): 31–8.

Bresser-Pereira, L.C., Oreiro, J.L., and Marconi, N. (2016) *Developmental Macroeconomics*, London: Routledge.

Carneiro, R.M. (2012) 'Velhos e novos desenvolvimentismos', *Economia e Sociedade* 21, special issue: 749–78.

Datafolha (2015) *'Avaliação Datafolha da Presidente Dilma'*, [online] December, Available from: https://www1.folha.uol.com.br/paywall/signup.shtml?https://www1.folha.uol.com.br/infograficos/2015/02/118652-avaliacao-datafolha-da-presidente-dilma.shtml. [Accessed 10 January 2024].

Forum (2016) 'Serra se enrola e inclui Argentina entre os BRICS', *Forum*, [online] 17 September, Available from: https://revistaforum.com.br/global/2016/9/17/serra-se-enrola-inclui-argentina-entre-os-brics-17429.html [Accessed 10 January 2024].

Grabel, I. (2018) 'Toward a pluripolar global financial architecture? The Bretton Woods institutions and the new landscape of developmental finance', *Review of Radical Political Economics*, 50(4): 1–7.

Ianoni, M. (2018) *Estado e Coalizões no Brasil (2003–2016): Social-desenvolvimentismo e neoliberalismo*, Rio de Janeiro: Contraponto.

IPEADATA (2023), Available from: http://ipeadata.gov.br/Default.aspx [Accessed 18 August 2023].

Lake, D.A., Martin, L., and Risse, T. (2021) 'Challenges to the liberal order: Reflections on international organization', *International Organization*, 75(2): 225–57.

Mishkin, F. (2000) 'What should central banks do?', *Federal Reserve Bank of St Louis Review*, 82(6): 1–13.

Musacchio, A. and Lazzarini, S.G. (2013) *Reinventing State Capitalism: Leviathan in Business, Brazil and Beyond*, Cambridge, MA: Harvard University Press.

Nölke, A. (2017) 'Brexit: Towards a new global phase of organized capitalism?', *Competition & Change*, 21(3): 230–241.

Nölke, A. (2022) *Post-Corona Capitalism: The Alternatives Ahead*, Bristol: Bristol University Press.

Nölke, A. and May, C. (2019) 'Liberal versus organised capitalism: A historical-comparative perspective', in T. Gerőcs and M. Szanyi (eds) (2019) *Market Liberalism and Economic Patriotism in the Capitalist World-System*, London: Springer.

Oreiro, J.L. and Paula, L.F. (2021) *Macroeconomia da Estagnação Brasileira*, Rio de Janeiro: Alta Books.

Paula, L.F. (2011) *Financial Liberalization and Economic Performance: Brazil at the Crossroads*, London: Routledge.

Paula, L.F., Modenesi, A., and Pires, M. (2015) 'The tale of the contagion of two crises and policy responses in Brazil: A case of (Keynesian) policy coordination?', *Journal of Post Keynesian Economics*, 37(3): 408–35.

Paula, L.F., Fritz, B., and Prates, D. (2017) 'Keynes at the periphery: Currency hierarchy and challenges for economic policy in emerging economies', *Journal of Post Keynesian Economics*, 40(2): 183–202.

Paula, L.F., Leal, J.L., and Ferreira, M. (2024) 'Financial subordination of peripheral emerging economies: A Keynesian-Structuralist approach', *Review of Keynesian Economics*, 12(1): 94–117.

Petry, J. (2023) 'Beyond ports, roads and railways: Chinese economic statecraft, the Belt and Road Initiative and the politics of financial infrastructures', *European Journal of International Relations*, 29(2): 319–351.

Petry, J. and Nölke, A. (2024) *The BRICS and the Global Financial Order: Liberalism Contested?*, Cambridge: Cambridge University Press.

Prates, D.M., Paula, L.F., and Fritz, B. (2020) 'Varieties of developmentalism: A critical assessment of the PT governments', *Latin American Perspectives*, 47(1): 45–64.

Saad-Filho, A. and Feil, F. (2023) 'From climate change to sustainable and inclusive economies: A policy agenda', *Critical Sociology*, 50(1): 49–63.

Sato, E. (2012) *Economia e Política das Relações Internacionais*, Belo Horizonte: Fino Traço.

Serra, J. (1982) 'Ciclos e mudanças estruturais na economia brasileira do pós-guerra', in L.G. Belluzzo and R. Coutinho (eds) *Desenvolvimento Capitalista no Brasil: Ensaios sobre a Crise*, São Paulo: Brasiliense.

Singer, A. (2018) *O Lulismo em Crise: Um Quebra-cabeça do Período Dilma (2011–2016)*, São Paulo: Cia das Letras.

UNCTAD (2015) *Trade and Development Report – 2015: Making the International Financial Architecture Work for Development*, Geneva: United Nations Conference on Trade and Development.

Williamson, J. (1990) 'What should the World Bank think about the Washington Consensus?' *The World Bank Research Observer*, 15(2): 251–64.

6

Relaxing the Survival Constraint: India's Financial Statecraft in Search of Domestic Autonomy

Anush Kapadia and Fathimath Musthaq

Introduction

In this chapter, we propose to understand financial statecraft as the use of monetary, financial, and regulatory levers to reduce a state's *survival constraint*, which necessarily has both domestic and international manifestations. The *state's* capacity to relax its domestic survival constraint rests on a set of social compacts or political settlements between the state and society. For India, we identify the evolving bargain between the state and the three dominant classes – big business, rich farmers, professional class – (Bardhan, 1999) as central to explaining India's financial statecraft. This political settlement yields a national *economy* with particular weaknesses, namely a heavy reliance on the import of oil, the import-demand for capital and consumer goods (the latter particularly driven by India's aspirational salaried class which results in chronic *current account deficits*), and domestically bound accumulation strategies particularly in non-tradable sectors by India's big businesses, which yields a stagnant economy with little innovation and marginal exports (Nölke et al, 2021). Meanwhile, rich farmers continue to rely on state subsidies while taxes on urban elites are low, contributing to a structural *fiscal deficit*. This is compounded by a highly mobilized and largely poor electorate that makes particularistic demands that yield particularistic welfare consumables. While this initial bargain has evolved over the years – capital becoming discursively dominant, the bureaucracy relatively less autonomous, some rich farmers morphing into businesses – the net result for India's survival constraint is relatively unchanged. The signal change is on the external account, with external *private* debt issued by a handful of large firms substituting for external public debt helping to relax the balance of payments constraint.

The political settlement in India thus produces a chronic current account deficit and a structural fiscal deficit which the state manages through a variety of state policies that we identify as financial statecraft. It manages the country's current account deficit through the nurturing of enclave sectors such as the IT and software industries, strict regulations on the capital account (favouring equity over debt flows), and extensive foreign exchange management (reserve accumulation and interventions in forex markets). Remittances are also a critical prop, so the Indian state is expanding the international use of its mobile payment technology in key remittance corridors.

We develop this idea of financial statecraft through a sympathetic critique of Armijo and Katada's original concept. Built on the idea of 'economic statecraft', the concept of financial statecraft carries with it an allegiance to foreign policy objectives (Armijo and Katada, 2015). In her rendering of the concept, Armijo includes foreign policy orientation as one of the three conditions for classifying a policy as financial statecraft, along with intentionality and the use of monetary and financial resources (Armijo, 2019). Armijo further elaborates: 'political leaders' actions that are primarily oriented towards achieving domestic goals thus fall outside of the scope of international financial statecraft' (Armijo, 2019, p 28).

An exclusive focus on foreign policy objectives might be limiting. As Baldwin (1985) notes, the study of statecraft originally encompassed both domestic policy objectives as well as foreign policy goals. It was merely an accident of history that students of international relations gravitated toward the concept and tied it to foreign policy goals while scholars of domestic politics more or less abandoned the term (Baldwin, 1985). Given that the original concept has the bandwidth to accommodate both dimensions, we argue limiting it to one impoverishes the analysis of financial statecraft, particularly for subordinate countries. For one thing, the present rendering of the concept contains an implicit bias towards 'offensive' measures, which is problematic given that subordinate countries are more likely to engage in 'defensive' financial statecraft. Furthermore, what can appear as offensive statecraft, such as the strategic management of outward capital flows (internationally oriented), can in fact be defensive measures to maintain the internal balance of forces or the political settlement (domestically oriented). For example, if we go by the original definition of financial statecraft, it is difficult to conclude that India does any financial statecraft, since none of it can be classified as pertaining to or furthering purely 'foreign policy' objectives. What appears as financial statecraft in India, such as attempts to launch an Indian rupee settlement mechanism in international trade, lobbying along with BRICS peers for more representation in global financial governance (Liu and Papa, 2022), the gradual liberalization of India's capital account, and its extensive monetary management, we argue, are primarily geared toward relaxing its survival constraint on both domestic and international fronts.

In reconceiving financial statecraft along these lines, we bring together insights from the 'international financial subordination' (IFS) and financial statecraft literatures. We read the state's survival constraint as another way of understanding IFS though in a slightly different but compatible vein from Alami et al (2023). Along with IFS scholars, we see India occupying a subordinate position in the global economy, and sharing with similarly subordinate states features such as low labour productivity, the production of low value-added goods, a regressive taxation system, a narrow fiscal base, and vulnerability to global liquidity shocks; in short, the makings of India's survival constraint. In a slightly different vein from IFS scholars, we argue that the survival constraint binds all agents in the global financial system, including the hegemon, but differentially. Monetary power *is* a unit's ability to bend this fundamental constraint further than others. States naturally differ in their abilities to relax their survival constraint, and economies differ in scale: these variations then generate a hierarchy of global currency and finance.

Armijo's five attributes of state capabilities viz financial statecraft (Chapter 3, this volume) can be read as the fruits of especially domestic collective action on the part of states to build military-industrial economies and polities in the context of an unequal global division of labour. These capabilities provide a salutary link to domestic political settlements within states that may or may not be institutionalized in ways that produce such capacities. As such, highlighting these capacities actually enables us to follow Alami in observing that 'financial statecraft and state–finance institutional arrangements in developing and emerging economies must be conceived as the *material condensation of two types of social relations, IFS and domestic class configurations*', (Alami, Chapter 2, this volume, emphasis in original).

Our application of Minsky's concept of the survival constraint to states and economies is a preliminary attempt to use India's financial statecraft to illustrate how IFS and domestic class configurations come together. Our proposal to use the concept of the survival constraint to reconceptualize financial statecraft does three things: 1) renders explicit the *intimate connection* between the domestic and the international survival constraints, which then 2) clarifies the *domestic political settlement* that shapes financial statecraft, and 3) makes explicit the *hierarchy* in the global economy by placing both 'offensive' and 'defensive' statecraft, or in the words of the editors of this volume, 'reach of state capacity' and 'degree of state capacity', respectively (Petry and Nölke, Chapter 1, this volume), on a continuum. In foregrounding the domestic political economy, we agree with Alami that 'being attentive to domestic class-based interests, strategies, and conflicts is essential to explaining the variegated ways in which states navigate and negotiate the constraints and pressures of IFS' (Alami, Chapter 2, this volume).

A state has to manage two survival constraints: that of its own balance sheet (fiscal account) and that of the national economy (current account). While the two balances are linked, the relationship is far from mechanical. Facing *deficits* on both fiscal and trade dimensions, the Indian state has evolved a set of institutional practices, 'financial statecraft', that manage these deficit constraints in a manner that reflects both the domestic political settlement and the country's location in the global division of labour. The state's capacity to relax the domestic survival constraint, and the terms on which it does so, create both limitations and possibilities for relaxing the nation's international survival constraint.

To build our case, in the second section, we first provide a reframing of financial statecraft that may be more applicable to subordinate, down-hierarchy countries, that is, most countries in the world. We do so, as previously mentioned, by building on Minsky's concept of the survival constraint, applying it to political units, and making explicit the relationship between the domestic and international survival constraint. We use the case of India to illustrate this approach to understanding financial statecraft. In the third section, we note the importance of embedding domestic politics into financial statecraft analysis by illustrating the political settlements that shape India's response to its fiscal and current account deficits. In the fourth section, we detail the ways in which India relaxes its survival constraints through the management of the capital account and interventions in financial markets, that is, through financial statecraft. We conclude in the fifth section by reflecting on the relationship between 'coping' with and relaxing the survival constraint.

Financial statecraft as relaxing the survival constraint

Hyman Minsky used the concept of a 'survival constraint' to show the pressures on economic units emanating from financial obligations; we apply this idea to political units (Kapadia, 2024). Capitalism is a cash nexus; all economic units require a positive cash inflow to survive to the next day. The source of this cash can be varied – savings, earnings, selling, or borrowing – but cash inflow has to be *greater* than cash outflow else the unit is dead. The configuration of the survival constraint binds all units together to form an interlocking set of balance sheets that is an economy, and in the international context, an interlocking set of national balance sheets that constitutes the world economy. But this interlocking is always *hierarchical*: some units have a more relaxed survival constraint than others thanks to historical legacies and (with national economies) their position in the global division of labour. Such balance sheets can in turn relax or tighten the constraint on other units.

Financial statecraft in reference to the fisc has two faces because states, like all balance sheets in principle, can raise funds domestically or internationally. Domestically, states can either tax or borrow; internationally, states can borrow either in their own currency or in world money. The more autonomous a state is domestically in terms of taxing and borrowing power, the less it has to rely on global finance. Even then, a state depending on domestic savers might crowd out private businesses, pushing them to finance globally and thereby creating other vulnerabilities that require a particular kind of financial statecraft to manage (of course, such private foreign borrowing might be repressed which might affect national productivity itself).

The question of financial statecraft comes down to the relation of the state to financial structures. Financial structures might come to be institutionalized in particular ways, so that the question of statecraft seems to devolve to a question about the relationship between the state and financial institutions. Institutions can of course aim to alter underlying structural features of an economy including financial ones. But focusing on institutions without bringing in the underlying structures gives us an incomplete picture.

As mentioned in the Introduction to this volume, states can have a range of relationships to international and domestic financial institutions from subordination to autonomy to influence. The editors define 'degree of state capacity' precisely in terms of the state's ability to 'exercise power vis-à-vis financial actors/markets' (Petry and Nölke, Introduction, this volume). In cash flow terms, if a state is subordinated to domestic financial actors, what this means is that it is unable to impose sufficient taxes or borrow sufficiently from these actors through their purchases of state debt. A state unable to relax its survival constraint domestically will then be compelled to do so internationally; it may then be forced into a financially subordinate position internationally.

The view from the survival constraint offers a way of understanding why hierarchy defines the international system. A state sits at the top of the *domestic* hierarchy of money because, as a legitimate political contract covering all economic units, it can force cash flows to itself (through taxation) at greater scale and robustness than other private balance sheets in its jurisdiction. A state's location in the *global* hierarchy of money similarly depends on the degree to which it is able to relax its survival constraint internationally. Having an 'offensive' or 'defensive' posture towards global finance rests centrally on the degree of financial autonomy a state and other balance sheets have at home. It also depends on the underlying trade balance of the economy which it governs. Defensive moves are those that seek to *relax* the state's survival constraint domestically and/or internationally. A state can be said to be acting offensively when it is using existing financial power, that is, an already relaxed survival constraint, to reshape international financial structures and influence other states.

Thinking through the survival constraint therefore helps us clarify what is meant in the literature by defensive and offensive forms of financial statecraft (Armijo and Katada, 2015) which this volume's editors have put in their own terms of autonomy (degree of state capacity) versus influence (reach of state capacity). Defensive moves are those that seek to *relax* the state and its economy's survival constraint domestically and/or internationally. Since money is fungible, relaxing the survival constraint can occur on either the domestic or international front. Benjamin Cohen's 'power to delay' (2008) thus applies equally to domestic finance (Cohen, 2008) viz a state's ability to overcome 'original sin' and borrow long in its own currency as it does when it borrows internationally. The *terms* on which the survival constraint is relaxed naturally differ substantially depending on whether it is domestic or foreign counterparties/currencies involved, but the function remains the same viz a relaxation of the survival constraint.

A state can be said to be acting offensively when it is using existing financial power, that is, an already relaxed survival constraint, to achieve some policy objective. Offensive action might take several forms: trying to get other state and non-state actors to transact in its currency, trying to recycle surpluses accumulated from trade in a way that pursues its economic and foreign policy objectives, blocking access to key financial infrastructure which the particular state controls. But none of these moves are conceivable for a state tightly disciplined by its survival constraint on either front.

A state that has little trouble attracting flows of capital into its debt is one with a highly relaxed survival constraint. It can enjoy such a position for various reasons: because it houses a substantial international financial centre (network capacity, in Armijo's terms), its economy represents a substantial piece of global GDP, or both, such as the current hegemon. Such a state is then in a position to act offensively in terms of its global financial statecraft. A country with substantial surpluses on its current account might on the other hand have a Dutch disease issue where it is trying to prevent currency appreciation and/or subsiding its exports, and/or looking for profitable/safe sources for its accumulated reserves. Either way, such a nation, for example China, is no longer severely constrained by its international survival constraint.

On a conceptual note, we think that it is difficult to definitively declare whether currency manipulation or banking sanctions are primarily internationally oriented unless a state is powerful enough to take on the role of rewarding and punishing other states. India lacks the sophisticated and liquid financial markets that the US has, or the large investible surplus of China. The resources at its disposal are rather meagre. What India has in terms of tools is the state's ability to regulate the financial system thanks to decades of financial repression managed by a relatively autonomous monetary bureaucracy at the Reserve Bank of India (RBI). Thus, for a down-hierarchy balance sheet country like India, notwithstanding its size and regional significance, the survival constraint poses critical challenges, particularly in light of twin deficits, in successfully executing offensive financial statecraft. Consequently, we may think of the Indian state as having considerable power and capacity to repress its domestic financial system, but with little international reach, which places it in quadrant C, 'domestic autonomy' (see Petry and Nölke, Introduction, this volume). Yet this is autonomy of a particular, subordinate kind. The political settlement underlying the Indian state means that it lacks fiscal capacity to tax powerful domestic constituencies. This puts greater pressure on the monetary and financial arms of statecraft to relax India's survival constraint through *debt* held by the nationalized banking system rather than taxation. Again, the nature of the political settlement has direct *financial* implications.

Political and material constraints

At first blush, it might seem odd to apply the survival constraint to a state. After all, the state has the power to tax. In a commodity money world, taxing in gold and silver money gives it direct access to resources. But, following the 'chartalist' argument (retailed now under 'Modern Monetary Theory', or MMT), a state can also issue fiat or chartal tokens that subjects can use to pay back the tax imposed on them, giving such tokens real economic value. A sovereign state can never have affordability issues according to this view.

The chartalist argument ignores two critical elements. First, chartalists ignore the central fact of politics. The institutionalization of taxation is perhaps the most elemental form of financial statecraft. Indeed, almost the entire burden of successful state formation rests on this; state capacity in general is largely *fiscal* capacity since fiscal power is a condition for all other powers, especially coercive powers. But taxation is always a *political* bargain. Fiscal capacity is a function of domestic social pacts and political settlements (Schumpeter, 1991). Important also to note here is that because the survival constraint is ultimately a liquidity constraint (does the unit have sufficient 'cash' to survive?), the modulation of a state's survival constraint comes down to the political economy of its relationship with merchant banking institutions, domestic or foreign. States always have a vested interest in controlling a merchant banking function for their debt. Indeed, the financial statecraft of successful, autonomous states revolves around managing its relationship to *domestic* creditors.

Thus, for all the talk of the American debt being held by foreigners, it is worth noting that for most rich nations, the vast bulk of their total state debt is held domestically; for example, foreign entities hold only about 33 per cent of all outstanding US government debt (PGPF, 2023). This is exactly the opposite for poorer nations whose public debt is largely held externally, increasingly in the hands of private creditors (World Bank Development Data Group, 2021). The financial statecraft of successful states entails cultivating a domestic creditor constituency. It is critical to emphasize this fact of domestically held debt lest we place too much emphasis on financial repression as the cause of sovereign debt being held domestically. Beyond financial repression, there are good financial reasons for domestic institutions to hold the debt of their own sovereign.

A state's merchant banking function, the means by which it relaxes its survival constraint, can take various institutional forms from central banks themselves buying debt to primary dealer systems, nationalized banks, or hedge funds. Central banks were of course invented to turn taxation power into financial power by issuing 'money' secured by state debt; this was especially useful as war finance. At their inception, central banks were very much political settlements between financial oligarchs and feudal state power. There is a synergistic relationship between states and finance up to a point since the successful marketing of state debt can benefit from a deep and liquid financial market for 'government stock'.

Yet more critical than the institutional form is the *nationality of the counterparty* to a state's debt: are a state's creditors largely foreign or domestic, and what are their exit options? One could approximate an index of international financial subordination based on whether a nation's debt is held primarily domestically or externally. Globalized finance is a source for funding state debt, especially for 'emerging' nations. But in a world of highly mobile and liquid capital searching for yield makes the already hard work of domestic state formation – the forging of political pacts to increase domestic fiscal/financial capacity – much harder to undertake for developing nations. When faced with a choice between cheaper but potentially hot-money debt denominated in a foreign currency and more expensive but stickier domestic debt, state elites and technocrats often find that they lack the time and space to build political coalitions and the robust institutions to source domestic debt. The survival constraint is a liquidity constraint, and liquidity kills you quick. This was exactly the situation in which Indian technocrats found themselves in the late 1980s, leading to an overloading of short-term, private external debt that made the country highly vulnerable to an external shock in 1991 (Joshi and Little, 1994).

The second oversight in chartalism pertains to global hierarchy. No nation, especially developing ones, are self-sufficient economically; a national economy has *material* constraints on what can be achieved domestically. Some basic national needs like food and fuel might have to be imported. While India overcame external reliance on food grain imports by the late 1960s thanks to its Green Revolution, it continues to depend on imports of petroleum, oil, and lubricants for a full 87 per cent of its needs (Ministry of Petroleum & Natural Gas, 2023). This naturally then forms a major component of its current account deficit and thus its balance of payments (RBI, 2023b). As one prominent economic journalist observes, the three traditional bugbears of the Indian economy have been the '3Fs': foreign exchange, food, and fuel (Damodaran, 2020).

Countries thereby require the rest of the world, not just their own taxpayers, to accept their creditworthiness to some extent. In a world of a global cash nexus, this means ensuring a sufficient inflow of whatever counts as world money (either from trade or finance) to access vital foreign goods and relax its material survival constraint. Economic and political settlements will have to be made internationally in order to source world money to access these vital goods. From this point of view, mercantilism is a completely rational response to relaxing a state's international survival constraint, especially for down-hierarchy countries. Yet, according to data from the RBI, over the past decade, India has run a current account deficit averaging $30 billion (see Figure 6.3).

The degree to which a state can relax its underlying survival constraint therefore revolves around three features: 1) the state's ability to tax and borrow domestically, 2) the economy's position on the trade account, and 3) the state's ability/willingness to attract foreign flows either in the form of (public/private) debt or private equity. As previously argued, each of these elements is embedded in a particular political economy. A state's ability to borrow domestically is primarily a function of its domestic political settlement. Politics affects the trade balance through the success or failure of domestic industrial policy. The attractiveness of a nation viz foreign investors depends on where it positions itself geopolitically and the degree to which powerful domestic actors support foreign investment in the country.

This understanding of the survival constraint gives us a framework to analyze any country's financial statecraft. Taking the Indian case, we begin by asking how India's domestic political settlement leaves its imprint on the two dimensions of the survival constraint: the *state's* fiscal capacity, on the one hand, and the *nation's* balance of trade, on the other.

India's political economy and its international survival constraint

> It was already clear by 1986 that we were in an internal debt trap which would soon engulf us in an external debt trap (Patel, 1992, p 43).

In this section, we unpack the political economy of India's domestic survival constraint, which then shapes its international survival constraint. We focus primarily on India's two deficits, the state's fiscal deficit and the nation's current account deficit, and how these are underpinned by the country's class configuration and political settlement. Our analysis will demonstrate that key to understanding India's recent international financial statecraft is the institutional *disarticulation* of its two deficits.

While the current account deficit has widened through the decades, the Indian state, through its fiscal-monetary machine, has managed to keep the public debt domestic, and considerably reduced external public debt relative to its peers, by shifting the external debt burden on to certain private entities that now borrow abroad in US dollars. On the one hand, this disarticulation is a signal achievement because it considerably relaxes the Indian *state's* survival constraint by precluding it from having to borrow abroad to fund the current account deficit. Yet the Indian state does socialize some of the risk taken on by these private borrowers through another element of financial statecraft, namely its management of the rupee. This shift from public to private external debt has occurred in an economic context of rising dependence on foreign imports, especially oil from the Gulf and consumer goods from China, and the continuing dearth of exports, furthering the *nation's* dependence on *private* balance sheets to relax India's international survival constraint. The secure embedding of some Indian *firms* in circuits of global capital has now become critical to relaxing the *nation's* survival constraint viz funding its current account deficit.

Fiscal deficit and financial statecraft

The nature of India's political settlement is such that the state's fiscal deficit is part of the deep structure (Bardhan, 1999). Elites constituencies in urban India are hard to tax; property transactions, for instance, are routinely undertaken with substantial 'black money' (Kumar, 2017). Rich farmers from dominant castes receive all manner of support prices and subsidized inputs, including fertilizer and credit. Compounding this, a machine-based, patronage politics plays out as a welter of particularizing welfare schemes are floated in exchange for electoral support at both central and federal ('state') levels (Chatterjee, 2019). On the revenue side, capitalists resort to baroque tax dodges through tax havens; they tend to strike particularist deals for particular favours and contracts rather than forming a collective tax settlement with the state. The inability to tax is coupled with the compulsion to spend largely on consumption rather than capital-forming items, resulting in structural deficits.[1]

Finding durable and secure funding for this deficit is therefore a critical enabler of India's political settlement itself. The institutional means to domestically fund this structural fiscal deficit were created back in the 1960s when Indian banks were nationalized. Nationalization meant that the government mandated two key operations that relaxed its survival constraint: first, it 'preempted' household savings that were lodged in

Figure 6.1: Ownership of central government securities

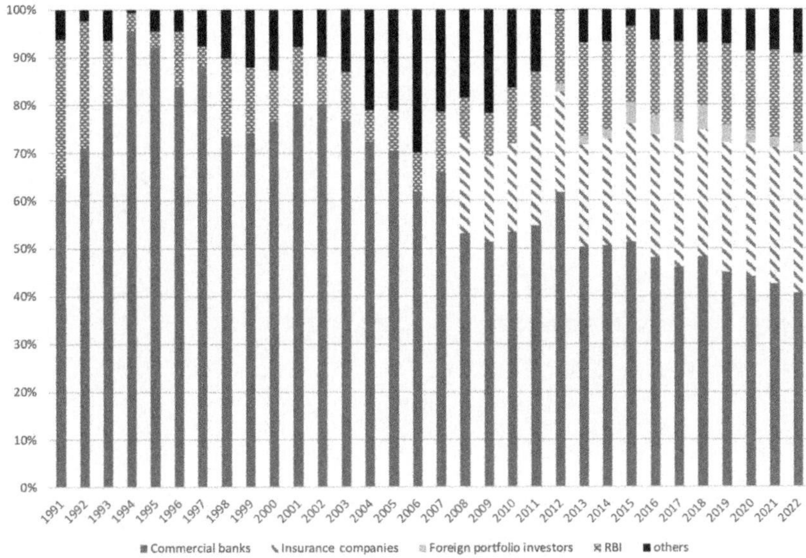

Source: RBI (nd)

these banks by declaring that a 'statutory liquidity ratio' of bank assets be in the form of government debt. This form of 'financial repression' was supplemented by a bank branch expansion programme that saw the expansion of the rural banks to monetize rural savings. Household savings, amounting to 20–25 per cent of GDP for much of the period, found their way into the nationalized banks that were then forced to fund the government deficit (see Figure 6.1). This 'fiscal-monetary machine' (Kapadia, 2017) enabled India to avoid the standard Third World debt problems for much of the postwar period, even at the cost of financial repression, because it limited the extent to which the Indian state had to seek savings abroad. Yet given the safety of government debt, banks routinely hold more than the required amounts of public debt on their books, illustrating that more than mere 'repression' is at work. Important to note here is that big businesses dominated this nationalized financial structure that mobilized the nation's savings (Bardhan, 1999), a trend that we continue to see to this day (Sengupta and Vardhan, 2023). Figure 6.1 shows that in 2022 domestic commercial banks held 37 per cent of total government securities (down from 55 per cent in 1991), whereas foreign investors held a mere 1.6 per cent.

The ability of the domestic fiscal monetary machine to deliver fiscal autonomy came under strain as the politics of the domestic survival constraint shifted in the 1980s, particularly in the later part of the decade with the rise of farmers movements, lower caste movements, and the

Figure 6.2: Long-term external debt: public and publicly guaranteed debt (PPG) vs private nonguaranteed debt (PrNG)

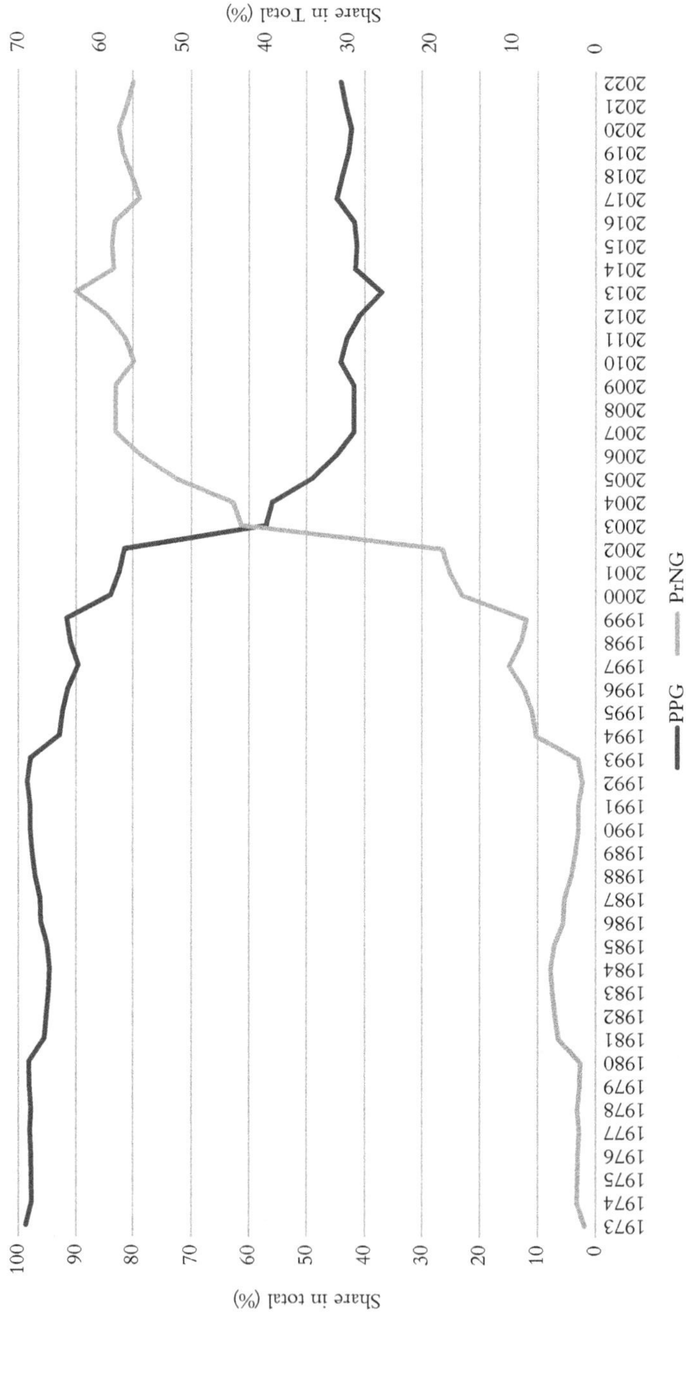

Source: World Bank International Debt Statistics

fracturing of one-party dominance and the cobbling together of a series of unstable coalition governments. Populism with subsidies, salary increases for public servants, and various other transfers meant that the fiscal deficit started to get out of hand. This then meant further pre-emption of household savings through the nationalized banking system. By the end of the decade, the combined pre-emptions into the fiscal debt stood at a full 53 per cent of bank assets. This started topping out into the central bank itself through direct monetization of the deficit, spilling inevitably into inflation (Mohan, 2008).

The fiscal-monetary machine had overheated, so the Indian state had to move to external debt in increasing amounts at the margin, thereby changing its mode of financial statecraft. With the survival constraint tightening domestically, it was actually loosening internationally in the 1980s. While 'concessional' finance became harder to access thanks to a round of Third-World debt workouts, private finance through recycled petrodollars now finally found its way into Indian sovereign debt just as its domestic debt engine was overheating. This was more expensive and for shorter durations than concessional debt, but it was still cheaper than domestic debt. As ever, the siren song of cheap global finance turned out to be deadly, and overexposure to short-term foreign sovereign debt left the country critically vulnerable such that even a modest oil shock in 1990–91 pushed it into a full-blown balance of payments crisis (Joshi and Little, 1994). Indian financial statecraft had made a critical error.

This episode is important since it appears to be seared into the minds of technocrats and central bankers such that exposure to short-term *sovereign* debt has never again been a feature of how the state manages its survival constraint. Subsequent to the policy error of the 1980s, Indian financial statecraft had given the Indian state substantial degrees of fiscal autonomy. There is discipline viz the state's internal survival constraint, and it comes in no small measure from the *ideology* of fiscal prudence that prevails in policy circles. Since the global financial markets share this ideology, there is also perhaps a sense among technocrats that if the fiscal deficit gets out of hand, there would be a risk of capital flight, especially from highly liquid portfolio flows, which could jeopardize the international survival constraint. But India's *domestic* fiscal-monetary machine means that when the state needs to ramp up debt to respond to crises like COVID-19, it can do so at a substantial scale (9 per cent of GDP) without a threat of capital flight.

With the partial opening of the capital account, a new configuration emerged whereby the temporary entwining of the two deficits during the 1980s, internal and external, was fundamentally undone. India's external debt situation had completely shifted by the early 2000s (see Figure 6.2). Whereas the earlier period saw the *nation's* current account deficit funded almost entirely by flows to *sovereign* debt from concessional sources with the capital account totally repressed, the current period sees a complete flip. The current account deficit remains (notwithstanding substantial invisibles earnings), but after the early 1990s balance of payments crisis, *sovereign* external debt is now negligible while *private* debt, still highly managed but allowed only for certain firms, has taken its place. How this private debt is sourced and its risks managed is an important element of India's financial statecraft.

Once the dust settled after post-crisis reforms, capital inflows came to be 'liberalized' with foreign sovereign debt run off, standing today at very moderate levels (Ministry of Finance, 2023). The fiscal deficit remains somewhat of an outlier in GDP terms compared to other emerging markets, but the real outlier is in terms of interest costs (Eichengreen et al, 2023, p 7). These elevated costs of domestic funds can perhaps be read as an insurance premium for a relaxed survival constraint and fiscal autonomy from foreign capital.

Current account deficit and the tightening international survival constraint

Fiscal autonomy is not the same thing as autonomy for the national economy as a whole. The current account deficit remains thanks to continued dependence on oil imports, a failed export policy, and import-substitution policies. While some portion of these imports are refined and re-exported, thereby earning foreign exchange, the vast bulk is consumed locally.

Cheap consumer goods, from textiles to electronics to key pharmaceutical inputs from the China trade, keep the salaried 'middle class' happy but do not create the jobs needed for the largest population in the world which depends on revenue expenditures on welfare by the state even as these expenditures are stagnant and even declining as a share of GDP thanks to fiscal orthodoxy. India's growth might be driven in part by these salaried masses, but it has largely been a jobless growth. The consumption that this class drives might now be reaching saturation point (Roy, 2019) and therefore declining as a source of aggregated demand even as COVID-19 ramped up existing inequalities.

The other perennial import is foreign oil, and even there the state attempted import substitution in the form of domestic extraction. This proved insufficient for domestic needs, and coupled with the import substitution industrialization strategy's inability to produce sufficient exports, meant that the current account deficit largely comprised oil imports (Banik and Velamuri, 2023), leaving the external account vulnerable to oil price shocks.

This current account deficit is therefore structural in a real-economy sense, and supported by the political settlement. The failure of industrial policy to either galvanize the export sector or successfully substitute imports tightens the international survival constraint. A brief tryst with a current account surplus in the early 2000s (see Figure 6.3) led to what turned out to be a false sense of export optimism and a rush for signing free trade agreements with ASEAN nations (Banik and Velamuri, 2023, p 39).

But since then, owing to jobless growth and a widening current account deficit, India has withdrawn from the Regional Comprehensive Economic Partnership with Asian economies and moved to bring in 'production-linked incentives' to import-substitute away some of its critical vulnerabilities. Many such industrial policy schemes have been floated from the National Manufacturing Policy of 2012 to 2015's Make in India Policy, yet the domestic political economy precludes a relationship of 'embedded autonomy' between state and business even while the trade account remains relatively open. Thus manufacturing remains stagnant at around 15 per cent of GDP (Chakraborty and Nagaraj, 2020). Many of India's new oligarchs draw their wealth from 'rent-thick', non-tradable sectors that depend centrally on crony-type relations with the state, sectors like mining, commodities, finance, infrastructure, real estate, steel, utilities, and telecoms services (Walton, 2020, p 232). The country's vulnerability on the trade account and the resulting loss of growth and jobs potential does not affect this class in their economic enclaves.

The inability to earn sufficient foreign exchange to pay for imports rounds out our perennial bugbears of the 3Fs (food, fuel, foreign exchange). The need for a foreign source of savings is driven by real-side factors but only at the margin. Prior to the 2000s, India's trade balance hovered in the negative territory but in the relatively safe zone of 2–3 per cent of GDP. This only went out of control thanks to exogenous shocks, the earliest being failed monsoons and a resulting food crisis that led to the requirement to import grains in the late 1950s (thus spurring the Green Revolution and self-sufficiency in grain stocks). For the bulk of the post-independence period, foreign savings to pay for imports were sourced from multilaterals for the most part on concessional terms. Today it is managed by a mix of invisible earnings and borrowed foreign exchange reserves.

The current account deficit would be a lot worse but for two contributions to invisibles/services earnings at opposite ends of the class spectrum. Software services of course grab the headlines, bringing in about 33 per cent of India's invisible earnings (see Figure 6.4). Yet Figure 6.5 speaks to the important role played by inward remittances. Inward remittances and local withdrawals from non-resident deposits together make up about 23 per cent of invisible earnings (RBI, 2023a). Thus, the hard-earned savings of India's workers abroad working in construction and other such work in Gulf Cooperation Council (GCC) countries, are comparable to those of the stars in the software world, between them bringing in over half of India's non-trade earnings. This source of invisibles earnings was not a feature of the pre-1990s world. But it also marks a failure of export-promotion and import-substitution policies

Figure 6.3: India's current account deficit (US$ millions)

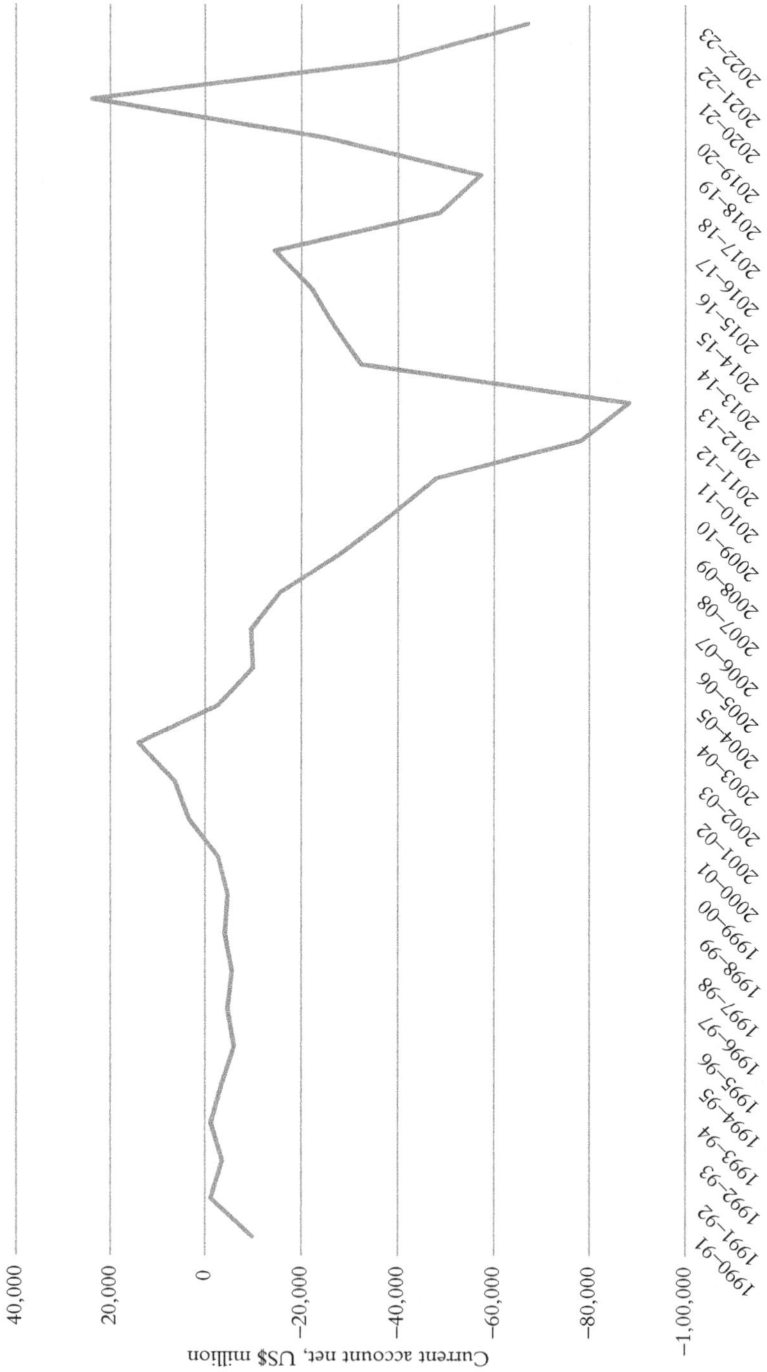

Source: RBI (nd)

Figure 6.4: Share of software services in India's invisible earnings

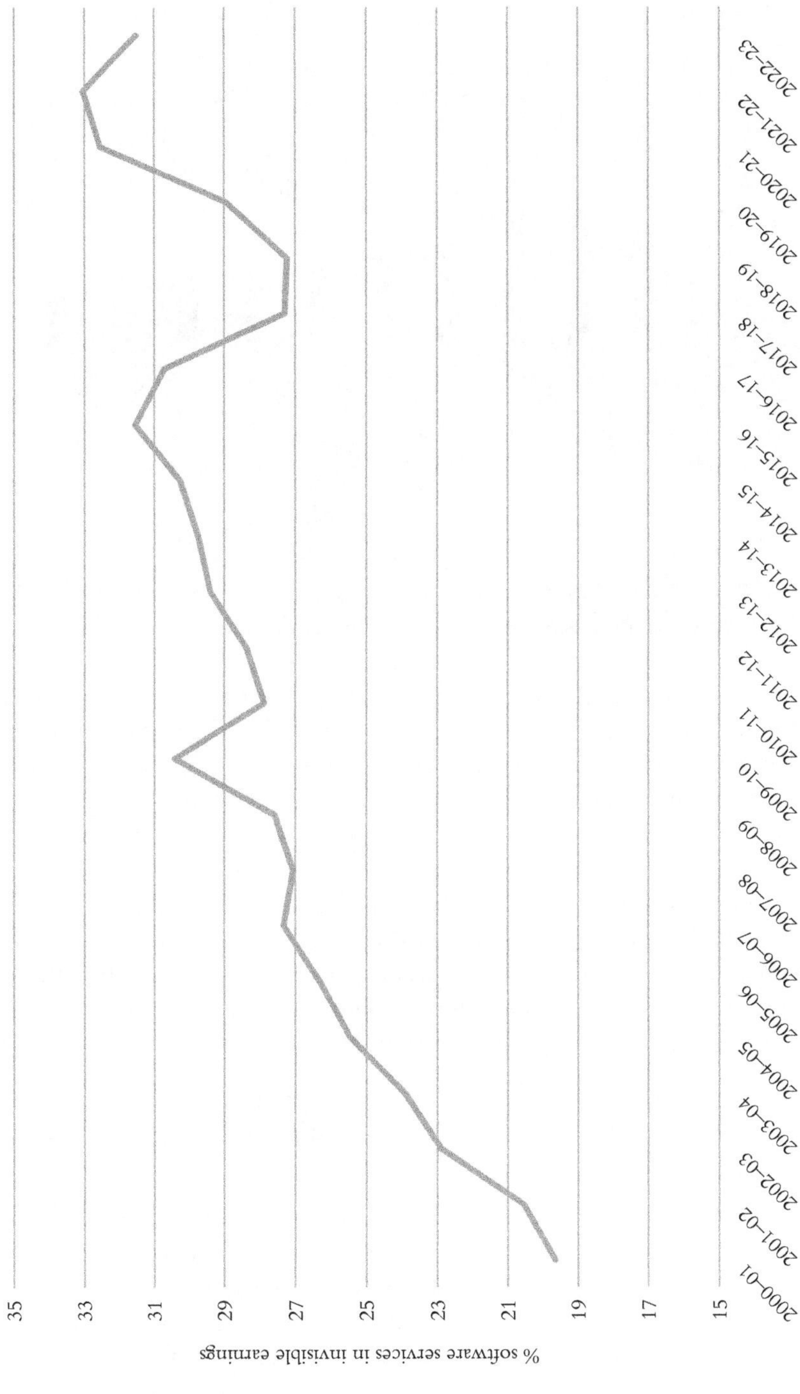

Source: RBI (nd)

Figure 6.5: Remittance inflows in 2022 (US$ billions)

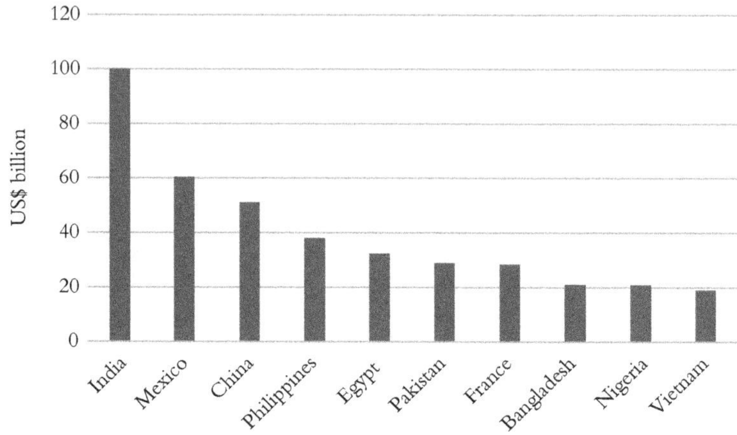

Source: World Bank staff estimates based on IMF balance of payments data

that one of India's key exports is its working poor, on the one hand, and its relatively upper caste/class white-collar software workers on the other, harvesting ill-distributed social capital.

The current account deficit and the fiscal deficit were thus somewhat entwined until the late 1990s, but at a relatively sustainable level barring exogenous shocks (the other way that the fiscal and currency account deficits get entwined is through the quasi-sovereign debt of public sector oil companies that are sold abroad). Thanks to financial repression and a closed capital account, this *foreign* borrowing initially took the form of *sovereign* borrowing of the Indian state rather than private corporate or household borrowing. However, in the 2000s, the state liberalized the capital account and thus began to manage its international survival constraint through a more sophisticated set of measures involving a turn to private debt, reserve accumulation, and foreign exchange interventions.

RBI relaxing the survival constraint through capital account management

The configuration of India's capital account reflects the balance between the RBI's attempt to manage the survival constraint, on the one hand, and big Indian capital's preferences for limited inward foreign direct investment (FDI) and unlimited outward expansion, on the other. The RBI, known for its cautious liberalization, thanks to lessons from its 1991 crisis and the 1997 Asian Financial Crisis, privileges direct investment over portfolio flows and equity over debt flows. And yet, notwithstanding the gradual liberalization of direct investments (which was heavily contested in the post-independence period), FDI flows lag behind the more volatile categories of foreign portfolio inflows and foreign-denominated borrowing by private firms. This reflects the historic and enduring resistance to foreign ownership in India. The RBI manages resulting vulnerabilities from 'hot money' flows by intervening in the foreign exchange market to stabilize the rupee, and sterilizing these interventions to meet its inflation target. These interventions to manage the survival constraint (financial statecraft) importantly provide a currency hedge to India's big businesses borrowing in dollars.

Breaking down the capital account into three distinct pieces – foreign portfolio investment (FPI), FDI, and 'other investment' of which external commercial borrowing constitutes an important piece – clarifies how India's political settlement asserts itself in the RBI's management of the capital account.

Whereas big businesses have historically opposed FDI and to a lesser extent FPI, they have largely favoured policies enabling cheap credit and outward expansion. Thus, it is not surprising that FDI inflows, while gradually liberalized since the 1991 crisis, and further liberalized in the early 2000s, have staggered behind both FPI and external commercial borrowings which in part reflects foreign investors' reluctance to commit to physical operations in India and the resistance of big business to FDI (Ye, 2014). Consequently, India continues to generate the lowest levels of FDI as share of GDP in the BRICS group, as shown in Figure 6.6.

The financing channels available to Indian firms speak to Indian policy makers' efforts to carve out autonomy by limiting exposure to global finance. First, India's big businesses get privileged access to credit from Indian public sector banks, which in 2022 delivered 58 per cent of total bank credit (Sengupta and Vardhan, 2023). More recently, however, the main beneficiaries of the new waves of credit through public sector banks have been politically well-connected firms in non-tradeable sectors such as energy, roads, and airports (Chatterjee, 2023). Meanwhile, the share of credit provided by foreign banks remained flat at 4 per cent in the period 2011–22 (Sengupta and Vardhan, 2023). A second avenue for financing is through India's two major stock exchanges: the National Stock Exchange and the Bombay Stock Exchange. As outlined by Petry (Chapter 9, this volume), the Indian state exercises considerable control over these exchanges by capping foreign ownership in exchange shares, as well as by limiting foreign participation through a lengthy application process and a complex regulatory structure.

A third channel for financing is through the external commercial borrowing route. In 2004, the RBI eased regulations such that external commercial borrowing could be used to fund joint ventures (JVs) and wholly owned

Figure 6.6: Inward FDI stocks as share of GDP

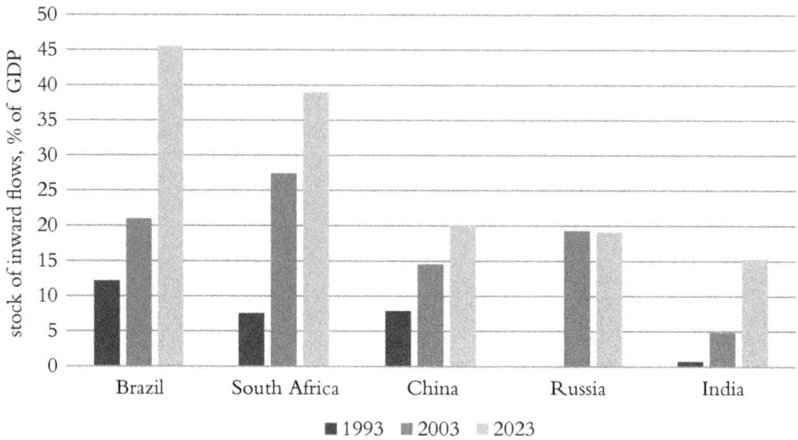

Source: UNCTAD

Figure 6.7: External commercial borrowing and its share in total external debt

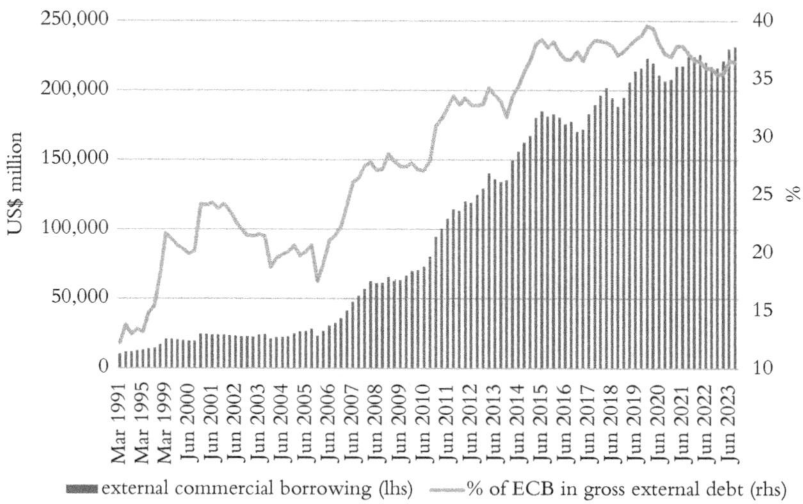

Source: RBI (nd)

subsidiaries. At the end of September 2023, India's total external debt was US$635 billion, 36 per cent of which constituted commercial borrowings, as shown in Figure 6.7. Since 2010, 90 per cent of firm issuance has been through the external commercial borrowing route (Acharya and Vij, 2020). Large conglomerates such as Mahindra & Mahindra and Sun Pharmaceuticals used proceeds raised through external commercial borrowing to drive their overseas expansion during the 2000s (Balcet and Bruschieri, 2010).

Notwithstanding liberalization, only a few large conglomerates who have outgrown the Indian banking system (which is anyway still largely geared to finance government dissaving) are allowed to take on such debt, a 'licence permit raj' for foreign debt is well intact. Thus, when debt gets out of hand, it is *private* debt held domestically that fails thanks to the oligarch's party, especially in infrastructure, spilling over into the banking system which saw a build-up of bad debt and eventually required a substantial bailout (Credit Suisse, 2012). This was followed by a crisis in the 'shadow banking' system of India, the so-called non-bank financial companies, and the real estate sector (Subramanian and Felman, 2019).

An important portion of India's capital account is thus made up by leveraging up private balance sheets on the external account. This requires a particular kind of financial statecraft (which we may think of as 'derisking') as private balance sheets are used to relax the national survival constraint, but with state-provided backstops (Musthaq, 2021). In a hotly contested set of actions, the RBI uses its extensive foreign exchange reserves to prop up the rupee. This makes sense in light of India's import bill and its role in the current account deficit. The RBI has intervened on multiple occasions to stem currency depreciation, notable among them the Lehman collapse in September 2008, the US long-term rating downgrade in August 2011 (18 per cent depreciation of rupee against US dollar), and the 'taper tantrum' in May 2013 (about 19 per cent depreciation of rupee against US dollar) (Khan, 2014). According to the IMF, between April and December 2008, foreign portfolio investors withdrew US$9–10 billion from India, with roughly US$4 billion in outflows in October alone (Acharya and Kulkarni, 2012). At the height of the crisis in October, the RBI sold US$18.6 billion on forex markets. Thus, despite a regulated capital account, India's subordinate status is made clear in periods of global liquidity shocks. As insurance, the RBI has accumulated a large trove of foreign exchange reserves, which by 2023 stood at US$563 billion, roughly 15 per cent of the GDP (RBI, nd).

Through currency interventions, the RBI provides an implicit currency hedge for external borrowing. The RBI's management of the rupee means that the oligarchs get a free hedge from the central bank, but few global players are willing to go long on the rupee (thanks to 'original sin') so the market for hedging rupee risk is broken, forcing the RBI to manage risk in the first place. But these 'permitted borrowers' benefit all the same (external commercial borrowing includes some public sector undertakings as well).

In the context of a worsening current account deficit and a depreciating rupee, it is no surprise that India held negotiations to implement a rupee settlement mechanism (as a means to limit foreign exchange outflows) in February 2022, following the West's sanctions on Russia. India's dependence on oil, and Russia's willingness to sell its oil at a highly competitive price, made this transaction attractive notwithstanding India's alliance with the US.

As articulated by observers, the Russia–Ukraine war presented an opportune moment for India to insist on export settlement in rupee (Sharma, 2023).

The realities of India's political economy, however, have stalled negotiations for a rupee settlement mechanism. First, without changes in the real economy, that is a substantial increase in exports, trading partners such as Russia are unlikely to use rupee as an invoicing currency. Talks to implement a rupee settlement mechanism were suspended in May 2023 in light of the trade gap in favour of Russia and Russian banks' unwillingness to hold rupees. Second, India's restrictive capital account and general financial repression also deter foreign actors from dealing in rupee. Meanwhile, rupee internationalization poses problems for India in terms of monetary policy autonomy. With increased rupee internationalization, the RBI has less discretion to manage the domestic money supply even while managing the rupee, as the trilemma would begin to bite. Rupee surpluses in the hands of nonresidents potentially increase nonresident holding of rupee assets which can heighten India's vulnerability to external shocks in the context of a current account deficit.

Thus, for all its efforts, India's trade profile, repressed financial system, and highly managed capital account are not suited to further embed the rupee payment settlement mechanism in global trade. According to a former governor of the RBI, currency internationalization does not depend on 'special government encouragement', but rather on creating the preconditions such as 'a deep and dynamic domestic financial market, a well-respected legal framework for contract enforcement, and stable and predictable macro and microeconomic policies'(Reddy, 2023).

Conclusion

This chapter expands the notion of financial statecraft to include the set of banking operations around debt and currency that states and their central banks undertake in order to manage their survival constraint, namely the requirement for liquid funds. For states, this turns on the acceptability of their debt domestically (managed by the central bank operating as the state's merchant banker) as well as its ability to form sociopolitical compacts domestically to tax (a broader issue of fiscal sociology). The economy's balance of trade generates another set of liquidity demands that the state and its bank have to manage, mainly through the decision by the fiscal authorities as to the denomination and duration of its external debt and by the central bank through its currency management and regulation of the capital account.

The India case shows how states can be both relatively fiscally autonomous even while constrained by the economy's underlying trade imbalances. The Indian state's domestic autonomy arrives not through the taxation but the debt route via the construction of a fiscal-monetary machine, a domestic banking system to intermediate between household savings and state borrowing. This machine operated well so long as the fiscal deficit thrown up by the underlying political settlement was within manageable bounds (and so long as savings rates remained relatively high). The point at which this deficit got out of hand and started filling up the domestic financial system, including the central bank, with too much debt, was the point at which the Indian state's fiscal autonomy was compromised as it borrowed internationally, from private sources and at ever-shorter tenures.

The resulting 1991 crisis led to a hasty retreat to the status quo ante, namely very little sovereign external debt. But the chronic current account deficit had by now ballooned even more and had to be managed. The solution, unavailable before the liberalization moment, was to allow more FDI and debt flows into a narrowly defined set of large businesses. Thus, notwithstanding the rhetoric of 'liberalization', the capital account remains heavily managed. What liberalization achieved was twofold: first, it opened up more strategies of financial statecraft to manage current account vulnerabilities since FDI and private debt flows were hitherto verboten. But correspondingly, it brought certain private firms into the orbit of global capital so that the solution to India's international survival constraint was found in 'globalization' along a very narrow channel.

Big business has used its dominance not to create a manufacturing base that can take advantage of the country's so-called demographic dividend but rather to take up residence in critical, non-tradeable enclaves. From here it helps run the state's patronage-welfare machine, but the balance between state and business is such that no productive industrial policy that could contain the current account deficit has yet emerged. Part of big business is piped into global capital for its debt needs but it has also mobilized capital from domestic banks, again largely for infrastructure projects operated through public–private partnerships. Domestically, bad private debt built up in the banking system as the public–private partnerships failed to deliver, leading to a protracted bailout even while most big capital owners fended off bankruptcy proceedings to hold on to their firms. The domestic banking system could not discipline the oligarchs, but such discipline is required for functional 'embedded autonomy'. In this way, India's political settlement sets out the broad parameters within which financial statecraft manages the state and nation's survival constraint.

Hence over the post-liberalization period, we have moved from a relatively undisciplined fiscal authority borrowing short-term internationally to a relatively undisciplined set of private balance sheets borrowing both internationally and domestically. The Indian state's fiscal autonomy funds the welfare machine and purchases regime legitimacy, while private capital is plugged in domestically and internationally but produces only enclave-based dominance without moving the manufacturing needle. Thus, India's international survival constraint remains relatively tight, accentuated by the failure of industrial policy, and the global ambitions of India's big businesses. It can plausibly be argued that India's financial statecraft seeks to sustain an ongoing model that manages external finance for key firms and therefore has internalized the power dynamics and hierarchies of international financial subordination (Alami, Chapter 2 this volume), and does so within the confines of its domestic political settlement.

As the IFS literature has observed, the post-Keynesian tradition foregrounds currency hierarchy but fails to adequately account for its emergence. The technical fact of hierarchy is anchored in a political economy account of domestic and international institutional formation including state formation. On the other hand, it is unclear how the IFS literature connects domestic and international class struggles with the technical capacities of certain currencies. Kvangraven's assertion in this volume (Chapter 11) that 'IFS is a reflection of a deeper underlying global division of labour' is of course true but perhaps does not go far enough. More than a 'reflection', IFS is an *outcome* of the interlocking of domestic and international political struggles that lead to more or less secure institutionalization of social power. Hierarchies emerge, ultimately, because of differing capacities for and trajectories of the institutionalization of collective action.

Needless to say, states often differ in their ability to relax their survival constraint precisely because they are locked into (neo-)imperial relations of trade and production. But it is critical to note that a radically unequal global division of labour is not the sole source of hierarchy in world money and finance. Capitalist money is an IOU whose value and robustness are predicated on the creditworthiness and scale of its issuer. Institutionalized collective action, economic or political, generates creditworthiness. Being subordinate in the world system makes this kind of collective action extremely difficult, which is why a hierarchical global economy is durably reproduced, but subordination or dominance is ultimately determined by our capacities for collective action in the face of these incredible inequalities. Indeed, to see things any other way would be to deny agency on the part of subordinate groups, something IFS scholars are rightly keen to avoid (see Kvangraven, Chapter 11, this volume).

Note

1 That said, the Indian state is not an outlier on the expenditure side viz the emerging market average; it is an outlier in terms of having a lower *revenue*-to-GDP ratio than its cohort (Eichengreen et al, 2023, p 9). India's structural fiscal deficit results from its pattern of expenditure combined with its *political* inability to sufficiently tax its citizens.

References

Acharya, V. and Vij, S. (2020) *Foreign Currency Borrowing of Corporations as Carry Trades: Evidence from India*, Cambridge, MA: National Bureau of Economic Research.

Acharya, V.V. and Kulkarni, N. (2012) 'What saved the Indian banking system: State ownership or state guarantees?' (SSRN Scholarly Paper ID 1987928), Rochester, NY: Social Science Research Network.

Alami, I., Alves, C., Bonizzi, B., Kaltenbrunner, A., Koddenbrock, K., Kvangraven, I., et al (2023) 'International financial subordination: a critical research agenda', *Review of International Political Economy*, 30(4): 1360–86.

Armijo, L.E. (2019) 'Financial Statecraft', in T.M. Shaw, L.C. Mahrenbach, R. Modi, and X. Yi-chong (eds) *The Palgrave Handbook of Contemporary International Political Economy* (1st edn), New York: Palgrave Macmillan, pp 27–43.

Armijo, L.E. and Katada, S.N. (2015) 'Theorizing the financial statecraft of emerging powers', *New Political Economy*, 20(1): 42–62.

Balcet, G. and Bruschieri, S. (2010) 'Acquisition of technologies and multinational enterprise growth in the automotive and the pharmaceutical industries: Drivers and strategies', in K.P. Sauvant, J.P. Pradhan, A. Chatterjee, and B. Harley (eds) *The Rise of Indian Multinationals: Perspectives on Indian Outward Foreign Direct Investment* (1st edn), New York: Palgrave Macmillan, pp 111–65.

Baldwin, D.A. (1985) *Economic Statecraft*, Princeton, NJ: Princeton University Press.

Banik, N. and Velamuri, S.R. (2023) 'The "what", "why", and "how" of a widening current account deficit', *Economic and Political Weekly*, 58(3).

Bardhan, P. (1999) *The Political Economy of Development in India: Expanded Edition with an Epilogue on the Political Economy of Reform in India* (2nd edn), Oxford and New York: Oxford University Press.

Chakraborty, J. and Nagaraj, R. (2020) 'Has India deindustrialised prematurely?', *Economic and Political Weekly*, 55(48).

Chatterjee, E. (2023) 'India's oligarchic state capitalism', *Current History*, 122(843): 123–30.

Chatterjee, P. (2019) *I Am the People: Reflections on Popular Sovereignty Today*, New York: Columbia University Press.

Cohen, B.J. (2008) 'The international monetary system: diffusion and ambiguity', *International Affairs*, 84(3): 455–70.

Credit Suisse (2012) *House of Debt. Equity Research.*

Damodaran, H. (2020) 'From "entrepreneurial" to "conglomerate" capitalism', *Seminar Magazine*, October, pp 33–37.

Eichengreen, B., Gupta, P., and Ahmed, A. (2023) 'India's debt dilemma', India Policy Forum, NCAER, Available from: https://www.ncaer.org/wp-content/uploads/2024/07/IPF2023-Paper-1.pdf [Accessed 14 February 2025].

Joshi, V. and Little, I.M.D. (1994) *India: Macroeconomics and Political Economy, 1964–1991*, Washington DC: World Bank.

Kapadia, A. (2017) 'The structure of state borrowing: Towards a political theory of control mechanisms', *Cambridge Journal of Regions, Economy and Society*, 10(1): 189–204.

Kapadia, A. (2024) *A Political Theory of Money*, Cambridge: Cambridge University Press.

Khan, H. (2014) 'Regulating capital account: Some thoughts', 9th Annual Conference of FEDAI, Cape Town, South Africa, [online] 12 April, Available from: https://www.rbi.org.in/Scripts/BS_ViewBulletin.aspx?Id=14902 [Accessed 24 February 2024].

Kumar, A. (2017) *The Black Economy in India*, Gurgaon, Haryana, India: India Penguin.

Liu, Z.Z. and Papa, M. (2022) 'Can BRICS de-dollarize the global financial system?', *Elements in the Economics of Emerging Market*, Available from: https://doi.org/10.1017/9781009029544 [Accessed 27 January 2025].

Ministry of Finance (2023) *Quarterly External Debt*.

Ministry of Petroleum & Natural Gas (2023) *Snapshot of India's Oil and Gas Data*, Available from: https://ppac.gov.in/uploads/whatsnew/1705401403_Snapshot%20of%20India%27s%20Oil%20&%20Gas%20data-Dec-23_web%20Upload.pdf [Accessed 14 February 2025].

Mohan, R. (2008) 'The role of fiscal and monetary policies in sustaining growth with stability in India', *Asian Economic Policy Review*, 3(2): 209–36.

Musthaq, F. (2021) 'Unconventional central banking and the politics of liquidity', *Review of International Political Economy*, 30(1): 281–306.

Nölke, A., ten Brink, T., May, C., and Claar, S. (2021) *State-Permeated Capitalism in Large Emerging Economies* (1st edn), London: Routledge.

Patel, I.G. (1992) 'New economic policies a historical perspective', *Economic and Political Weekly*, 27(1–2).

PGPF (2023) 'The federal government has borrowed trillions. Who owns all that debt?', *Peter G. Peterson Foundation*, [online], Available from: https://www.pgpf.org/blog/2023/05/the-federal-government-has-borrowed-trillions-but-who-owns-all-that-debt [Accessed 24 February 2024].

RBI (2023a) 'Data on India's invisibles for first quarter (April–June) 2023–24', Reserve Bank of India, [online], Available from: https://rbi.org.in/Scripts/BS_PressReleaseDisplay.aspx?prid=56737 [Accessed 1 March 2024].

RBI (2023b) *Developments in India's Balance of Payments during the First Quarter (April–June) of 2023–24*, Reserve Bank of India.

RBI (nd) 'Database on Indian Economy', [online], Available from: https://cimsdbie.rbi.org.in/DBIE/#/dbie/home [Accessed 1 March 2024].

Reddy, Y.V. (2023) 'The rupee as an international currency', The India Forum, [online] 21 June, Available from: https://www.theindiaforum.in/rupee-international-currency [Accessed 14 February 2025].

Roy, R. (2019) 'Demand, supply and growth slowdowns', *Business Standard*, 6 December, Available from: https://www.business-standard.com/article/opinion/demand-supply-and-growth-slowdowns-119120600037_1.html [Accessed 14 February 2025].

Schumpeter, J.A. (1991) 'The crisis of the tax state', in J.A. Schumpeter (ed) *The Economics and Sociology of Capitalism*, Princeton, NJ: Princeton University Press.

Sengupta, R. and Vardhan, H. (2023) 'India's credit landscape in a post-pandemic world', in I. Gupta and M. Das (eds) *Contextualizing the COVID Pandemic in India* (India Studies in Business and Economics), Singapore: Springer Nature Singapore, pp 273–95.

Sharma, V.B. (2023) 'Explainer: How feasible is RBI's push to settle international trade in rupees?', *The Wire*, [online] 10 January, Available from: https://thewire.in/economy/explainer-rbi-rupee-settlement-international-trade [Accessed 27 January 2024].

Subramanian, A. and Felman, J. (2019) 'India's great slowdown: What happened? What's the way out?' (Working Paper), Cambridge, MA: Center for International Development, Harvard University.

Walton, M. (2020) 'An Indian gilded age? Continuity and change in the political economy of India's development', in E. Chatterjee and M. McCartney (eds) *Class and Conflict: Revisiting Pranab Bardhan's Political Economy of India*, Oxford: Oxford University Press, pp 223–55.

World Bank Development Data Group (2021) *Assessment on Public Sector Domestic Debt*, Washington DC: World Bank.

Ye, M. (2014) *Diasporas and Foreign Direct Investment in China and India*, New York: Cambridge University Press.

7

Seeking Autonomy Beyond Subordination: Chinese Financial Statecraft and the e-CNY

Christopher A. McNally

Introduction: A new era of financial statecraft

The war in Ukraine is one among several recent factors causing turmoil and transformation in the global economy. It is triggering rapid and profound adjustments by rerouting basic supplies, ranging from oil and gas to food staples, fertilizers, and various metals. These disruptions are only in part due to the armed conflict. Western countries have levied extensive sanctions against Russia that are introducing additional uncertainty and instability, not only to trade and financial ties with Russia, but also affecting the wider global political economy.

The bigger picture indicates a coming sea change in several key commodity trades that could reshape geoeconomics. Most notable will be the energy trade. Another key evolution is likely to occur in international finance. Of all the sanctions levied against Russia, those in the financial realm are biting the hardest and are likely to cause the most severe consequences, both intended and unintended.

These financial sanctions aim to cripple the Russian economy, even to the extent of causing a crisis. As with other developing and emerging market economies (DEEs), Russia remains in a subordinated position within the International Monetary System (IMS) dominated by Western powers. As a result, before the war Russian authorities sought to create a buffer to extinguish a potential financial crisis. They amassed more than US$630 billion in foreign exchange reserves to be able to defend the value of the rouble and keep the Russian economy afloat (Martin, 2022). However, a considerable part of the reserves is held in international assets domiciled in the US, Europe, and Japan.

In an unprecedented move in terms of scale and swiftness, Russian foreign exchange assets were frozen shortly after the onset of the war. Russia was robbed of its ability to protect the rouble internationally and had to institute sky-high interest rates and severe capital controls. These stabilized the situation and allowed the rouble to regain its footing. But the longer-term consequences of Russia losing control over part of its reserves and being cut off from the Western financial system remain to be seen.

Perhaps the biggest unknown of how the sanctions play out is what this means for the future of the IMS, especially the US dollar's role within it. Prognostications range from a possible decline in the dollar's importance to the strengthening of American hegemony and thus US dollar dominance. Certainly, from the point of view of late 2024, the dollar's status seems quite assured. It remains the world's most sought-after haven.

Nevertheless, the swift and almost absolute nature of Western financial sanctions has alarmed many DEEs. Large parts of the Russian financial system have been barred from the Society for Worldwide Interbank Financial Telecommunication (SWIFT) currency exchange messaging system, making international payment transactions difficult to process. Most unsettling, though, are the sanctions levied on Russia's foreign reserves, implying that direct control is more important than mere ownership.

China and India, both with markets that have provided Russia an outlet for its exports, worry about the reach of the West's sanctions. Countries on good terms with Washington and Brussels might have little to fear, yet many DEEs are concerned that they could be next. This creates an incentive to reduce reliance on the US dollar and diversify holdings.

Barry Eichengreen (2022) ponders the possibility of a large shift of global foreign exchange reserves away from US Treasury bonds, thereby reducing the reliance of countries like China on the US dollar. However, he contends that this is highly unlikely to occur. While the dominance of the US dollar has fallen from around 70 per cent of total global reserves around 2000 to less than 60 per cent today, the shift has been within Western currencies. In fact, the movement has been toward the Canadian and Australian dollars, South Korean won, and the Swedish krone. Given the West's united front against Russia, there is no escape. Moreover, gold and the Chinese currency, the renminbi or yuan, cannot act as good substitutes. Put simply, there is no ready alternative payment infrastructure available besides that centred on Western currencies.

Alas, one can easily imagine scenarios, such as a Chinese attack on Taiwan, that could destabilize the global financial system to a breaking point. As Eichengreen (2022) warns, the resulting Western sanctions and exclusion from SWIFT 'would be an economic catastrophe for China and the world economy'. It is therefore an understatement that we are living through unprecedented times in terms of how the global financial system evolves.

In such an interconnected world everyone sits to some extent in the same boat. There is no safe distance from the ricochet effects of financial sanctions.

Despite the many unknowns, one thing is evident: Western sanctions vis-à-vis Russia have propelled financial statecraft to a new level. The instruments employed and their scope have undergone massive expansion and become central to economic statecraft in general. What the liberal international economic order saw as a public good, the infrastructures and ecosystems enabling the smooth functioning of global finance, have now been turned into economic weapons of unprecedented reach and effect.

As indicated earlier, financial statecraft is a subset of economic statecraft. David Baldwin (2020) argues that any time economics is used as an instrument of international politics, it constitutes 'economic statecraft', the facilitation of foreign policy goals through economic means. Armijo and Katada (2015, p 43) have further defined financial statecraft as 'the intentional use, by national governments, of domestic or international monetary or financial capabilities for the purpose of achieving ongoing foreign policy goals, whether political, economic, or financial' (see also Armijo, Chapter 3, this volume).

Tools of financial statecraft can take many forms. They can imply positive (inducing) or negative (restricting) sanctions. They can be purely 'bilateral' or then 'systemic' in scope. And they can also be 'offensive' or 'defensive' in nature (Andrews, 2006, p 19; Cohen, 2008; 2018; Armijo and Katada, 2015, pp 46–7). The practice of financial statecraft has gained such prominence in recent decades due to the 'weaponization' of the US dollar by successive US administrations. For instance, US sanctions on Banco Delta Asia, a Macau-based bank, in March 2007 effectively severed North Korea's access to foreign exchange by scaring other banks in Macau away from doing business with Pyongyang. Iran has similarly been squeezed economically by its inability to access the US dollar-based international financial system.

America's effective control over vast swaths of the IMS generate unprecedented leverage to exercise financial statecraft. The whole globe, but especially DEEs, are in a subordinate position. As the introduction to this volume and the chapter by Ilias Alami elaborate, 'international financial subordination' suggests a 'relation of domination, inferiority and subjugation between different spaces across the world market, expressed in and through money and finance, which penalizes actors in DEEs disproportionally' (Alami et al, 2023, p 4; also see Alami, Chapter 2, as well as Kvangraven, Chapter 11, both this volume).

The concept of international financial subordination calls forth the hierarchical nature of global financial and monetary relations, where DEEs often remain stuck at the bottom (Kaltenbrunner and Painceira, 2018). DEEs therefore suffer unduly from recurring financial crises and are often 'forced' to accumulate USD reserves to insulate themselves from financial shocks, both domestic and external.

China is no exception. But more so than in other DEEs, Chinese policies have acquired the contours of a form of proactive or offensive financial statecraft to counter the adverse effects of its subordinate global position (see Petry and Nölke, Chapter 1, as well as Ehlke, Salzer, and Westermeier, Chapter 10, this volume). With the rapid rise of the Chinese economy, Chinese authorities have begun to explore novel applications to extend their international economic influence. This has created a unique form of Chinese financial statecraft (see Nölke, 2023; Petry, 2023).

The next section briefly conceptualizes the nature and logic of China's emergent financial statecraft. It highlights two major factors shaping it and outlines some of its major contours. In the third section, I introduce Chinese efforts to launch the world's first major central bank digital currency (CBDC), the e-CNY, also colloquially referred to as the digital yuan. The fourth part of the article investigates the implications of the e-CNY for yuan internationalization. It analyzes the potential broader ramifications of launching the e-CNY for the future of the IMS, including the yuan's and dollar's roles within it. The chapter ends with several concluding remarks that explore the future of Chinese financial statecraft as it relates to the introduction of the e-CNY, including the opportunities and possible threats it could create for the yuan's global status.

China's emergent financial statecraft

Two crucial factors shape the practice of Chinese financial statecraft. First, China's subordinated position within the IMS. Second, the evolution of China's domestic politico-economic arrangements, namely, the institutional logics of its unique form of state capitalism or Sino-capitalism. These factors shape both the intents and methods of Chinese financial statecraft.

The situation that Russia faced after the unprecedented sanctions of 2022 drives home the extent to which DEEs remain in a subordinated position in international finance. The US dollar continues to dominate cross-border payments. Financial intermediation is provided by institutions either domiciled in the US or its allies (Eichengreen, 2011; Norrlof, 2014; Cohen, 2018). This puts the US at the centre of infrastructures undergirding financial connectivity between different places and entities (Petry, 2023). Although financial markets are usually seen as neutral exchange mechanisms, US dollar dominance reproduces American hegemony and provides manifold opportunities to exercise statecraft for Washington.

Like other DEEs, especially export-oriented economies in East Asia, China relies heavily on the global financial infrastructure. Even though it is now the second largest global economy, there is no escaping the reach of American financial hegemony. As China reformed and opened up in the 1980s and 1990s, policy makers adopted an export- and investment-led growth model like other East Asian economic success stories. This involved a relatively closed capital account and control over the exchange rate.

Such a strategy created large export surpluses, which the Chinese government invested primarily in US dollar-denominated financial assets. Ironically, China's success as an exporter and international investment destination forced it to integrate with and use the IMS dominated by the US dollar. As long as this is the case, China remains exposed to two crucial vulnerabilities.

First, a large chunk of China's state savings is tied up in assets at the mercy of US monetary policy, making China vulnerable to the debasement of the US dollar. Second, China remains at considerable risk of becoming a target of US financial sanctions. Given the recent example of Russia, this could mean the quasi-confiscation of a large chunk of its foreign reserves, complicating its conduct of exchange rate and monetary policy. Perhaps even more ominous would be a cut-off from SWIFT. Given the linkages between trade networks and international currencies, such a cut-off could obliterate Chinese exports and potentially induce a financial crisis within China.

These risks always existed, but they have become more prominent over the last decade. Already after the global financial crisis of 2008 Chinese authorities sought ways to tackle external vulnerabilities. They pursued means to foster greater international usage of the yuan. This was to assure an additional route of trade finance while hoping to increase China's economic autonomy over time.

Most analyses see these efforts as having made little headway. Although different reasons have been proffered for why this is the case, a full opening of the capital account and freeing of the yuan's exchange rate are seen as necessary preconditions in the dominant techno-economic perspective (see Kennen, 1983; Chinn and Frankel, 2005). Such liberalization, though, risks destabilizing China's domestic growth regime (Bowles and Wang, 2013; Otero-Iglesias and Vermeiren, 2015; Prasad, 2017; 2021; Subacchi, 2017; Cohen, 2018).

To protect domestic financial stability, China has only opened its capital account very gradually and cautiously. Up until this day, capital flows across Chinese borders face controls – they are channelled in designated 'pipelines' that are subject to Chinese regulation and quotas (McNally and Gruin, 2017; Petry, 2021). In addition, the yuan's exchange rate is not fully determined by the market since the People's Bank of China (PBoC) continues to deploy various tools to manage it.

The potential of the yuan to become a significant international currency is thus thorny and complex. China has actually muddled through the process of currency internationalization to a considerable extent. While liberalizing both its exchange rate and capital account, various institutional safeguards are in place that allow authorities to exert ultimate control. This combination continues to assure a relatively high degree of monetary autonomy (McNally and Gruin, 2017), but it complicates full-throttle internationalization. Without the breadth and depth of investment options offered by the US dollar or even euro, a yuan-based ecosystem for international trade settlement, payments, investment, and reserve diversification remains in its infancy.

Nevertheless, the pressure on China to develop an international currency is larger now than ever before. Seeking independence from the US dollar and thus the reach of American extraterritorial jurisdiction has become a pressing matter of national security. At the same time, Chinese authorities remain unwilling to open up the capital account fully and let the yuan move freely. This requires the maintenance of some measure of capital controls.

To overcome this contradiction, Chinese approaches have drawn on the institutional arrangements and experiences pioneered domestically under Sino-capitalism (McNally, 2012; 2019). As Nana de Graaff (2020, p 209) points out, China's international economic positioning is rooted in a domestic political economy that is interlinked with an evolving global economy and crucially mediated by elite networks and elite strategies. As a result of this hybridization and bricolage, Chinese policies have adapted some liberal tenets of financial management but seek work-around solutions that often rely on state coordination and guidance.

The comparative capitalism literature (Jackson and Deeg, 2008; Clift, 2021) incorporates important insights that can be leveraged to understand Chinese approaches. Various strands of the literature have distinguished among major types of capitalism. The logic of Sino-capitalism is most closely related to conceptualizations of state capitalism (Naughton and Tsai, 2015; Alami and Dixon, 2020; Nölke et al, 2020), which examine the specific roles and power of the state within different national configurations of capitalism, as well as variations in state capacity and different patterns of interaction between state and capital.

Sino-capitalism functions as a refurbished form of state capitalism (Naughton and Tsai, 2015; McNally, 2017). However, its dynamics have so far balanced state coordination with bottom-up networked modes of entrepreneurship, private ownership, and local initiative. Sino-capitalism is thus driven by a unique juxtaposition of state capitalism with decentralized market competition and private capital accumulation (McNally, 2012; 2019).

By using the insights generated in the literature, Sino-capitalism emerges as statist in proclivity, but not averse to employing neoliberal market solutions when deemed necessary. Therefore, despite its statist logic, Sino-capitalism recognizes the considerable benefits market competition and international economic integration bring.

In addition, insights on variations in institutional configurations of state–finance relationships developed in this volume provide conceptual tools to understand the evolution of yuan internationalization and the role of the e-CNY within it. Accordingly, Chinese authorities are using considerable state capacity to negotiate a novel pathway between full-blown economic liberalization and draconian state control to carve out a sphere of international monetary autonomy. This pathway aims to establish an ecosystem of Chinese clearing banks, global financial centres, and designated 'pipelines' to effectively channel capital into and out of China, fostering greater availability of various investment products denominated in the yuan (McNally and Gruin, 2017; McNally, 2020).

As with the evolution of the domestic political economy, this approach utilizes a combination of policy experimentation with long-term policy prioritization. Full-scale economic liberalization according to an ideal-type is consciously eschewed in favour of innovative tinkering and work-around solutions (Heilmann, 2018). Oversight by the central state is tempered by localized policy trials that at times engender innovative bottom-up policy solutions. Experimentation tends to include various pilot zones and projects that leave ample room for local ingenuity, learning, and ad hoc tinkering to generate experimental institutions and regulations (see Tsai, 2007; Dickson, 2008).

Sino-capitalism's hybrid institutional arrangements have enabled Chinese policy makers to develop successful reform logics. These logics are now finding expression at the international level and can serve as an analytical vehicle for understanding China's emergent financial statecraft, including strategies to internationalize the yuan and launch the e-CNY.

To sum up, although Sino-capitalism incorporates aspects of liberalization, including financial liberalization, liberalizing impulses are bound by deliberate efforts to keep state control intact. The logic of Sino-capitalism therefore seeks work-around solutions that incorporate partial liberalization under continued state guidance.

As these domestic politico-economic logics are applied to internationalizing the yuan, Chinese policy makers have aimed at not upsetting crucial state control that assures economic, especially financial, stability. Rather than neoliberal solutions that incorporate full-scale liberalization, the capital account and exchange rate remain carefully managed. The goal is to leave sufficient state control intact to assure less volatility and preserve monetary independence.

This way, strategies employed to internationalize the yuan have reproduced elements of the Sino-capitalist logic. Targeted liberalization, policy experimentation, and institutional hybridization have been widely employed. For example, the building of offshore yuan markets only transpired after strategic collaborations between Chinese state actors and international financial centres, institutions, and networks. Luxembourg is an interesting example of this, as well as the efforts by the City of London to grab a larger share of the growing yuan business.

Launching the e-CNY or digital yuan

Chinese authorities have sought to chart a middle course between pursuing exchange rate stability, free cross-border capital flows, and domestic monetary autonomy. They have employed active policy intervention to stabilize foreign exchange markets with the purpose of diminishing volatility and cross-border speculation. This has been combined with targeted and selective capital account opening while retaining monetary independence. However, limits on convertibility have hampered yuan internationalization.

It is for this reason that most analysts do not see the yuan rivalling the US dollar any time soon. Perhaps the most fascinating and little understood aspect of Chinese efforts to chart a middle course while internationalizing the yuan is the launch of a CBDC. This digital version of legal tender was first officially designated as the 'digital currency/electronic payments' (DCEP) project but has now been renamed the e-CNY (Stephan, 2022).

Over the past decade, the digital payments market in China has developed rapidly to become a world leader (Ehlke, Salzer, and Westermeier, Chapter 10 this volume). The PBoC is intent on utilizing this advanced infrastructure to create the first major state-backed CBDC in the world (Deutsche Bank, 2020). CBDCs differ from both physical cash and traditional electronic payments in that they tend to be programmable digital tokens. These digitally individual tokens can serve as the statutory, digital version of cash in circulation.

The PBoC has been conducting research on a digital yuan since 2014, illustrating the priority Chinese policy makers attach to this effort. Spearheading these efforts is the PBoC's Digital Currency Research Institute, a research team within China's central bank dedicated to investigating the digital yuan or e-CNY (Stephan, 2022). The institute was established in 2016 and focused in its early days on replicating the technology underlying private cryptocurrencies, such as Bitcoin and Ethereum. This technology is known as distributed ledger technology (DLT) or 'blockchain' technology.

All DLT-based digital currencies are managed in a decentralized manner by protocols hammered out among private parties with no centralized authority. Their tamper-proof characteristics rely on a multitude of nodes 'validating' all information on the blockchain. The PBoC Digital Currency Research Institute filed more than 60 patents related to blockchain in its first year. However, research then moved away from DLT in favour of a centralized platform model. The e-CNY is issued and supervised centrally by the PBoC. As such, it is more similar to the structure utilized by Chinese payment apps Alipay and WeChat Pay.

The Institute's deputy head Di Gang stated in 2021 that the Institute had developed a blockchain-based distributed ledger for the e-CNY, but that several technical hurdles prevented broader scalability (Stephan, 2022). In fact, scalability is perhaps the Achilles heel of blockchain technology applied to a widely used currency, since the computing power needed to validate every single transaction in different nodes is enormous. Nonetheless, the e-CNY does make use of some of the technologies developed in the crypto community and beyond. It uses trusted computing and special encryption based on hardware and software integration. This creates a programmable digital currency that boasts much greater security, practically removing the possibility of counterfeiting. Most importantly, given its digital nature, all transactions are visible and traceable.

This expresses perhaps the digital yuan's greatest future advantage. Its traceability could provide the PBoC with unprecedented real-time insight on the creation, accounting, and circulation of money in the Chinese economy. Depending on how the PBoC utilizes, processes, and examines this data, it could revolutionize monetary policy. A CBDC, for example, could generate much needed data in an economic downturn, which could enable authorities to more easily pinpoint economic sectors in most dire need of monetary support. In contrast, monetary operations undertaken in the West in recent years, such as quantitative easing (QE), are rather crude tools that push money out into the economy regardless of need. Such a sledgehammer approach carries grave risks, since currency over-issuance can create financial bubbles and inflation.

High levels of financial transparency can also help lower financial risks, since banks can better track and analyze the businesses of their borrowers and, with this, non-performing assets. Theoretically, stresses and risks to the financial system can be detected early on and addressed in a targeted manner. The e-CNY could also make it easier to fight financial crimes including corruption, money laundering, the financing of terrorism and, perhaps most significantly, tax evasion. All this implies lower costs to run financial infrastructures and much greater transparency and traceability regarding financial transactions.

There are drawbacks to this brave new world of money. Some commentators in the West see the digital yuan as another effort by the Chinese Communist Party (CCP) to exert greater control over Chinese citizens (Keram, 2021). Based on information released so far, anonymity is only assured in smaller transactions between users, while the PBoC can trace every movement of the e-CNY given its electronic footprints. No wonder that the introduction of digital money raises distinct privacy concerns. Even in China, these are likely to create some societal pushback to total surveillance (see Ehlke, Salzer, and Westermeier, Chapter 10, this volume).

The launch of the e-CNY also replicates other efforts by central authorities to build infrastructural arrangements and control mechanisms that sustain the state's hegemony over finance. Comparable efforts to balance financialization with state control can be found in various areas of Chinese financial reform, such as capital markets and other fintech innovations (Gruin, 2019; Petry, 2020). By enhancing financial surveillance and monitoring, the e-CNY can more efficiently handle crucial aspects of socio-economic stability, such as the build-up of excessive financial risks. The aim is to steer economic development and ensure social stability by perfecting rather than reducing state power.

At this point in time, the e-CNY still remains officially in an experimental phase and is not yet ready for a full rollout. As with domestic reforms, the PBoC has pursued a classical trial and error approach (Heilmann, 2018). First, the digital yuan was piloted in a number of major cities throughout 2021. Then, at the start of 2022, the PBoC made actual digital yuan wallets available on the iOS and Android app stores in China.

On 10 January 2023 the PBoC included e-CNY in currency circulation reports for the first time, revealing that the digital yuan represented roughly 0.13 per cent of the 10.47 trillion yuan ($1.54 trillion) in circulation at the end of 2022. This indicates a low adoption rate for the e-CNY. The process of widening digital yuan use also involves various trials set to expand geographically and in terms of use cases. For instance, the e-CNY received smart contract functionality alongside a series of newly unveiled use cases in January 2023. These included buying securities and making offline payments (Coghlan, 2023).

E-CNY infrastructure is also being integrated with China's leading domestic mobile payments providers, Alipay and WeChat Pay. As China began CBDC trials, some argued that the PBoC's intention in launching the digital yuan was to replace the dominant electronic payment operators with a government version. However, the PBoC insists that the introduction of the digital yuan will not reduce the market share of Alipay and WeChat Pay. Rather, the e-CNY is supposed to 'complement' these providers (South China Morning Post, 2022a).

In reciprocity, Alipay and WeChat Pay are also committed to promoting the e-CNY. Alipay has now added a button on its app that enables users to search for and download the official e-CNY wallet within its platform (South China Morning Post, 2022a). Once integrated, users can make purchases with e-CNY on the app. In essence, besides the initial set-up, no one would notice that they are using a digital currency instead of a more traditional electronic payment. WeChat Pay, operated by Tencent Holdings, has also set up a similar e-CNY wallet feature.

It is important to note here the digital yuan's two-tier design. Supporting infrastructure is provided by the PBoC. However, the front end is managed by payment providers and banks, both private and state-owned. Since the digital yuan equals cash in circulation, it is fully backed by the PBoC and completely risk free. The digital wallets customers open are not considered bank accounts and have no interest payments. Under this system, only banks can convert digital yuan into bank deposits and vice versa. This includes digital-only banks like Tencent-backed WeBank and Ant-backed MyBank. This set-up ensures the continued centrality of banks in the Chinese financial system and is likely to prevent financial disintermediation, one of the fears with launching CBDCs.

Although there still remain a host of uncertainties, including technical hurdles, privacy concerns, low rates of adoption, as well as regulatory and legal challenges, the digital yuan represents a fundamental and deliberate initiative by Chinese authorities to revolutionize money itself. Quite ironically, a technology that was invented to circumvent centralized coordination and power could trigger a substantial enhancement of monetary surveillance and, hence, state authority.

The e-CNY and yuan internationalization

The PBoC has assured other countries that the e-CNY is not a threat to existing national currencies. For example, Zhou Xiaochuan, the former governor of the PBoC, stated that the e-CNY is designed to focus on domestic transactions and not to replace SWIFT. The digital yuan 'may not necessarily be up to the job' if it was suddenly asked to undertake the role of cross-border payments (Qin, 2022).

Zhou's remarks are likely part of a concerted Chinese government campaign to clamp down on any speculation regarding the digital yuan's international role. It is intended to assuage foreign observers and underplay potential threats this new technology could pose to existing financial infrastructures, especially the SWIFT system. The reality, though, is murky, multifarious, and nuanced. The digital yuan could provide a breakthrough technology for China to successfully internationalize its currency. But there are a number of factors which could undermine such an effort, including technical and geopolitical.

An interesting academic debate concerns whether the digital yuan could aid China in internationalizing the yuan. On one side stand those who argue that the launch of a CBDC will make little difference. For China to successfully internationalize the yuan, authorities have to fully liberalize the capital account. This in turn requires deep and liquid debt markets functioning within a relatively stable regulatory regime.

Eswar Prasad (2020), for example, argues that the yuan will only become prominent as an international currency after the Chinese government removes major restrictions on capital flows: 'the DCEP on its own will not be a game changer that elevates the renminbi's role in international finance.' Similarly, Eichengreen (2011; 2022) has consistently argued that the odds of the US dollar's role being replaced are low given the lack of credible alternatives.

These doubts about the e-CNY's part in furthering yuan internationalization follow the dominant techno-economic perspective, which lays out relatively monolithic constraints and stark trade-offs in establishing a widely accepted reserve currency (Kennen, 1983; Chinn and Frankel, 2005). And there is also a political dimension. Prasad (2021) not only argues that China has to follow the conditions laid out by the techno-economic perspective, but also holds that the absence of a strong rule of law culture and the centralized power of the CCP imply less international trust for the furnishing of a Chinese reserve currency.

These analyses make valid points. The lack of a fully liberalized capital account and, more generally, the lack of international creditors' full trust and faith in the politico-economic stability of China make the yuan as a safe-haven currency a tricky proposition. However, legal and institutional certainty in international finance is relative. For example, efforts by central banks to slightly diversify their holdings, such as by the Bank of Israel, can make a difference (Avis, 2022). Just a small percentage of currency reserves migrating to the yuan could be substantial in total.

Moreover, while there are distinct reasons to distrust the sanctity and security of property rights in China, the same goes for international holders of US dollars. The freezing of the Russian Central Bank's assets has stoked worries that global finance has crossed a red line (Martin, 2022). Central banks, sovereign wealth funds, and high net worth individuals residing in countries with potentially troubled relations with the US must be re-evaluating the security of their holdings.

The 'weaponization' of the US dollar by successive US administrations threatens to undermine the very fundament of the global system. Joseph Yam Chi-Kwong, the former chief executive of the Hong Kong Monetary Authority (HKMA), thinks it is a 'stupid and crazy' strategy. In his view, such moves create capital controls on people who use the US dollar (South China Morning Post, 2022b). The make-up of the international financial infrastructure as an open public good is called into question.

Given this backdrop, China continues to seek pathways to internationalize the yuan. This process remains based on the logic of Sino-capitalism. It aims to attenuate the stark trade-offs the literature posits for the monetary trilemma by seeking controlled financial openness and lower exchange rate volatility paired with continued monetary independence.

China's unique calibration relies on the establishment of a financial ecosystem facilitating global yuan trade. This financial infrastructure is still in its infancy, but it makes use of both state-coordinated efforts and private initiatives. One example involves the launching of the Shanghai oil futures contract as well as changing economic relations with the Gulf Cooperation Council (GCC), and especially Saudi Arabia (McNally, 2020). During his visit to Saudi Arabia in late 2022, Chinese President Xi Jinping explicitly called for the greater use of the Shanghai market for pricing GCC oil and suggested invoicing some oil exports by the GCC in yuan.

The e-CNY constitutes a central element of such an effort to build new financial infrastructures. Given the inherent complexity and risks associated with launching a financial innovation as far-reaching as a CBDC, its initial introduction is focused domestically. However, there are various initiatives underway to test the e-CNY's international role. In February 2022, the PBoC announced expanding the digital yuan pilot programme to Hong Kong for retail payments (Qin, 2022). Since Hong Kong is already the largest offshore yuan distribution centre, the conversion to e-CNY could serve as an important spring board for its internationalization.

The PBoC is also a member of the mBridge project that is exploring cross-border CBDC payments between itself and the Bank of Thailand, the Central Bank of the United Arab Emirates, and the HKMA. This project further involves the Bank of International Settlements (BIS) and private sector participants such as Goldman Sachs, HSBC, Société Générale, and China's biggest state-owned banks. The project aims to lower costs and improve the speed of international transactions using CBDCs (Gkritsi, 2021).

The e-CNY could further function to buildout existing financial infrastructures to manage China's capital account. The 'pipelines' in use now (for example, the Stock and Bond Connects between Hong Kong and the mainland) could be managed with greater ease, and thus expanded with the use of the e-CNY. Enhanced transparency and traceability of capital flows could allow the PBoC to rapidly flag suspicious behaviour and large speculative capital movements. In times of crisis, the PBoC could target certain flows, creating sophisticated capital controls that are highly effective, yet more subtle and less intrusive than at present (Greene, 2021).

The e-CNY thus fits China's strategy for capital account opening: to broaden channels for capital flows while keeping overall control. In this context, the e-CNY could help the Cross-Border Interbank Payment System (CIPS) that China has established gain wider acceptance. Although CIPS has already been functioning for eight years, its transactions and membership remain far behind those of Western clearing houses (Nölke, 2023). CIPS also depends on SWIFT for most cross-border messaging.

Recent events may encourage more participation in CIPS. If integrated, the use of a digital yuan international payments system in combination with CIPS could expand the yuan's international ecosystem. It follows the Chinese strategy of creating not only spatial, but also digital infrastructures centered on China (Nölke, 2023). In 2019, the PBoC actually made clear that launching the digital yuan is aimed at protecting China's foreign exchange sovereignty (Huang, 2019). If the e-CNY's ease-of-use rivals that of established Chinese payment apps, it could usher in increased global adoption of the yuan.

This raises an additional aspect regarding all digital currencies. They are not just simple means of exchange but are also part of wider platforms with a multitude of functions and applications. The competition among CBDCs will in part depend on the platforms associated with them. As with so much else, the governance of data flows, storage, and access creates a host of thorny technological, legal and, ultimately, geopolitical issues.

Since the e-CNY will have to interact with other CBDCs and digital payment systems, CBDC interoperability and interchange are likely to emerge as new areas of global cooperation. The mBridge project depicted earlier is one such example. Another is SWIFT itself. It has launched a major effort to integrate different CBDC systems. As Nick Kerigan, Head of Innovation at SWIFT, noted, 'Different systems and different CBDCs will need to be able to efficiently work together, or it will hamper the ability of businesses and consumers to make frictionless cross-border payments using CBDCs' (SWIFT, 2022).

In the case of China, the logic of Sino-capitalism is likely to balance statist inclinations with the need to foster private capital accumulation and global integration. Although the future remains murky, the e-CNY's significance for global monetary affairs could be substantial. Nevertheless, given the dominance of existing Western financial infrastructures, China seems to have decided that it has to continue working within established systems, such as SWIFT and the BIS. This does not mean that Beijing has given up on developing a complimentary set of China-centred institutions. The e-CNY is part of wider efforts to forge a new financial ecosystem. This system is likely to work closely with existing Chinese payment apps, Alipay and WeChat Pay (Ehlke, Salzer, and Westermeier, Chapter 10, this volume). It will also collaborate with SWIFT and the system of correspondence banking that incorporates a very prominent role for US banks and the US dollar. But it could be sufficiently autonomous to lie beyond the reach of US sanctions, and thus form an alternative global payments infrastructure.

Put differently, once a global multi-CBDC arrangement or even just an efficient payment system incorporating CBDCs, such as the mBridge project, is operable, it could provide a cheap and fast alternative to SWIFT. This would diminish the dominant role of the US dollar and consequently the reach of US extraterritorial jurisdiction (Campbell, 2021; Nölke, 2023). Quite profoundly, a successful payment system incorporating the e-CNY could ameliorate the subordinated position of China in the IMS. Other DEEs could benefit as well, since they would have the opportunity to collaborate based on a newer, much more efficient infrastructure that cuts out many incumbents.

In summary, the process of how the e-CNY emerges internationally will be negotiated and probed over time. As before, the logic of Sino-capitalism fosters an experimental, cautious, and bit-by-bit trial and error approach.

This caution is due to technological/legal, but also geopolitical, concerns. Chinese authorities have been playing down the e-CNY's international role, since it could become another point of contention with the US (Qin, 2022).

This strategy makes sense. The major force that could undermine the e-CNY's international adoption is early political pressure from existing incumbents, first and foremost the US, but also various banks and financial centres. All of these are likely to see their status threatened. One example is the US domestic ban on payment functions of Tencent's WeChat App, that is, WeChat Pay. A concerted effort, as with the Russia sanctions, to undermine the international usage of the e-CNY could spell its premature downfall on the international stage.

Conclusion: A brave new world of money

The-CNY has been launched experimentally and adopted in several dozen major Chinese cities and regions. But it still faces a host of legal, political and technical uncertainties. Perhaps its greatest strength may be seamless integration with existing payment apps, making its domestic use straightforward for the consumer. The e-CNY's international adoption faces much greater headwinds in comparison to its domestic application.

Arguments concerning the e-CNY's influence on yuan internationalization span the gamut. It might make no difference whatsoever, since the major obstacles to yuan internationalization of a closed capital account, insufficiently deep and liquid domestic financial markets, and a host of legal and security issues remain. However, this rather bleak view ignores the history of Chinese financial reform and yuan internationalization to date. Chinese policy makers, in fact, aim to establish a new ecosystem or infrastructure for trading and investing the yuan, first domestically, and then internationally (Nölke, 2023; Petry, 2023).

The various examples noted earlier, including the mBridge project (Gkritsi, 2021) and the integration of the digital yuan into existing Chinese payment platforms, create opportunities to forge a new digital ecosystem that extends beyond China. Other ongoing efforts, such as close collaboration with SWIFT and the expansion of CIPS, are complementing this new ecosystem. As with domestic politico-economic logics, international use is likely to be quite limited for the e-CNY at first. One clear focus could be importers/exporters directly dealing with the Chinese market. The ease of use and lower costs of a new digital platform could entice foreign traders to denominate more trade with China in yuan. Given the importance of Chinese trade for the global economy, this could be a viable strategy to spread the use of the yuan internationally.

Trade invoicing in yuan among DEEs is likely to be in conjunction with the Belt and Road Initiative (BRI) and its focus on infrastructure financing

(Petry, 2023). Since the backbone of the e-CNY's ecosystem will remain independent of other global payment systems, its role as an alternative payment mechanism could be in and of itself an incentive to use it, especially for DEEs.

This factor is likely to play into invoicing oil in yuan. China remains the largest oil importer globally. Offering yuan obligations to pay for trillions of dollars of oil imports, especially from key OPEC members like Saudi Arabia, could create a large shift in how global commodity trades are financed. Already this has occurred for Russia, as more and more of its international trade is being conducted in yuan and roubles.

Precisely because China is now the biggest trading partner of the GCC, invoicing oil in yuan will change the nature of oil export revenue recycling. Instead of most revenues flowing into international US dollar markets, the petrodollar recycling loop could be diminished. Oil export revenues would pay for Chinese imports in yuan and flow into yuan markets (McNally, 2020). However, Washington still holds important cards, especially its deep security relationship with key GCC members, including arms exports.

In addition, the lack of global norms around CBDCs and the fluid nature of this fintech innovation open further spaces for China to engage with the over 100 governments already developing their own CBDCs (Heath, 2022). The digital yuan could foster an alternate monetary ecosystem with China at its centre, yet spanning the globe. A sort of template for this is provided by China's private sector digital payment incumbents, AliPay and WeChat Pay. As they become part of the digital yuan's ecosystem, their established payment efficiency, ease of use, and already near global reach could fashion new avenues for yuan internationalization.

Seen from the perspective of comparative capitalism (Jackson and Deeg, 2008; Clift, 2021), the e-CNY's characteristics of traceability and thus unprecedented real-time insight into the movement of money will condition new interactions between the logics of market efficiency and the logics of state capitalism (Alami and Dixon, 2020; Nölke et al, 2020). Depending on how the PBoC utilizes, processes, and analyzes newly available data, the e-CNY could enhance state surveillance of monetary affairs – a state capitalist logic – while at the same time enabling new use applications that foster digital ecosystems and markets.

Poignantly, applications of the digital yuan could transform China's management of international capital flows, enabling a much more fine-tuned calibration of the yuan's internationalization process. In fact, the e-CNY could serve as a work-around solution to unfettered capital account liberalization. Chinese authorities can retain control and full surveillance while allowing almost free capital movements across their borders.

Finally, continuous experimentation and integration under the logic of Sino-capitalism make the pitfalls of the e-CNY's first-mover status less risky. Chinese authorities are prone to constantly adjust and seek areas of collaboration/interlinkage. Already several avenues are being explored to make the e-CNY compatible with other initiatives and international financial ecosystems. Such efforts are likely to accelerate in coming years, as the breadth and intensity of financial sanctions against Russia mean that many governments owning large amounts of US dollars are likely to question their control over these funds. Chances are higher now than ever for a metamorphosis of the IMS.

Although financial markets and infrastructures are usually seen as neutral exchange mechanisms, control over their operation and functioning can serve as tools of financial statecraft (Fichtner, 2017; Petry, 2023). Bernards and Campbell-Verduyn (2019) note how markets are always organized for specific purposes. Whoever is in charge of them gains control over key infrastructural nodes yielding significant power to shape not only financial but also political outcomes. The financial infrastructures of the neoliberal system evidently reproduce US hegemony and enable an extremely effective exercise of financial statecraft by Washington.

Chinese policy is facing this subordinated role in the IMS. However, the launch of the e-CNY shows that China is not a helpless victim of financial subordination. Rather, Chinese authorities seek to proactively exert international influence. Aspects of market-based (neoliberal) finance are combined with efforts to enhance state capacity. In this manner, the domestic logics of Sino-capitalism condition a gradual, cautious, and experimental approach instead of a collision course. Work-around solutions are pursued while continuing to operate within the neoliberal IMS. The launch of the digital yuan reflects in this manner a unique Sino-capitalist mode of financial statecraft.

Ultimately, the e-CNY is part of ongoing efforts by the CCP to construct an efficient and stable financial system while preserving political supremacy and control over macrosocial development (McNally, 2020; Gruin, 2021). The PBoC's objectives in launching the digital yuan are thus manifold, ranging from a substantial improvement of financial efficiency and greater financial fairness to the enhancement of state authority and supervision of monetary operations. The development of the e-CNY reflects the logic of Sino-capitalism, combining aspects of market-based neoliberal finance with efforts to enhance state surveillance (McNally, 2020; Gruin, 2021). In fact, the nature of CBDCs is ideally suited to these dual objectives. Full adoption of the e-CNY will create much more insight and control over capital flows, possibly triggering a paradigmatic shift, not just technological, but also in terms of financial platforms, regulations, and the very nature of money.

In this manner, the e-CNY will enable the Chinese government to create new market infrastructures and technological standards. Such state-guided action is distinct from a reliance on direct planning or command-and-order instruments of economic governance. The state is intimately involved in forging new markets and infrastructures, expanding the innovative opportunities these provide. Market efficiency rationalities are amalgamated with state capitalist logics, ushering in a new era of state–market interaction that transcends the neoliberal / neo-statist dichotomy with yet unclear global repercussions.

References

Alami, I. and Dixon, A.D. (2020) 'State capitalism(s) redux? Theories, tensions, controversies', *Competition & Change*, 24(1): 70–94.

Alami, I., Alves, C., Bonizzi, B., Kaltenbrunner, A., Koddenbrock, K., Kvangraven, I., et al (2023) 'International financial subordination: A critical research agenda', *Review of International Political Economy*, 30(4): 1360–86.

Andrews, D.M. (2006) 'Monetary power and monetary statecraft', in D.M. Andrews (ed) *International Monetary Power*, Ithaca: Cornell University Press.

Armijo, Leslie Elliot and Katada, Saori N. (2015) 'Theorizing the financial statecraft of emerging powers', *New Political Economy*, 20(1): 42–62.

Avis, D. (2022) 'Israel adds yuan to $206 billion reserves in 'philosophy' change', *Bloomberg*, 17 April, Available from: https://www.bloomberg.com/news/articles/2022-04-20/israel-adds-yuan-to-206-billion-reserves-in-philosophy-change [Accessed 13 February 2025].

Baldwin, D.A. (2020) *Economic Statecraft* (New edn), Princeton, NJ: Princeton University Press.

Bernards, N. and Campbell-Verduyn, M. (2019) 'Understanding technological change in global finance through infrastructures', *Review of International Political Economy*, 26(5): 773–89.

Bowles, P. and Wang, B. (2013) 'Renminbi internationalization: A journey to where?', *Development and Change*, 44(6): 1363–85.

Campbell, C. (2021) 'How China's digital currency could challenge the almighty dollar', *Time*, 11 August, Available from: https://time.com/6084146/china-digital-rmb-currency/ [Accessed 13 February 2025].

Chinn, M. and Frankel, J. (2005) 'Will the euro eventually surpass the dollar as leading international reserve currency?' (NBER Working Papers no 11510), Cambridge, MA: National Bureau for Economic Research.

Clift, B. (2021) *Comparative Political Economy: States, Markets and Global Capitalism*, London: Palgrave Macmillan.

Coghlan, J. (2023) 'China's digital yuan gets smart contract functionality alongside new use cases', *Cointelegraph*, 20 January, Available from: https://cointelegraph.com/news/china-s-digital-yuan-gets-smart-contract-functionality-alongside-new-use-cases [Accessed 13 February 2025].

Cohen, B.J. (2008) 'The international monetary system: Diffusion and ambiguity', *International Affairs*, 84(3): 455–70.

Cohen, B.J. (2018) *Currency Statecraft: Monetary Rivalry and Geopolitical Ambition*, Chicago: The University of Chicago Press.

De Graaff, N. (2020) 'China Inc. goes global. Transnational and national networks of China's globalizing business elite', *Review of International Political Economy*, 27(2): 208–33.

Deutsche Bank (2020) 'Central bank digital currencies – money reinvented', *CIO Special Report*.

Dickson, B. (2008) *Wealth into Power: The Communist Party's Embrace of China's Private Sector*, Cambridge: Cambridge University Press.

Eichengreen, B. (2011) *Exorbitant Privilege: The Rise and Fall of the Dollar and the Future of the International Monetary System*, Oxford: Oxford University Press.

Eichengreen, B. (2022) 'The international financial consequences of Mr Putin', *East Asia Forum*, 8 May, Available from: https://eastasiaforum.org/2022/05/08/the-international-financial-consequences-of-mr-putin/ [Accessed 13 February 2025].

Fichtner, J. (2017) 'Perpetual decline or persistent dominance? Uncovering Anglo-America's true structural power in global finance', *Review of International Studies*, 43(1): 3–28.

Gkritsi, E. (2021) 'mBridge reveals 15 use cases and 22 heavyweight participants', *CoinDesk*, 4 November, Available from: https://www.coindesk.com/policy/2021/11/05/mcbdc-bridge-reveals-15-use-cases-and-22-heavyweight-participants [Accessed 13 February 2025].

Greene, R. (2021) 'Beijing's global ambitions for central bank digital currencies are growing clearer', *Carnegie Endowment for International Peace*, Available from: https://carnegieendowment.org/research/2021/10/beijings-global-ambitions-for-central-bank-digital-currencies-are-growing-clearer?lang=en [Accessed 13 February 2025].

Gruin, J. (2019) 'Financializing authoritarian capitalism: Chinese fintech and the institutional foundations of algorithmic governance', *Finance and Society*, 5(2): 84–104.

Gruin, J. (2021) 'The epistemic evolution of market authority: Big data, blockchain and China's neostatist challenge to neoliberalism', *Competition & Change*, 25(5): 580–604.

Heath, R. (2022) 'Watch out for China's digital yuan', *Politico*, 13 May, Available from: https://www.politico.com/newsletters/digital-future-daily/2022/05/13/watch-out-for-chinas-digital-yuan-00032475 [Accessed 13 February 2025].

Heilmann, S. (2018) *Red Swan: How Unorthodox Policy-Making Facilitated China's Rise*, Hong Kong: Chinese University Press.

Huang, E. (2019) 'China's new digital currency could encourage worldwide use of the yuan, says CEO', *CNBC*, 12 September, Availabe from: https://www.cnbc.com/2019/09/13/chinas-new-cryptocurrency-and-yuan-rmb-internationalization.html [Accessed 13 February 2025].

Jackson, G. and Deeg, R. (2008) 'From comparing capitalisms to the politics of institutional change', *Review of International Political Economy*, 15(4): 680–709.

Kaltenbrunner, A. and Painceira, J.P. (2018) 'Subordinated financial integration and financialisation in emerging capitalist economies: The Brazilian experience', *New Political Economy*, 23(3): 290–313.

Kennen, P.B. (1983) 'The role of the dollar as an international reserve currency' (Occasional Papers no 13), Group of Thirty.

Keram, A. (2021) 'China wants to take the entire country cashless — and surveil its citizens even more closely', *The Washington Post*, 2 March, Available from: https://www.washingtonpost.com/opinions/2021/03/02/china-digital-yuan-currency-surveillance-privacy/ [Accessed 13 February 2025].

Martin, P. (2022) 'Putin's biggest mistake of the Ukraine war? Trusting the Western financial system', *The Conversation*, [online] 7 March, Available from: https://theconversation.com/putins-biggest-mistake-of-the-ukraine-war-trusting-the-western-financial-system-178635 [Accessed 13 February 2025].

McNally, C. (2012) 'Sino-capitalism: China's reemergence and the international political economy', *World Politics*, 64(4): 741–76.

McNally, C. (2017) 'Rebalancing the economy, refurbishing the state: The political economic logic of Sino-capitalism in contemporary China', *Revue de la regulation (Regulation Review)*, Spring.

McNally, C. (2019) 'Theorizing Sino-capitalism: Implications for the study of comparative capitalisms', *Contemporary Politics*, 25(3): 313–33.

McNally, C. (2020) 'The chaotic mélange: neo-liberalism and neo-statism in the age of Sino-capitalism', *Review of International Political Economy*, 27(2): 281–301.

McNally, C. and Gruin, J. (2017) 'A novel pathway to power? Contestation and adaptation in China's internationalization of the RMB', *Review of International Political Economy*, 24(4): 599–628.

Naughton, B. and Tsai, K.S. (eds) (2015) *State Capitalism, Institutional Adaptation, and the Chinese Miracle*, New York: Cambridge University Press.

Nölke, A. (2023) 'Geoeconomic infrastructures: Building Chinese-Russian alternatives to SWIFT', in B. Braun and K. Koddenbrock (eds) *Capital Claims: Power and Global Finance*, London: Routledge.

Nölke, A., ten Brink, T., May, C. and Claar, S. (2020) *State-permeated Capitalism in Large Emerging Economies*, London: Routledge.

Norrlof, C. (2014) 'Dollar hegemony: A power analysis', *Review of International Political Economy*, 21(5): 1042–70.

Otero-Iglesias, M. and Vermeiren, M. (2015) 'China's state-permeated market economy and its constraints to the internationalization of the RMB', *International Politics*, 52(6): 684–703.

Petry, J. (2020) 'Financialization with Chinese characteristics? Exchanges, control and capital markets in authoritarian capitalism', *Economy and Society*, 49(2): 213–38.

Petry, J. (2021) 'Same same, but different: Varieties of capital markets, Chinese state capitalism and the global financial order', *Competition & Change*, 25(5): 605–30.

Petry, J. (2023) 'Beyond ports, roads and railways: Chinese economic statecraft, the Belt and Road Initiative and the politics of financial infrastructures', *European Journal of International Relations*, 29(2): 319–51.

Prasad, E.S. (2017) *Gaining Currency: The Rise of the Renminbi*, Oxford: Oxford University Press.

Prasad, E.S. (2020) 'China's digital currency will rise but not rule', *Project Syndicate*, 25 August, Available from: https://www.project-syndicate.org/commentary/china-digital-currency-will-not-threaten-dollar-by-eswar-prasad-2020-08 [Accessed 13 February 2025].

Prasad, E.S. (2021) *The Future of Money: How the Digital Revolution Is Transforming Currencies and Finance*, Cambridge, MA: Harvard University Press.

Qin, N. (2022) 'Former Chinese central bank chief says digital yuan is for retail transactions', *Yahoo News*, 17 April, Available from: https://finance.yahoo.com/news/former-chinese-central-bank-chief-064915840.html [Accessed 13 February 2025].

South China Morning Post (2022a) 'China digital currency: leading mobile payment apps Alipay, WeChat Pay install new features to help widen e-CNY roll-out', *South China Morning Post*, 5 May, Available from: https://www.scmp.com/tech/big-tech/article/3176812/china-digital-currency-leading-mobile-payment-apps-alipay-wechat-pay [Accessed 13 February 2025].

South China Morning Post (2022b) '"Crazy" US sanctions against China, Russia "weaponise" financial markets, threaten to undermine dollar, former HKMA chief Joseph Yam says', *South China Morning Post*, 11 April, Available from: https://www.scmp.com/business/banking-finance/article/3174030/crazy-us-sanctions-against-china-russia-weaponise [Accessed 13 February 2025].

Stephan, A. (2022) 'Stanford Knowledge Base: Digital Currency Research Institute (字货币研究所) of the People's Bank of China', *Stanford Cyber Policy Center*, 8 March, Available from: https://digichina.stanford.edu/work/knowledge-base-digital-currency-research-institute-of-the-peoples-bank-of-china/ [Accessed 13 February 2025].

Subacchi, P. (2017) *The People's Money: How China is Building a Global Currency*, New York: Columbia University Press.

SWIFT (2022) 'New experiments pave way for international payments using CBDCs', *SWIFT*, 19 May, Available from: https://www.swift.com/news-events/news/new-experiments-pave-way-international-payments-using-cbdcs [Accessed 13 February 2025].

Tsai, Kellee (2007) *Capitalism Without Democracy: The Private Sector in Contemporary China*, Ithaca, NY: Cornell University Press.

PART III

8

The Role of the State in Subordinate Financialized Capitalism: Comparing Financialization of Brazilian and Turkish Firms

Annina Kaltenbrunner, Elif Karaçimen, and Joel Rabinovich

Introduction

Since the beginning of the 21st century, the role of the state and the financialization of the global economy have emerged as focal points of academic inquiry. Those studies focusing on state capitalism and economic statecraft especially have highlighted the renewed and increasing visibility of the state's involvement in economic activities. As well as emphasizing the rising role of sovereign wealth funds, state-owned enterprises, and national development banks (for example, Alami and Dixon, 2020; Alami et al, 2022), this literature encompasses the analysis of widespread state interventions in the aftermath of global financial crises and the growing economic and geopolitical influence, including the potential challenge to Western-centric capitalism, of state-led development models in the Global South (notably from China; see for example, Bremmer, 2010; Petry, 2023). These analyses of diverse empirical instances reflect the literature's broader conceptual engagement with the state's augmented role in emerging and capitalist economies (ECEs).

Many of these contributions have highlighted the transnational and externally facing aspect of state involvement in ECEs. For example, Nölke et al (2021) highlight that developing countries have always faced a trade-off between autonomy and external pressures, whereas Haberly and Wójcik

(2017) argue that state intervention in the Global South is more calculated and internationally extroverted. Yet so far the specific nature and role of the state in countries which assume a subordinate position in global money and financial markets remains undertheorized and underanalyzed. A recent literature on international financial subordination (IFS) has started to conceptualize this systemic and structural international monetary and financial subordination of ECEs and the role of the state therein (for example, Alami et al, 2023; Santos, 2023). This subordination reflects the inherently hierarchical structure of the global financial system, where ECEs occupy subordinate positions that influence their capacities, limitations, and forms of state intervention.

While insightful, this literature still lacks detailed studies on how states in these subordinate positions manage financial dynamics. We fill this gap with an in-depth empirical investigation of the role of the Brazilian and Turkish states in mediating the financial operations of Brazilian and Turkish non-financial corporations (NFCs) over the last 20 years.

Theoretically, we adopt a historical materialist approach to state theory, building on the profound insights offered by Alami (2019a), Alami et al (2023), and Yalman et al (2019). This approach, we believe, enables a deeper investigation into the nuances of state intervention in the contemporary capitalist landscape. This foundational understanding sets the stage for a detailed examination of the state's role in shaping the financialization processes of ECEs NFCs as key agents of domestic capital accumulation. While an extensive literature on the financialization of NFCs in advanced economies shows trends like increased holdings of financial assets, higher debt-to-equity, and a move to market-based financing (Davis, 2016; Fiebiger, 2016; Orhangazi, 2008), research on ECEs is less developed. Existing studies suggest that NFCs in ECEs not only hold substantial financial assets, particularly cash (Demir, 2007; Kalinowski and Cho, 2009; Correa et al, 2012; Powell, 2013), but also engage in significant international borrowing (Duarte, 2019), indicating a pattern of subordinate financialization (Kaltenbrunner et al, 2024). However, the intricacies of how state interventions intersect with these financialization trends in ECEs remain underexplored.

Our research seeks to fill this gap and to unravel how state interventions impact the evolving financial behaviours of NFCs within ECEs, set against the backdrop of IFS-induced pressures. To do so, we conduct a detailed comparative case study of the strategic interventions employed by the Brazilian and Turkish states to facilitate or constrain the engagement of their NFCs with (international) financial markets. Brazil and Turkey are two of the largest emergin markets, with significant domestic financial markets and increasing levels of integration into the global economy (see also Machado et al, Chapter 5 in this volume). They also host world-leading companies competing in several countries (Khanna and Palepu, 2006) with potentially explosive external debt levels (IMF, 2015). We posit that the policies of ECE states concerning NFCs' financial behaviours exhibit a strategic, yet contradictory, nature, marked by an oscillation of enabling, mitigating, and restricting actions. This dynamic is vividly illustrated through the intricate trade-offs and challenges these states encounter in promoting domestic capital accumulation (and thus their NFCs engagement with financial markets), while having to shield globally integrated capital groups against the vulnerabilities arising from global financial markets.

Specifically, the study contributes to our understanding of state interventions in ECEs in three key ways: first, it sheds light on the strategic essence of state interventions in Brazil and Turkey, underscored by the shifts in policy responses to global financial conditions. Both Brazil and Turkey enacted liberalization measures during periods of global liquidity surplus in the early 2000s to attract foreign capital flows. However, the post-global financial crisis (GFC) era saw a pronounced shift towards more active state involvement, with policies explicitly designed to influence the financial activities of NFCs, reflecting a strategic adaptation to the changing global financial landscape.

Secondly, the inherent contradictions in the policies of ECEs' states are vividly illustrated by the complex trade-offs and dilemmas that these states encounter in their efforts to stimulate domestic capital accumulation, while also trying to shield themselves from the vulnerabilities posed by global financial markets. This dynamic is especially pronounced in the period post-2016, where both Brazil and Turkey exhibit shifts in their policy approaches. Brazil, for instance, after having actively promoted domestic firm borrowing before the GFC, made a strategic pivot by reducing National Bank for Economic and Social Development (BNDES) lending and increasing interest rates, pushing firms towards international capital markets to seek financing. During the same period, Turkey adjusted its policy framework to tighten foreign exchange borrowing and introduced tax incentives aimed at promoting the retention of Turkish lira. These policy shifts underscore the inherent contradictions in ECEs' state interventions, emphasizing their struggle to navigate the competing priorities of integrating into the global financial system while striving to sustain domestic capital accumulation.

Thirdly, our analysis reveals how each state's approach to navigating the challenges and opportunities presented by IFS reflects their unique capital accumulation and class dynamics, along with their integration into the world economy. In Brazil, a change in government and subsequent austerity measures, particularly post-2015, led to a drastic cut in BNDES lending (see also Machado et al, Chapter 5 in this volume). This strategic pivot within the state's financial intervention policies was aimed at realigning the country with global financial norms, representing the interests of financial bourgeois while reinforcing commodity-exporting sectors (Mello Filho and de Santos, 2022). Conversely, Turkey's approach, reflecting its heavy reliance on imports for production and vulnerability to capital outflows, exchange rate fluctuations, and inflation, focused on augmenting the role of public banks to alleviate the increasing debt burden on the private sector. Notably, in Turkey, capital groups that have leveraged domestic credit channels and incentives have progressively gained prominence. These groups, involving those with strong ties to ruling political circles, have further solidified their influence within the economy (Güngen and Akçay, 2023).

Our arguments are developed over five sections. Following this introduction, the second section provides a brief review of the literature on the rising role of the state in ECEs, and the emerging research agenda on IFS. Building on this foundation, the same section advances our theoretical framework that integrates debates on the state's growing role, drawing on a historical materialist approach to dissect the state's influence on capital accumulation under global financial pressures. In the third section, the text then delves into detailed case studies of Brazil and Turkey, showcasing the evolving financial behaviours of NFCs, the effects of global market dynamics, and the periods of significant global capital flows shaping state policies. The fourth section concludes by reflecting on the complex effects of state interventions in NFC financing.

The rising role of the state in emerging capitalist economies

For many scholars, increased state intervention has come back, some even arguing that it implies a new form of state capitalism.[1] Although what is precisely meant by state capitalism varies considerably in the current literature (see Alami and Dixon, 2020 and Alami et al, 2022 for excellent overviews and a critical discussion), this literature thematizes the apparent renewal and visibility of the state's role in the economy. In the context of ECEs, this increased visibility comprises phenomena such as the growth and (global) importance of various forms of 'state-capital hybrids' such as sovereign wealth funds, state-owned enterprises, and national development banks (Musaccio and Lazarini, 2014; Dolfsma and Grosman, 2019; Alami and Dixon, 2020); extensive state interventions following global (financial) shocks (Carney, 2015); and the rising importance and geopolitical influence – as well as potential threat to Western-dominated capitalism – of state-led development regimes (in particular China) (Bremmer, 2010; McNally, 2013).

These different empirical phenomena are also reflected in varied conceptual takes on the seemingly more prominent role of the state in ECEs. In Comparative Capitalism, authors have focused on national varieties of capitalism where the state assumes a more prominent role in production and investments, and state–business relations are more developed. Broadly, in this literature state-led varieties of capitalism are seen as an alternative to neoliberalism and catch-up economic development in the Global South (for example, Nölke, 2014; Nölke et al, 2021). In contrast to the traditional developmental state though, these forms of state-permeated capitalism do not operate through a powerful, centralized steering committee, but through close cooperation and competition between various state and business coalitions at the national and sub-national level held together by mechanisms of loyalty and trust, rather than market-mechanisms (Nölke et al, 2021).

This literature explicitly considers the pivotal transnational dimension of state capitalism in ECEs. For example, Nölke et al (2021) highlight that developing countries have always faced a trade-off between autonomy and external pressures, and that the development strategies of large emerging economies are highly dependent on their embeddedness into global economic structures that provide decisive barriers and options for particular growth strategies, and require the protection of national capitalist institutions against external shocks. Moreover, the authors highlight the importance of understanding the rising role of the state within the changing nature of this international context, in particular developing countries' increased transnationalization through transnational corporations (TNCs) and global financial flows.

The transnational element and the reconfiguration of the state under conditions of globalization and financialization to achieve development objectives has also been considered in the Global Political Economy literature. For example, Carney (2015) argues that the strength of one-party regimes, and their use of state-owned corporations, has to be seen in the context of reducing the instabilities arising from increased financial globalization. From a Polanyian perspective, Haberly and Wójcik (2017) explain the rise of big government financial development in developing countries as an attempt to maintain social security and national sovereignty in the face of increased financialization and globalization, which in these countries is more calculated and internationally extroverted. Importantly, these state actions – in particular in the form of state-owned enterprises and reserve accumulation – are not typically an outright attack on market disciplinary regulatory restructuring or global economic integration, but seek to achieve a balanced synthesis of these competing impulses to sustain the processes of neoliberalism, globalization, and financialization. This analysis aligns with the insights provided by Alami's chapter (Chapter 2, this volume), which elucidates how such state actions, including the operation of state-owned enterprises and reserve accumulation, are strategic responses within the confines of the international financial system, aiming not to counteract but to synthesize global economic trends to support neoliberalism, globalization, and financialization.

Finally, the financial statecraft literature has highlighted the use of domestic or international monetary and financial capabilities by ECE governments to achieve foreign policy goals (for example, Armijo and Katada, 2015; Petry, 2023). These interventions can be either 'offensive' – including measures such as bribes and sanctions – or defensive, that is 'to protect the status quo preserving their country's domestic economic and political autonomy' (Armijo and Katada, 2015, p 47). As discussed by Armijo (Chapter 3 this volume), ECEs often rely on defensive strategies and collective actions to navigate entrenched global financial hierarchies, reflecting their structural limitations within the global financial architecture. These strategies can further be 'bilateral' or 'systemic' and utilize either monetary or financial means. For example, Petry (2023) shows how the construction of Chinese financial infrastructures in the context of the Belt and Road Initiative can be seen as offensive and defensive (as well as bilateral and systemic) forms of economic statecraft to challenge the current liberal order.

While these discussed contributions provide valuable insights into ECE states more prominent and visible role in the contemporary era, they generally lack a specific theory of the state in ECEs (see also Alami and Dixon (2020) for a general critique of a missing state theory in the state capitalism literature).[2]

An emerging body of literature on ECEs' international financial subordination (IFS) has started to systematically theorize and conceptualize the subordinate integration of ECEs into international money and financial markets, including the role of the state therein (Alami, 2019b; Alami et al, 2023; Bonizzi et al, 2022). Alami et al (2023) define IFS as 'a relation of domination, inferiority, and subjugation between different spaces across the world market, expressed in and through money and finance, which penalizes actors in DEEs disproportionally' (p 1363). Though manifest through different empirical phenomena, such as heightened external vulnerability and exchange rate volatility, structurally higher interest rates, and the need to accumulate low yielding reserves, the key dimensions of IFS are (a) that it is both structural and systemic to the global economy (rather than due to domestic policy failures or institutional weaknesses), and (b) that it creates both constraints on agency, and a persistent value transfer from the periphery to the core (see also Alami, Chapter 2, this volume).

Traditionally, particularly in the post-Keynesian strand of this literature, ECEs' subordinate integration into international money and financial markets had been identified as a fundamental constraint which biases ECE states' priorities towards external rather than internal policy objects. These constraints include, for example, the need to offer higher interest rates to attract foreign capital, the need to accumulate wasteful foreign exchange reserves, or the necessity to intervene in foreign exchange markets, which has unwanted consequences for domestic monetary and financial conditions (for example, Kaltenbrunner and Painceira, 2015; de Paula et al, 2017).

More recently, drawing on Marxist state theory, authors in this tradition have argued for an understanding of the state in subordinate financialized capitalism which goes beyond identifying the constraints IFS imposes for policy space, to one that anchors IFS and its relationship with the state in a broader theoretical understanding of the role of the state in capitalist society (Alami, 2019b; Yalman et al, 2019; Bedirhanoğlu, 2021; Alami et al, 2023). This literature complements and builds on previous studies that emphasize the significant impact of state interventions and regulatory frameworks on the financialization of ECEs, as highlighted in the works of Lapavitsas (2013), exploring the reconfiguration of regulatory and supervisory frameworks; Painceira (2021), focusing on the creation of sovereign debt markets; Karwowski and Centurion-Vicencio (2018), examining new fiscal and monetary policy frameworks; and Aalbers (2017), highlighting the linkages between state restructuring and the financialization of housing.

Among these, Alami et al (2023), following Clarke (1991), put forward a view of the state 'as playing a key role in processing global capitalist class relations, in politically containing social antagonisms, and in securing the general conditions for accumulation within national territories' (p 1375). In this view, states attempt to negotiate IFS 'in ways that are more or less consistent with their accumulation strategies and attempts to engineer particular social contracts between classes' (p 1375).

We continue this research by further theorizing the role of the state in IFS. In particular, we stress the seemingly contradictory actions of ECE states as they attempt to mediate between global economic pressures and the need to maintain domestic capital accumulation amidst capitalism's systemic contradictions. In a capitalist economy, individual capitalists relentlessly strive to accumulate capital through the sale of products produced by workers, necessitating continuous competition to reduce production costs. As argued by Clarke (1988), this competitive dynamic often results in overaccumulation and realization challenges for individual capitalists. In this instance, the collective interest of the capitalist class (capital-in-general), which is chiefly aimed at preserving the rate of profit, often diverges from the goals of individual capitalists or 'particular capitals', who are primarily focused on maximizing their own profits. This divergence sometimes leads to actions that may conflict with the broader requirements for the stability and overall profitability of the entire capitalist system. While the market adjusts commodity values based on their abundance or scarcity to mediate between these individual and collective interests, it cannot fully reconcile their inherent conflicts and systemic contradictions (Clarke, 1988).

This discord necessitates significant state intervention to secure the interests of capital-in-general by enforcing market rules, inherently intertwined with the power of money as capital. However, while the state plays a key role in upholding the rule of money, it is simultaneously constrained by the broader social power of money and related social relations (de Brunhoff, 1976). Elaborating on this, Alami (2019b) explains that the international flow of money and finance reflects and imposes global capital accumulation conditions and competitive discipline of capital value on different national economies, an impact which is mediated through their balance of payments and exchange rate mechanisms. The impact of international money and finance flows on national economies is particularly relevant in understanding the state's contradictory role in ECEs amidst their integration into global markets, representing critical contradiction for state management. So, it becomes clear that the state's role extends beyond managing domestic capitalist conflicts, but also needs to address the complexities of global market integration (Clarke, 2001). Von Braunmühl (1978) further emphasizes that the nature of state interventions is significantly influenced by how a country is woven into the global economic fabric, with each nation's approach being shaped by its unique position and role in the world market, alongside the broader dynamics of global capital accumulation.

Therefore, inconsistent and controversial state interventions should be viewed as the norm rather than an anomaly, and, in our view, they represent a unique characteristic of subordinate financialization. This perspective is supported by studies such as Alami's (2019a) analysis of Brazil and Apaydin and Çoban's (2023) examination of Turkey, who illustrate the nuanced and often contradictory nature of state policies within the framework of financialization in emerging economies. The next section extends this theoretical empirical work with our comparative study of the dynamic and at times seemingly contradictory interventions of the Brazilian and Turkish states into NFCs engagement with (international) financial markets.

State mediated financialization of NFCs in Turkey and Brazil

Building on the theoretical framework discussed earlier, this section critically examines how the state's role in managing the contradictions of capital accumulation and its navigation of global finance capital are reflected in the financialization of Brazilian and Turkish NFCs. As highlighted in the introduction, while the changing financial operations and practices of NFCs in advanced economies have received considerable attention, there is significantly less work on the financial behaviour of ECE firms.

Given the dominant role of global finance capital for ECEs, our analysis proposes that the state's role in NFCs' financialization processes aligns closely with global financial cycles and can be divided into three distinct sub-periods:

1. The first period, spanning from 2003 to 2008, characterized by high global liquidity and culminating in the global financial crisis (GFC) of 2008.
2. The second period, from 2009 to 2015, marked by a surge in international market liquidity as major economies employed strategies like lowering interest rates and adopting quantitative easing to mitigate the impacts of the GFC.
3. The third period, running from 2016 to the present, characterized by a phase of comparatively reduced global liquidity and punctuated by significant systemic events, including the emerging markets sell-off in 2018 and the COVID-19 pandemic in 2020 (IMF, 2020).

While these global phases of liquidity fundamentally shaped state interventions in Brazil and Turkey to maintain capital accumulation in the context of the structural conditions imposed by IFS, it is also important to recognize that the extent and nature of these interventions varied significantly due to the countries' distinct characteristics of domestic capital accumulation and class relations. For example, Machado et al in Chapter 5 of this volume show that the ambiguous contestation of the current global financial order 'reflects Brazil's internal political dynamics, where there has been an alternation of power between governments more or less aligned with the underlying ideology of the liberal financial order'.

2003–08: State restructuring in the interest of finance capital

The initial phase under examination reveals that state interventions are not only characteristic but also essential in navigating the complexities of international financial subordination. Far from being at odds with IFS, such interventions – including the reorganization of the regulatory and supervisory framework for financial activities, the management of cross-border finance, the establishment of sovereign debt markets, and the development of public–private partnerships (PPPs) – have been pivotal in facilitating the engagement of NFCs from ECEs within the global capital circuits and the hierarchical, unstable global financial system.

This period under review begins with Brazil and Turkey experiencing severe financial crises between the end of the 1990s and early 2000s. These crises were primarily due to a sudden halt or reversal in global financial flows to ECEs. Post-crisis policy design in both countries aimed to benefit from the expansion of the global financial market, and to meet the profit expectations of financial investors. This required significant adjustments in the role of the state (Reis and Oliveira, 2023). Following IMF guidelines, both countries implemented tight fiscal and monetary policies. These included inflation targeting regimes plus floating exchange rates, reserve accumulation, and the establishment of central bank independence, paired with a fiscal policy focused on maintaining primary budget surpluses and extensive privatizations. Additionally, a repressive labour regime became an integral part of the policy framework in both countries (Bozkurt-Güngen, 2018; Reis and Oliveira, 2023; Akçay, 2024).

In this policy environment, Brazil and Turkey both saw domestic credit expansion and high growth rates, lasting until the global financial crisis in 2008 (Arestis et al, 2016; Karaçimen, 2014). Simultaneously, in both countries, as a result of the strong growth, an increase in NFCs' profits and their accumulation of cash and short-term investments occurred. As shown by Kaltenbrunner et al (2024) rather than reinvesting those earnings, firms held onto those cash reserves as a defensive strategy against a potential change in global financial conditions; a process which the authors characterize as subordinate financialization.

Further, during this period, NFCs in both countries significantly increased their indebtedness. The IMF (2015) reports that between 2007 and 2014, Brazil and Turkey witnessed the fourth and second highest increases, respectively, in total NFC debt among all ECEs, with China experiencing the highest increase and Chile ranking third. Existing evidence shows that prior to the GFC, this increase in debt was primarily aimed at supporting capital expenditures in an environment of high growth rates and lucrative investment opportunities, in the context of abundant global liquidity (Özmen et al, 2012; Finello Corrêa et al, 2017; Kaltenbrunner et al, 2024). This trend of expanding gross fixed capital formation in tandem with the rise in credit to NFCs is clearly illustrated in Figure 8.1.

However, whereas both countries experienced substantial increases in debt – fundamentally enabled by the cheap financing conditions on global financial markets – there were also notable differences in their trajectories. In Brazil, while bank credit remained the most important source of finance, bond issuance also became an important source of firm financing (Figure 8.2). A significant share of these bonds were issued offshore on international financial markets. In the case of Turkey, according to information from the Central Bank of Turkey, issued bonds represented less than 1 per cent of total liabilities in the 2000s and 2010s. In the period following the 2001 crisis, as the potential for profit from financing public debt diminished due to shrinking budget deficits and falling interest rates, Turkish banks shifted their focus more towards their core business activity: providing finance to the private sector (Karaçimen, 2014).

The observed differences between Brazil and Turkey can be attributed to variations in state intervention into financial markets. In Brazil, domestic regulations prohibit banks from lending in foreign currency, which compelled Brazilian firms to seek cheaper financing abroad. This regulatory landscape changed significantly with a law introduced in 2022, which relaxed these restrictions, as will be discussed. Even with this relaxation, the contrast

Figure 8.1: Credit to non-financial firms and gross capital formation

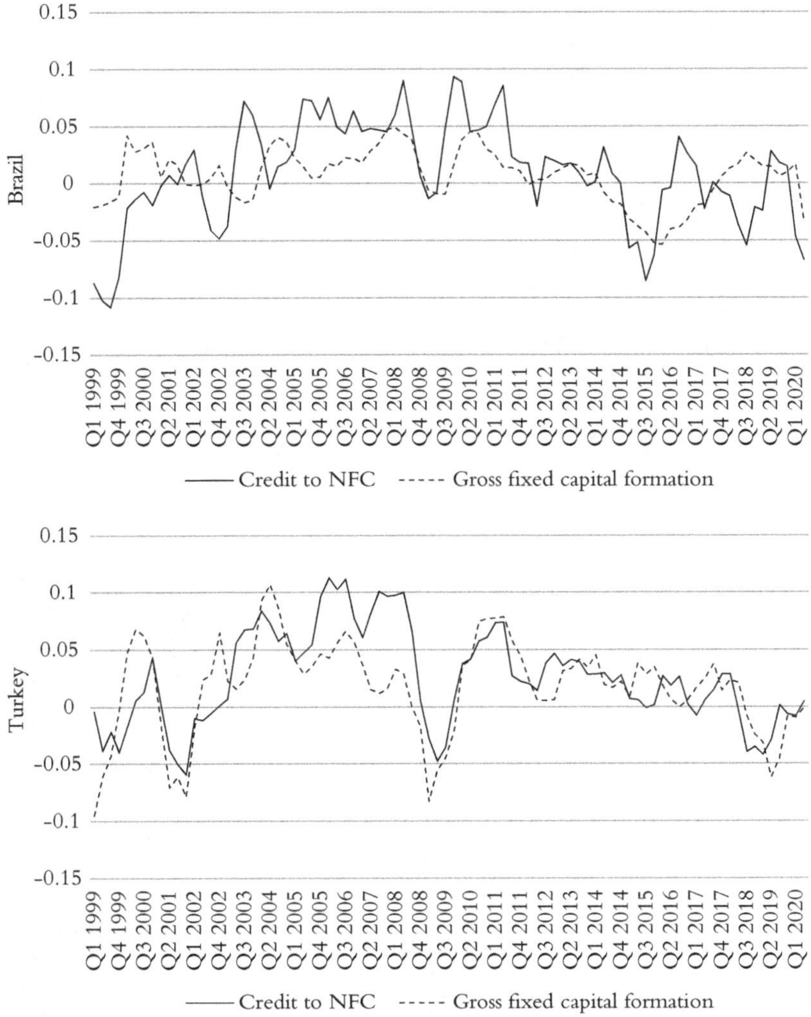

Source: BIS and OECD, reproduced from Kaltenbrunner et al (2024)

with Turkey is stark, where no such lending restrictions existed, enabling banks to more freely facilitate foreign currency lending. Further, Turkey also presents a different scenario, because foreign banks and the foreign branches of domestic banks have emerged as major financing avenues abroad for Turkish NFCs (Karaçimen, 2014). This reliance is partly attributed to the underdevelopment of domestic bond markets in Turkey, which renders Turkish NFCs relatively inexperienced in such financial mechanisms.

Thus, the period from 2003 to 2008 signified a critical juncture in Brazil and Turkey and highlights the influence of global liquidity abundance on state

Figure 8.2: Bond issuance in the domestic market, Brazilian nationals and Brazilian residents in international markets (US$ million)

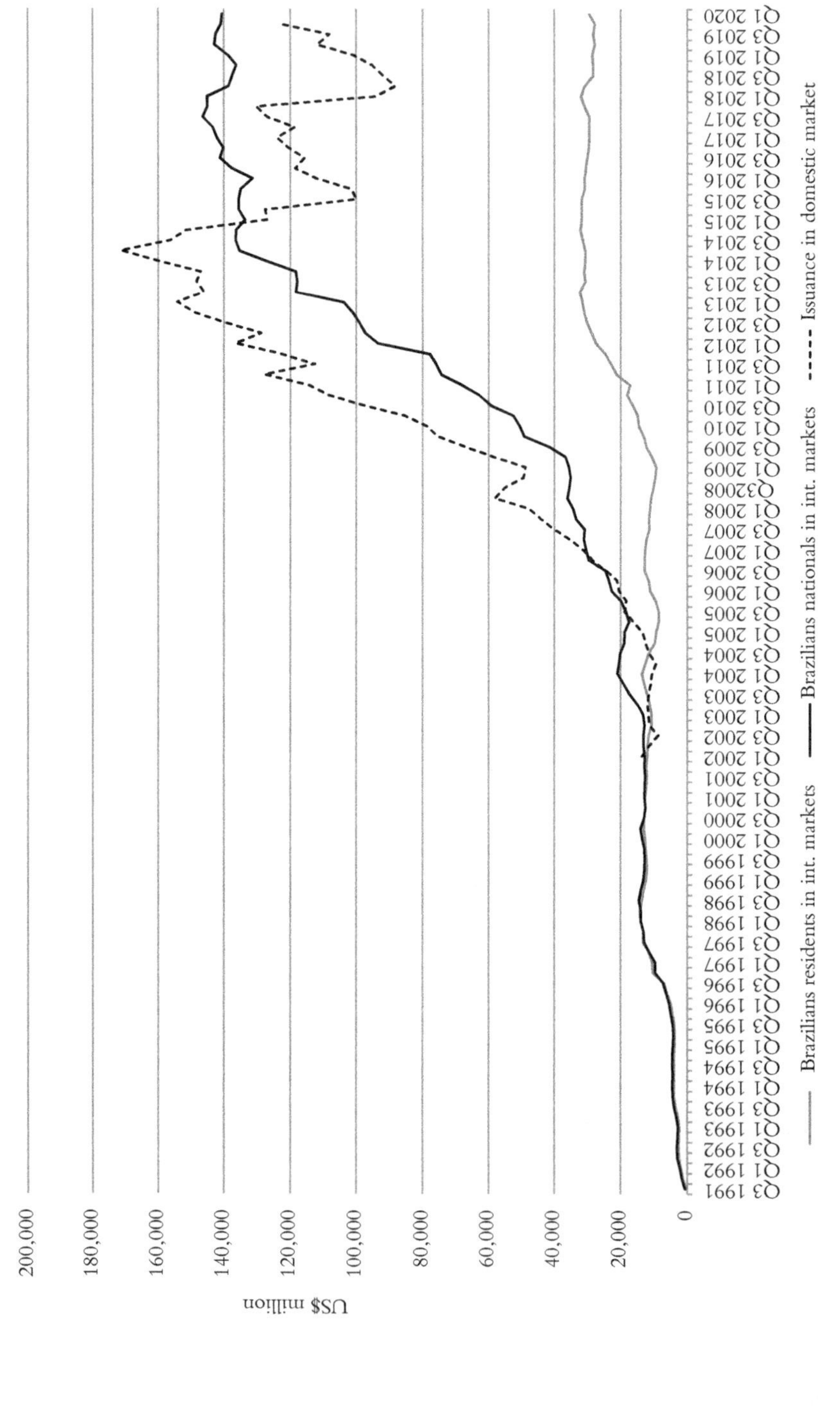

Source: BIS, reproduced from Kaltenbrunner et al (2024)

restructuring towards accommodating the interest of finance capital. During this transformative era, the strategies adopted by both countries were aimed at attracting and maintaining a steady influx of foreign capital, despite an increasing reliance on transnational finance. Such state interventions in financial markets had tangible effects on corporate strategies reflected in a substantial surge in external debt in both countries (accompanied by a significant accumulation of cash to protect against a change in global financial conditions). The distinct approaches adopted by Brazil and Turkey – Brazil's restrictive regulations on foreign currency lending versus Turkey's established reliance on foreign banks and branches – in turn show the variegated landscape of financial market interventions at the backdrop of different financial and productive structures.

2009–15: Government-led credit expansions

The onset of the second period is marked by a notable stagnation in profitability, as evident in the gross capital formation figures (Figure 8.1). This stagnation, coupled with the challenges of repaying debt post-GFC, signalled the beginning of a new phase. For example, in Turkey, the share of foreign currency debt in GDP almost doubled after 2004, reaching around 16 per cent in 2008, and half of this debt was due to mature in 2009 and 2010 (33 per cent and 17 per cent of the total, respectively) (Rawdanowicz, 2010). During this time, governments in both Brazil and Turkey intervened to facilitate the continuous borrowing of NFCs, thus mediating their financialization. Again, the specific policy measures differed: whereas Brazil focused on public credit through the BNDES due to private banks' hesitance, the Turkish state enabled foreign currency loans for firms without foreign exchange income through regulatory changes in 2009, significantly shifting corporate borrowing and increasing banking sector debt.

In Brazil, while bank credit predominantly drove the increase in lending before the crisis, post-crisis financing saw a major role played by directed public credit, particularly through the BNDES. This shift was partly due to the private banks' growing reluctance to lend and also a result of a countercyclical policy measure. The National Treasury, which only contributed 7 per cent of the total funds lent by BNDES in 2007, increased its share to 49 per cent by 2016, peaking at 58 per cent in 2014 (Torres Filho, 2018). By 2016, BNDES accounted for over 50 per cent of all credit with maturities extending beyond five years.

In Turkey, although NFCs were already engaging in significant foreign exchange (FX) borrowing, particularly from international sources, a crucial regulatory change in 2009 significantly influenced corporate borrowing practices. This policy shift directed NFCs towards sourcing their FX loans from domestic banks, marking a pivotal turn in the landscape of corporate finance within the country. The new regulation allowed firms without FX income to obtain FX loans from resident banks, provided these loans were at least US$5 million and had a duration of more than one year. This ease of access to foreign currency loans led to an increase in FX indebtedness through domestic banks. Consequently, Turkish NFCs shifted from borrowing directly from FX financial markets, as was the norm previously, to relying more on the domestic banking sector, which, in turn, increased its international borrowing to channel funds to NFCs. As a result, the external debt of the banking sector saw a substantial increase, growing from around 8 per cent of the GDP to 29 per cent by September 2015 (IMF, 2016). Additionally, the Central Bank of Turkey introduced the reserve options mechanism in 2011. This innovative tool allowed banks to hold a portion of their required reserves in foreign currency, further facilitating domestic banks' credit expansion by enabling them to borrow from international markets at lower interest rates (Boratav and Orhangazi, 2022).

This period highlights the delicate balance states must strike in facilitating corporate access to capital while managing the risks associated with increased foreign exchange exposure, illustrating the complex interplay between national policies and the pressures of the global financial system. As global financial conditions became more insecure, and accumulated financial fragilities began to bite, the Brazilian and Turkish states intervened to maintain domestic capital accumulation. These interventions, in turn, reflected existing structures of accumulation. In both Brazil and Turkey, post-GFC, government support for sectors like construction, energy, transport, and mining notably increased, reflecting the state's crucial role in channelling financial resources to these areas (Ebenau and Liberatore, 2013; Orhangazi and Yeldan, 2021). It is worth mentioning that the facilitation of external funds through PPPs is a crucial part of this process, demonstrating state mediation's significance in the escalation of FX debt among NFCs (Kaltenbrunner et al, 2024).

2016–present: Divergent state policies: Brazil's neoliberal turn vs Turkey's fiscal challenge

The economic landscapes of both Brazil and Turkey witnessed substantial disruption in 2015 due to capital flight from ECEs, triggered by the devaluation of the Chinese renminbi. During this period, both countries contended with diminished global market liquidity, leading their economies to experience stagnation that has persisted up to the present. Moreover, a crisis of profitability became apparent in both nations (Marquetti et al, 2023; Mutlu, 2023). In response to these shared challenges and in alignment with the overarching interests of capital, both Brazil and Turkey underwent significant policy shifts, which disproportionately affected the working classes (Mello Filho and de Santos, 2022; Yeldan et al, 2023). Though these policy shifts, which will be discussed later, may seem to have clashed with the interests of financiers and certain capital groups, they still generally upheld one of the main pillars of neoliberalism: free capital mobility (see also Chapter 2 by Alami and Chapter 9 by Petry, both this volume). Thus, the state continued to act in the general interest of capital in line with the imperatives of financialized capitalism, even if it implemented seemingly contradictory policies.

In this last phase, the policy shifts diverged substantially between the two countries. In Brazil, the state adopted a firm embrace of neoliberal policies, particularly following a severe recession in 2015. Conversely, Turkey experienced a considerable deterioration in fiscal balance during this period, as the government assumed the risks associated with high private debt.

These economic conditions also led to contrasting state interventions in the financial behaviour of NFCs in each country, reflecting their distinctive capital accumulation characteristics and class dynamics. In Brazil, despite the government's initial expansion of public banking, the Temer administration's post-2015 austerity policies led to a significant reduction in the role of public banking in corporate financing. In 2016 the credits offered by BNDES started to be restricted. The BNDES increased its interest rates by switching from TJLP (*Taxa de Juros de Longo Prazo* –long term interest rate) to TLP (*Taxa de Longo Prazo* – long term rate). While the former was defined by the National Monetary Council, in accordance with the government's economic policy, the latter automatically followed the market rate for the 5-year Treasury bonds added to the Extended Consumer Price Index. The BNDES was also forced to pay back to the Treasury and became a target of a strong media campaign that associated it with companies involved in political corruption (Torres Filho, 2018). Between 2018 and 2020, public bank total loans fell by R$24 billion, a reduction of 35 per cent (Mello Filho and de Santos, 2022). In Brazil, the transition towards austerity and a diminished role for public banking, particularly after 2015, coupled with a rise in private funding through bond issuances since 2017 (Aparecida et al, 2022), reflects a strategic pivot within the state's financial intervention policies. This change highlights a complex strategy aimed at aligning with global financial norms while addressing domestic capital groups' demands for fiscal austerity.

In contrast, Turkey, facing severe currency crises in 2018 and 2021 due to capital flow fluctuations, took a different approach and implemented drastic measures.[3] Turkey experienced a portfolio outflow of US$15.4 billion in 2015, primarily from short-term funds, and its currency depreciated by 25 per cent against the dollar over the year, placing it among the most vulnerable ECEs, alongside Argentina (Bonfield, 2016). The Turkish government, grappling with the high external debt of its companies and significant currency depreciation, restricted NFCs' borrowing in foreign currency and phased out mechanisms that facilitated FX credit expansion.

The reserve option mechanism, which facilitated FX credit expansion for domestic banks, was gradually phased out starting in 2016, culminating in its complete abolition by 2022. Further, a crucial regulatory change came in 2018, reversing the 2009 regulation that had allowed NFCs without FX revenue to obtain FX loans. However, in a move to support a credit-driven model of capital accumulation, Turkey augmented the role of public banks, especially in FX loan expansion. The shift in the composition of loans from private to public banks and from Turkish lira to foreign currencies is clearly evident in Table 8.1, showcasing a marked contrast to Brazil's approach.

This strategy in Turkey was a response to the country's heavy reliance on imports for production, making it particularly vulnerable to capital outflows, exchange rate fluctuations, and inflation. To address these economic challenges, the Turkish government strategically enhanced the role of public banks, complemented by targeted incentives, to reduce the burgeoning debt load on the private sector. This approach significantly favoured capital groups that maintain close ties to the ruling political elite (Güngen and Akçay, 2023). Such a strategy was designed not just to counter Turkey's economic vulnerabilities but also to bolster specific capital factions, demonstrating a deliberate coordination between state policies and the interests of prominent domestic capital groups. This approach starkly contrasts with Brazil's, where the dynamics of capital accumulation were influenced by the country's strong export earnings. These earnings played a crucial role in maintaining the value of Brazil's currency, despite global economic pressures. As a result, Brazil adopted a strategy that differed from Turkey's, with its economic policies and banking sector adjustments reflecting its unique financial landscape and capital accumulation characteristics. Its strategic shift in financial intervention policies aimed to align with international financial standards, catering to the interests of

Table 8.1: Composition of bank loans to NFCs (except small and medium sized enterprises), Turkey

	2004	2009	2018	2019	2020	2021
Public (%)	**57.3**	**61.1**	**73.4**	**71.2**	**70.1**	**73.9**
Public TL (%)	74.5	63.6	36.2	40.4	42.6	35.2
Public FX (%)	25.5	36.4	63.8	59.6	57.4	64.8
Private (%)	**42.7**	**38.9**	**26.6**	**28.8**	**29.9**	**26.1**
Private TL (%)	57.4	54.7	63.9	62.6	58.2	65.5
Private FX (%)	42.6	45.3	36.1	37.4	41.8	34.5

Source: Turkish Central Bank

the financial bourgeoisie and bolstering the commodity-exporting sectors (Mello Filho and de Santos, 2022).

As the contradictions, stemming from global economic pressures and the imperative to sustain domestic capital accumulation, heightened with the capital outflows in 2018 and 2020, state intervention intensified in both countries, again taking different routes. The most prominent change in Brazil was the granting of Central Bank autonomy in 2021, showing its commitment to the neoliberal agenda, sustaining a capital accumulation regime supported by capital flows, and prioritizing the interests of finance capital. According to (Mello Filho and de Santos, 2022), together with the rigid fiscal regime, Central Bank autonomy reflects an intensified subordination of the institutional form of the state in Brazil to the monetary and financial regime. Additionally, the introduction of a new Brazilian law towards the end of 2022 removed several barriers to operations in foreign currency. This legislation enabled Brazilian banks to offer loans denominated in foreign currencies to both foreign and local firms, thereby facilitating the financing of imported or exported goods and services. However, it is important to note that domestic bank accounts in foreign currency remain restricted to specific sectors and require prior authorization from the Central Bank.

Turkey, on the other hand, took an opposite path, as the resources to sustain a capital accumlation regime that is foreign-capital dependent and credit-driven and to favour the interests of government-aligned bourgeois classes became extremely difficult, the government moved further away from the neoliberal programme. The sustaining of Turkey's global economic integration faced amplified contradictions following a second currency crisis towards the end of 2021. To counter the further depreciation of its currency, the state escalated its intervention, adopting measures that were at times at odds with its prevailing capital accumulation strategy. One of the most dramatic of its regulations was the imposition of limitations on foreign currency transactions of NFCs (Pitel, 2022). Another major measure demonstrating the direct interference of the state into the financial practices of NFCs was the introduction of the KKM instrument (FX-protected deposit accounts), which is an innovative instrument of the Turkish government protecting the savings of customers with foreign currency deposits in USD, EUR, and GBP or gold deposit accounts against changes in exchange rates, provided that they are converted into Turkish lira. In 2022, the government approved a corporate income tax exemption on gains from investing in KKM accounts to persuade NFCs to hold more lira rather than foreign currency. These strategic moves highlight the state's navigation through inherent contradictions – between fostering a capital inflow-driven accumulation regime and attempting to enhance confidence in the national currency.

Conclusion

The analysis of the state-mediated financial subordination of NFCs in Brazil and Turkey offers deep insights into the complexities of managing domestic capital accumulation amid global economic integration pressures. At the start of the 2000s, during a period of global liquidity surplus, both countries enacted liberalization measures to attract foreign capital flows. Yet, the post-GFC era marked a strategic shift, with intensified state interventions influencing the financial behaviours of NFCs. In Brazil, the lowering of BNDES rates encouraged public borrowing by NFCs, while in Turkey, 2009 regulations facilitated foreign currency borrowing for NFCs without FX earnings, and the 2011 reserve option mechanism supported domestic credit expansion. The period post-2016 saw heightened contradictions in policy measures; Brazil's BNDES reduced lending and increased rates, prompting firms to turn towards more favourable international markets. Conversely, in Turkey, the 2018 reversal of the 2009 regulation, termination of the reserve option mechanism, and introduction of tax exemptions on KKM accounts illustrate the state's efforts to balance capital inflow-driven accumulation with national currency stability to sustain its domestic capital accumulation. This nuanced analysis underscores the intricate interplay between national economic strategies and global finance, highlighting adaptive yet contradictory policies by states facing global financial pressures. Rather than simply reacting to external constraints, these strategies reveal how Brazil and Turkey's states actively operate within the hierarchical structure of the global financial system, reinforcing their positions within subordinate financialized capitalism. This result shows the value of differentiation between different types of state actions as highlighted in the financial statecrafts literature. As we show, these can alternate between defensive and offensive actions depending on the state of the global financial cycle, and the complex interplay between external pressures and the need to sustain domestic capital accumulation. The role of the state in mediating the behaviour of NFCs demonstrates significant variation, which can be attributed to the unique class constellations and capital accumulation regimes within Brazil and Turkey, shaped by their distinct strategies of global integration. In Turkey, where the economic structure is marked by import reliance, exchange rate fluctuations, and inflation, state intervention has been oriented towards supporting public banks. This strategy is designed to lighten the debt burden on the private sector, complemented by targeted incentives. It reflects the government's intention to support capital groups with substantial ties to the political elite, showcasing how state interventions are strategically aligned with the interests of these influential domestic factions. Conversely, Brazil's strategy, informed by its class configuration dominated by powerful export-oriented agribusiness and mining sectors, capitalizes on robust export earnings to maintain its currency value against global pressures. The resultant economic policies and banking sector strategies in Brazil are thus tailored to sustain and enhance the interests of these dominant classes and financial bourgeois, leveraging the country's export strength to navigate economic challenges. This strategic differentiation not only underscores the distinct financial landscapes of Turkey and Brazil but also highlights how state policies are interwoven with the interests and power dynamics of different class groups within each country, influencing their approach to managing financialization's impacts.

Lastly, the critical examination of state interventions in NFC financing over the observed period reveals profound implications for financial subordination, demonstrating that such policies have not only heightened firms' vulnerabilities to FX-debt and market fluctuations but also directed fund allocations in ways that deepen financial subordination. In Turkey, the notable rise in FX-denominated deposits starkly contrasts with the strategic placement of investments abroad, whereas in Brazil, a significant portion of capital was channelled into non-productive activities, including the repayment of reais-denominated debts to the BNDES (Kaltenbrunner et al, 2024). This nuanced analysis highlights the intricate impact of state policies on the financial strategies and vulnerabilities of NFCs, situated within the expansive framework of global financial integration.

Notes

1. In light of the historical implications of 'state capitalism' as observed in the political economies of the Soviet Union, pre-1979 China, and economic development strategies in peripheral regions post-World War II (van Apeldoorn et al, 2012), our analysis intentionally avoids this term. However, the literature's focus on the transnational aspect of state involvement in ECEs provides a rich basis for our examination of the state's role in the context of IFS.
2. An exception to the general lack of a specific state theory in state capitalism literature is van Apeldoorn et al (2012), who utilize Marxian state theory and Polanyi's insights to underscore the state's integral role in capital accumulation. Particularly, they note how neoliberal globalization's contradictions and crises have necessitated a more pronounced state role in both the capitalist core and periphery, leading to outward-looking, economically expansionist state action in the Global South, as seen in countries like China and Russia.
3. In recent years, substantial state interventions in Turkey have been analyzed through the lens of 'authoritarian consolidation' (Akçay, 2021) and an 'authoritarian mode of financialization' (Karas and Dönmez, 2023). Additionally, Bedirhanoğlu (2021) contends that the Justice and Development Party (AKP) government has been compelled to operate beyond the usual political limitations set by the Turkish state's parliamentary system to effectively address these unique challenges.

References

Aalbers, M.B. (2017) 'The variegated financialization of housing', *International Journal of Urban and Regional Research*, 41(4): 542–54.

Akçay, Ü. (2021) 'Authoritarian consolidation dynamics in Turkey', *Contemporary Politics*, 27(1): 79–104.

Akçay, Ü. (2024) 'Revisiting the rise and decline of authoritarian neoliberalism: A political economy analysis of AKP's initial decade', *Journal of Balkan and Near Eastern Studies*, 26(6): 972–87.

Alami, I. (2019a) 'Post-crisis capital controls in developing and emerging countries: Regaining policy space? A historical materialist engagement', *Review of Radical Political Economics*, 51(4): 629–49.

Alami, I. (2019b) *Money, Power and Financial Capital in Emerging Markets*, London: Routledge.

Alami, I. and Dixon, A.D. (2020) 'State capitalism(s) redux? Theories, tensions, controversies', *Competition & Change*, 24(1): 70–94.

Alami, I., Babic, M., Dixon, A.D., and Liu, I. (2022) 'Special issue introduction: What is the new state capitalism?', *Contemporary Politics*, 28(3): 245–63.

Alami, I., Alves, C., Bonizzi, B., Kaltenbrunner, A., Koddenbrock, K., Kvangraven, I., et al (2023) 'International financial subordination: a critical research agenda', *Review of International Political Economy*, 30(4): 1360–86.

Aparecida, L.B.D., Lazzarini, S.G., and Bortoluzzo, A.B. (2022) 'Long-term financing: Exploring the recent advances in the Brazilian bond market', *Revista de Administração Contemporânea*, 26(2): e210076.

Apaydin, F. and Çoban, M.K. (2023) 'The political consequences of dependent financialization: Capital flows, crisis and the authoritarian turn in Turkey', *Review of International Political Economy*, 30(3): 1046–72.

Arestis, P., Baltar, C.T., and Prates, D.M. (2016) 'Brazilian economic performance since the emergence of the Great Recession: The effects of income distribution on consumption', *Panoeconomicus*, 63(2): 157–74.

Armijo, L.E. and Katada, S.N. (2015) 'Theorizing the financial statecraft of emerging powers', *New Political Economy*, 20(1): 42–62.

Bedirhanoğlu, P. (2021) 'Global class constitution of the AKP's "authoritarian turn" by neoliberal financialization' in E. Babacan, M. Kutun, E. Pınar, and Z. Yılmaz (eds) *Regime Change in Turkey: Neoliberal Authoritarianism, Islamism and Hegemony*, New York: Routledge.

Bonfield, C. (2016) 'The Turkish economy in 2015', *Centre for Strategic Studies*, [online] 24 February, Available from: https://www.csis.org/analysis/turkish-economy-2015-0 [Accessed 31 January 2025].

Bonizzi, B., Kaltenbrunner, A., and Powell, J. (2022) 'Financialised Capitalism and the Subordination of Emerging Capitalist Economies', *Cambridge Journal of Economics*, 46(4): 651–78.

Boratav, K. and Orhangazi, Ö. (2022) 'Neoliberal framework and external dependency versus political priorities, 2009–2020', in E. Özçelik and Y. Özdemir (eds) *Political Economy of Development in Turkey: 1838–Present*, Singapore: Springer, pp 287–314.

Bozkurt-Güngen, S. (2018) 'Labour and authoritarian neoliberalism: Changes and continuities under the AKP governments in Turkey', *South European Society and Politics*, 23(2): 219–38.

Bremmer, I. (2010) *The End of the Free Market: Who Wins the War between States and Corporations?*, New York: Portfolio.

Carney, R.W. (2015) 'The stabilizing state: State capitalism as a response to financial globalization in one-party regimes', *Review of International Political Economy*, 22(4): 838–73.

Clarke, S. (1988) *Keynesianism, Monetarism and the Crisis of the State*, Aldershot: Edward Elgar.

Clarke, S. (1991) 'State, class struggle, and the reproduction of capital', in S. Clarke (ed) *The State Debate*, Wiesbaden: Springer, pp 183–203.

Clarke S. (2001) 'Class struggle and the global overaccumulation of capital', in R. Albritton, M. Itoh, R. Westra, R., and A. Zuege (eds) *Phases of Capitalist Development: Booms, Crises and Globalisations*, London: Palgrave, pp 76–92.

Correa, E., Vidal, G., and Marshall, W. (2012) 'Financialization in Mexico: Trajectory and limits', *Journal of Post Keynesian Economics*, 35(2): 255–75.

Davis, L.E. (2016) 'Identifying the 'financialization' of the nonfinancial corporation in the US economy: A decomposition of firm-level balance sheets', *Journal of Post Keynesian Economics*, 39(1): 115–41.

De Brunhoff, S. (1976) *Marx on Money*, New York: Urizen.

Demir, F. (2007) 'The rise of rentier capitalism and the financialization of real sectors in developing countries', *Review of Radical Political Economics*, 39(3): 351–59.

de Paula, L.F., Fritz, B., and Prates, D.M. (2017) 'Keynes at the periphery: Currency hierarchy and challenges for economic policy in emerging economies', *Journal of Post Keynesian Economics*, 40(2): 183–202.

Dolfsma, W. and Grosman, A. (2019) 'State capitalism revisited: a review of emergent forms and developments', *Journal of Economic Issues*, 53(2): 579–86.

Duarte, C.B. (2019) 'Corporate debt expansion in emerging countries after 2008: Profile, determinants and policy implications' in L.-P. Rochon and V. Monvoisin (eds) *Finance, Growth and Inequality*, Aldershot: Edward Elgar, pp 179–209.

Ebenau, M. and Liberatore, V. (2013) 'Neodevelopmentalist state capitalism in Brazil and Argentina: Chances, limits and contradictions', *dms–Der Moderne Staat–Zeitschrift für Public Policy, Recht und Management*, 6(1): 17–18.

Fiebiger, B. (2016) 'Rethinking the financialisation of non-financial corporations: A reappraisal of US empirical data', *Review of Political Economy*, 28(3): 354–79.

Finello Corrêa, M., de Medeiros Lemos, P., and Feijo, C. (2017) 'Financeirização, Empresas Não Financeiras e o Ciclo Econômico Recente da Economia Brasileira', *Economia e Sociedade*, 26(spe): 1127–48.

Güngen. A. and Akçay, Ü (2023) 'Growth models, power blocs and authoritarianisms in Turkey and Egypt in the 21st century' (IPE Berlin Working Papers), Berlin: Institute for International Political Economy.

Haberly, D. and Wójcik, D. (2017) 'Earth incorporated: Centralization and variegation in the global company network', *Economic Geography*, 93(3): 241–66.

IMF (2015) 'Corporate leverage in emerging markets. A concern?', *Global Financial Stability Report*, Washington, DC: International Monetary Fund.

IMF (2016) 'Turkey selected issues', *IMF Country Report No 16/105,* Washington, DC: International Monetary Fund.

IMF (2020) *Global Financial Stability Report: Markets in the Time of COVID-19*, Washington, DC: International Monetary Fund.

Kalinowski, T. and Cho, H. (2009) 'The political economy of financial liberalization in South Korea: State, big business, and foreign investors', *Asian Survey*, 49(2): 221–42.

Kaltenbrunner, A. and Painceira, J.P. (2015) 'Developing countries' changing nature of financial integration and new forms of external vulnerability: the Brazilian experience', *Cambridge Journal of Economics*, 39(5): 1281–306.

Kaltenbrunner, A., Karaçimen, E., and Rabinovch, J. (2024) 'The changing financial practices of Brazilian and Turkish firms under financial subordination, a mixed-methods analysis', *Socio-Economic Review*, 22(4): 1967–94.

Karaçimen, E. (2014) 'Financialization in Turkey: The case of consumer debt', *Journal of Balkan and Near Eastern Studies*, 16(2): 161–80.

Karas, D. and Dönmez, P. (2023) 'Crises of authoritarian financialization: Monetary policy in Hungary and Türkiye in the polycrisis', in M. Yağcı (ed) *Central Banking in a Post-Pandemic World*, London: Routledge, pp 186–220.

Karwowski, E. and Centurion-Vicencio, M. (2018) 'Financialising the state: Recent developments in fiscal and monetary policy' (HAL SHS Working Papers), Available from: https://halshs.archives-ouvertes.fr/halshs-01713028 [Accessed 31 January 2025].

Khanna, T. and Palepu, K.G. (2006) 'Emerging giants: Building world-class companies in developing countries', *Harvard Business Review*, 84(10).

Lapavitsas, C. (2013) *Profiting without Producing: How Finance Exploits Us All*, London: Verso Books.

Marquetti, A., Maldonado Filho, E., Miebach, A., and Morrone, H. (2023) 'An interpretation of the Brazilian economy from the profit rate: 1950–2020', *Brazilian Journal of Political Economy*, 43(2): 309–34.

McNally, C.A. (2013) 'The challenge of refurbished state capitalism: Implications for the global political economic order', *dms–Der Moderne Staat–Zeitschrift für Public Policy, Recht und Management*, 6(1): 9–10.

Mello Filho, M.S.B. and de Santos, D.O. (2022) 'Crisis and reconfiguration: Economic and political changes in the Brazilian accumulation regime in the XXI century', *Analyser les transformations de l'Amérique latine*, 33(2).

Mutlu, O. (2023) 'Türkiye ekonomisinde sermaye birikim dinamikleri: Üretken olmayan emek, artık değer oranı ve kârlılık', *Praksis*, (63): 283.

Musacchio, A. and Lazzarini, S.G. (2014) *Reinventing State Capitalism: Leviathan in Business, Brazil and Beyond*, Cambridge, MA: Harvard University Press.

Nölke, A. (2014) *Multinational Corporations from Emerging Markets: State Capitalism 3.0*, Wiesbaden: Springer.

Nölke, A., ten Brink, T., May, C., and Claar, S. (2021) *State-Permeated Capitalism in Large Emerging Economies* (1st edn), London: Routledge.

Orhangazi, Ö. (2008) 'Financialisation and capital accumulation in the non-financial corporate sector: A theoretical and empirical investigation on the US economy: 1973–2003', *Cambridge Journal of Economics*, 32(6): 863–86.

Orhangazi, Ö. and Yeldan, A.E. (2021) 'The re-making of the Turkish crisis', *Development and Change*, 52(3): 460–503.

Özmen, E., Şahinöz, S., and Yalçın, C. (2012) 'Profitability, saving and investment of non-financial firms in Turkey', Central Bank of the Republic of Turkey, Working Paper No 12/14.

Painceira, J.P. (2021) *Financialisation in Emerging Economies: Changes in Central Banking*, London: Routledge.

Petry, J. (2023) 'Beyond ports, roads and railways: Chinese economic statecraft, the Belt and Road Initiative and the politics of financial infrastructures', *European Journal of International Relations*, 29(2): 319–51.

Pitel, L. (2022) 'Turkey dials up the pressure on banks as lira slides', *Financial Times*, [online] 11 May, Available from: https://www.ft.com/content/32999c60-d0ab-44cc-a0d0-2b2496b06ed3 [Accessed 13 May 2024].

Powell, J. (2013) 'Subordinate financialisation: A study of Mexico and its non-financial corporations', PhD Thesis, SOAS, University of London.

Rawdanowicz, L. (2010) 'The 2008–09 crisis in Turkey: Performance, policy responses and challenges for sustaining the recovery' (OECD Economics Department Working Papers, No 819), OECD Publishing.

Reis, N. and de Oliveira, F.A. (2023) 'Peripheral financialization and the transformation of dependency: A view from Latin America', *Review of International Political Economy*, 30(2): 511–34.

Santos, A.C. (2023) 'Conceptualising state financialisation: from the core to the periphery', *New Political Economy*, 28(1): 142–54.

Torres Filho, E.T. (2018) *O BNDES em uma encruzilhada: Como evitar sua desmontagem*, Instituto de Estudos para o Desenvolvimento Industrial.

van Apeldoorn, B., de Graaff, N.A., and Overbeek, H.W. (2012) 'The reconfiguration of the Global State–Capital Nexus', *Globalizations*, 9(4): 471–86.

von Braunmühl, C. (1978) 'On the analysis of the bourgeois nation-state within the world market context: An attempt to develop a methodological and theoretical approach', in J. Holloway and S. Picciotto (eds) *State and Capital: A Marxist Debate,* London: Edward Arnold, pp 160–77.

Yalman, G.L., Marois, T., and Güngen, A.R. (2019) *The Political Economy of Financial Transformation in Turkey*, London: Routledge.

Yeldan, A.E., Boratav, K., and Köse, A.H. (2023) 'Türkiye'de derinleşen yapısal kriz eğilimi ve kâr İtilimli enflasyonun dinamikleri', *İktisat ve Toplum Dergisi*, (158): 8–30.

9

Tools of Subordination and/or Statecraft? A Comparative Analysis of Stock Markets in Large Emerging Markets

Johannes Petry

Introduction

Since the 1980s, stock markets have emerged as a key financial infrastructure in the global economy and as important drivers of economic growth (Lavelle, 2004). Between 1978 and 2020, the number of listed companies tripled from 13,712 to 43,248 while their market capitalization increased from 23.1 per cent to 134.6 per cent of global GDP (World Bank, 2021). The spread of capital markets changed how corporate governance, financing, and ownership of companies functions globally and is central to financialization processes that have engulfed not only the core but also the periphery of the global economy (Bonizzi, 2013). While in 1978 only 9 per cent (1,257) of listed companies were from non-high income countries, 39 per cent (16,870) of these companies are listed in emerging/developing economies by 2020.

Stock markets are crucial intermediaries that structure national financial systems' integration into the global financial system (Petry, 2020b). Importantly, they essentially act as catalysts, potentially serving both as a source of subordination as well as statecraft for these emerging markets. On the one hand, stock markets can exacerbate financial subordination (Bonizzi and Kaltenbrunner, 2018). By enabling easy access for global institutional investors, they contribute to subsuming countries to the vagaries of global capital flows (Naqvi, 2019). On the other hand, they can curtail the power of global capital and states can organize markets in ways that direct market outcomes towards certain state objectives and policies (Chen and Rithmire,

2020), hence facilitating financial statecraft. This chapter argues that whereas stock markets in more neoliberal financial systems are more likely to suffer from the adverse effects of international financial subordination, more state-capitalist financial systems offer the possibility of increasing resistance and exercising statecraft through stock markets (despite global financial hierarchy). Thus, how stock markets are organized matters greatly for the social outcomes they produce (Petry et al, 2023).

This chapter investigates the relationship between stock markets, subordination, and statecraft in six large emerging markets – Brazil, Russia, India, China, South Africa, and South Korea – through investigating the ownership of stock exchanges and listed companies as well as restrictions on capital flows. In a first step, this chapter analyzes the differential institutional embeddedness of stock exchanges and its corresponding effect on the organization of markets. Whether stock exchanges themselves are owned by foreign or domestic actors, the state, or financial investors is crucial for the incentive structure that informs how exchanges organize markets. In a second step, the chapter analyzes the ownership structure of the respective stock markets and the associated different social outcomes. Whether institutional investors, corporations, or the state own the majority of companies' shares, and whether these are domestic of foreign actors, greatly influences the dynamics of these markets. The chapter illustrates that a larger influence of foreign and institutional investors facilitates the effects of subordination, whereas greater non-financial and domestic ownership provides greater scope for developmental activities. Finally, the chapter takes a closer look at how these countries structure foreign investor access differently – which might intensify or impede the power of foreign institutional investors, depending on whether they can access a local market freely or whether restrictions and regulations are in place.

This research investigates data about the structure and institutional configurations of stock markets derived from Bloomberg Terminal data, regulatory documents, and secondary literature.[1] The chapter is structured as follows. The second section discusses the conceptual relationship between stock markets, subordination, and statecraft. The third section then conducts an empirical investigation of ownership patterns in stock markets – focusing on stock exchanges, listed companies, and foreign investor access. The fourth section concludes and outlines avenues of future research.

Stock markets between subordination and statecraft

Stock markets are one of the institutional foundations of modern capitalism and one of the core technologies of financial globalization (Weber et al, 2009). Especially since the 1980s, countries around the world have created stock markets in their efforts to facilitate economic growth and development

(Lavelle, 2004). By 2020, almost every country in the world – from Malawi to Bhutan – had established a stock market.[2] But why do stock markets matter for financial subordination and statecraft?

On the one hand, stock markets offer a large potential for financial statecraft. While conventionally economic/financial statecraft is defined as a state's ability to achieve foreign policy objectives (Armijo and Katada, 2015; Baldwin, 2020; Armijo, Chapter 3, this volume), other authors highlight its domestic dimension (also Kapadia and Musthaq, Chapter 6, this volume). Weiss and Thurbon (2021, p 475), for instance, argue for repurposing the concept of economic statecraft to also incorporate domestic economic activities by states; this widening of the concept, they argue, 'draws attention to cases in which states become involved in domestic economic activities, in efforts to counter geopolitical and/or geoeconomic challenges'. Especially in countries where the government plays a more important role in managing the economy, finance has often been utilized for developmental purposes (Thurbon, 2016; Grabel, 2017; Rethel and Thurbon, 2020; Pape and Petry, 2024).

This logic also applies to stock markets. The state might for instance exercise (a degree of) control through ownership stakes in listed companies, shaping corporate strategy in line with government objectives (Wang, 2015; Nem Singh and Chen, 2018). Through control over financial infrastructures and regulatory initiatives, the state might also facilitate the financing and growth of particular industries that are viewed as strategically important for national development (Musacchio and Lazzarini, 2013; Malkin, 2022; Petry et al, 2023). Thus, by facilitating the professionalization, financing, and internationalization of domestic companies, furthering industrial policy, or building up important industries (Chen and Rithmire, 2020, Omarova, 2024)[3] – even expanding these activities internationally (Petry, 2023) – stock markets can potentially increase a state's reach and capacity.

On the other hand, stock markets can equally facilitate financial subordination. Alami et al (2023, p 1363) define international financial subordination as 'a relation of domination, inferiority and subjugation between different spaces across the world market, expressed in and through money and finance, which penalizes actors in DEEs [developing and emerging economies] disproportionally.' The global financial system is structured hierarchically, dominated by the US and other Western economies, with emerging and frontier markets (that is, countries with less developed financial systems) at the bottom of the food chain (Bonizzi et al, 2022; Cerpa Vielma and Dymski, 2022). While this is most often discussed in relation to currencies (de Paula et al, 2017), this is also the case for stock markets.

The global spread of stock markets has often been equated with the diffusion of neoliberal financial norms and practices like shareholder value orientation (Lazonick and O'Sullivan, 2000; Harvey, 2005) as well as the correspondingly growing global power of Anglo-American institutional investors (Harmes, 1998; Gabor, 2021; Petry et al, 2021). Through the dissolution of capital controls (Abdelal, 2007) and the spread of market-based forms of finance (Carroll and Jarvis, 2013), developing countries are increasingly integrated into a system of 'market rule' (Soederberg, 2007; Peck et al, 2012). In this system, (especially foreign institutional) investors increasingly exercise power vis-à-vis states as increasingly volatile investment flows disrupt economic activity (Naqvi, 2019), shape government policy (Fichtner et al, 2022), and limit fiscal space (Hardie, 2012). Stock markets can thus reproduce existing financial hierarchies and limit state capacity and reach.

Stock exchanges are thus essentially catalysts, crucial intermediaries that inform the positionality of emerging markets with respect to patterns of subordination and statecraft. Of course the spread of capital markets brings with it problems associated with financialization like rising wealth inequality and higher degrees of financial speculation (Pike and Pollard, 2010), but these processes are not necessarily linked to neoliberalism (Davis and Walsh, 2017; Petry, 2020a). So, when are stock markets a source of subordination and when do they contribute to statecraft?

This chapter argues that ownership – of the stock exchange itself which creates the rules of the game according to which markets function, of the companies listed on the stock market, as well as restrictions on foreign ownership/market participation – plays a crucial role. The adverse effects of international financial subordination are more prevalent if institutional investors, especially foreign entities, have a dominant role and unhindered access in the ownership of the stock exchange itself as well as the ownership of listed companies. Such a setup likely reinforces neoliberal financial norms like shareholder value orientation and intensifies the probability of volatile financial flows that reduce state reach and capacity.

Reversely, stock markets more likely act as a source of statecraft when the state retains a degree of ownership over stock exchanges and listed companies. While reaping the benefits of market-based financial systems – like raising capital, professionalizing corporate governance, and gaining international recognition – the state would be better able to curtail the power of global finance and better able to fend off short-term oriented practices like shareholder value orientation or volatile capital flows. It might even be able to direct market outcomes for facilitating national development objectives.

In emerging markets whose political economies lean more towards neoliberal norms and institutional configurations, the negative effects of subordination are therefore likely intensified through stock markets. By contrast, stock markets in more state-capitalist institutional settings are more likely to strengthen state reach and capacity by enabling the exercise of various forms of financial statecraft. This does not suggest that statecraft and subordination are opposite poles on a continuum (see also Alami, Chapter 2, this volume). All emerging markets are subject to global financial hierarchies. But it is the institutional embeddedness of stock markets that informs whether these markets act as catalyst for intensifying the effects of subordination and/or for facilitating statecraft.

Empirical analysis: stock markets in large emerging markets

Based on these considerations, this chapter analyses the structure of stock markets in six of the largest emerging markets globally – Brazil, Russia, India, China, South Africa, and South Korea (for a detailed case selection, see Petry et al, 2023). Given the growing economic and political importance of emerging markets within global capital markets, a closer analysis of their stock markets is thus warranted.

Ownership of stock exchanges

Exchanges are crucial for the functioning of national financial systems, serving as 'anchors' for financial centres and gateways to global markets (Wójcik, 2012). While the terms 'stock exchange' and 'stock market' are often used interchangeably, there is an important distinction to be made. While they organize a particular marketplace (that is, the stock market), stock exchanges are powerful actors in their own right. They are complex organizations whose task is the provision of financial infrastructures that enable the functioning of stock markets in the first place (Petry, 2021). While stock markets are used by investors to allocate financial assets, provide corporate financing, and facilitate economic growth, certain infrastructural arrangements must exist to *enable* these transactions (Bowker and Star, 1999; Bernards and Campbell-Verduyn, 2019): from market data, indices, financial products, and trading platforms to clearing, exchanges shape the infrastructural arrangements of capital markets. By providing these financial infrastructures, exchanges shape capital markets, their development, characteristics, and dynamics (Petry, forthcoming).

How exchanges are governed, by whom they are owned, and which constraints and incentives they face thus influences the kinds of markets that they create. When exchanges are largely owned by institutional investors, they are much more likely to be subject to shareholder value orientation and to organize markets in ways that facilitate the profit-oriented interests of (foreign) institutional investors, like easing and facilitating global investor access – thus further intensifying subordination. By contrast, when domestic, and especially state, entities are dominant owners of exchanges, they are much more likely to not follow these subordinating practices but instead decrease the power of global capital – for example through trading and ownership restrictions – and even facilitate other national development objectives.

Between emerging markets we can thus observe considerable variation in stock exchange ownership (Figure 9.1). In China, exchanges are fully state-owned entities. As 'frontline regulators' they are part of the regulatory apparatus as the government views them as crucial nodal points in managing the financial system in order to achieve state objectives (Petry, 2020a). Consequently, rather than profit maximization, the performance of Chinese stock exchanges is evaluated based on their contribution to and achievement of state objectives. Since many of the exchanges' operational staff and management are also party members, the state-directed logic of exchanges' key performance indicators is exacerbated (Collins and Gottwald, 2014). Rather than a facilitator of subordination, exchanges in China have been central in allowing the state to manage its capital markets to achieve state objectives (Bell and Feng, 2009; Petry, 2020a).

While the Korea Exchange (KRX) is no longer completely in public ownership, the institutional arrangements of their ownership are still very conductive to state influence (Thurbon, 2016). Up until 2015, KRX was designated as a 'public institution' as the government was concerned that 'allowing the KRX to operate as a private company could lead to reckless management' (Song, 2013), and it was as such subject to regular government inspections and parliamentary scrutiny, and the government could appoint top executives and determine its budget. While the exchange has since become a 'private entity' again, its shares are not freely tradable but divided between trading members, most of which are Korean with foreign brokers like JP Morgan only holding 9 per cent of outstanding shares while government-owned financial institutions still hold 5 per cent. In addition, KRX was only made private again under the condition that it would be controlled and supervised by Korea's Financial Services Commission (Yoon, 2015), and KRX management is still politically appointed with most CEOs having previously served at different regulators or the Ministry of Finance (see also Lim, 2010). While formally private, the state very much remains in control of Korea's stock exchange.

In Russia's Moscow Exchange (MOEX), various state institutions like the Russian Central bank, SberBank, and state development corporation (VEB.RF) are the three largest shareholders, jointly holding 30.1 per cent of outstanding shares, and only around half of MOEX's shares are in free-float and can be publicly traded. While foreign entities hold 60.3 per cent in Russia's MOEX, no foreign shareholder owns more than 5.3 per cent of outstanding shares and foreign ownership is capped to prevent foreign control. Importantly, foreign investors have not been allowed to sell Russian stock holdings since the Ukraine invasion in 2022; they are thus stuck and cannot exercise shareholder powers. The power of global investors is thus

Figure 9.1: Stock exchange ownership in large emerging markets

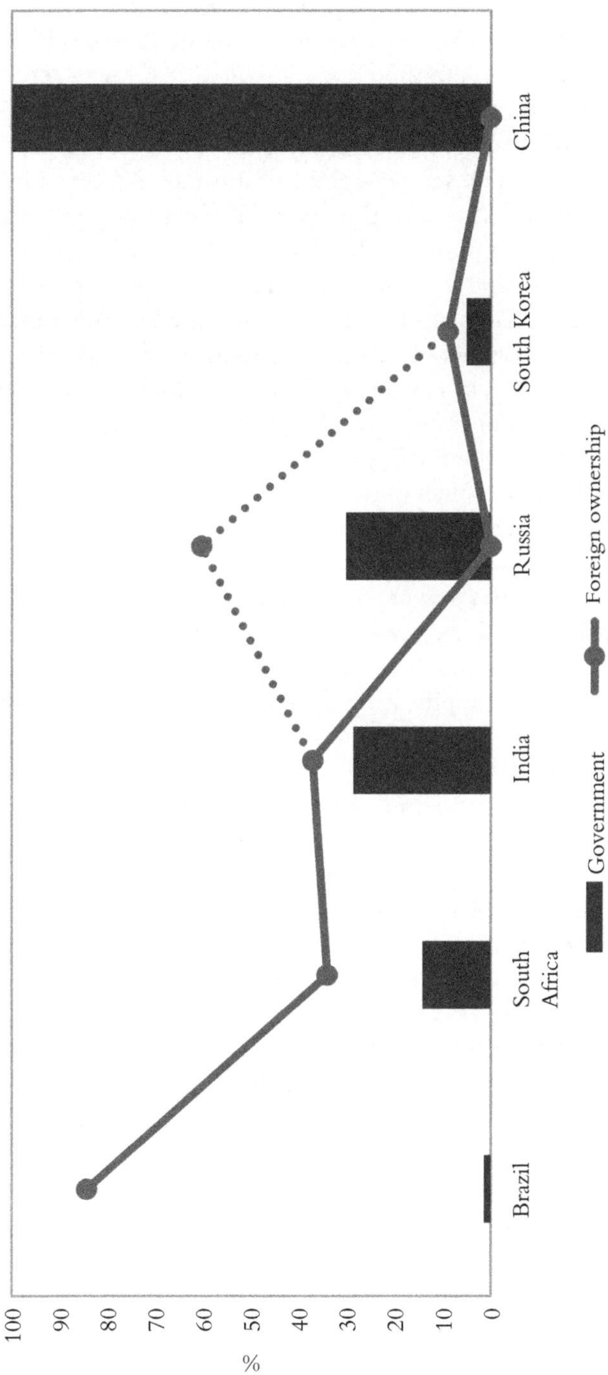

Source: Based on data from exchange websites, annual reports, policy documents[4]

rather limited, and instead the state has been able to utilize MOEX as a developmental tool to control capital allocation (Viktorov and Abramov, 2022), a pattern that can also be observed in Russia's banking system (Midhura and Ageeva, 2022).

The story is similar in India. In the main stock exchange, the National Stock Exchange of India (NSE), the state owns 28.62 per cent of the exchanges' shares.[5] The state-owned Life Insurance Corporation of India, State Bank of India (SBI), and the Stock Holding Corporation of India are NSE's three single largest shareholders, holding 10.72 per cent, 7.56 per cent, and 4.44 per cent of outstanding shares, respectively. Only 51 per cent of the exchange's shares can be publicly traded, while the remaining 49 per cent is distributed between different stakeholder groups. Foreign institutional investors only hold 25.15 per cent of shares,[6] and foreign ownership is capped at 49 per cent in order to prevent foreign control of the market. While not directly beholden to the state as in China and (to some degree) Russia, the exchanges will act on behalf of the regulators when instructed. This was, for instance, the case when India's exchanges banned the use of stock market data for offshore derivatives after the Indian securities regulator had voiced concerns about pricing power (Mukherjee, 2018). This is in line with other studies that illustrate how the commanding height of Indian finance and banking are still very much subject to state control, which has not been significantly diluted despite limited liberalization attempts (Jayadev et al, 2018; Nölke et al, 2022).

This stands in stark contrast to the cases of South Africa and Brazil. In South Africa, state ownership of the Johannesburg Stock Exchange (JSE) stands at only 14.2 per cent, while foreign ownership stands at 33.9 per cent. The structure of the largest shareholders is much more mixed, consisting of three domestic asset managers – NintyOne (14.8 per cent), PSG Asset Management Services (9.8 per cent), and Allan Gray (6.8 per cent) – and the state-owned Public Investment Corporation (14.2 per cent), as well as Goldman Sachs (5.6 per cent) and Vanguard (3.51 per cent). Consequently, the state has little control over the JSE, and instead the exchange's business model is much more geared towards facilitating the needs of institutional investors. It does not come as a surprise that South Africa's stock market has been described as one of the most financialized among emerging markets (see Bond, Chapter 4, this volume).

In Brazil, state ownership of the stock exchange (B3) is basically non-existent, with the Brazilian treasury holding a mere 1.33 per cent of outstanding shares. In contrast, foreign institutional investors reign supreme, with players like Capital Group (10.9 per cent), T. Rowe Price (5.4 per cent), Baillie Gifford (5.4 per cent), and BlackRock (4.9 per cent) counting as the exchange's largest shareholders. Together, foreign ownership accounts for 84.3 per cent of B3's shares. It is thus no surprise that the state was not able to utilize B3 for its national development policies – historically relying on its national development bank (BNDES) – and instead the exchange has been a driver of financialization processes within the country (Lavinas et al, 2022).

These different ownership patterns have important consequences for how exchanges manage capital markets. Profit considerations and shareholder value orientation are dominant drivers of exchange activities when state ownership is low and foreign institutional investor ownership is high. In contrast, the performance of exchanges, their personnel, and management is (partially) measured by how they contribute towards certain state objectives in more state-capitalist settings which restrict foreign ownership and where the state has an important hold over the trading platform (Petry et al, 2023). This relationship also extends to the ownership of those companies that are listed on the respective market.

Ownership of listed companies

Different types of owners have very different preferences and thus different effects with respect to the relationship between subordination and statecraft. Similar to privately owned banks, institutional investors are much more likely to facilitate short-term financial objectives (for example, shareholder value orientation), whereas state ownership is more likely to facilitate other objectives like growing national champions or facilitating industrial policy by channelling capital to certain parts of the economy.[7] Moreover, a larger share of foreign (institutional) investors also likely increases the pressures of financial subordination on listed companies.

Importantly, state influence over corporate ownership manifests through different channels. While state ownership might be hidden through different layers of investment structures, some types of ownership are more susceptible to state influence than others. In China, Russia, India, and Brazil, next to the government, holding companies (4–12 per cent), corporations (19–25 per cent), and individuals (4–11 per cent) own significant company shares. State-owned enterprises, for instance, often hold shares in other corporations, either directly or via holding companies (Wang, 2015). Further, exercising influence on individual owners (for example, Russian oligarchs, Chinese party members, Indian business families) is much easier than influencing foreign asset managers or hedge funds, especially in economic systems where socio-economic ties between political and business elites are crucial coordination mechanisms (Nölke et al, 2022). By analyzing the listed companies in each of the studied countries' main stock market index, we can thus observe significant variation in patterns of ownership structures between countries (Figure 9.2).[8]

South Africa has the stock market that is most exposed to the effects of financial subordination, with 66.6 per cent foreign ownership, most of

Figure 9.2: Stock market ownership in large emerging markets

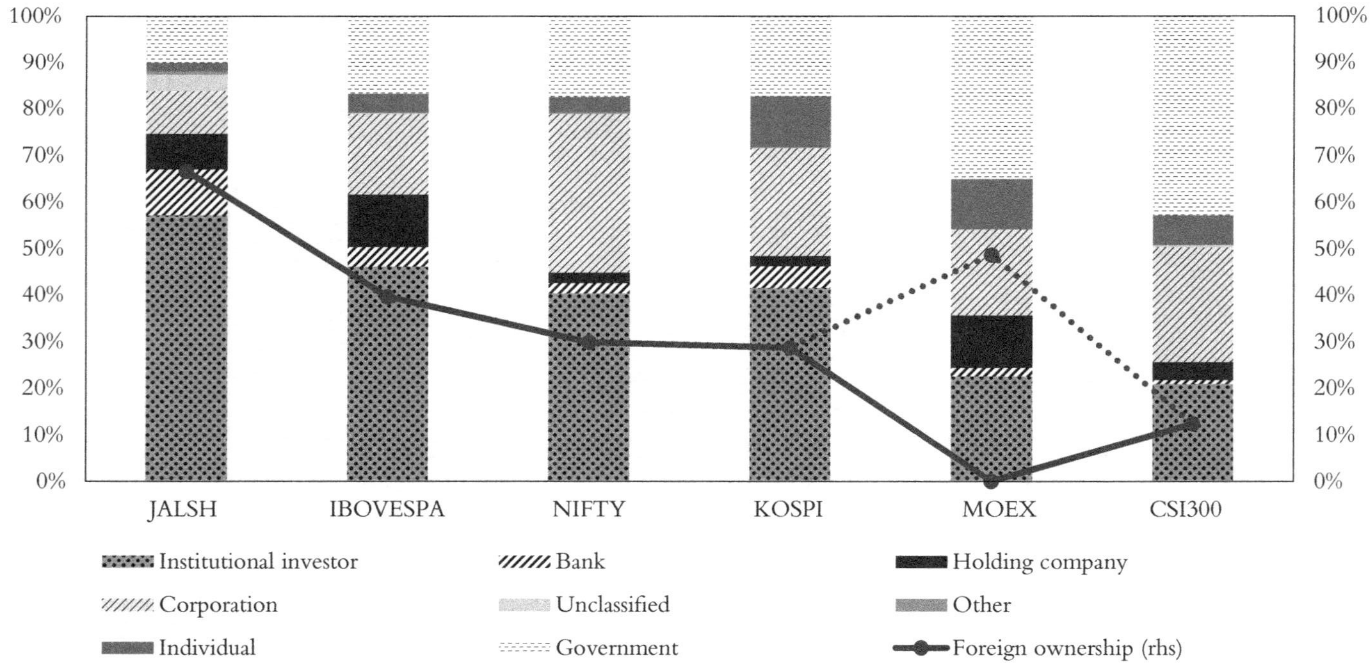

Source: Bloomberg Terminal ownership data[9]

which are institutional investors. BlackRock is the single largest investor (7 per cent) in companies listed in South Africa's main stock market index (the JALSH index), other major investors being Vanguard (5.2 per cent), Capital Group (2.7 per cent), or JP Morgan (1.8 per cent). In contrast, state ownership is only 10 per cent, mostly held by the Public Investment Corporation (6.5 per cent), South Africa's pension fund and second largest investor. As Isaacs and Kaltenbrunner (2018) argue, this structure of the South African stock market has facilitated new forms of external vulnerability as the global financial cycle facilitates volatile capital flows. This has significantly contributed to the financialization of listed corporations in South Africa as well as an investment strike, as South Africa's capital market functions mainly for satisfying the profit needs of investors rather than raising funds and facilitating national economic development (Karwowski, 2018; Bond, Chapter 4, this volume).

In Brazil, the situation is slightly more mixed. Institutional investors hold almost half of all company shares (46.6 per cent) in the Ibovespa index, with BlackRock (5 per cent), Vanguard (3.6 per cent), and Capital Group (2.7 per cent) among the largest shareholders. However, the Brazilian government itself is the single largest shareholder with 7.9 per cent of shareholdings (albeit this is concentrated in state-owned electricity and oil companies), and overall state ownership is moderately large with 16.9 per cent. Foreign ownership is 39.6 per cent of all outstanding stocks, most of which is concentrated in a few large corporations (for example, Anheuser-Busch InBev), banks, and asset managers. Especially as the government sought to grow the stock market from the 2000s onwards, by reducing capital gains tax and facilitating foreign participation in the market, Brazilian companies became much more sensitive to stock market valuations and changing international investor sentiments (Lavinas et al, 2022; also Nölke et al, 2022). While the state plays a larger role than in South Africa, the Brazilian market is still dominated by foreign financial players, facilitating its international financial subordination (see also Lange Machado et al, Chapter 5, this volume).

While the structure of India's stock market ownership is similar, there are important differences to Brazil (see also Nölke et al, 2022). First, foreign ownership only accounts for 29.9 per cent and is thus much lower than in Brazil or South Africa. As the largest foreign institutional investors, Vanguard, BlackRock, and Capital Group only hold 2.2 per cent, 1.9 per cent, and 1.6 per cent of shares, respectively. These asset managers are accompanied by large global non-financial corporations like Unilever or Suzuki whose ownership stakes derive from joint ventures and subsidiaries that they have created in India. Overall, the share of institutional investors is smaller at only 40.3 per cent while the government accounts for 17.4 per cent of shareholdings, with significant direct and indirect ownership stakes in many listed Indian companies. The most important category of shareholders, however, are corporations, which account for 34 per cent of outstanding shares. These are mostly cross-shareholdings between conglomerates like Tata, the single largest shareholder in India's stock market, which owns 9.8 per cent of the total market. While the government does not have an outsized role, the smaller size of both foreign and institutional investors likely reduces financialization pressures on listed companies, especially as a large bulk of shareholdings are essentially long-term block holdings within Indian business conglomerates.

The picture is similar in South Korea. Foreign ownership here also only accounts for 28.8 per cent, most of which are institutional investors, with BlackRock, Vanguard, and Fidelity owning 4.5 per cent, 3.3 per cent, and 1.7 per cent of outstanding shares, respectively. Instead, the single-largest shareholder in almost every Korean company is the government-owned National Pension Fund (NPS), owning 10.9 per cent of the entire stock market. Importantly, the NPS has been known to continuously pursue developmental financial strategies (Lee and Grimes, 2022) and thus plays an important role as anchor investor in Korean firms. Similarly, the Korea Development Bank (KDB) is a main investor in several strategically important companies like Hyundai Merchant Marine (shipping), Korea Electric Power Corporation (electricity), and Hanwha Ocean (shipbuilding). In addition, cross-shareholdings between large Korean conglomerates (chaebol) and the families running these firms also contribute to a significant ownership concentration in the hands of more long-term strategic investors which severely mitigates foreign influence (Kalinowski, 2009), with Samsung, LG, SK, and Hyundai accounting for 15.2 per cent, 10.8 per cent, 4.7 per cent, and 4.2 per cent of stock market ownership, respectively. Rather than foreign and institutional investors, the state and Korean chaebol dominate Korea's stock market.

In Russia and China, the picture is again very different. In Russia, the state is the largest owner, with state-owned institutions holding 34.9 per cent of all outstanding shares. In contrast, BlackRock and Vanguard each only hold around 2 per cent of shares, and institutional investors overall only hold 22.5 per cent of company shares. Instead shareholdings are dominated by Russian and foreign non-financial corporations (18.5 per cent) as well as oligarchs (10.9 per cent) and their holding companies (11.3 per cent). Given the close network ties between the oligarchs and the government (Lane, 2008), the state's influence over corporate Russia is even larger as oligarchs have to toe the state line. And while foreign ownership seems high at 48.7 per cent, a large portion of this are Cyprus-based Russian offshore investors (15.9 per cent). In addition, the government has restricted foreign investors from selling their Russian company stock holdings after the Ukraine invasion in 2022; international institutional investors thus basically have capital tied in Russia involuntarily. While pre-2022, the Russian state had been somewhat more exposed to the effects of financial subordination, similar to the overall development of its financial system, the state has retained the upper hand in Russia's stock markets.

Finally, the Chinese stock market is the most state-controlled one. State-owned institutions – government entities, enterprises, and financial companies – hold a total of 42.7 per cent of outstanding company shares in the CSI300 index, while private non-financial companies account for another 24.5 per cent of shareholdings. However, the state also has increasing influence on these kinds of actors as the authorities have been promoting the presence and power of 'party organizations' (*dang zuzhi*) to boost private sector compliance with government priorities.[10] Similarly, many of the larger individual investors that own 6.2 per cent of shares are party members and thus more likely to follow government instructions. Institutional investors only account for 20.8 per cent of all shareholdings, while foreign investors merely hold 12.4 per cent of outstanding shares.[11] Out of our sample, Chinese stock markets are thus least vulnerable to external financial flows and investor sentiment and instead the state is most likely to utilize stock markets for national development objectives. In 2019, the Chinese government for instance created a new market segment, the so-called STAR market, to raise funds for strategically important technology companies that are aligned with government policy. By 2022, the market had become the largest initial public offerings (IPO) market in the world, facilitating the funding of tech companies in line with government policy such as 'Made in China 2025' (Malkin, 2022). Overall, we can again observe significant variation with respect to ownership patterns in these six stock markets.

Management of foreign investment

In addition to the ownership structure of stock exchanges and listed companies, countries can also create various mechanisms to keep global investors at bay. Since foreign institutional investors strive to maximize their investment returns, free capital movement is crucial for international investors' ability to withdraw funds. Thereby, as the IMF (Bakker and Chapple, 2002, p 39) noted, 'capital account liberalization can act as a useful disciplinary mechanism to promote the pursuit of stable and sustainable macroeconomic policies'. However, in the absence of restrictions on capital flows and investor access, mechanisms of financial subordination are exacerbated as such unfettered access can lead to foreign investors dominating local stock markets, thus increasing pressures for adopting liberal policies (Harmes, 1998) while often also introducing considerable volatility (Bonizzi and Kaltenbrunner, 2018). While completely isolating from global investors is hardly possible nor desirable, states can regulate their markets in ways that enable resistance towards pressures to conform with the expectations

Table 9.1: Capital flow restrictions in large emerging markets

	Brazil	**Russia**	**India**	**China**	**South Africa**	**South Korea**
foreign investor registration	limited; mandatory but no centralized system	yes; investors need contract with Russian broker	yes; mandatory centralized (GIFT City, FII/FPI)	yes; mandatory centralized (Connect, RQFII/QFII)	no; no centralized system	Yes; mandatory centralized (IRC system, KRX-Link)
monitoring of foreign trading / stock ownership	no	yes; foreign ownership monitored	yes; foreign ownership monitored	yes; trading/ownership monitored (SAFE, CFMMC)	no; only for foreign takeovers	Yes; trading/ownership monitored (FIMS)
foreign trading (% of total volume)	high (47%)	high (50%; pre-2022)	limited (12%)	limited (10–15%)	high (46%)	limited (19%)

Sources: Bloomberg Terminal, Eikon Terminal, exchange websites/annual reports, policy documents

of profit-oriented global investors and manage foreign investor access in order to maintain state autonomy. Again, we can observe significant variety between the six markets under investigation (Table 9.1).

A first step is investor access. In China, South Korea, and India foreign investors have to go through a rather lengthy application process (also MSCI, 2020). Here, foreign investors can only enter domestic capital markets after obtaining regulatory approval as qualified foreign institutional investors (RQFII/QFII in China, FII/FPI in India, IRC in Korea)[12] or through dedicated investment channels (China Stock Connect, India GIFT City, KRX-Eurex Link). In contrast, Brazil and South Africa only register the foreign exchange transactions of capital entering the country, without any comprehensive system. Russian authorities require foreigners to enter agreements with licensed Russian brokers (which enables a degree of oversight), and after February 2022 only 'friendly countries' – that is only those countries who have not evoked sanctions against Russia – are allowed to actively trade on MOEX. A similar pattern exists for the monitoring of foreign investor trading and ownership. Utilizing their existing registration systems, in China, India, Korea, and Russia the exchanges/authorities monitor foreign ownership levels and trading activities (for example, SAFE/CFMMC in China, FIMS in Korea),[13] whereas no similar systems exist in Brazil or South Africa.

While from a neoliberal perspective, an open, active market for corporate control is an important feature for facilitating shareholder value orientation (profit creation), in state-capitalist capital markets strategic companies are often protected from foreign control in order to facilitate the creation of national champions. Foreign ownership for any listed Chinese company is, for instance, capped at 30 per cent of its (free float) shares. Up until April 2020, investments in India's stock market had equally been regulated with foreigners only allowed to hold 10–49 per cent of listed companies, albeit these regulations had been relaxed in recent years; but still, many restrictions still apply.[14] In Russia, pre-2022 foreigners could only own 25–50 per cent of strategically important companies active in Russian media, banking, infrastructures (for example, railways, pipelines, electricity, telecommunications), commodities (for example, mining), or with military ties (for example, weapons, aviation, encryption) (Hogan Lovells, 2021). Since international investor assets have essentially been frozen since the Ukraine invasion, foreign influence within the domestic market is now quite impossible in Russia's war economy. Limited restrictions – albeit with higher investment limits – also exist in South Africa, whereas investment into Brazilian and Korean companies is relatively liberalized with only a few restrictions on banking, mining, telecommunication, media, and healthcare. However, an important difference here is that the structure of Korea's stock market – with continued state influence and control as well as large cross-shareholdings between Korean families/business groups (chaebol) – prevents increased foreign influence despite seemingly liberal policies (Kalinowski, 2009), whereas Brazil's more liberal system is much more exposed to financial volatility and foreign investor influence (Nölke et al, 2022).

These infrastructural arrangements also translate into the actual activities of foreign investors in these markets. In 2019, foreign investors accounted for 46–50 per cent of trading volume in Brazil, Russia (pre-2022), and South Africa, while only accounting for 12–19 per cent in India, Korea, and China, and have been basically non-existent in Russia since February 2022 as only 'friendly countries' are allowed to actively trade on MOEX. Overall, whereas Brazil and South Africa are relatively open to foreign investors, Korea and India are much more closed, while China and Russia maintain the most stringent controls.

Conclusion

What is the relationship between stock markets, subordination, and statecraft? This chapter has argued that stock exchanges act as crucial intermediaries between their respective home countries and a hierarchically structured global financial system. On the one hand, exchanges can facilitate the achievement of developmental policies, providing states with an important lever of financial statecraft. This is especially the case in more state-capitalist economic systems where the state has a strong hold on financial markets and has the ability to restrict the power of global finance. On the other hand, when prioritizing shareholder value orientation and facilitating more volatile capital flows by foreign institutional investors, stock exchanges can intensify the negative effects of financial subordination. Financial systems that are built on more liberal economic principles are more prone to such pressures.

By analyzing their institutional configuration, ownership patterns, and capital flow management practices, this chapter illustrates stark differences in the functioning of stock markets across emerging markets, resulting in significant variation in how stock markets mediate these countries' relationships with subordination and statecraft. In Brazil and especially South Africa, stock markets likely intensify financial subordination as foreign institutional investors play a dominant role in the ownership of stock exchanges as well as listed companies and few restrictions exist to keep them at bay; the state plays little to no role in these markets and stock markets contribute to these countries' subordinate position within the global financial system. In contrast, the state is more powerful in Indian and Korean stock markets, with many restrictions placed on foreign investors, and this is even more so the case in Russia. In all cases the institutional setting of stock markets facilitates autonomy from global finance, reducing external vulnerabilities and strengthening domestic and/or state control. Finally, Chinese stock markets are most closely aligned with a state-capitalist model of market organization. The state rules supreme in these markets and foreign investors have little power in this setup. In addition, the state is able to utilize stock markets for facilitating certain national development objectives, especially with respect to industrial strategy.

Overall, the patterns of stock market ownership holdings in the studied large emerging markets correspond to their position with respect to subordination and statecraft as mapped throughout this volume. China has the ability to utilize its stock market for national development objectives and engage in some forms of statecraft (McNally, Chapter 7 this volume). In contrast, the story for the other countries is one of degrees of autonomy and subordination. Russia, Korea, and India (Kapadia and Musthaq, Chapter 6 this volume) are able to reduce external vulnerabilities and secure a certain degree of autonomy from global markets, while in Brazil (Lange Machado et al, Chapter 5 this volume) and especially South Africa (Bond, Chapter 4 this volume) stock markets intensify the effects of international financial subordination. Importantly, these positions also correspond to whether these countries play a role in contesting the liberal global financial order more broadly (Petry and Nölke, 2024), warranting further research between subordination, statecraft, and their potential impact on global financial structures.

As one of the institutional foundations of modern capitalism, stock markets act as catalysts for both subordination and statecraft. National institutional configurations refract pressures emanating from the hierarchical global financial system in different ways, and outcomes largely depend on these markets' institutional embeddedness. Of course, this chapter is not an exhaustive treatment of this subject. Beyond stock markets, other aspects of capital markets – from bonds to futures and foreign exchange trading – require more careful examination in this respect. In addition, a more systematic analysis of global stock markets is warranted. Especially given that we could observe significant variation within the group of large emerging markets, a more thorough exploration of global varieties of capital markets in both developed and emerging economies could provide fruitful insights in contemporary debates about the variegated relationships between state, finance, and capitalism.

Notes

1 The author also draws on 90 interviews that were conducted with stock exchanges across the world (Chicago, Delhi, Frankfurt, Hong Kong, London, Seoul, Shanghai, Singapore, Tokyo, and Zurich). While these are not directly quoted in the text, they provided important background information on the role and different institutional configurations of stock markets.

2 The list of countries without a stock exchange is very small and most of these fall into one of the following categories: city states (for example, Monaco, Vatican), small island states (for example, Vanuatu, Kiribati), socialist countries (for example, North Korea, Cuba), poor, war-torn countries (for example, South Sudan, Afghanistan), or least developed countries (for example, Liberia, Madagascar).

3 Of course such attempts need not be successful and can also fail, as described by (Gomez, 2009).

4 The dotted line depicts foreign ownership of the Russian stock exchange; however, since February 2022 these assets have essentially been frozen and exercising any form of influence is not possible.

5 NSE is a much more liquid market than India's second exchange, the Bombay Stock Exchange (BSE); here both foreign and government ownership is lower and local stakeholders hold a larger share of stocks; the same limitations for foreign investment and free float apply.

6 The largest foreign shareholder is also a state-owned entity; a subsidiary of Temasek, Singapore's sovereign wealth fund, holds 5 per cent of shares.

7 In China, India, and Russia, for instance, state-owned banks ultimately hold 50 per cent, 70 per cent, and 72 per cent of bank assets, respectively, while only accounting for 41 per cent Brazil and 4 per cent in South Africa (Petry and Nölke, 2024).

8 This analysis is based on an analysis of individual company's shareholder data extracted from the Bloomberg Terminal. Importantly, main stock market indices usually only contain the largest companies in each stock market that jointly account for the majority of market capitalization. The tendency for internationalization for these large companies is much higher than for smaller listed companies.

9 The dotted line depicts foreign ownership of the Russian listed companies; however, since February 2022 these assets have essentially been frozen and exercising any form of influence is not possible.

10 Source: https://macropolo.org/party-committees-private-sector-china/?rp=m (Accessed 4 February 2025).

11 An important clarification is that this is foreign ownership of the CSI 300 index, not the entire Chinese stock market (which is around 4–5%).

[12] China: Qualified Foreign Institutional Investors/RMB Qualified Foreign Institutional Investors; India: Foreign Institutional Investors/Foreign Portfolio Investors; Korea: Investment Registration Certificate.

[13] China: State Administration of Foreign Exchange/China Futures Market Monitoring Center; Korea: Foreign Investment Management System.

[14] See: https://www.rbi.org.in/fiilist/index.html (accessed 10 March 2021).

References

Abdelal, R. (2007) *Capital Rules: The Construction of Global Finance*, Ithaca: Cornell University Press.

Alami, I., Alves, C., Bonizzi, B., Kaltenbrunner, A., Koddenbrock, K., Kvangraven, I., et al (2023) 'International financial subordination: A critical research agenda', *Review of International Political Economy*, 30(4): 1360–86.

Armijo, L.E. and Katada, S.N. (2015) 'Theorizing the financial statecraft of emerging powers', *New Political Economy*, 20(1): 42–62.

Bakker, A. and Chapple, B. (2002) *Advanced Country Experiences with Capital Account Liberalization*, Washington, DC: International Monetary Fund:

Baldwin, D.A. (2020) *Economic Statecraft: New Edition*, Princeton, NJ: Princeton University Press.

Bell, S. and Feng, H. (2009) 'Reforming China's stock market: Institutional change Chinese style', *Political Studies*, 57(1): 117–40.

Bernards, N. and Campbell-Verduyn, M. (2019) 'Understanding technological change in global finance through infrastructures', *Review of International Political Economy,* 26(5): 773–89.

Bonizzi, B. (2013) 'Financialization in developing and emerging countries', *International Journal of Political Economy,* 42(4): 83–107.

Bonizzi, B. and Kaltenbrunner, A. (2018) 'Liability-driven investment and pension fund exposure to emerging markets: A Minskyan analysis', *Environment and Planning A: Economy and Space,* 51(2): 420–39.

Bonizzi, B., Kaltenbrunner, A., and Powell, J. (2022) 'Financialised capitalism and the subordination of emerging capitalist economies', *Cambridge Journal of Economics,* 46(4): 651–78.

Bowker, G.C. and Star, S.L. (1999) *Sorting Things Out: Classification and its Consequences*, Cambridge, MA: MIT Press.

Carroll, T. and Jarvis, D.S.L. (2013) 'Market building in Asia: Standards setting, policy diffusion, and the globalization of market norms', *Journal of Asian Public Policy,* 6(2): 117–28.

Cerpa Vielma, N. and Dymski, G. (2022) 'A core–periphery framework for understanding the place of Latin America in the global architecture of finance', *Cambridge Journal of Economics,* 46(4): 629–50.

Chen, H. and Rithmire, M. (2020) 'The rise of the investor state: State capital in the Chinese economy', *Studies in Comparative International Development*, 55(3): 257–77.

Collins, N. and Gottwald, J.-C. (2014) 'Market creation by Leninist means: The regulation of financial services in the People's Republic of China', *Asian Studies Review,* 38(4): 620–38.

Davis, A. and Walsh, C. (2017) 'Distinguishing financialization from neoliberalism', *Theory, Culture & Society,* 34(5–6): 27–51.

De Paula, L.F., Fritz, B., and Prates, D.M. (2017) 'Keynes at the periphery: Currency hierarchy and challenges for economic policy in emerging economies', *Journal of Post Keynesian Economics,* 40(2): 183–202.

Fichtner, J., Heemskerk, E.M., and Petry, J. (2022) 'The new gatekeepers of financial claims: States, passive markets, and the growing power of index providers', in B. Braun and K. Koddenbrock (eds) *Capital Claims: Following Finance Across Borders*, London: Routledge, pp 107–29.

Gabor, D. (2021) 'The Wall Street consensus', *Development and Change,* 52(3): 429–59.

Gomez, E.T. (2009) 'The rise and fall of capital: Corporate Malaysia in historical perspective', *Journal of Contemporary Asia,* 39(3): 345–81.

Grabel, I. (2017) *When Things Don't Fall Apart: Global Financial Governance and Developmental Finance in an Age of Productive Incoherence*, Cambridge, MA: MIT Press.

Hardie, I. (2012) *Financialization and Government Borrowing Capacity in Emerging Markets*, Basingstoke: Palgrave Macmillan.

Harmes, A. (1998) 'Institutional investors and the reproduction of neoliberalism', *Review of International Political Economy,* 5(1): 92–121.

Harvey, D. (2005) *A Brief History of Neoliberalism*, Oxford: Oxford University Press.

Hogan Lovells (2021) 'The law on foreign investments in Russian strategic companies', *Hogan Lovells*, [online], Available from: https://www.hoganlovells.com/~/media/hogan-lovells/pdf/publication/law-on-foreign-investments-in-russian-strategic-companies_pdf.pdf [Accessed 6 May 2024].

Isaacs, G. and Kaltenbrunner, A. (2018) 'Financialization and liberalization: South Africa's new forms of external vulnerability', *Competition & Change,* 22(4): 437–63.

Jayadev, A., Mason, J.W., and Schröder, E. (2018) 'The political economy of financialization in the United States, Europe and India', *Development and Change*, 49(2): 353–74.

Kalinowski, T. (2009) 'The politics of market reforms: Korea's path from Chaebol Republic to market democracy and back', *Contemporary Politics*, 15(3): 287–304.

Karwowski, E. (2018) 'Corporate financialization in South Africa: From investment strike to housing bubble', *Competition & Change,* 22(4): 413–36.

Lane, D. (2008) 'From chaotic to state-led capitalism', *New Political Economy,* 13(2): 177–84.

Lavelle, K.C. (2004) *The Politics of Equity Finance in Emerging Markets*, Oxford: Oxford University Press.

Lavinas, L., Araujo, E., and Gentil, D.L. (2022) 'Brazil: Stock markets and corporate credit now driving financialization?', *Theoretical Economics Letters*, 12(4): 1074–94.

Lazonick, W. and O'Sullivan, M. (2000) 'Maximizing shareholder value: A new ideology for corporate governance', *Economy & Society*, 29(1): 13–35.

Lee, Y. and Grimes, W.W. (2022) 'Manifesting the embedded developmental state: The role of South Korea's national pension service in managing financial crisis', *Review of International Political Economy*, 30(5): 1933–56.

Lim, H. (2010) 'The transformation of the developmental state and economic reform in Korea', *Journal of Contemporary Asia*, 40(2): 188–210.

Malkin, A. (2022) 'The made in China challenge to US structural power: Industrial policy, intellectual property and multinational corporations', *Review of International Political Economy*, 29(2): 538–70.

Mishura, A. and Ageeva, S. (2022) 'Financialisation and the authoritarian state: The case of Russia', *Cambridge Journal of Economics*, 46(5): 1109–40.

MSCI (2020) *Global Market Accessibility Review 2020*, June, Available from: https://www.msci.com/documents/1296102/1330218/MSCI_2021_Global_Market_Accessibility_Review_Report.pdf/d88d8bc0-a882-58c7-35f0-bef191e0ebe2 [Accessed 4 February 2025].

Mukherjee, A. (2018) 'MSCI, India's Singapore ban just handed you a big whip', *Economic Times*, 12 February, Available from: https://economictimes.indiatimes.com/markets/stocks/news/msci-indias-singapore-ban-just-handed-you-a-big-whip/articleshow/62882763.cms?from=mdr [Accessed 4 February 2025].

Musacchio, A. and Lazzarini, S.G. (2013) *Reinventing State Capitalism: Leviathan in Business, Brazil and Beyond*, Cambridge, MA: Harvard University Press.

Naqvi, N. (2019) 'Manias, panics and crashes in emerging markets: An empirical investigation of the post-2008 crisis period', *New Political Economy*, 24(6): 759–79.

Nem Singh, J. and Chen, G.C. (2018) 'State-owned enterprises and the political economy of state–state relations in the developing world', *Third World Quarterly*, 39(6): 1077–97.

Nölke, A., May, C., Mertens, D., and Schedelik, M. (2022) 'Elephant limps, but jaguar stumbles: Unpacking the divergence of state capitalism in Brazil and India through theories of capitalist diversity', *Competition & Change*, 26(3–4): 311–33.

Omarova, S.T. (2024) 'Finance as a tool of industrial policy: A taxonomy of institutional options', *Roosevelt Institute*, 12 February, Available from: https://rooseveltinstitute.org/publications/finance-as-a-tool-of-industrial-policy/ [Accessed 4 February 2025].

Pape, F. and Petry, J. (2024) 'East Asia and the politics of global finance: A developmental challenge to the neoliberal consensus?' *Review of International Political Economy*, 31(1): 224–52.

Peck, J., Theodore, N., and Brenner, N. (2012) 'Neoliberalism resurgent? Market rule after the great recession', *South Atlantic Quarterly*, 111(2): 265–88.

Petry, J. (2020a) 'Financialization with Chinese characteristics? Exchanges, control and capital markets in authoritarian capitalism', *Economy & Society*, 49(2): 213–38.

Petry, J. (2020b) 'Securities exchanges: Subjects and agents of financialization', in P. Mader, D. Mertens, and N. Van Der Zwan (eds) *The Routledge International Handbook of Financialization*, London: Routledge, pp 253–64.

Petry, J. (2021) 'From national marketplaces to global providers of financial infrastructures: Exchanges, infrastructures and structural power in global finance', *New Political Economy*, 26(4): 574–97.

Petry, J. (2023) 'Beyond ports, roads and railways: Chinese economic statecraft, the Belt and Road Initiative and the politics of financial infrastructures', *European Journal of International Relations*, 29(2): 319–51.

Petry, J. (forthcoming) 'Exchanges: Infrastructures, power and the differential organisation of capital markets', in B. Brandl, M. Campbell-Verduyn, and C. Westermeier (eds) *Cambridge Global Handbook of Financial Infrastructure*, Cambridge: Cambridge University Press.

Petry, J. and Nölke, A. (2024) *BRICS and the Global Financial Order: Neoliberalism Contested?*, Cambridge: Cambridge University Press.

Petry, J., Fichtner, J., and Heemskerk, E.M. (2021) 'Steering capital: the growing private authority of index providers in the age of passive asset management', *Review of International Political Economy*, 28(1): 152–76.

Petry, J., Koddenbrock, K., and Nölke, A. (2023) 'State capitalism and capital markets: Comparing securities exchanges in emerging markets', *Environment and Planning A*, 55(1): 143–64.

Pike, A. and Pollard, J. (2010) 'Economic geographies of financialization', *Economic Geography*, 86(1): 29–51.

Rethel, L. and Thurbon, E. (2020) 'Introduction: Finance, development and the state in East Asia', *New Political Economy*, 25(3): 315–19.

Soederberg, S. (2007) 'The "new conditionality" of socially responsible investing strategies: The politics of equity financing in emerging markets', *New Political Economy*, 12(4): 477–97.

Song, S.-H. (2013) 'KRX to keep public institution status', *Korea JoongAng Daily*, 31 January, Available from: https://koreajoongangdaily.joins.com/2012/10/21/economy/CEOs-seen-as-living-on-borrowed-time/2961120.html [Accessed 4 February 2025].

Thurbon, E. (2016) *Developmental Mindset: The Revival of Financial Activism in South Korea*, Ithaca: Cornell University Press.

Viktorov, I. and Abramov, A. (2022) 'The rise of collateral-based finance under state capitalism in Russia', *Post-Communist Economies,* 34(1): 15–51.

Wang, Y. (2015) 'The rise of the "shareholding state": Financialization of economic management in China', *Socio-Economic Review,* 13(3): 603–25.

Weber, K., Davis, G.F., and Lounsbury, M. (2009) 'Policy as myth and ceremony? The global spread of stock exchanges, 1980–2005', *Academy of Management Journal,* 52(6): 1319–47.

Weiss, L. and Thurbon, E. (2021) 'Developmental state or economic statecraft? Where, why and how the difference matters', *New Political Economy,* 26(3): 472–89.

Wójcik, D. (2012) *The Global Stock Market: Issuers, Investors, and Intermediaries in an Uneven World*, Oxford: Oxford University Press.

World Bank (2021) *World Development Indicators*, Washington, DC: World Bank Group, Available from: https://databank.worldbank.org/source/world-development-indicators [Accessed 4 February 2025].

Yoon, J.-Y. (2015) 'KRX lifted from public corporation status', *Korea Times,* 29 January, Available from: https://www.koreatimes.co.kr/www/biz/2025/02/602_172716.html [Accessed: 4 February 2025].

10

Increasing State Capacity through Central Bank Digital Currencies: A Comparative Account of the Digital Yuan and the Digital Rouble

Roxana Ehlke, Tim Salzer, and Carola Westermeier

Introduction

Across the globe, central banks are either actively exploring or are already engaged in developing central bank digital currencies (CBDCs). CBDCs introduce a new kind of public money into the monetary system, but – perhaps more importantly – they also provide new ways of storing and circulating money outside of the established international financial system (Kuehnlenz et al, 2022). CBDCs are widely seen to be motivated by geo-economic dynamics. They have the potential to facilitate international transactions that no longer rely on the use of the US dollar and therefore on clearing institutions under US jurisdiction. Therefore, they could become an instrument to evade the reach of Western, and especially US, sanctions, and to shield domestic and cross-border transactions from foreign interference (Westermeier, 2023, de Goede and Westermeier, 2022).

While the term of CBDC suggests that it is a coherent and unified concept, the motivations for central banks to develop a digital currency vary from case to case, ranging from the strengthening of 'traditional' monetary sovereignty (Chia and Helleiner, 2024) to preserving autonomy in the digital realm (Westermeier, 2024). The overarching term of central bank digital currency encompasses a large bandwidth of substantially different initiatives, designating either the digitization of cash – in the case of so called 'retail

CBDCs' – or the modernization of the technology for interbank transactions within a given currency zone – 'wholesale CBDCs' – as well as the overhaul of cross-border payment infrastructures – 'mCBDCs', a shorthand for 'multiple CBDCs'.

So far, typologies of CBDCs have been insufficient when it comes to the political rationales behind the different projects. In most cases, distinctions are mostly based on technical criteria and leave certain crucial aspects in the shadow, most crucially, how these different initiatives are conditioned by and likely to affect domestic and transnational relations of power, both between the respective administrations and the domestic private sector as well as between different countries. This chapter aims to fill this gap by examining the CBDC projects of two countries that openly challenge the current hegemonic financial order: China and Russia. Due to their strained relationship with the United States, the CBDC projects under development in Russia and China have frequently been framed as geopolitical endeavours (Nölke, 2022; McNally, Chapter 7, this volume). Building on Petry and Nölke's conceptual framework (Chapter 1, this volume), the present chapter makes further forays into the study of the politics of CBDCs by systematically comparing the projects developed by central banks in the People's Republic of China and the Russian Federation, that is, two regimes that have in the past repeatedly attempted to challenge American political and economic hegemony through the construction of new payment circuits. Following Nölke and Petry's appeal, we integrate both domestic and international dimensions into this comparison.

For this analysis, we focus on reports and other forms of communication on the two projects. Distinguishing the chapter from prior published works, the chapter provides insight into the domestic discourses in the original languages to assess the role of CBDCs in state capitalism. As argued by the literature on central banks, we interpret public statements by the central banks as strategic communications (Holmes, 2014). These statements are carefully crafted to avoid possible misinterpretations. Hence, they provide insights into the rationales that are used to legitimize the introduction of the new currency. Reports and commentaries by other financial and political actors are used to contextualize central banks' statements in a broader perspective.

In the remainder of this chapter, we will discuss both the main drivers and motivations to develop a domestic CBDC in both Russia and China as well as the distinct mechanisms of implementation in each of the two countries. To do so, we will first focus on the aims of both the Russian and the Chinese central banks with respect to the global economy. We will argue that while both CBDCs can be considered as tools of defensive financial statecraft that widen the possible scope of action in the realm of foreign policy (Armijo and Katada, 2015), the international implications of the projects figure much more prominently in Russian statements. Then, we will address domestic goals which central banks pursue by developing a CBDC. As state-controlled infrastructures, CBDCs could extend the degree of state capacity vis-à-vis the domestic financial sector. Finally, we will discuss specific constraints linked to the institutional order of their respective domestic economies with which both the Russian and the Chinese central bank are confronted and which affects the precise mechanism whereby the payment system reform is implemented.

The international dimension of the digital yuan and the digital rouble

Since the 2008 financial crisis, the payments industry has experienced rapid and transformative changes, with numerous new players entering the market and new technologies – most notably blockchain – being applied to payment processing (see Maurer, 2012; Nelms et al, 2018; Westermeier, 2020). Organizations like the Bank for International Settlements (BIS) often cite the development of CBDCs as a natural response to these technological advancements and an effort to bridge existing efficiency gaps in payment systems (for example, BIS, 2023; Skingsley, 2023). However, by framing the rise of CBDCs purely as a result of technological progress, commentators tend to overlook the influence of political and geopolitical factors.

Indeed, while in political discourse, money and the monetary system have often been presented as technical matters par excellence, since the turn of the millennium, a succession of geopolitical and monetary crises have led to a gradual politicization of monetary matters. This politicization of the existing international monetary order has become manifest in two closely intertwined ways. The global financial crisis of the late 2000s has lent new impetus to criticism of the global currency hierarchy and, in particular, the dollar's position at its apex. Similarly, the enforcement of economic sanctions in and through financial infrastructures has turned the technological systems undergirding the global economy into a contentious issue. These developments are relevant for the CBDC projects in both Russia and China as the following paragraphs will elaborate.

The financial crisis, the geopoliticization of financial infrastructures, and dollar hegemony

During the global financial crisis, it became apparent how different spaces in the world economy were exposed to the crisis's repercussions in highly differing ways, indicating their subordinated position in global finance in relation to the Western, and especially US, core. In this context, the 'exorbitant American privilege' resulting from the dollar's status as international currency has once more risen to prominence (Eichengreen, 2011). Indeed, the crisis illustrated that, due to the dollar's status as global reserve currency, a breakdown of the American financial industry would wreak havoc across the entire globe. Similarly, as the financial crisis unfolded, it became evident that the capacity and responsibility to prevent and manage financial crises rests to a non-negligible extent with the Federal Reserve, a US institution, which had progressively cemented its status as the role of a backstop for the entire global financial system over the second half of the twentieth century (Mehrling, 2011; McDowell, 2017).

Following the global financial crisis, a variety of political initiatives to either circumvent the dollar or to openly challenge its status as global reserve currency have been mushrooming across the globe. Russia and China, as members of the BRICS group, have been particularly proactive in this respect (Liu and Papa, 2022). First, through their advocacy in established international organizations such as the International Monetary Fund (IMF) and the BIS (Zhou, 2009), the BRICS countries have brought about tangible if not necessarily revolutionary changes in the functioning of the global monetary system as evidenced by the inclusion of the renminbi in the IMF's Special Drawing Rights currency basket (Liu and Papa, 2022). Both Russia and China have attempted to bypass the dollar by building new exchange circuits that do not rely on the dollar for their mutual trade relations or for foreign trade with specific countries, such as the member states of the Shanghai Cooperation Organization (Nölke, 2022). Furthermore, Latin American countries have established their own alternative payment circuit for regional trade that bypasses American-dominated infrastructures (Fritz et al, 2023). More recently, BRICS leaders even discussed the topic of creating a common currency, that could undermine the dollar's global role, during the BRICS summit in Johannesburg in 2023 (Gojdka and Munzinger, 2023).

Over the last two decades, not only the currency hierarchy, but also the technical infrastructures undergirding the global financial system have become a focus of political tensions. This has especially been the case in the realm of payments and their associated technologies. While in the past, scholars in this field remarked, with some degree of self-mockery, that payments were generally considered to be a particularly dull or geeky topic (Maurer, 2012), the repeated instrumentalization of financial infrastructures for Western security interests has led to a sea change in how payment technologies and payment providers are perceived. As has become apparent, American political and economic hegemony is sedimented in financial infrastructures which function as intelligence providers in the American global war against terrorism and represent the sine qua non to implement Western economic sanctions (de Goede, 2012; de Goede and Westermeier, 2022; Mulder, 2022; Langenohl and Burghardt, 2024).

In Russia, the possibility that Western powers might use their hegemony in financial infrastructures for foreign policy aims has been a particularly powerful instigator of policy change over the 2010s (for example, Ehlke, forthcoming). After the Iranian and North Korean banks were disconnected from the SWIFT (Society for Worldwide Interbank Financial Telecommunication) network as part of Western sanctions policy in 2012 and 2017, respectively, the Russian government reacted by initiating the construction of a domestic financial messaging service, the System for the Transfer of Financial Messages (SPFS) (Shagina, 2021). The urgency of establishing a viable alternative payment system was starkly demonstrated when the US-based payment services Visa and Mastercard, which had dominated the market for card payments in Russia since the early 2000s and on whose systems the card payment services of the country's largest banks relied (Guseva and Rona-Tas, 2014), blocked the payments of card holders from some Russian banks after Russia's annexation of Crimea in 2014 (BBC, 2014). This led to the creation of the National System of Payment Cards (NSPC), which is fully owned by the Bank of Russia. It serves as the operator of the Mir national payment system and constitutes the operational and payment clearing house for processing bank card transactions within Russia (Kochergin and Iangirova, 2020; AO 'NSPK', 2023).

Similarly, in China, over the 2010s, a domestic alternative to SWIFT has been brought into operation. In 2015, the Chinese Cross-Border Interbank Payment System (CIPS) began the clearing and settlement of renminbi payments. While as of 2023 the SWIFT infrastructure is still used for cross-border transactions, the CIPS could be operated without it in the future. Furthermore, announcements have been made about the coming interoperability of the CIPS with Russia's SPFS (Shagina, 2021; Nölke, 2022).

Even before the recent enthusiasm for CBDCs, both the People's Republic of China and Russia, alongside other BRICS countries, have engaged in collective financial statecraft. In order to bypass the dollar and develop alternative technological infrastructures for international trade, both countries have created their own multilateral platforms ('outside option', see Armijo, Chapter 3, this volume) and have also tried to bring about change within the existing institutional framework ('inside option', ibid) for global economic governance. An overarching aim in these endeavours has been to decrease asymmetrical vulnerabilities caused by the dependence on the use of the US dollar in international settlements. CBDCs, despite being presented as a natural result of technological progress and the development of the 'digital economy' in statements by international organizations such as the BIS, prolong those existing initiatives at reconfiguring the international payment system and decreasing the reliance on the dollar and American-controlled infrastructures. In this context, the development of CBDCs is understood by many as a potential pathway towards the materialization of the de-dollarization agenda in international trade and finance.

CBDCs as financial statecraft?

As a result of the infrastructural geopolitics at play in and through the international financial architecture, many commentators, academic and not, expect that the development of CBDCs in China and Russia aim to shield their domestic economies from foreign interference, at least to some extent, and that the desire for control and autonomy drives both projects (for example, Shagina, 2021; Prokopenko, 2023).

In the case of the digital rouble, the currency's potential advantages in terms of cross-border payments have been a major topic since the beginning of the project (Bank of Russia, 2020, p 8; 2021, p 7; 2022a, p 116). The Central Bank of Russia (CBR) recognized that the development of settlement and payment infrastructures is key to mitigating geopolitical risks (Bank of Russia, 2022b, p 12). The long-looming and, after Russia's invasion of Ukraine in 2022, effective disconnection of Russia from the SWIFT network has been cited repeatedly in the context of the development of the digital rouble (TASS, 2020; 2023). Minister of Finance Anton Siluanov described CBDCs in general as a possible means for cross-border payments which takes away the possibility of 'unfriendly countries' interfering in the processes of international payments (Kuzmicheva, 2023a). The digital rouble has been described as a means to lessen the dependence on the US dollar in international settlements (Tyotkin, 2020a). The CBR already explicitly advocated for the digital rouble as an alternative to SWIFT from the start of the programme in 2020. Given the number of countries with ongoing CBDC projects, the vice governor of the CBR Olga Skorobogatova assumes that interconnected CBDCs will eventually become able to perform the role of the network (RBC, 2020). In this context it has also been framed as a project of national self-respect and sovereignty (Kuzmicheva, 2022; Skorobogatova, 2022).

Russian authorities have specifically announced their intention to use the digital rouble in bilateral settlements with China. According to the chairman of the State Duma Committee on the financial market, Anatoly Aksakov, a successful collaboration with China with regard to digital rouble's international connectivity is supposed to make the project attractive for other countries and undermine US power in the global financial system (Reuters, 2022; Vakhitova, 2022). In January 2023, the CBR proposed two models to create trans-border interconnectivity of the digital rouble. One of those models is based on bilateral agreements on the integration of CBDC platforms, while the other one relies on a single shared hub-platform that connects the CBDC platforms of different countries. In the beginning, the first model shall be pursued with China (Buylov, 2023b).

By contrast, in the People's Republic of China, the geopolitical significance of the digital yuan is rarely ever thematized in an explicit manner (see Salzer, forthcoming). Issues such as the renminbi's internationalization and the issue of dollar hegemony or economic sanctions are conspicuously absent from the discourse of central bankers, even though the Chinese CBDC is potentially relevant for both topics (McNally, Chapter 7, this volume). The People's Bank of China (PBoC) already participates in pilot projects, such as the mBridge initiative (BIS Innovation Hub, 2021), in which CBDCs are used as instruments for cross-border transactions. However, instead of taking up this thematic thread, representatives of the PBoC have repeatedly insisted that the digital yuan was primarily oriented towards the domestic market. Nevertheless, discussions about geopolitics do occur in the broader ecosystem of economic experts around the central bank. Thus, the journal *China Finance* published by the Chinese central bank has featured several articles in which contributing authors overtly criticize the international payment system built on top of the SWIFT infrastructure, which is said to mainly privilege American interests, and promote the digital yuan as one possible alternative (孙立坚 and 杨洁萌, 2020). While international considerations connected to the Chinese CBDC are thus implicit, domestic ambitions are voiced more prominently.

When comparing public statements about their respective CBDCs by monetary authorities in the two countries, it becomes evident that they do not address geopolitics and the implications for the international financial system to the same extent. While in Russia the topic of sanctions and the unconcealed geopolitical confrontation with the West are central to the discourse around the digital rouble, in China, the absence of current sanctions allows for keeping the geopolitics out of the spotlight when discussing the CBDC. In the Russian context, the political authorities explicitly present their work on the digital Rouble as an endeavour with wide-ranging geopolitical implications and as an overt challenge to dollar hegemony. In the context of the sanctions, this policy complements other measures of defensive financial statecraft, like the introduction of capital controls to stabilize the value of the rouble (Prokopenko, 2023). In the People's Republic, to the contrary, public statements about the currency tend to downplay the possible implications of the new currency, even though many foreign and local observers anticipate that the digital yuan might effectively affect the international currency hierarchy. The country's lower degree of financial subordination and expanding creditor and currency capabilities (Armijo, Chapter 3, this volume), as evidenced in the RMB's inclusion in the Special Drawing Rights currency basket (Liu and Papa, 2022), its more prominent role as international means of settlement (for example, SWIFT, 2024), and the proliferation of bilateral swap agreements involving the PBoC (Song and Xia, 2020), make an offensive role of the digital yuan in international finance more plausible.

This difference with respect to how the Russian and the Chinese central banks present their own CBDC projects leads to a divergence in how both assess the relevance of CBDCs more generally. For instance, the Russian Central Bank tends to imply that the digital yuan as well as the digital rouble are part of a grand strategy of undoing dollar hegemony, while the Chinese central bank constantly downplays this latter point. As a matter of fact, the Russian central bank has repeatedly presented the digital rouble as a way to create a shared monetary architecture together with the PBoC, while the PBoC has made no such statement and has repeatedly emphasized the domestic orientation of the project.

Increasing state capacity domestically

While much of the discussion concerning the digital rouble and the digital yuan focuses on the international drivers of the projects, Russian and Chinese authorities to differing degrees have also justified the projects by referring to specific challenges in the domestic realm. In both countries, there is considerable overlap regarding the domestic purposes that central banks communicate. In both cases, the central bank aims to supplant cryptocurrencies, to increase the state's monitoring or surveillance capacities. Furthermore, in Russia as well as in the People's Republic of China, public authorities attempt to strengthen their grips over the domestic financial sector. Yet the fact that the two banks are embedded in two very different institutional environments provide reasons why they pursue certain idiosyncratic goals. Thus, the precise mechanisms through which authorities attempt to achieve their goals differ as the following explains.

Cryptocurrencies and social surveillance

In both countries, CBDCs have been framed as alternatives to cryptocurrencies, and work on their development has in both cases gone hand in hand with stricter regulations of cryptocurrency mining and trading as well as progressive restrictions of its use for payments. In the aftermath of the global financial crisis in the late 2000s, China had become one of the principal locations for Bitcoin mining. Yet, over the 2010s, Chinese regulators implemented a series of legal changes which have led to the decline of both mining and trading in China, beginning in 2013 with an official statement declaring that Bitcoin was a risky asset due to its fluctuating value and that it hence did not represent a form of money (State Council, 2013). Nevertheless, over chiefly the same period, then-governor of the PBoC Zhou Xiaochuan repeatedly praised the merits of Bitcoin in public, declaring that its emergence heralded the beginning of a new era in monetary history, the age of digital money. According to Zhou, the history of money was marked by a tendency towards progressive dematerialization of currencies. Money thus had taken different forms over time, first commodity money, then fiat paper money, and ultimately digital money (罗兰, 2016). Belonging to the same developmental stage in monetary history as cryptocurrency, the digital yuan would nevertheless avoid the pitfalls of existing privately issued currencies, which, according to Zhou, had developed too quickly (冯虎, 2018)

Similarly, the CBR has emphasized the threats that cryptocurrencies entail, arguing that neither cryptocurrencies nor stablecoins constituted a form of money (Bank of Russia, 2020, p 10). The tendency towards the use of cryptocurrencies was 'seriously jeopardis[ing] Russians' well-being' (Bank of Russia, 2022c, p 2). Beyond the potential for private investors to incur losses, the use of cryptocurrencies would endanger the stability of the financial system. An increased holding of cryptocurrencies would have effects similar to dollarization and undermine the country's monetary sovereignty. According to the CBR, high investment in cryptocurrencies furthermore contributed to a decapitalization of the Russian stock market and a decrease of investments in the real economy. At the same time, it would decrease the rouble's value and create liquidity, market, and credit risks for the banking system. Against this background, the CBR recommended a comparatively restrictive legislation on cryptocurrencies (Bank of Russia, 2022c, pp 20–4, 29).

After a boom in cryptocurrency trading and mining, Russian legislators became concerned with drafting new regulations for the market in 2018. The aim was to create requirements for customer verification to counter money laundering and terrorist financing involving cryptocurrencies (Partz, 2018). The law 'On Digital Financial Assets' of 2020 forbids the use or acceptance of cryptocurrencies as a means of payment in the Russian Federation, while trading is still allowed (Tyotkin, 2021). Nevertheless, the rather strict approach to cryptocurrencies and stablecoins has repeatedly been criticized, especially from within the Ministry of Finance, due to concerns about negative impacts on the Russian economy and the potentials to use cryptocurrencies to circumvent US-dominated financial infrastructures. This led to further legislation allowing cryptocurrency mining and its use in cross-border settlements in an experimental regime under the CBR's supervision (Baydakova, 2022; Bloomberg, 2024; Kommersant, 2024). In 2020, the CBR had presented the digital rouble as an explicit alternative to cryptocurrencies, as it was meant to provide the same technological conveniences as cryptocurrencies while being publicly backed (Bank of Russia, 2022c, pp 4, 8). The fact that other countries are currently developing CBDCs is given as another factor that could undermine the value of the rouble. The implementation of the digital rouble shall serve as an alternative and thus contribute to the stability of the currency's value (Bank of Russia, 2020, pp 21–2).

Furthermore, in the People's Republic as well as in Russia, CBDCs have been associated with the goal of increasing the state's capacity for social control and surveillance. Two technical features of a digital currency are relevant in this respect. First, in both countries, the introduction of the new digital currency would move a certain share of retail transactions directly onto a centralized ledger of the central bank, which is likely to provide regulators with access to a greater amount of data than before. Secondly, the currency could potentially be made interoperable with so-called 'smart contracts', that is, automated payments which are executed or not depending on a previously specified external condition.

In the Chinese case, the precise privacy implications of the CBDC are somewhat difficult to assess. Official statements underline the distinction between different kinds of wallets with varying upper limits regarding both transactions and deposits. The higher the limit, the more demanding are the prerequisites concerning the identification of users. Yet, even lower-level wallets are linked to a telephone number, so that completely anonymous transactions are impossible, a fact that is explicitly stated in official statements and justified in reference to anti-money laundering and countering the financing of terrorism guidelines (Atlantic Council, 2022).

However, the precise advantage for the PBoC remains unclear with respect to traceability when comparing the digital yuan to existing payment applications such as WeChat Pay and Alipay. While the expansion of the mobile payments industry in the 2000s and early 2010s had been made possible by a business model in which the operations of payment companies were somewhat obscure to regulators, this has since changed. In the early years of the industry, data generated by mobile payments via third-party payment apps was in certain cases difficult for the central bank to access: in the balance sheets of the banking system, transactions made via such applications appeared, if at all, only as movements between accounts at different banks held by the payment company. Individual-level data, that is, information about the nature of the purchase as well as the identity of both buyers and sellers, was controlled by the payments providers and was hence not automatically made available to regulators. While this configuration occasioned several conflicts between the PBoC and the relevant companies over the conditions of financial data sharing, a 2017 reform established a state-controlled national clearing house through which mobile payments have since been processed. In this sense, past reforms have already led to a substantial increase of overall transparency of digital payments for the Chinese central bank, even in the absence of a state-run digital currency (Xing et al, 2018, p 1221; Ba, 2022, pp 211–20). However, the digital yuan might differ from conventional digital payment methods in that it is said to be compatible with smart contracts, so that the central bank could potentially earmark the digital currency for specific payments and hence facilitate the regulation of monetary practices by including or excluding certain purchases from the space of feasible transactions. Yet, for the time being, to the best of our knowledge, no further official specifications about the subjects have been made by Chinese authorities.

Similarly in the Russian case, there had already been a high degree of transparency of non-cash payments prior to the digital rouble but its development is nevertheless supposed to increase the possibilities of financial oversight. In the context of the first sanctions against Russian financial actors after the annexation of Crimea in 2014, the CBR created the Operations and Payment Clearing Centre. This clearing facility belongs to the CBR-owned NSPC, which also operates Russia's 'Mir' card payment system and has been processing domestic transactions including by international card payment providers between 2015 and 2022 (Kochergin and Iangirova, 2020; AO 'NSPK', 2023). Still, increased control over transactions is explicitly presented as a positive feature that comes with the new form of money, especially in discussions about its uses for the transfer of government funds (Bank of Russia, 2021, p 19). Minister of Finance Anton Siluanov underlined the potential of the digital rouble to trace all transactions and this way prevent means from being misappropriated (Kuzmicheva, 2023a). The digital rouble was even described as a way to replace cash altogether. According to then first deputy governor of the CBR Sergey Shvetsov, cash was being used predominantly for semi-legal economic activities or when card payment is not possible. Therefore, cash constituted 'dirty and infectious' money (Korneev, 2021). In early publications on the digital rouble, it was suggested that government disbursements for public tenders would be earmarked for the intended area of spending to decrease possibilities for corruption and embezzlement of government funds (Bank of Russia, 2020, pp 15–16; 2022a, p 115; Ivatkina, 2022). First deputy governor Skorobogatova announced that to this end smart contracts were central to the motivation for creating the digital rouble (Tyotkin, 2020b).

The discussion of potential applications of smart contracts also extended to government programmes of social transfer payments (Tyotkin, 2020b), leading to further controversies. In a parliamentary discussion on a basic income for families with children, a possible future circumscription of digital roubles to a spending for 'important social purchases' (State Duma, 2024, 13th question) was cited as an argument in favour of such basic income. The possibility to limit the use of social transfers to a predetermined set of goods and services however was met with some criticism, for example by scientists and representatives of the banking industry, arguing that it would infringe civil liberties and rights (Tosunyan, 2020; Pshenichnikov, 2022, p 45). In reaction, Skorobogatova first declared that there would be no general earmarking and that digital roubles will not be limited in their acceptance, but in September 2023 the CBR announced that the question of digital rouble earmarking will be postponed (TASS, 2023). A circumscription of possible spending areas of the digital rouble, defined via smart contracts, shall be approached carefully, according to the CBR's deputy governor Alexey Zabotkin, since such measures would negatively affect the value of the digital rouble vis-à-vis other forms of the currency (Bezrukova, 2023). In an explanatory webinar on the digital rouble project, the director of CBR's department for the national payment system Alla Bakina said that limitations on digital rouble spending regarding sets of goods were not planned and would be in contradiction with the logics of the project (Luzgin, 2023).

The digital yuan and the domestic financial sector: blurring the public–private boundary

The fundamental architecture of the digital yuan is based on a collaboration between domestic private actors and the central bank, and the PBoC has thus taken several steps to limit the potential threat of the digital yuan to the domestic banking sector. First, the digital yuan is non-interest-bearing to avoid a decline in bank deposits following its introduction (范一飞, 2018). Furthermore, digital yuan wallets come with a tight upper limit restricting the maximum amount for each account holder, so that even if customers were to temporarily lose trust in the banking sector, they could only shift a limited proportion of their bank deposits into their accounts (Atlantic Council, 2022). Through these safeguards, the public–private partnership at the centre of the existing financial system was meant to be preserved, and the digital yuan would essentially serve as a means of payment rather than a store of value, that is, as a substitute for cash rather than for deposits. The precise contours of what came to be called the digital yuan's 'two-tier model' of public–private cooperation were explicated in a research article published in 2017 by the then-head of the Digital Currency Institute Yao Qian (姚前, 2018). Thus, the fundamental principle holds that certain designated private firms – banks as well as payment providers and telecom companies – open accounts at the central bank to purchase digital yuan from the PBoC in exchange for bank deposits. After having acquired a certain amount of the currency, they could then credit digital yuan into their clients' wallets to enable them to make purchases with it.

The digital yuan showcases that the establishment of a CBDC does not necessarily lead to a straightforward expansion of state capacity at the expense of private actors. Rather, with the progressive restructuration of the Chinese payments landscape, the boundary between the PBoC and mobile payments providers becomes increasingly fuzzy, making the distinction between the two altogether less relevant. This blurring of boundaries occurs from two opposite directions. On one side, the third-party payment providers (TPPPs) are progressively integrated into the payment infrastructure managed by the central bank as their technology is hardwired into the supporting system of the digital yuan. Indeed, as the main technology providers for the new currency, both WeChat Pay and Alipay are made indispensable for the operation of the new payment infrastructure and their monopolistic position in retail payments is even further consolidated. In the current situation, Alipay is said to be contributing its integrated development environment as well as its distributed database system, OceanBase (Liu, 2021). Moreover, as of December 2022, their applications serve as user interfaces for customers who want to make payments with the digital yuan.

On the other hand, the PBoC interferes in a more substantial manner in the operations of the TPPPs. Since the late 2010s, the bank has thus been imposing a set of new regulations on the largest actors in the industry with respect to the management of their customers' funds, limiting their capacity to take on financial risk. Hence, the companies are progressively transformed into mere supporting systems for the transfer of digitized official currency, and the industry's operating model, which had allowed it to expand so quickly in its early years, is being completely overhauled. As researchers at the IMF have argued, Chinese digital payment companies have been de facto CBDC providers since 2020, that is, even before the official launch of the digital yuan. This has been the case because, since 2020, Chinese TPPPs have been obliged by the PBoC to deposit the totality of their customers' funds into central bank reserve accounts. As a result, with respect to the anchor of their value, money stored in TPPP accounts has become indistinguishable from CBDC deposits, since the former are fully backed by reserves.

To summarize, in China, the PBoC has tried to further consolidate its relationship with the two dominant private players in the field of payments by developing the digital yuan in collaboration with the domestic technology giants and by creating a single technical infrastructure which ties them even more closely to state organizations. In this sense, the private–public cooperation underpinning the Chinese CBDC is yet another example of how the Chinese party-state succeeds to strengthen its grip over de jure private domestic entities.

Russia: Increasing state capacity through centralization

The plans for the digital rouble also show that preserving the existing financial system aligns with the development of financial state capacity: the digital rouble, like the digital yuan, is envisioned as a two-tiered model. This model would maintain the relationship of commercial banks to their customers (Bank of Russia, 2021, p 8). The CBR constitutes the first tier of the system as the issuer of the digital rouble and the operator of the platform where digital rouble wallets are located and transactions are carried out. Tier two is comprised of the commercial banks that open digital rouble wallets on the platform for their clients and perform transactions upon their clients' request. The federal treasury is also part of tier two, holding its own wallet for budgetary reasons (Bank of Russia, 2021, pp 9–10). In this way the CBDC shall be made accessible for households and businesses while preserving the existing financial system (Bank of Russia, 2022a, p 116). Commercial banks act as intermediaries between their clients and the CBR's digital rouble platform by incorporating a software module into their mobile applications which permits access to the digital rouble wallet and transfers of digital roubles to cash or non-cash. The CBR provides the software module (Bank of Russia, 2021, pp 8–10).

Very similar to the Chinese case, the CBR claims explicitly that the digital rouble will not alter the existing two-tier financial system. It stresses that the commercial banks were involved in an extensive feedback process surrounding the project. Private and market actors were invited to provide feedback on an October 2020 consultation paper by addressing potential risks, benefits, and the implementation timeline; that feedback was to be included in the further planning and conception of the CBDC (Bank of Russia, 2020, pp 4–5, 40). According to the CBR, a majority of respondents were in favour of a rapid introduction of the digital rouble to keep pace with the development of digital technologies and a global trend to introduce CBDCs (Skorobogatova and Zabotkin, 2021).

Despite this feedback process, there was criticism from parts of the banking industry. In open letters to the CBR in 2020 and 2023, the Association of Russian Banks, which the largest Russian banks had abandoned in 2017 over disagreements concerning representation (Tegin, 2017), expressed concerns regarding the effect that the CBDC could have on the market and the commercial banks. The issues raised related for example to questions concerning the obligations of the commercial banks, the reimbursement of banks for costs connected to the introduction and operation of the CBDC, and the role of the CBR as an independent regulator and simultaneous actor in the payment market (Tosunyan, 2020; Buylov, 2023a). In other instances, commercial banks had voiced concerns about the possible competition between the digital rouble and the established banking system (RBC, 2021). Studies by the rating agency Moody's, as well as by Sberbank, concluded that the digital rouble will lead to a significant decrease in banks' liquidity and creditworthiness, that will lead to higher interest rates (Tyotkin, 2020c; Chernyshova, 2020).

The CBR addressed these concerns but mostly declared them as being unwarranted. A sudden outflow of liquidity from bank deposits to digital rouble wallets is not expected since the introduction will be gradual. Any risks to financial stability or liquidity issues in the banking sector could be addressed by means of monetary policy (Bank of Russia, 2020, pp 10–11; 2021, pp 25–6; 2022a, p 119; Krivosheya and Semerikova, 2021, p 8). Also, a limit will be imposed on monthly additions to the digital rouble wallet (Kuzmicheva, 2023b). Still, the CBR has considered the possibility that the digital rouble's partial replacement of other forms of money in circulation would negatively affect the liquidity and lead to an increased competition in the banking sector. Rather than endangering the banks' business model, this should raise innovative potential in the market and contribute to the development of the financial system (Bank of Russia, 2020, pp 4–8, 16; 2021, pp 25–6; 2022a, pp 119–20; Grishenko et al, 2021; Kuzmicheva, 2023c).

The wider developmental trajectories in the Russian economy towards an authoritarian state-controlled capitalism have to be taken into account to understand the potential structural impacts of the digital rouble. After the disruptive privatizations in the 1990s, the state returned as an active economic actor in the early 2000s. This entailed an economy-wide increase of state ownership and control (for example, Vernikov, 2014; Viktorov and Abramov 2016; Mishura and Ageeva, 2022). In this context financialization and innovations in financial technologies further strengthen large state-owned banks (Mishura and Ageeva, 2022). The financial sector is increasingly taking the shape of a 'financial vertical' (Khmelnitskaya, 2014) in which the state controls a big part of financial flows through near-monopolistic financial institutions. Aside from an increasing geographical concentration in the Moscow area, the formation of the financial vertical entails an expanding market share of the largest banks – facilitated by the Bank of Russia's 'cleaning policy' to remove banks of questionable stability from the system to increase stability and governability – and an increasing weight of state-controlled banks vis-à-vis private and (partly) foreign-owned banks (Mishura and Ageeva, 2022).

With the emergence of financial innovations, large state-controlled banks are often in a pioneer position, giving them a head start in adopting innovations in relation to smaller and private banks and putting them in the position of contributing to the shaping of the market and regulatory environment (Mishura and Ageeva, 2022). It is therefore likely that the introduction of the CBDC will also contribute to a further centralization of the Russian banking sector. Even though the pilots of the digital rouble cannot be limited to the 'national champions' among the banks, since those prototypes are meant to ensure the functioning of the CBDC in the entire banking sector, the increasing competition that the digital rouble engenders will most probably follow the logics of the 'financial vertical' in increasing the clout of state-owned entities.

Conclusion

This chapter has presented three distinct arguments through an examination and comparison of the Russian and Chinese CBDC projects. First, while both CBDC projects are potential instruments to undermine the role of the US dollar in global finance, there are considerable differences in the way the communication around the projects addresses this issue. While both administrations have expressed criticism of the global dominance of the US dollar previously, this critique is specifically addressed within the context of the CBDC project only in Russia. After Russia's aggression against Ukraine and the unfolding sanctions against the country, this rationale of countering international financial subordination (Alami et al, 2023; Alami, Chapter 2, this volume) is especially pronounced in the discourse on the digital rouble. In this context, the digital rouble primarily has a character of defensive financial statecraft. The discourse typically refers to the potential of bilateral cooperation with China, which could permit the digital rouble to unfold its offensive potential by undermining US hegemony in global finance. Conversely, communication regarding the digital yuan sidesteps addressing the rivalry with the US prominently. At the same time, China has been articulating its criticism of the USD's global role very clearly and its position in the global economy makes a potential use of offensive financial statecraft based on the digital yuan much more plausible than it would be the case for the digital rouble. The difference here can be explained by the varying degrees of international financial subordination of the two countries that translates into differences regarding the reach of their financial statecraft through CBDCs.

Second, in China and in Russia the CBDC projects increase the degree of state capacity. In both countries, the fear of losing monetary sovereignty due to the spread of private cryptocurrencies is a concern for state authorities. Additionally, the technological potential for enhanced surveillance, social control, and effectiveness in combating corruption and illicit transactions also influences the reasoning behind the adoption of a CBDC.

Third, the specific mechanisms by which state capacity is enhanced differ. The CBDC projects in both countries impact various entities differently based on the structure of their respective domestic financial sectors. In Russia, the project concerns mainly the banking industry, whereas in the Chinese case, telecommunications companies as well as fintechs and traditional financial institutions are impacted. Central banks can use CBDC projects to increase their leverage over the financial industry in different ways: either by increasing competition on an unlevel playing field to induce further concentration within the domestic financial sector, as it will likely happen in Russia, or by enrolling strategically important corporations into the projects to better monitor them, as in China. As of 2024, the current state of the project in Russia suggests a potential for additional centralization of the domestic financial sector around state-controlled entities. In China, to the contrary, the central bank obtains desirable outcomes not by directly competing with traditional institutions but by furthering the integration of the domestic industry into the central bank's payment system.

In conclusion, the development of the digital rouble and the digital yuan are guided by the aim of strengthening state control over the financial sector and society at large. The central role of the state as an economic actor in both countries is reflected in the ways that development of the CBDC increases the degree of state capacity. While in the case of China, this high degree of state capacity is also coupled with a potential international influence of the digital yuan (see also McNally, Chapter 7, this volume), the digital rouble serves to strengthen the domestic autonomy of the state which had already been pronounced in this state capitalist formation. The international motivations surrounding the digital rouble nevertheless hint at a subordination of this project in the context of the bilateral relationship with China.

Acknowledgements

The authors acknowledge funding by the Collaborative Research Centre 'Dynamics of Security' (SFB/TRR 138). Very helpful comments in this chapter were provided by Andreas Langenohl and the participants of the workshop 'Payment Infrastructures and Multidimensional Inequalities' at Weizenbaum Institute Berlin on 13 and 14 April 2023. Research assistance was provided by Nils Jansen.

References

Alami, I., Alves, C., Bonizzi, B., Kaltenbrunner, A., Koddenbrock, K., Kvangraven, I., et al (2023) 'International financial subordination: a critical research agenda', Review of International Political Economy, 30(4): 1360–86.

AO 'NSPK' (2023) 'О компании АО «НСПК»', [online] 23 July, Available from: https://www.nspk.ru/about/company/ [Accessed 23 July 2023].

Armijo, L.E. and Katada, S.N. (2015) 'Theorizing the financial statecraft of emerging powers', *New Political Economy*, 20(1): 42–62.

Atlantic Council (2022) 'Atlantic Council-UC San Diego conference on digital currency in China and the Asia Pacific', Atlantic Council, [online] 14 February, Available from: https://www.atlanticcouncil.org/event/conference-on-digital-currency-in-china-and-the-asia-pacific/ [Accessed 7 April 2024].

Ba, S. (2022) *The New Cycle and New Finance in China*, Singapore: Springer Nature Singapore.

Bank for International Settlements (2023) 'III. Blueprint for the future monetary system: improving the old, enabling the new', in *Annual Economic Report 2023,* [online] 20 June, Available from: https://www.bis.org/publ/arpdf/ar2023e3.htm [Accessed 13 November 2024].

Bank of Russia (2020) *A Digital Ruble: Consultation Paper*, Moscow: Bank of Russia, [online], Available from: https://www.cbr.ru/statichtml/file/113008/consultation_paper_201013_eng.pdf [Accessed 12 November 2024].

Bank of Russia (2021) *Digital Ruble Concept*, Moscow: Bank of Russia, [online], Available from: https://www.cbr.ru/Content/Document/File/120239/dr_cocept.pdf [Accessed 11 November 2024].

Bank of Russia (2022a) *Основные направления единой государственной денежно-кредитной политики на 2023 год и период 2024 и 2025 годов: Проект от 27 сентября 2022 года*, Moscow: Bank of Russia, [online], Available from: http://www.cbr.ru/about_br/publ/ondkp/ [Accessed 4 November 2022].

Bank of Russia (2022b) *Russian Financial Market Development Program for 2022–2024*, Moscow: Bank of Russia, [online], Available from: https://www.cbr.ru/content/document/file/132531/fm_development_program_2022-2024.pdf [Accessed 11 November 2024].

Bank of Russia (2022c) *Cryptocurrencies: Trends, Risks, and Regulation – Consultation Paper*, Moscow: Bank of Russia, [online], Available from: https://www.cbr.ru/Content/Document/File/132242/Consultation_Paper_20012022_eng.pdf [Accessed 11 November 2024].

Baydakova, A. (2022) 'Russian government introduces crypto bill to parliament over central bank objections', Coindesk, [online], 21 February, Available from: https://www.coindesk.com/policy/2022/02/21/russian-government-introduces-crypto-bill-to-parliament-over-central-bank-objections [Accessed 4 February 2025].

BBC (2014) 'Visa and Mastercard block Russian bank customers', *BBC News,* [online] 21 March, Available from: https://www.bbc.com/news/business-26678145 [Accessed 2 July 2023].

Bezrukova, A. (2023) 'Банк России рассмотрит вопрос об «окрашивании» цифровых рублей', *РБК Крипто,* [online] 5 September, Available from: https://www.rbc.ru/crypto/news/64f73cef9a794773a28203a5 [Accessed 5 April 2024].

BIS Innovation Hub (2021) 'Inthanon-LionRock to mBridge: building a multi CBDC platform for international payments', *BIS*, [online] 28 September, Available from: https://www.bis.org/publ/othp40.htm [Accessed 8 January 2024].

Bloomberg News (2024) 'Russia races to legalize crypto as sanctions weigh on firms', Bloomberg, [online], 30 July, Available from: https://www.bloomberg.com/news/articles/2024-07-30/russia-races-to-legalize-crypto-as-sanctions-weigh-on-companies [Accessed 4 February 2025].

Buylov, M. (2023a) 'Цифровому рублю не хватает статуса', *Коммерсантъ,* [online] 7 August, Available from: www.kommersant.ru/doc/6147368 [Accessed 6 April 2024].

Buylov, M. (2023b) 'Цифровой рубль собрался за границу', *Коммерсантъ,* [online] 9 January, Available from: https://www.kommersant.ru/amp/5758849 [Accessed 7 April 2024].

Chernyshova, Y. (2020) 'М Сбербанк спрогнозировал отток до ₽4 трлн из банков в цифровой рубль', *РБК*, [online] 15 December, Available from: https://www.rbc.ru/finances/15/12/2020/5fd86d479a79470af8e7e4f9 [Accessed 6 April 2024].

Chia, C. and Helleiner, E. (2024) 'Central bank digital currencies and the future of monetary sovereignty', *Finance and Space*, 1(1): 35–48.

de Goede, M. (2012) *Speculative Security: The Politics of Pursuing Terrorist Monies*, Minneapolis, MN: University of Minnesota Press.

de Goede, M. and Westermeier, C. (2022) 'Infrastructural Geopolitics', *International Studies Quarterly*, 66(3): sqac033.

Eichengreen, B. (2011) *Exorbitant Privilege: The Rise and Fall of the Dollar and the Future of the International Monetary System*, Oxford: Oxford University Press.

Fritz, B., Kaltenbrunner, A., Mühlich, L., and Orsi, B. (2023) 'South-South monetary regionalism: a case of productive incoherence?', *New Political Economy*, 28(5): 818–31.

Gojdka, V. and Munzinger, P. (2023) 'Brics-Staaten wollen eigene Währung: Ersetzen diese Länder bald den Dollar?', *Süddeutsche.de*, [online] 28 August, Available from: https://www.sueddeutsche.de/wirtschaft/brics-waehrung-dollar-alternative-1.6171793 [Accessed 3 April 2024].

Grishenko, W., Morosov, A., Petreneva, E., and Sinyakov, A. (2021) *Что изменится для банков и их клиентов с введением цифрового рубля. Аналитическая записка*, Moscow: Bank of Russia.

Guseva, A. and Rona-Tas, A. (2014) *Plastic Money. Constructing Markets for Credit Cards in Eight Postcommunist Countries*, Palo Alto: Stanford University Press.

Holmes, D.R. (2014) *Economy of Words: Communicative Imperatives in Central Banks,* Chicago: University of Chicago Press.

Ivatkina, M. (2022) 'Совершенно новые деньги: как изменится наша жизнь с введением цифрового рубля?', *абзац* [online] 16 August, Available from: https://absatz.media/ekonomika/9712-sovershenno-novye-dengi-kak-izmenitsya-nasha-zhizn-s-vvedeniem-cifrovogo-rublya [Accessed 5 April 2024].

Khmelnitskaya, M. (2014) 'Russian housing finance policy: state-led institutional evolution', *Post-Communist Economies*, 26(2): 149–75.

Kochergin, D.A. and Iangirova, A.I. (2020) 'Development of a Russian national payment card system in the midst of economic sanctions', *Problems of Economic Transition*, 62(4–6): 272–85.

Kommersant (2024) 'Путин легализовал майнинг и внешнеторговые расчеты в криптовалюте', *Коммерсантъ*, [online] 8 August, Available from: https://www.kommersant.ru/doc/6880183 [Accessed 4 February 2025].

Korneev, A. (2021) 'В Банке России спрогнозировали замену «заразных денег» цифровым рублем', *РБК Крипто,* [online] 3 June, Available from: https://www.rbc.ru/crypto/news/60b8d8df9a7947264254843f [Accessed 5 April 2024].

Krivosheya, E. and Semerikova, E. (2021) 'Central bank digital currencies (CBDC): Taxonomy, design and Russian specifics', *Skolkovo*, [online], Available from: https://www.skolkovo.ru/researches/cifrovye-valyuty-centralnyh-bankov-tipologiya-dizajn-i-rossijskaya-specifika/ [Accessed 6 April 2024].

Kuehnlenz, S., Orsi, B., and Kaltenbrunner, A. (2022) 'Central bank digital currencies and the international payment system: The demise of the US Dollar?', *Research in International Business and Finance*, 64: 101834.

Kuzmicheva, A. (2022) 'Глава РСПП выступил за ускоренное внедрение цифрового рубля', *РБК Крипто,* [online] 29 November, Available from: https://www.rbc.ru/crypto/news/6385f90a9a7947262933abf0 [Accessed 5 April 2024].

Kuzmicheva, A. (2023a) 'Силуанов назвал срок выпуска в обращение цифрового рубля', *РБК Крипто,* [online] 24 April, Available from: https://www.rbc.ru/crypto/news/644660b29a7947e37306e80d [Accessed 4 April 2024].

Kuzmicheva, A. (2023b) 'Глава ЦБ назвала лимит пополнения кошелька с цифровыми рублями', *РБК Крипто,* [online] 20 April, Available from: https://www.rbc.ru/crypto/news/644109ba9a7947a889f79be4 [Accessed 6 April 2024].

Kuzmicheva, A. (2023c) 'Набиуллина предсказала усиление конку ренции банков из-за цифрового рубля', *РБК Крипто,* [online] 28 April, Available from: https://www.rbc.ru/crypto/news/644bc2f59a7947196edbd84f [Accessed 7 April 2024].

Langenohl, A. and Burghardt, K. (2024) 'Non-traditional finance and the infrastructural imagination of geoeconomic hegemony: The case of Russia's war in Ukraine', *Journal of Global Security Studies*, 9(3).

Liu, C.-W. (2021) 'The Chinese fintech boom and the consolidation of recentralized authoritarian capitalism', *Asian Survey,* 61(6): 971–98.

Liu, Z.Z. and Papa, M. (2022) *Can BRICS De-dollarize the Global Financial System?* (1st edn), Cambridge: Cambridge University Press.

Luzgin, A. (2023) 'Банк России не будет устанавливать огранич ений для цифрового рубля', *РБК Крипто,* [online] 18 October, Available from: https://www.rbc.ru/crypto/news/652f96849a79476fa6e957b1 [Accessed 5 April 2024].

Maurer, B. (2012) 'Payment: Forms and functions of value transfer in contemporary society', *The Cambridge Journal of Anthropology*, 30(2): 15–35.

McDowell, D. (2017) *Brother, Can You Spare a billion? The United States, the IMF, and the International Lender of Last Resort*, New York: Oxford University Press.

Mehrling, P. (2011) *The New Lombard Street: How the Fed Became the Dealer of Last Resort*, Princeton, NJ: Princeton University Press.

Mishura, A. and Ageeva, S. (2022) 'Financialisation and the authoritarian state: the case of Russia', *Cambridge Journal of Economics*, 46(5): 1109–40.

Mulder, N. (2022) *The Economic Weapon: The Rise of Sanctions as a Tool of Modern War*, New Haven/London: Yale University Press.

Nelms, T.C., Maurer, B., Swartz, L., and Mainwaring, S. (2018) 'Social payments: Innovation, trust, Bitcoin, and the sharing economy', *Theory, Culture & Society*, 35(3): 13–33.

Nölke, A. (2022) 'Geoeconomic Infrastructures', in B. Braun and K. Koddenbrock (eds) *Capital Claims: Power and Global Finance* (1st edn), London: Routledge, pp 147–66.

Partz, H. (2018) 'Russia: State duma considers law "on digital financial assets", echoes US regulations', *Cointelegraph,* [online] 21 March, Available from: https://cointelegraph.com/news/russia-state-duma-considers-law-on-digital-financial-assets-echoes-us-regulations [Accessed 5 April 2024].

Prokopenko, A. (2023) 'Russia's capital controls are designed to aid Putin's 2024 re-election', *Carnegie Endowment for International Peace*, [online] 19 October, Available from: https://carnegieendowment.org/russia-eurasia/politika/2023/10/russias-capital-controls-are-designed-to-aid-putins-2024-re-election?lang=en [Accessed 12 November 2024].

Pshenichnikov, W.W. (2022) 'Обзор основных положений концепций цифрового рубля', *Современная экономика: проблемы и решения*, (2): 35–49.

RBC (2020) 'ЦБ увидел в цифровых валютах потенциального конкурента SWIFT – Поможет ли третья форма рубля нивелировать угрозу санкций для международных расчетов', *РБК*, [online] 23 December, Available from: https://www.rbc.ru/finances/23/12/2020/5fe31a799a79476e537cdf8a [Accessed 5 April 2024].

RBC (2021) 'Эксперты назвали главные риски внедрения цифрового рубля в России – Новая форма валюты может остаться невостребованным «нишевым продуктом»', *РБК*, [online] 12 January, Available from: https://www.rbc.ru/finances/12/01/2021/5ffc4caf9a79470d03a85b55 [Accessed 5 April 2024].

Reuters (2022) 'Russia plans to use digital rouble in settlements with China, says lawmaker', *Reuters Media*, [online] 26 September, Available from: https://www.reuters.com/markets/currencies/russia-plans-use-digital-rouble-settlements-with-china-says-lawmaker-2022-09-26/ [Accessed 10 March 2022].

Salzer, T. (forthcoming) 'A brief infrastructural history of currency digitalization in the People's Republic of China, 2000s–2020s', in C Westermeier, M. Campbell-Verduyn, and B. Brandl (eds) *The International Handbook of Financial Infrastructure*, Cambridge: Cambridge University Press.

Shagina, M. (2021) 'How disastrous would disconnection from SWIFT be for Russia?', *Carnegie Endowment for International Peace*, [online] 28 May, Available from: https://carnegiemoscow.org/commentary/84634, last updated on 1 July 2023 [Accessed 12 November 2024].

Skingsley, C. (2023) 'Shaping the future financial system in the public interest', Keynote speech at the 'Exploring central bank digital currency: evaluating challenges and developing international standards' conference, 28 November, Washington DC, Available from: https://www.bis.org/speeches/sp231128.htm [Accessed 13 November 2024].

Skorobogatova, O. (2022) 'Первый зампред ЦБ: ограничения тарифов на эквайринг пока не принесли пользы потребителям', *ТАСС*, [online] 23 June, Available from: https://tass.ru/interviews/15000261 [Accessed 4 April 2024].

Skorobogatova, O. and Zabotkin, A. (2021) 'Концепция цифрового рубля', *Press conference on the digital ruble concept*, Moscow: Bank of Russia.

Song, K., and Xia, L. (2020) 'Bilateral swap agreement and renminbi settlement in cross-border trade', *Economic and Political Studies*, 8(3): 355–73.

State Council of the People's Republic of China (2013) '人民银行等五部委发布关于防范比特币风险的通', [online] 5 December, Available from: https://www.gov.cn/gzdt/2013-12/05/content_2542751.htm [Accessed 5 April 2024].

State Duma (2024) Shorthand of the meeting on 17 January 2024, 6th session of the 8th legislative period, 13th question, Novichkov, Nikolai Vladimirovich, party: 'Spravedlivaya Rossiya – za pravdu', [online] Available from: http://transcript.duma.gov.ru/node/6289/ [Accessed 12 November 2024].

SWIFT (2024) 'RMB Tracker January 2024. Monthly reporting and statistics on renminbi (RMB) progress towards becoming an international currency', *SWIFT*, [online], Available from: https://www.swift.com/fr/node/11096 [Accessed 5 April 2024].

TASS (2020) 'В ЦБ заявили, что цифровые валюты могут потеснить SWIFT на рынке международных переводов', *ТАСС*, [online] 23 December, Available from: https://tass.ru/ekonomika/10333241 [Accessed 5 April 2024].

TASS (2023) 'ЦБ сообщил, что цифровые рубли не будут 'окрашиваться' для отслеживания операций с ними', *ТАСС*, [online] 6 April, Available from: https://tass.ru/ekonomika/17466641 [Accessed 5 April 2024].

Tegin, M. (2017) '«Большая восьмерка» выходит из Ассоциации российских банков', *Ведомости*, [online] 17 July, Available from: https://www.vedomosti.ru/finance/articles/2017/07/17/724096-tosunyan [Accessed 13 May 2023].

Tosunyan, G.A. (2020) 'Письмо АРБ Председателю ЦБ РФ Набиуллиной Э. С. по докладу Банка России «Цифровой рубль»', 30 December.

Tyotkin, M. (2020a) '«Жесткий контроль за доходами граждан». Каким будет цифровой рубль', *РБК Крипто,* [online] 19 October, Available from: https://www.rbc.ru/crypto/news/5f8d809e9a7947960e2843b8?from=copy [Accessed 5 April 2024].

Tyotkin, M. (2020b) 'ЦБ: цифровой рубль позволит использовать смарт-контракты при госплатежах', *РБК Крипто,* [online] 23 December, Available from: https://www.rbc.ru/crypto/news/5fe336af9a79477c77550cc6 [Accessed 5 April 2024].

Tyotkin, M. (2020c) 'Moody's предсказало отток средств со счетов банков из-за цифрового рубля', *РБК Крипто*, [online] 11 November, Available from: https://www.rbc.ru/crypto/news/5fab888e9a794748ec8fbae9 [Accessed 6 April 2024].

Tyotkin, M. (2021) 'Закон о цифровых активах вступил в силу. Что изменилось', *РБК Крипто,* [online] 1 January, Available from: https://www.rbc.ru/crypto/news/5fedaf549a794784d89eb416 [Accessed 5 April 2024].

Vakhitova, G. (2022) 'Цифровой рубль может заменить систему международных расчетов', *Российская Газета*, [online] 1 December, Available from: https://rg.ru/2022/12/01/vozmut-v-oborot.html [Accessed 5 April 2024].

Vernikov, A. (2014) '"National champions" in Russia's banking services market', *Problems of Economic Transition*, 57(4): 3–25.

Viktorov, I. and Abramov, A. (2016) 'The state capture of Russian non-bank financial institutions and markets after the 2008 crisis', *Competition & Change*, 20(1): 3–20.

Westermeier, C. (2020) 'Money is data – the platformization of financial transactions', *Information, Communication & Society*, 23(14): 2047–63.

Westermeier, C. (2023) 'From flows towards updates: Security regimes and changing technologies for financial surveillance', *Review of International Studies*, 49(4): 615–36.

Westermeier, C. (2024) 'The digital euro: A materialization of (in) security', *Review of International Political Economy*, 31(5): 1–24.

Xing Q., Hei, J., and Pu, L. (2018) 'Analysis on the influence of the introduction of NetsUnion on the Third-Party Payment and UnionPay in China', *Proceedings of the 2018 2nd International Conference on Education Science and Economic Management (ICESEM 2018),* Xiamen: Atlantis Press.

Zhou, X. (2009) 'Reform the international monetary system', BIS, [online] 23 March, Available from: https://www.bis.org/review/r090402c.pdf [Accessed 3 April 2024].

罗兰(2016) '数字货币离我们还有多远　取代纸币大势所趋已经提上央行日程', *The People's Daily*, [online] 17 February, Available from: http://paper.people.com.cn/rmrbhwb/html/2016-02/17/content_1654423.htm [Accessed 5 April 2024].

孙立坚 and 杨洁萌 (2020) '中国法定数字货币发展新机遇', 中国金融, 17: 65–7.

冯虎 (2018) '周小川：数字货币要可靠了以后再进行推广', 中国经济网 [online], Available from: http://www.ce.cn/xwzx/gnsz/gdxw/201803/09/t20180309_28410782.shtml [Accessed 7 April 2024].

范一飞 (2018) '关于数字央行货币几点考虑', 财新, [online] 26 January, Available from: https://finance.caixin.com/m/2018-01-26/101203131.html [Accessed 7 April 2024].

姚前 (2018) '央银行数字货币原型系统实验研究', 软件学报, 29(9): 2716–32.

11

Afterword: The Relevance of Global Capitalism for Studying Statecraft and Financial Subordination

Ingrid Harvold Kvangraven

At a moment where emerging economies' share of global GDP has risen drastically, and where this shift has called into question the dominance of the West in the contemporary world order, how this 'rise' remains structured within a hierarchically organized global economy – and the nature of variations within the Global South – is an important research and political question. As defined by the editors, this book aims to combine insights from literatures on financial subordination, financial statecraft, and comparative capitalism to begin to answer this question. In this afterword, I hope to engage critically, yet constructively, with this aim and the book's contributions, to ultimately push the research agenda on the nature of states in the Global South within a hierarchically structured world forward.

The need for a greater understanding of how international financial subordination (IFS) shapes states of the Global South is an important one and Petry and Nölke's book is a step towards broadening and developing this understanding. As one of the authors who put forward the concept of IFS (Alami et al, 2023), I am particularly glad to see so much engagement with the concept and attempts to broaden and deepen the debate about it and how it relates to other concepts from other theoretical traditions. As with all concepts that are picked up by a wide range of traditions, there is a risk that it loses some of its original meaning in the process of transmission. One problem with concepts spreading through different traditions and disciplines is that the link between theory and politics that originally constituted the concept can be weakened or even torn apart. This has crucial implications because, as I will outline, IFS as an umbrella concept originally emerged from radical traditions working with critical theoretical understandings of capitalism, with crucial political implications. Separating IFS from the politics and theoretical traditions from which it emerged should, therefore, be resisted. In light of this, a part of my engagement here is with IFS in general and how IFS can be abused, misused, and misread in various ways, and what the implications of that are for our understanding of global capitalism. I also connect these debates to broader discussions of Eurocentrism and decolonization in the social sciences in general to investigate to what extent IFS and financial statecraft literatures contribute to reinforcing or resisting Eurocentrism in the social sciences.

In short, my call in this afterword is for research going forward to explicitly outline the theory of capitalism that underlies any attempt to understand states and finance in the Global South and to critically reflect on and discuss these theoretical foundations. This is important not only for scholarly rigour, but also for clarifying the political stakes of the debates about IFS and statecraft.

Conceptual ground-clearing: which IFS?

While deepening and widening the debate about finance from the vantage point of the Global South is a welcome aim, I would argue that some conceptual ground-clearing is important for the debate going forward, to avoid authors speaking past each other and misunderstandings of what IFS entails.

Debates about what shapes and drives state interventions in the Global South, as well as their implications, are ultimately underpinned by differences in understandings of global capitalism. The question then arises: how do each of these literatures understand capitalism? What are their underlying theoretical foundations? The chapters in the book are quite rich on empirical observations and discussions of characteristics of the international economic order and ideal types to consider, but the contributions are not always clear on the more fundamental question of how capitalism is understood, and what this means for their analysis, conclusions, and political implications. Based on this, I would like to call attention to three issues to grapple with in future research, namely, first, the reading of IFS that is being evoked; second, the theoretical underpinnings of various contributions; and third, how the various theoretical engagements relate to the uneven development of capitalism, which is central to IFS.

First, IFS – as originally formulated by Alami et al (2023) and as also pointed out by Alami in this volume – does not deny agency of actors in the Global South. This misunderstanding comes from Palma's (2023) misreading, but has been repeated since then by others, including by contributors to this volume. It is worth reiterating, then, that literature within IFS does not consider actors of the Global South as passive, but that IFS is rather a research agenda that seeks to uncover the power relations that shape conditions of policy making in the Global South, including power relations internalized by state actors. IFS recognizes that there is an asymmetry between how states in the Global North and South can handle crises and contradictions of capitalist accumulation, thus recognizing that IFS can also be a catalyst for institutional and financial innovation (Alami, Chapter 2, this volume). As such, within an IFS agenda, the state has always been an important actor that has through history acted to mediate, mitigate, facilitate, and/or resist features of IFS – depending on the geographical, political, and historical specificity of the state. As we propose in Alami et al (2023), inquiries of IFS and its relationship with the state would be best situated in a broader theoretical understanding of the role of the state in capitalist society, where the state is a reflection of social relations and plays an important role in politically containing social antagonisms, and in securing the general conditions for accumulation within national territories.

Crucially, within an IFS framework, cases of state activism or 'financial statecraft' are not necessarily understood as an attempt to challenge IFS itself. Indeed, Alami's chapter (Chapter 2, this volume) shows very clearly that most often policies such as capital controls, financial regulation, or expansion of state-owned banking or financial entities do not challenge IFS as a global structure, but rather reflect ways that states manage IFS. Indeed, such policies are most often carried out while states simultaneously *deepen* the global division of labour through commitments to broader neoliberal agendas. As such, these policies do not challenge the contemporary structure of IFS, but rather reinforce it (albeit in a way that aims to limit the build-up of financial vulnerabilities and fragilities).

This understanding differs from those that simply see the global economic structure as an 'external constraint' or who see states as more or less autonomous agents which face a variety of challenges related to the international financial system that constrain them from pursuing their stated goals (for example, as is the case of some of the statecraft literature, as outlined by Armijo in Chapter 3 of this volume). Such assumptions are often rooted in (late) neoclassical, (neo-)Weberian, (post-)Keynesian, or realist understandings of capitalism, which see the state as separate and detached from the social relations that underpin it. As such, pairing IFS and financial statecraft together, as is attempted to do in this volume, may not always be theoretically possible if/when the theoretical foundations of the concepts are incompatible. Indeed, the reality of state intervention often not challenging the structural underpinning of IFS calls into question the binary opposition between state power/agency and financial market constraints that often appears in some international political economy (IPE) and comparative capitalism literature (Alami, 2018; Alami et al, 2023), including literature on financial statecraft. As such, merging some superficial understanding of IFS – ultimately informed by a misreading of the theoretical traditions of IFS – with literatures that ultimately have a completely different view of the state in capitalism risks actually undermining the theoretical insights from the IFS research agenda itself.

This leads us to the second point, which is that while the IFS research agenda has some key theoretical and conceptual building blocks defined, it is also ultimately an umbrella concept of a research agenda that has three main strands – post-Keynesian analyses of currency hierarchies, dependency theory, and Marxist political economy. As such, clarifying the theoretical foundations underlying any scholar's engagement with IFS would be helpful to advance a rich and theoretically rigorous debate about states and IFS. Putting forward an explicit formulation and discussion of theoretical foundations will also help distinguish between theoretical frameworks that may be incompatible. For example, the varieties of capitalism approach, including the more recent model of 'hierarchical market economies', is in fundamental contradiction with radical theories emerging from the Global South such as dependency theory. Indeed, dependency theory critics have taken the varieties of capitalism literature to task for both perpetuating methodological nationalism and for being fundamentally ahistorical (see Ebenau, 2012, for a comprehensive critique). In this case, arguing that IFS can be helpful for analyzing the structure of the global financial system, while varieties of capitalism literature can be used to explain variations in degree and reach of state capacity, can end up being contradictory and inconsistent, rather than enriching. To what extent the categories of comparative capitalism, state capitalism, or variety of capitalism literature will be fruitful for pushing forward our understanding of IFS and the state in the Global South will therefore depend on to what extent they are actually compatible with the strand of IFS that is being evoked. Indeed, making the stakes of the theories more clear would help to expose the political implications of these debates and differences as well, which at times are papered over in some discussions of IFS and financial statecraft.

Of course, the debates about states in global capitalism in the context of IFS are bigger than simply the literature on financial statecraft and comparative capitalism. Indeed, some of the contributions in the book study variations of state intervention without engaging with the financial statecraft literature at all, but rather taking a historical materialist approach to their understanding of the state (for example, Kaltenbrunner et al, Chapter 8, this volume), demonstrating that it is possible to study the state in IFS without drawing on comparative capitalisms literature or financial statecraft. The motivation for combining financial statecraft and IFS specifically, and the specific insights that could potentially emerge from such a merge, could, thus, be further elaborated on and discussed.

Third, and finally, understanding IFS requires uncovering structures that have been shaped historically through imperialism and the development of capitalism as an uneven and global system (Alami et al, 2023). It is tempting to focus on the novelty of the times in which we live. However, for a better understanding of our contemporary moment, we are best off historicizing the structures that have shaped society. This is important because it can allow us to better understand to what extent a phenomenon represents something structurally and qualitatively 'new' or whether we are observing new innovations of surface phenomenon that are based on an existing structure. For example, although we have witnessed new forms of financialization in recent decades, the tendency of finance to not necessarily promote production – an important concern in much of the financialization literature in the Global North – has a long history in the Global South that is often overlooked in the financialization debates, making the claims of novelty exaggerated (Koddenbrock et al, 2022). As such, historicizing financial statecraft could be a helpful path for future research to establish how state intervention has changed over time and whether the financial sanctions against Russia that are a focus of several of the chapters represent a qualitatively new phase of financial statecraft, if yes, how so, and which fundamental structures of the global economy shaping statecraft remain intact.

What's more, understanding the limits, potentials, and the underlying forces of financial statecraft would require an understanding of global capital accumulation and how different countries have been integrated into the global and uneven division of labour. It is, thus, important to not analyze financial 'statecraft' separate from the underlying forces that generate uneven development across the globe, producing different outcomes, constraints, and limits in the Global North and South. Failing to do so can lead us to Eurocentric ideas about what is 'lacking' in the Global South when compared to policies and institutions in the Global North without taking into account the structural forces that have produced and reproduce these differences (Pierre, 2012). This leads us to the discussion of Eurocentrism in studies of economics, finance, and the state.

Decolonizing economics, finance, and the state

Eurocentrism permeates the social sciences, and studies of finance, the state, and the Global South are no different (Amin, 2009; Koddenbrock et al, 2022). Eurocentrism is a distorted understanding of political economy that assumes that national political economies function in an endogenous and rational manner (Amin, 2009). At its core is an assumption of how capitalism evolved in Europe as an endogenous phenomenon isolated from global structural forces of oppression such as imperialism, dispossession, and exploitation, and an assumption that the rest of the world can follow a similar path, if only the right kind of institutions and policy mix is pursued (Dutt et al, 2025). This view of capitalism ignores the unevenness that the system was built on at its inception and the unevenness that it continues to reproduce – an unevenness that is central for to understanding IFS. Once one sees IFS as something that is baked into the capitalist system itself and that is continually reproduced, it becomes difficult to buy the idea that IFS itself can be challenged through statecraft or that the system can be made fair and flat through renegotiations of global governance structures. There has not been much critical engagement with ways in which some of the categories and assumptions in the financial statecraft or comparative capitalism literature may themselves reproduce certain forms of Eurocentrism. I give a few reflections on this here, but systematic critical exploration requires a much deeper discussion by scholars more directly engaged with those literatures.

Let us first consider how the state itself is conceptualized. In a Eurocentric conception of the state, the state is seen as autonomous and exogenous and in charge of the development of its population. Development, within this view, can happen through a series of policy-fixes pursued by the state and with help from international institutions. This contrasts with a non-Eurocentric view of the state which considers how the state evolved with the development of capitalism to secure capital accumulation, rather than existing as an autonomous or exogenous institution that can intervene in a neutral manner in the economy. The common assumption that countries of the Global South were able to embrace the Westphalian national state model of sovereignty once colonialism was over, is, thus, fundamentally Eurocentric and misguided, given that the Westphalian national state assumes a kind of sovereignty that has never been available for countries of the Global South, or even countries of the Global North, for that matter (Getachew, 2019). States of the Global South have always been shaped by imperialism and this has persisted even after the end of decolonization (Getachew, 2019; Galvan-Alvarez et al, 2020; Benyera, 2024). As such, when state capacity is defined as 'the ability of incumbent political leaders to conceptualize and implement public policies plausibly related to some desired goal' (Armijo, Chapter 3, this volume), this can be considered a Eurocentric understanding of the state as it sees autonomy and exogeneity of the state as a possibility. Attempting to merge this with an IFS agenda as defined by Alami et al (2023) would lead to theoretical inconsistencies and rather reinforce the Eurocentrism that the IFS agenda attempts to counter.

Let us next consider what a Eurocentric understanding of the global economy would entail and how this might relate to the discussion in this book. A Eurocentric understanding of the global economy is one that is abstracted from power relations and the inherent unevenness of capitalism (Dutt et al, 2025). Such an understanding assumes that it is possible for capitalism to be fair and produce relatively equal outcomes, and that countries of the Global South can catch up with the Global North if given the policy space to do so. Such an understanding focuses political attention on the institutions governing the global economy such as international financial institutions, rather than focusing on the dynamics of capitalism itself. There are hints at such an understanding in the overview of the statecraft literature presented by Armijo. For example, the main policy conclusion that emerges from Armijo's chapter is that countries of the Global South should direct their financial statecraft towards negotiating reform of the global financial governance system as a way to combat international financial subordination.

There have, of course, historically been attempts to reform global governance from Global South states, such as the New International Economic Order (NIEO) proposed in the 1970s – which ultimately did not materialize given the prevailing global power dynamics and global class structures supporting the status quo (Amin, 1984). The problem is that governance institutions are themselves reflections of uneven development. As such, targeting the reflections – or symptoms – of uneven development, rather than challenging uneven development itself at its roots, is unlikely to lead to the desired result. It becomes an idealist view if the assumption is that academics and policy makers can put forward ideas that will change the global system, rather than uncovering the material basis that has shaped the nature of those institutions to begin with. Once we consider that IFS is a reflection of a deeper underlying global division of labour, it also becomes clear that it cannot be 'combatted' through financial statecraft or bargaining at the international level. Any fundamental challenge to IFS will need to entail challenging the global capitalist system itself.

Further, targeting the global governance institutions as the main vehicle of injustice also assumes that if we live in a world where governance institutions *do not* favour Global North economies but rather allow for policy space for countries of the Global South, then catch-up will be possible. This is problematic because it does not consider the fact that capitalism itself is inherently uneven and it has been so since its conception. The idea that all states can be prosperous and equal is a dangerous one given that it does not properly take into account the underlying forces in capitalism that produce dispossession, exploitation, and unevenness. This is not to say that global governance institutions such as the IMF, the World Bank, and the World Trade Organization do not contribute to reproducing inequalities in very problematic and harmful ways – they most certainly do – but rather that the theory of capitalism that informs our scholarship lead us to very different ways of searching for and locating the underlying sources of inequality and IFS. And there are real political implications of these scholarly differences.

References

Alami, I. (2018) 'Money power of capital and production of "New State Spaces": A view from the global south', *New Political Economy*, 23(4): 512–29.

Alami, I., Alves, C., Bonizzi, B., Kaltenbrunner, A., Koddenbrock, K., Kvangraven, I.H., and Powell, J. (2023) 'International financial subordination: a critical research agenda', *Review of International Political Economy*, 30(4): 1360–86.

Amin, S. (1984) 'Self-reliance and the new international economic order', in Herb Addo (ed) *Transforming the World Economy? 9 Critical Essays on the New International Economic Order*, London: Hodder and Stoughton in association with the United Nations University.

Amin, S. (2009) *Eurocentrism: Modernity, Religion, and Democracy: A Critique of Eurocentrism and Culturalism*, Pambazuka Press (original work published 1988).

Benyera, E. (2024) 'The state in Africa is a colonial state', *Developing Economics*, 27 August.

Dutt, D., Alves, C., Kesar, S., and Kvangraven, I.H. (2025) *Decolonizing Economics – An Introduction*, London: Polity Press.

Ebenau, M. (2012) 'Varieties of capitalism or dependency? A critique of the VoC approach for Latin America', *Competition & Change*, 16(3): 206–23.

Galvan-Alvarez, E., Birk Laursen, O., and Ridda, M. (2020) 'Decolonising the state: subversion, mimicry and criminality', *Postcolonial Studies*, 23(2): 161–9.

Getachew, A. (2019) *Worldmaking After Empire: The Rise and Fall of Self-Determination*, Oxford: Princeton University Press.

Koddenbrock, K., Kvangraven, I.H., and Sylla, N.S. (2022) 'Beyond financialisation: the longue durée of finance and production in the Global South', *Cambridge Journal of Economics*, 46(4): 703–33.

Palma, G. (2023) 'Ricardo was surely right: the abundance of "easy" rents leads to greedy and lazy elites. Rentier-capitalism as an exercise in "non-creative" destruction. A tribute to Geoff Harcourt', *Review of Political Economy*, online first.

Pierre, J. (2012) *The Predicament of Blackness: Postcolonial Ghana and the Politics of Race*, Chicago, IL: University of Chicago.

Index

References to figures appear in *italic* type, while references to tables appear in **bold** type.